Rethinking Culture and Creativity in the Digital Transformation

This book discusses the role of digital technologies in the growth and development of cultural organizations and the creative sector. It includes contributions by authoritative scholars who address this topic through different perspectives, methodologies and approaches.

The first part of the volume focusses on theoretical contributions that identify the main transformations caused by the digital revolution, the use of data, outlining new possible analytic frameworks and future lines of research. The second part of the volume presents empirical contributions applied to different fields in the study of the cultural and creative sectors. These range from analyses of traditional cultural organizations such as museums, the evolution of trajectories in the fashion industry, techno-creative communities, digital services for tourism, to cultural and creative industries and wealth and creative work.

This edited volume will be of great value to scholars in the fields of Economics and Management including Economic Geography and Economic Development. Students and researchers interested in learning more about new technologies and their impact on cultural and creative sectors will also benefit from this book. This book was originally published as a special issue of *European Planning Studies*.

Luciana Lazzeretti is Full Professor in Management at the Department of Economics and Management of the University of Firenze, Italy.

Stefania Oliva is Research Fellow in Management at the Department of Economics and Management of the University of Firenze, Italy.

Niccolò Innocenti is Research Associate at the Florence School of Regulation of the European University Institute, Italy.

Francesco Capone is Associate Professor in Management at the Department of Economics and Management of the University of Firenze, Italy.

Rethinking Culture and Creativity in the Digital Transformation

Edited by
Luciana Lazzeretti, Stefania Oliva,
Niccolò Innocenti and Francesco Capone

LONDON AND NEW YORK

First published 2023
by Routledge
4 Park Square, Milton Park, Abingdon, Oxon OX14 4RN

and by Routledge
605 Third Avenue, New York, NY 10158

Routledge is an imprint of the Taylor & Francis Group, an informa business

Introduction, Chapters 1–10 © 2023 Taylor & Francis
Chapter 11 © 2022 Marie Delaplace, Leïla Kebir, Marjolaine Gros-Balthazard and François Bavaud. Originally published as Open Access.

With the exception of Chapter 11, no part of this book may be reprinted or reproduced or utilised in any form or by any electronic, mechanical, or other means, now known or hereafter invented, including photocopying and recording, or in any information storage or retrieval system, without permission in writing from the publishers. For details on the rights for Chapter 11, please see the chapter's Open Access footnote.

Trademark notice: Product or corporate names may be trademarks or registered trademarks, and are used only for identification and explanation without intent to infringe.

British Library Cataloguing in Publication Data
A catalogue record for this book is available from the British Library

ISBN13: 978-1-032-36506-0 (hbk)
ISBN13: 978-1-032-36508-4 (pbk)
ISBN13: 978-1-003-33237-4 (ebk)

DOI: 10.4324/9781003332374

Typeset in Minion Pro
by Newgen Publishing UK

Publisher's Note
The publisher accepts responsibility for any inconsistencies that may have arisen during the conversion of this book from journal articles to book chapters, namely the inclusion of journal terminology.

Disclaimer
Every effort has been made to contact copyright holders for their permission to reprint material in this book. The publishers would be grateful to hear from any copyright holder who is not here acknowledged and will undertake to rectify any errors or omissions in future editions of this book.

Contents

Citation Information		vii
Notes on Contributors		ix

Introduction: rethinking culture and creativity in the digital transformation 1
Luciana Lazzeretti, Stefania Oliva, Niccolò Innocenti and Francesco Capone

1 What is the role of culture facing the digital revolution challenge?
Some reflections for a research agenda 10
Luciana Lazzeretti

2 Data-driven arts and cultural organizations: opportunity or chimera? 31
Massimiliano Nuccio and Enrico Bertacchini

3 Valuing culture and creativity impacts in a global technological era:
reshaping the analytical framework 49
Pedro Costa

4 Museums and digital technology: a literature review on organizational issues 69
Francesca Taormina and Sara Bonini Baraldi

5 Is innovation in ICT valuable for the efficiency of Italian museums? 88
Calogero Guccio, Marco Ferdinando Martorana, Isidoro Mazza,
Giacomo Pignataro and Ilde Rizzo

6 Exploring the marriage between fashion and 'Made in Italy' and the key role
of G.B. Giorgini 110
Luciana Lazzeretti and Stefania Oliva

7 Path renewal dynamics in the Kyoto kimono cluster: how to revitalize
cultural heritage through digitalization 129
Silvia Rita Sedita and Tamane Ozeki

8   Anatomy of a techno-creative community – the role of brokers, places, and
    events in the emergence of projection mapping in Nantes   148
    Etienne Capron, Dominique Sagot-Duvauroux and Raphaël Suire

9   The impact of cultural and creative industries on the wealth of countries,
    regions and municipalities   170
    Rafael Boix Domenech, Blanca De Miguel Molina and Pau Rausell Köster

10 Exploiting the technology-driven structural shift to creative work in
    regional catching-up: toward an institutional framework   191
    Ben Vermeulen and Eleonora Psenner

11 Uses and practices of digital services in a situation of mobility: evolution
    versus revolution? The case of the Champs Elysées   217
    Marie Delaplace, Leïla Kebir, Marjolaine Gros-Balthazard and François Bavaud

    Index   237

Citation Information

The chapters in this book, except for Introduction, were originally published in the journal *European Planning Studies*, volume 30, issue 9 (2022). When citing this material, please use the original page numbering for each article, as follows:

Introduction
Rethinking culture and creativity in the digital transformation
Luciana Lazzeretti, Stefania Oliva, Niccolò Innocenti and Francesco Capone
European Planning Studies, DOI: 10.1080/09654313.2022.2052018

Chapter 1
What is the role of culture facing the digital revolution challenge? Some reflections for a research agenda
Luciana Lazzeretti
European Planning Studies, volume 30, issue 9 (2022), pp. 1617–1637

Chapter 2
Data-driven arts and cultural organizations: opportunity or chimera?
Massimiliano Nuccio and Enrico Bertacchini
European Planning Studies, volume 30, issue 9 (2022), pp. 1638–1655

Chapter 3
Valuing culture and creativity impacts in a global technological era: reshaping the analytical framework
Pedro Costa
European Planning Studies, volume 30, issue 9 (2022), pp. 1656–1675

Chapter 4
Museums and digital technology: a literature review on organizational issues
Francesca Taormina and Sara Bonini Baraldi
European Planning Studies, volume 30, issue 9 (2022), pp. 1676–1694

Chapter 5
Is innovation in ICT valuable for the efficiency of Italian museums?
Calogero Guccio, Marco Ferdinando Martorana, Isidoro Mazza, Giacomo Pignataro and Ilde Rizzo
European Planning Studies, volume 30, issue 9 (2022), pp. 1695–1716

Chapter 6
Exploring the marriage between fashion and 'Made in Italy' and the key role of G.B. Giorgini
Luciana Lazzeretti and Stefania Oliva
European Planning Studies, volume 30, issue 9 (2022), pp. 1717–1735

Chapter 7
Path renewal dynamics in the Kyoto kimono cluster: how to revitalize cultural heritage through digitalization
Silvia Rita Sedita and Tamane Ozeki
European Planning Studies, volume 30, issue 9 (2022), pp. 1736–1754

Chapter 8
Anatomy of a techno-creative community – the role of brokers, places, and events in the emergence of projection mapping in Nantes
Etienne Capron, Dominique Sagot-Duvauroux and Raphaël Suire
European Planning Studies, volume 30, issue 9 (2022), pp. 1755–1776

Chapter 9
The impact of cultural and creative industries on the wealth of countries, regions and municipalities
Rafael Boix Domenech, Blanca De Miguel Molina and Pau Rausell Köster
European Planning Studies, volume 30, issue 9 (2022), pp. 1777–1797

Chapter 10
Exploiting the technology-driven structural shift to creative work in regional catching-up: toward an institutional framework
Ben Vermeulen and Eleonora Psenner
European Planning Studies, volume 30, issue 9 (2022), pp. 1798–1823

Chapter 11
Uses and practices of digital services in a situation of mobility: evolution versus revolution? The case of the Champs Elysées
Marie Delaplace, Leïla Kebir, Marjolaine Gros-Balthazard and François Bavaud
European Planning Studies, volume 30, issue 9 (2022), pp. 1824–1843

For any permission-related enquiries please visit:
www.tandfonline.com/page/help/permissions

Notes on Contributors

François Bavaud, Institut de géographie et de durabilité, University of Lausanne, Lausanne, Switzerland.

Enrico Bertacchini, Department of Economics and Statistics "Cognetti de Martiis", Università degli Studi di Torino, Torino, Italy.

Rafael Boix Domenech, Department of Economic Structure, University of Valencia, Valencia, Spain.

Sara Bonini Baraldi, DIST – Interuniversity Department of Regional and Urban Studies and Planning, Polytechnic of Turin, Turin, Italy.

Francesco Capone, Department of Economics and Management of the University of Firenze, Italy.

Etienne Capron, GRANEM, University of Angers, Angers, France.

Pedro Costa, ISCTE – University Institute of Lisbon/DINÂMIA'CET-iscte, Lisboa, Portugal.

Blanca De Miguel Molina, Department of Business Organisation, Universitat Politècnica de València, Valencia, Spain.

Marie Delaplace, Lab'Urba – EUP, Gustave Eiffel University, Marne la Vallee, France.

Marjolaine Gros-Balthazard, Pacte – Social Science Research Center, Grenoble Alpes University, Grenoble, France.

Calogero Guccio, Department of Economics and Business, University of Catania, Catania, Italy.

Niccolò Innocenti, Florence School of Regulation, European University Institute, Italy.

Leïla Kebir, Institute of Geography and Sustainability (IGD), University of Lausanne, Lausanne, Switzerland.

Luciana Lazzeretti, Department of Economics and Management of the University of Firenze, Italy.

Marco Ferdinando Martorana, Department of Economics and Business, University of Catania, Catania, Italy.

Isidoro Mazza, Department of Economics and Business, University of Catania, Catania, Italy.

Massimiliano Nuccio, Department of Management, BLISS Digital Impact Lab, Ca'Foscari University of Venice, Venezia, Italy.

Stefania Oliva, Department of Economics and Management of the University of Firenze, Italy.

Tamane Ozeki, Department of Creative City, Osaka City University, Osaka, Japan.

Giacomo Pignataro, Department of Economics and Business, University of Catania, Catania, Italy; Department of Management, Economics and Industrial Engineering, Politecnico di Milano, Milano, Italy.

Eleonora Psenner, Institute for Geography, Leipzig University, Leipzig, Germany; Landesverband der Kultur- und Kreativwirtschaft Sachsen e.V., Leipzig, Germany; Institute for Regional Development, EURAC Research, Bolzano, Italy.

Pau Rausell Köster, Econcult, Departament d'Economia Aplicada, Universitat de València, Valencia, Spain.

Ilde Rizzo, Department of Economics and Business, University of Catania, Catania, Italy.

Dominique Sagot-Duvauroux, GRANEM, University of Angers, Angers, France.

Silvia Rita Sedita, Department of Economics and Management, University of Padova, Padova, Italy.

Raphaël Suire, LEMNA, University of Nantes, Nantes, France.

Francesca Taormina, DIST – Interuniversity Department of Regional and Urban Studies and Planning, Polytechnic of Turin, Turin, Italy.

Ben Vermeulen, Institute of Economics, University of Hohenheim, Stuttgart, Germany; Institut für Qualifizierende Innovationsforschung & -Beratung GmbH (IQIB), Bad Neuenahr-Ahrweiler, Germany.

Introduction: Rethinking culture and creativity in the digital transformation

Luciana Lazzeretti, Stefania Oliva, Niccolò Innocenti and Francesco Capone

ABSTRACT
The relationship between culture and economy is facing a new phase based on an increasing connection between culture, creativity and technological innovation. A New Era is beginning where cultural organisations may face different challenges that emerged from the diffusion of digital technology. The digital revolution has pervaded and transformed not only various industrial sectors, but the whole of society. The most evident consequences are in terms of new forms of representation of cultural heritage, growing creative capacity and new market niches. This edited collection seeks to enlarge this debate with the aim of offering a wide discussion of topics related to the role of new technologies and innovation for cultural and creative sectors and organisations. In particular, the objective is twofold: (a) understanding new dynamics generated by digital transformation and how they may affect the cultural and creative industries and organisations; (b) identifying the new challenges in the development of new trajectories for cultural and creative sectors in the Digital Era.

1. Introduction

Over the last decades, a stream of literature on the cultural and creative economy has been devoted to investigating its role in local development, economic growth, innovation and wealth (Potts 2016; Gong and Hassink 2017; Lazzeretti, Capone, and Innocenti 2017; Boix Domenech, De Miguel Molina, and Rausell Köster 2021). Culture and creativity have been studied as resources for the regeneration of products, sectors and places and elements to favour the transformation of the economic structure of cities and regions (Scott 2006; Cooke and Lazzeretti 2008; Pratt 2008; Lazzeretti and Oliva 2020). However, the relationship between culture and economy is facing a new phase based on an increasing connection between culture, creativity and technological innovation (Vermeulen and Psenner 2022). We are beginning a New Era where cultural organisations must face different challenges that emerged from the diffusion of digital technology (Lazzeretti 2020; De Bernard, Comunian, and Gross 2021; Nuccio and Bertacchini 2021).

This rapid revolution leads cultural institutions to rethink their role in the contemporary economic context. Productive forms change and new intangible added values are generated based on symbolic value and identity where creativity, technology transfer and craftsmanship are crucial components. The combination of craftsmanship and new technologies (Sedita and Ozeki 2021) stimulates a new ecosystem for innovation, capable of creating value and different typologies of entrepreneurship (Chandna and Salimath 2020). The digital revolution requires responding to a new public demand for cultural content from the digital communities and social networks.

Beyond the traditional topics of economic enhancement and conservation of culture and creativity, issues related to social and environmental problems have gained attention, together with the increasing role attributed to new technologies to cope with profound changes in modern society and the world economic crisis (Cruz and Teixeira 2021). The digital revolution has pervaded and transformed not only the various industrial sectors but large segments of society (Floridi 2014). The most evident consequences are in terms of new representations of cultural heritage, growing creative capacity and new market niches (Capron, Sagot-Duvauroux, and Suire 2021; Delaplace et al. 2022). The traditional cultural sectors, through the processes of digitization, have nourished both the possibilities for experimental art and culture and the possibilities of enhancement, new business modules and governance (Costa 2022).

This uncertain context has shown the great potential of digital tools in promoting new ways for experiencing cultural heritage and has allowed cultural and creative organizations to maintain the engagement with their audience. Creative workers have revealed an unexpected resilience (Massi, Vecco, and Lin 2020) as in the case of economic crisis or natural disasters (De Propris 2013; Oliva and Lazzeretti 2017).

Technological change in the creative industries has had an impact on the entire production network, transforming the dynamics of the sector and the industrial structure and altering the relationship between the different actors, interconnecting producers and users (Jones, Lorenzen, and Sapsed 2015). In the new scenario created by digital technologies, innovations are driven by users, thanks to the increasing accessibility of content, the decrease in production costs and the new role of the user-producer (Sacco, Ferilli, and Tavano Blessi 2018).

Furthermore, destructive innovation has pushed numerous activities to change their business models to meet new consumption models and fill the regulatory vacuum left by institutions that do not always manage to keep up with the evolution of the technological context (Mangematin, Sapsed, and Schüßler 2014; Landoni et al. 2020).

Despite that scholars have recognized the potential of cultural and creative industries and organisations in favouring innovation and growth in the wider economy, particularly when supported by highly related sectors (Innocenti and Lazzeretti 2019), it is not clear what the direction of the new industrial and technological trajectories are that can be generated starting from the digital transformation. Moreover, although the digital transformation has created new opportunities for growth and innovation, many challenges still exist for cultural and creative organizations, museums and their territorial contexts (Taormina and Baraldi 2022; Guccio et al. 2020).

First, the increasing use of digital tools has highlighted the social disparities of local communities, excluding from information and services part of society due to the increase of the digital divide. Moreover, the unregulated production of information has led to serious issues related to the spread of 'post-truth' or 'fake news' that comes from a 'feeling-based' communication and dissemination of information (Cooke 2021). This is in parallel with the issues related to the privacy of user data and transparency in their management.

However, despite online platforms having increasingly interconnected artificial intelligence and human components reaching a growing number of participants, concerns arise about the autonomy of individual decisions (Cristianini, Scantamburlo, and Ladyman 2021). The increasing use of social media, moreover, poses serious questions concerning the 'attention economy', where the clicks and followers on social media may represent a comparable 'currency' through the phenomenon of 'celebrities', increasing even more inequalities (Banks 2022; Cooke and Nunes 2021). This may lead to problems related to the measurement of the cultural value and forms of 'spectacularization' of cultural heritage. This phenomenon has involved cities of art and high-cultural places where the risk for the loss of identities of places (Lazzeretti 2012), favoured by policies for increasing competitiveness of places, is still higher with the digital revolution (Strom 2020).

Despite these criticisms affecting all sectors in a general framework of a lack of regulation in some of the dimensions concerning the relationship between new technologies, artificial intelligence and society, they can prejudice the possibilities offered to cultural and creative industries and organisations for their growth and development.

Given these considerations, the Special Issue seeks to enlarge this debate with aim of offering a wide discussion of topics related to the role of new technologies and innovation for the cultural and creative sectors and organisations. In particular, the objective is twofold: (a) understanding the new dynamics generated by digital transformation and how they may affect the cultural and creative industries and organisations; (b) identifying the new challenges in the development of new trajectories for cultural and creative sectors in the Digital Era.

2. Contents of the Special Issue

The present Special Issue represents a selection among the papers that were presented during the first edition of the 'Rethinking culture and creativity in the technological era' International Workshop that was held at the University of Florence in February 2020. This special issue is composed of 11 papers that were the most connected with the idea of rethinking the role of culture and creativity in the actual challenging times that see the increasing importance of the digital transformation, however, also throughout the Special Issue, we may distinguish different perspectives and trajectories.

The first three papers cover theoretical aspects of the issues related to the intersection between culture and creativity with the digital transformation, the use of data and new analytical frameworks.

The first paper, by Lazzeretti represents a deep reflection and a theoretical discussion regarding the role of culture and the revolution brought by the digital transformation. An intersection that has started to be considered as a game-changer also respect to societal norms and values. To discuss and respond to the questions raised regarding the role of culture in facing the digital revolution, the author followed the approach firstly suggested by the seminal work of Lester and Piore (2004), developing an open conversation with scholars from different disciplines that lasted more than one year and a half, following a narrative approach. The paper defines the algorithmic society as a 'narrative of the past', a society where the influence of algorithms (AI), that have predictive nature based on past data, is so pervasive that has a relevant impact also on the cultural aspects of that society. While a new phase of the evolution of the relationship between society, culture and economy is added here. This new phase is related to the relationship between culture and technology and is addressed as a 'narrative of the future' because it is based also on the imaginative capacity of the components of the community. The paper concludes by presenting a research agenda focused on the need to rethink policies, particularly those related to the conservation and enhancement of culture, keeping in mind the relevance of the imaginative capacity and creating and maintaining diversity.

The second paper, authored by Nuccio and Bertacchini deals with the role of data analytics in favouring the innovative capacity of arts and cultural organizations (ACOs), an area where the adoption of data ecosystems is considered one of the slowest. Given for granted the strong impact of the digital revolution over the last years on the organizations working on cultural and creative sectors, the authors discuss the relevance of data analytics and how these could be a new innovation enhancer for a potential and act as an enabler of Artificial Intelligence (AI) capacity to affect these sectors. The conceptual framework relies on the works by Bakhshi and Throsby (2012) to understand and categorize the impact of data analytics on innovation in customer relations, value creation and business models, also favouring the creation of value for both stakeholders and customers of arts and cultural organizations.

While the third paper by Costa presents a new analytical framework for valuing culture and creativity. Particularly with the ongoing changes driven by the new technological era, it is always more complex to clearly identify the value creation of cultural activities. The paper combines the work developed in four European and national research projects, to question and improve the actual measurements tools applied to valuing the impact of culture in society. A multidimensional grid is developed to value the impacts of the creative activities through the lens of territorial development using five different pillars: the cultural value, the economic value, the social value, the environmental value and finally the citizenship and participation value. All these dimensions are additionally split into sub-dimension and subsequently into 75 indicators to take into account the multidimensionality and complexity of this task. This grid will be finally systematised in a digital tool to enable the agent of cultural activities to self-assess their value creation.

Then the second group of papers has a focus on museums, discussing how the museums deal with the new digital technologies and if innovations regarding information and communications technology (ICT) are able to favour the efficiency of museums.

The first of these two papers, authored by Taormina and Bonini Baraldi presents an extensive literature review regarding the organizational issues related to the use of digital technologies in museums. The paper adopts a systematic literature review method, analyzing 94 sources composed by papers, project reports, conferences and books then attributed to the three analyzed domains, precisely new business models, emerging professional and organizational issues and finally digital strategy to consolidate and organize the pre-pandemic literature on the role of digital technologies for museums drawing some interesting paths. Showing that technological innovations and integration in museums are usually gradual rather than radical, authors suggest that the digital transformation on museums is really complex and not only from a technical point of view but also concerning organizational issues, particularly due to the largely acknowledged scarcity of resources.

The second paper, by Guccio, Martorana, Mazza, Pignataro and Rizzo, deals with the effect of ICT in favouring the efficiency and performance of museums in Italy. While the role of ICT in the wider economy has been studied extensively, less hype was dedicated to the relevance for museums. The paper, through an empirical analysis based on extensive data regarding ICT adoption and performance of more than 100 Italian state-owned museums, shed light on the positive effect of ICT on museums performance also differentiating between ICT online services and 'in situ' services showing that the latter are able to attract visitors more than the former.

Also the third group of papers is composed of two papers. These are focused on two case studies that deals with fashion and digitalization, the first one showing how this may lead to the rise of a cultural phenomenon, the 'Made in Italy', while the second showing that digitalization may help to favour the revitalization of the Kyoto kimono cluster. The first paper, by Lazzeretti and Oliva followed a textual analysis based on the data drawn from the G.B. Giorgini Archive and from an analysis of the frequency of the most relevant terms identified by the textual analysis on three online archives of digitalized newspaper and books that represented the international press. The evidence clearly shows the relevance of the first fashion shows organized in Florence by Giovanni Battista Giorgini between 1951 and 1967 in favouring the emergence of the 'Made in Italy' and the Italian Fashion Industry. One other relevant result is the relevance of the city Florence in those years for the fashion industry, strongly related to the presence of artisans in the leather and textile sector as well as to the attractive role of the cultural heritage present in the city. Using data preserved and made available through the use of digitalization of archives, newspapers and books, the paper shows that such sources may represent new opportunities to study culture thanks to the use of new technologies.

The second paper by Sedita and Ozeki as already mentioned, discusses the importance of the digitalization of the cultural heritage focusing on the capacity to revitalize a cultural sector after a declining period. The study deals with the Kyoto kimono cluster and followed a narrative approach applied to case study research to explain the new trajectories of development followed through the digitalization that occurred during the last years. The revitalization of the cluster was possible due to the combined effect of public and private initiatives driven by initial funding through public projects for the digitalization of cultural heritage that favoured the insurgence of entrepreneurial activities that gave rise to the path renewal of the cluster through new products, new concepts and experiences. Notwithstanding the introduction of new ideas and concepts, the symbolic and traditional aspects of the kimono were preserved and made available to a wider public and revitalized after a period of stagnation.

The fourth group of papers is connected to the role of places and services and based on two different cases for the French country. The first of these papers, authored by Capron, Sagot-Duvauroux and Suire through an in depth exploratory case study, based on the projection mapping community in the city of Nantes shows the important role of events and places on intermediary platforms in forming a community of innovation and confirming the relevance of local knowledge and geographical brokers located at the intersection of distinct knowledge bases in enabling the insurgence of new techno-creative practices.

While the second paper by Delaplace, Kebir, Gros-Balthazard and Bavaud discusses the use of digital services for different types of people, particularly related to mobile tourism services. The analysis through different statistical methods is based on a survey conducted on one of the most touristic areas of Paris in 2018 (the Champs Elysées). The idea is that, even if mobile and more in general digital services had a tremendous impact on tourism in general and even more on tourist behaviour, little is known about how this impacts the tourist experience of the destination and to understand if based on the typology of user the mobile technologies are only an extension of classic digital practices or more specific.

Finally, the last two papers deal with the role of cultural and creative industries or creative workers for the wealth or catching up of regions, giving interesting policy suggestions and implications. The first paper by Boix, De Miguel Molina and Köster presents an empirical analysis investigating the overall impact of cultural and creative industries (CCIs) on the per capita income and if this shows relevant differences using a different geographical unit of analysis. Results show a positive effect of CCIs on wealth at all scales. However some interesting differences may be identified as the study is performed over different continents and thus comprising both developed and developing countries, showing that the level of development plays an important role in the effect of CCIs on wealth, then to a more accurate level on 275 European regions and at the municipality scale, considering more than 500 Valencian municipalities. The strength of the works is that the results are robust to all the different scales analyzed and the positive effect of the CCIs is generally stronger as much as we move from less developed to more developed groups at all the geographical levels considered.

The paper that closes the special issue, authored by Vermeulen and Psenner, departs from the idea that technological evolution and relevant changes in these are able to drive a structural shift toward creative work and this is even more relevant regarding the actual digital revolution. The paper widely explores the framework of institutions governing the regional catching-up between regions that produce these new technologies, defined 'making regions', and those that are not able to produce these technologies and are only able to use them, 'applying regions', in this technology-driven structural shift. The authors identify three functions that drive this change, related to regional innovations and entrepreneurship, educational institutions and labour market.

3. Outlook for further research

In concluding this introduction to the Special Issue and trying to indicate some possible developments in the debate, we refer first of all to the research agenda outlined and to the numerous risks and opportunities mentioned that concern the evolution of the relationship between economy, culture, society and technology (Lazzeretti 2020). To these, the many and interesting insights that emerge from various contributions collected are added. Some of the results cannot be generalized as they are valid only for certain countries, regions or specific technologies. Hence, they need to be confirmed (or proven irrelevant) in different contexts.

However, this leaves space and provides promising avenues for future research, considering the rapidly expanding r-evolution brought by AI that during the last years is expanding also in cultural and creative sectors. Leaving open the questions regarding how the society will react to the already acknowledged dark sides in these areas that are so strongly related to the cultural and social identities of communities.

Disclosure statement

No potential conflict of interest was reported by the author(s).

ORCID

Luciana Lazzeretti http://orcid.org/0000-0002-9759-2289
Stefania Oliva http://orcid.org/0000-0003-2933-4795
Niccolò Innocenti http://orcid.org/0000-0001-8421-5479
Francesco Capone http://orcid.org/0000-0003-2000-3033

References

Banks, D. 2022. "The Attention Economy of Authentic Cities: How Cities Behave Like Influencers." *European Planning Studies* 30 (1): 195–209. doi:10.1080/09654313.2021.1882947.
Boix Domenech, R., B. De Miguel Molina, and P. Rausell Köster. 2021. "The Impact of Cultural and Creative Industries on the Wealth of Countries, Regions and Municipalities." *European Planning Studies*. doi:10.1080/09654313.2021.1909540.
Capron, E., D. Sagot-Duvauroux, and R. Suire. 2021. "Anatomy of a Techno-Creative Community–The Role of Brokers, Places, and Events in the Emergence of Projection Mapping in Nantes." *European Planning Studies*. doi:10.1080/09654313.2021.1959901.
Chandna, V., and M. Salimath. 2020. "When Technology Shapes Community in the Cultural and Craft Industries: Understanding Virtual Entrepreneurship in Online Ecosystems." *Technovation* 92-93: 102042. doi:10.1016/j.technovation.2018.06.005.
Cooke, P. 2021. "'The Dark Triad' Story of Widespread Entrepreneurial Decline and a Future Recovery Discourse." *Dislocation: Awkward Spatial Transitions* 253. doi:10.4324/9781003133551
Cooke, P., and L. Lazzeretti, eds. 2008. *Creative Cities, Cultural Clusters and Local Economic Development*. Cheltenham: Edward Elgar. doi:10.4337/9781847209948.
Cooke, P., and S. Nunes. 2021. "Post-Coronavirus Regional Innovation Policies: From Mega to Giga and Beyond Through Sustainable Spatial Planning of Global Tourism." *European Planning Studies*, 1–19. doi:10.1080/09654313.2021.1936463.
Costa, P. 2022. "Valuing Culture and Creativity Impacts in a Global Technological Era: Reshaping the Analytical Framework." *European Planning Studies*. doi:10.1080/09654313.2021.2023109.
Cristianini, N., T. Scantamburlo, and J. Ladyman. 2021. "The Social Turn of Artificial Intelligence." *AI & SOCIETY*, 1–8.
Cruz, S., and A. Teixeira. 2021. "Spatial Analysis of New Firm Formation in Creative Industries Before and During the World Economic Crisis." *The Annals of Regional Science*, 1–29. doi:10.1007/s00168-021-01052-3.
De Bernard, M., R. Comunian, and J. Gross. 2021. "Cultural and Creative Ecosystems: A Review of Theories and Methods, towards a New Research Agenda." *Cultural Trends*, 1–22. doi:10.1080/09548963.2021.2004073.

Delaplace, M., L. Kebir, M. Gros-Balthazard, and F. Bavaud. 2022. "Uses of Digital Services in Tourism: Evolution versus Revolution? The Case of the Champs-Elysées." *European Planning studies*.

De Propris, L. 2013. "How Are Creative Industries Weathering the Crisis?" *Cambridge Journal of Regions, Economy and Society* 6 (1): 23–35. doi:10.1093/cjres/rss025

Floridi, L. 2014. *The Fourth Revolution: How the Infosphere Is Reshaping Human Reality*. Oxford: OUP.

Gong, H., and R. Hassink. 2017. "Exploring the Clustering of Creative Industries." *European Planning Studies* 25 (4): 583–600. doi:10.1080/09654313.2017.1289154.

Guccio, C., M. Martorana, I. Mazza, G. Pignataro, and I. Rizzo. 2020. "Is Innovation in ICT Valuable for the Efficiency of Italian Museums?" *European Planning Studies*. doi:10.1080/09654313.2020.1865277.

Innocenti, N., and L. Lazzeretti. 2019. "Do the Creative Industries Support Growth and Innovation in the Wider Economy? Industry Relatedness and Employment Growth in Italy." *Industry and Innovation* 26 (10): 1152–1173. doi:10.1080/13662716.2018.1561360

Jones, C., M. Lorenzen, and J. Sapsed, eds. 2015. *The Oxford Handbook of Creative Industries*. Oxford: OUP.

Landoni, P., C. Dell'era, F. Frattini, A. Petruzzelli, R. Verganti, and L. Manelli. 2020. "Business Model Innovation in Cultural and Creative Industries: Insights from Three Leading Mobile Gaming Firms." *Technovation* 92-93: 102084. doi:10.1016/j.technovation.2019.102084.

Lazzeretti, L. 2012. "The Resurgence of the "Societal Function of Cultural Heritage". An Introduction." *City, Culture and Society* 3 (4): 229–233. doi:10.1016/j.ccs.2012.12.003

Lazzeretti, L. 2020. "What is the Role of Culture Facing the Digital Revolution Challenge? Some Reflections for a Research Agenda." *European Planning Studies*. doi:10.1080/09654313.2020.1836133.

Lazzeretti, L., F. Capone, and N. Innocenti. 2017. "Exploring the Intellectual Structure of Creative Economy Research and Local Economic Development: A Co-Citation Analysis." *European Planning Studies* 25 (10): 1693–1713. doi:10.1080/09654313.2017.1337728.

Lazzeretti, L., and S. Oliva. 2020. "Exploring the Marriage between Fashion and 'Made in Italy' and the Key Role of G.B. Giorgini." *European Planning Studies*. doi:10.1080/09654313.2020.1833842.

Lester, R., and M. Piore. 2004. *Innovation. The Missing Dimension*. Cambridge, MA: Harvard University Press.

Mangematin, V., J. Sapsed, and E. Schüßler. 2014. "Disassembly and Reassembly: An Introduction to the Special Issue on Digital Technology and Creative Industries." *Technological Forecasting and Social Change* 83: 1–9. doi:10.1016/j.techfore.2014.01.002

Massi, M., M. Vecco, and Y. Lin. 2020. "Digital Transformation in the Cultural and Creative Sectors." In *Digital Transformation in the Cultural and Creative Industries*, 1–9. Routledge.

Nuccio, M., and E. Bertacchini. 2021. "Data-Driven Arts and Cultural Organizations: Opportunity or Chimera?" *European Planning Studies*. doi:10.1080/09654313.2021.1916443.

Oliva, S., and L. Lazzeretti. 2017. "Adaptation, Adaptability and Resilience: The Recovery of Kobe after the Great Hanshin Earthquake of 1995." *European Planning Studies* 25 (1): 67–87. doi:10.1080/09654313.2016.1260093

Potts, J. 2016. *The Economics of Creative Industries*. Edward Elgar Publishing. doi:10.4337/9781785361517.

Pratt, A. 2008. "Creative Cities: The Cultural Industries and the Creative Class." *Geografiska Annaler: Series B, Human Geography* 90 (2): 107–117. doi:10.1111/j.1468-0467.2008.00281.x

Sacco, P. L., G. Ferilli, and G. Tavano Blessi. 2018. "From Culture 1.0 to Culture 3.0: Three Socio-Technical Regimes of Social and Economic Value Creation through Culture, and their Impact on European Cohesion Policies." *Sustainability* 10 (11): 3923. doi:10.3390/su10113923.

Scott, A. 2006. "Creative Cities: Conceptual Issues and Policy Questions." *Journal of Urban Affairs* 28 (1): 1–17. doi:10.1111/j.0735-2166.2006.00256.x.

Sedita, S., and T. Ozeki. 2021. "Path Renewal Dynamics in the Kyoto Kimono Cluster: How to Revitalize Cultural Heritage through Digitalization." *European Planning Studies*. doi:10.1080/09654313.2021.1972938.

Strom, E. 2020. "Revisiting the Arts as a Socially Innovative Urban Development Strategy." *European Planning Studies* 28 (3): 475–495. doi:10.1080/09654313.2019.1639398.

Taormina, F., and S. Baraldi. 2022. "Museums and Digital Technology: A Literature Review on Organizational Issues." *European Planning Studies*. doi:10.1080/09654313.2021.2023110.

Throsby, D. 2012. "New Technologies in Cultural Institutions: Theory, Evidence and Policy Implications." *International journal of cultural policy* 18 (2): 205–222. doi:10.1080/10286632.2011.587878.

Vermeulen, B., and E. Psenner. 2022. "Exploiting the Technology-Driven Structural Shift to Creative Work in Regional Catching-Up: Toward an Institutional Framework." *European Planning Studies*. doi:10.1080/09654313.2022.2028737.

What is the role of culture facing the digital revolution challenge? Some reflections for a research agenda

Luciana Lazzeretti

ABSTRACT
The article aims to explore the dialectic relationship between digital transformation and societal changes through a cultural and creative approach. The debate between an algorithmic society representation (as a narrative of the past) and a new strategic role of culture (as a narrative of the future) is still largely unexplored. In order to achieve the purpose of the research, the article wants to respond to the following research questions: what is the role of culture facing in the digital revolution? What opportunities and threats are created for the enhancement and preservation of culture and creativity? An open conversation in formal and informal environments has been mobilized from September 2018 until February 2020 with scientists and humanists following a narrative approach. The reflections derived and a comprehensive analysis of the literature on AI and data science have led to a review of models of culture-driven economic development. We propose a new research agenda for the preservation and enhancement of culture able to frame the opportunities and face the threats of the digital revolution.

1. Introduction

This is the time of narratives and storytelling. This is the time of surfing and multitasking. In the Era of Complexity, men and women look for simple solutions to increasingly complex issues. Decision processes change thanks to the application of Artificial Intelligence (AI), algorithms, robots and the Internet of Things (IoT) (Acemoglu and Restrepo 2018; Russell and Norvig 2016; Höller et al. 2014; Ford 2015). Metrics and rankings are produced to justify or to take more objective final decisions (Espeland and Sauder 2007; Domingos 2015). On the other hand, qualitative tools, as subjective representations and perceptions which were once the prerogative of the 'humanities', are now progressively used in many branches of Economics, animating the debate between algorithms and narratives (Thaler 2018; Shiller 2017). In particular, narratives represent an alternative but valid tool in the 'culture of education' (Bruner 1996), and in the 'narrative of the future' to address the increasingly topical issue of uncertainty (Bernardi, Huinink, and Settersten 2019; Vignoli et al. 2020).

We are in the 'summer' of AI, where algorithms and big data as paradigmatic innovations can shape not only scientific progress but also to forge societal values and norms. Now, more than ever, it becomes essential to understand the techno-economic paradigm shift we are facing to frame possible future scenarios (Agrawal, Gans, and Goldfarb 2019; WIPO 2019).

According to Cristianini (2014) a paradigm shifts when a scientific community changes its values, goals, and methods and the spread of these innovations has marked the transition from a knowledge-driven society to a data-driven society.

This is not to affirm a mechanistic view of human evolution expressed by a predetermined set of data. On the contrary, as sustained by Halevy, Norvig, and Pereira (2009) 'The Data are in the Wild':

> The biggest successes in natural-language-related machine learning have been statistical speech recognition and statistical machine translation. The reason for these successes is not that these tasks are easier than other tasks; (…) a large training set of the input-output behavior that we seek to automate is available to us in the wild. (Halevy, Norvig, and Pereira 2009)

This continuous relation between scientific progress and society as a whole is stressed by Kaplan (2016), who questions whether or not AI represents an autonomous discipline or just a field of application of computer science, considering its impact at the socio-economic level.

The example of mobile phones' impact on social behaviour reported by Von Hippel in 'Democratizing Innovation' (2005) concretely exemplifies the effects of this paradigm shift. This is particularly relevant for the enabling functions and features of mobile phones, able to process different kind data (body performances, localization of activities and qualitative data as perceptions, etc.) favouring the exchange of information and influencing the decision process at a relatively low monetary cost. On the other side, we experiment with new kinds of social costs (isolation, new forms of interactions, etc.) that affect human behaviour and brain activities.

The living and working environments of individuals have therefore changed and are integrated into a *unicum* made up of parts that are difficult to distinguish and that involve the experiences made in the physical and virtual worlds that together represent the iso-sphere where the fourth industrial revolution (Floridi 2014) and a new 'humanology' are taking place (Harari 2016). Regarding this dystopia, related to the relationship between man and machine, the Israeli historian Harari in Homo Deus revives the debate on humanology and write: 'it is at the same time, the ecology of the humans and the anthropology of the machines and the study of the mutual redistribution of their functions' (Harari 2016).

It is precisely the dialectic relationship between digital transformation and societal changes the horizon of this paper, which aims, embracing a cultural and creative approach, to foster the debate between an algorithmic society representation (as a narrative of the past) and a new strategic role of culture (as a narrative of the future) exploring a still virgin ground (Amabile 2019). Our research questions are the following: what is the role of culture in the digital revolution? What opportunities and threats are created for the enhancement and preservation of culture and creativity?

We have constructed an open conversation (Lester and Piore 2004) in formal and informal environments with some scientists and humanists that lasted from September 2018 until February 2020 according to a narrative approach.[1] Our reflections led us to review the models of culture-driven economic development and to propose a new research agenda for the preservation and enhancement of culture able to frame the opportunities and face the threats of the digital revolution.

The paper is structured as follows. Section 2 discusses the rise of the algorithm society. Section 3 presents the conservation and technological enhancement of culture, while Section 4 analyses culture as a resource and digital creative capacity. Section 4 presents the dark side of digital revolution. The paper ends with some final reflections for a research agenda.

2. The rise of algorithmic society: a narrative of the past

With the term 'algorithmic society' we refer to that society where the impact of AI is so significant that it influences not only the economic and organizational aspects typical of business contexts but also the political, social and above all cultural aspects of a community of people living in a given territory, influencing fundamental aspects of their life, as consumption and work environment.

At the end of the twentieth century, the solid Fordist capitalism was substituted by the concept of *liquid capitalism* (Bauman 2013), characterized first by the multimedial and then by financial domains. Currently, we are in a new phase defined 'documedial' capitalism by the philosopher Ferraris (Ferraris 2017; Paini and Ferraris 2018). This new capitalism is based on the 'registration' of documents. Documents/goods are exchanged on the web where information represents the strategic resources to be processed.

The famous American constitutionalist Balkin (2017) defines the algorithmic society as a society organized around social and economic decision-making by algorithms, robots, and AI agents with a renewed vigour for the three laws of robotics by Isaac Asimov. Some authors, referring to cybernetics and the concept of 'black box', call it Black society (Pasquale 2015), others prefer to discuss 'algorithmic regulation' starting from the concept of AI as 'social machine' (Cristianini and Scantamburlo 2020).

Notwithstanding the explanatory power of the abovementioned definitions, the framework described represents a narrative of the past, within which the choices of the future are based on the predictive nature of the algorithms and the information related to the past collected by Big Data. Concerning these approaches, the peculiarity of our assumptions consist in discussing in a complex and interconnected multidisciplinary perspective, the three dimensions of the transformation of the algorithmic society: social, economic and cultural, through the lens of the economy of culture and local development. In such a society many things change including the value system, the concept of experience, the way of doing research, the forms of work. Oil is no longer the main energy source: information is 'the new oil'.

In this respect, in this paper the term 'digital transformation' to define the complex and rapid transformation caused by the development of artificial intelligence. This involves not only society but also the economy, the enhancement and preservation of culture and the related models of culture-driven economic development. It has been defined by some writers as a 'digital insurrection' (Baricco 2013) and can be retraced by referring to the narration of its protagonists, places and innovations that generated it. It is a Californian story, a story of a community with its values, a *community in action* as the philosopher Hannah Arendt (1958) would say, which started at the time of the war in Vietnam and continued until today. According to her, the action has to take place in public spaces: now on web space and the *community in action may construct its identity* through social networks.

It all began in California in the late 1960s thanks to an initiative of a group of engineers, hackers, males, white guys, a kind of hippy. A typology of people, completely different from the imaginary of these professions depicted in Europe (Isaacson 2011); it was effectively represented in a recent London exhibition 'California: Designing Freedom' (2017), accompanied by an interesting interview with Google's Head of Design, Matias Duarte.[2]

The research they conducted then continued in at least two other places that are symbolic of the digital revolution: Switzerland and Japan. In Europe, at CERN in Geneva, the WEB was born thanks to the English physicist Berners-Lee (Berners-Lee and Fischetti 2001) and in Japan, with the explosion of the Manga industry, we have the invention of the PlayStation and the development of the video game industry (Aoyama and Izushi 2003).

All these innovations were born in those places that regional science and creative economy literature has described as 'creative milieu' or cultural or creative districts whether they are cities, regions, businesses, universities or districts. We cannot forget that the digital revolution cradle is the Silicon Valley, already described in the past itself as a Marshallian industrial district adjacent to the classic Los Angeleno Hollywood creative district of cinema. Creative territories long observed and studied by regional and creative economy economists such as Allen Scott, Michael Storper and Ann Markusen. These are places where physical and cognitive proximity combine, where multi-ethnic and multicultural communities coexist and where the innovative capacity of culture and creativity generate what today could be defined as 'a creative district of the third millennium'. Here, innovative bottom-up initiatives originated by *cross-fertilization* processes proliferate. Art and science, artists and technologists find the synthesis in iconic products, such as Apple's personal computer, an example of the blend between technology and design. In these places, innovators such as Mark Zuckerberg found the entrepreneurial and financial energies they had not encountered in the places where ideas were born (Harvard University, Boston), as the emblematic story of the birth of Facebook reminds us (Kirkpatrick 2011). These are all places where creative thinking has been able to combine the competitive advantages of localization with those of globalization generating a new category of so-called 'ubiquitous' and multiple products, new technologies and new forms of work.

Paradigmatic innovations have emerged (personal computer, iPhone, iPad, PlayStation, etc.) that have transformed not only machines but also society, starting from the language used, natural and artificial together. An emblematic example is that of social networks, which have evolved rapidly to increasingly simplified forms of communication: from the increasingly short written ones (Facebook, Twitter), to images (Instagram), up to representations of emotions (emoticons), new hieroglyphics of postmodern sign language as also adopted on Facebook.

It is the era of Steve Jobs, Tim Berners-Lee, Mark Zuckerberg, including Kutaragi, who have conquered the world. It is the story of a rebellion that was born local but aspiring to a global dimension from the beginning, without the support of particular theories. The synthesis of this change can be summed up in the vision of the world as a game, or rather as a video game, where adults/children live a condition of increasingly binding duality between real and virtual worlds, between reality and fiction.

In this transformation, we are witnessing a mutation in the function of gaming, which prefigures a training scheme for an entire society. Here the global video game industry gains the podium among the main cultural and creative industries of recent years capable of combining cultural and technological contents and involving networks of companies and consumers of all ages.

In this context, the dimension of videogames can also have double implications, positive (therapeutic) and negative (alienation), as Turkle (1995) reminds us in her book 'Life on the Screen'.

We are at the dawn of a new era, within which with enough data, the numbers speak for themselves characterized by the end of theories (Anderson 2008).

Starting from this scenario we will discuss the impact this transformation has had on culture and creativity and culture-driven development models for conservation and enhancement. A narrative of the where future choices are based not only on data from the past but also on the imagination capacity of individuals.

3. Conservation and technological enhancement of culture: a narrative of the future

Socio-economic transformations have also had an impact on the cultural transformations of the algorithmic society. It is, therefore, necessary to rethink also the models of local development based on the strategic trinomial culture, economy, society of the past adding a fourth pillar: technology. Some examples of cyber-physical idea-structures have already emerged such as the smart city and industry 4.0, but there is still a lack of theoretical models able to properly re-ontologise and re-epistemologise the human project, emphasizing the human component in its design and execution phases (Floridi 2020).

We recall in this regard the recent contribution of Sacco, Ferilli, and Tavano Blessi (2018) which addresses the issue of the evolution of culture and technology for the creation of value by envisioning three socio-technical regimes: Culture 1.0, a pre-industrial model that developed under the aegis of 'patronage' in its many forms; Culture 2.0., where cultural and creative activities produce value and profit through products and services; Culture 3.0, characterized by the active cultural participation of consumer users and the emphasis given to their ability to create social and economic value, where explicit reference is made to the role of technology.

In previous studies, four fundamental phases were identified in the evolutionary process of the relationship between culture, economy and society: the preservation of culture, the economic enhancement of culture; the cultural enhancement of the economy and finally the social enhancement of culture.

In a starting phase, the importance of culture as an asset to be preserved, was highlighted then instead it was considered as a resource to be economically valued, like other productive factors, developing economic models of sustainable local development such as cultural districts and clusters. Also, the studies relative to the innovation processes have changed. During the first two phases they focused mainly on technology transfers and end-users, then, thanks also to contribution of culture, the attention was focused rather on innovative ideas, shifting to the early stages of the innovation process and concentrating on the relationship between creativity, innovation and entrepreneurship.

After the economic and financial crisis of 2008, a fourth phase of the relationship between culture, economy and society began in Europe, which brought society back to the centre of the debate by rediscovering the role of the social enhancement of culture for social cohesion and inclusion, for democracy, well-being and environmental sustainability. In the meantime, in the rest of the world, models based on the economic valorization of culture were spreading, with different times and hybridization of forms. These aspects have been extensively investigated in numerous studies and research assuming as units of analysis: local systems – cities, States, regions, districts and clusters; cultural and creative industries; museums and other cultural organizations, and their implications for innovation, resilience, entrepreneurship, both in Europe and elsewhere (Lazzeretti 2004; Cooke and Lazzeretti 2008; Lazzeretti 2012; 2013; Cooke and Lazzeretti 2019; Lazzeretti and Vecco 2018).

But when we thought we had reached the end of the process, putting the last piece – from culture to economy first and from economy to society later – we could not do it. Accordingly, the digital revolution and the advent of the algorithmic society have changed the reference scenarios and timescales and with them also the models of local development previously built and a fifth phase was opened: 'Enhancement and technological preservation of culture' (Figure 1).

A phase that requires taking charge of both aspects of conservation and technological enhancement of culture at the same time, and not separately as in the past. With a concept of Janus-faced culture, understood both as a 'digital resource and capacity' able to generate value from an economic and social point of view. Able to preserve assets and generate new products and services and sectors or renew existing ones. However, also culture as a 'shield' useful to face the risks of the digital revolution. Both aspects refer to the same principle, the 'Protection and Enhancement of Diversity' and assign a strategic role to 'Territories'.

In the era of the anthropology of machines and the ecology of humans, it is necessary to reset everything and go back to the beginning, to the natural world and the availability of resources. There are therefore three categories we have to create value, culture and development: Natural Resources, Human Resources and also Machines. In this way we will be able to imagine new models of sustainable culture-driven development aimed at the preservation, conservation and technological enhancement of Diversity, be it Natural, Human, Artistic, Cultural and Digital, where the latter represents the synthesis of the interaction between humans and machines.

Even the reference to Places will have to change: they can be at the same time 'Anchors of Memory' to the real world; or 'Traps of Imagination' in the virtual world. Following Bauman's liquid capitalism, the territorial dimension supplies important tools to face the risks of globalization, such as cities of art, places full of meaningful relationships and history, harbingers of culture and development (Lazzeretti 2005).

Now, in algorithmic society, they could be means to face risks of digitization, memory loss, self-consciousness, alienation. But these same spaces could also be the exact opposite. Territory in the twentieth century meant discussing economies of agglomeration, local communities, physical proximity, local development. Then Globalization transformed the division of labour, introduced economies from the global value chain, created a global

Conservation ■ Culture as an asset to preserve and conserve (stock) • Cultural organizations **Focus: conservation/safeguard of the heritage**	**Economic enhancement of culture** ■ Culture as an economic factor of production and driving force for development • Cultural districts and clusters • Cultural industries and organizations **Focus: Local economic development process**
Cultural enhancement of the economy ■ Culture as capacity and resource for innovation and creativity • Creative cities • Creative clusters and districts • Cultural industries and cultural and creative organizations **Focus: innovative process**	**Social enhancement of culture** ■ Culture as an asset for social development • Preservation of identity and authenticity • Education, dissemination of knowledge • Integration and social cohesion • Democracy and well-being • Sustainability, Resilience **Focus: Culture-based sustainable capitalism**
Enhancement and technological preservation of culture	
Technological enhancement of culture ■ Culture as a digital resource ■ Culture as a Digital Creative Ability Policies for value creation and development	**Technological conservation/safeguarding of culture** ■ Culture as a tool to face the risks of the digital revolution Policies for the protection of Diversity and the activation of the Territories
Focus: Digital revolution and "documedial" capitalism	

Figure 1. The five phases of the evolution of the relationship between society, culture, economy and technology. Source: Author's elaboration.

consumer and expanded the concept of proximity (Boschma 2005). Everything merged and thanks also to new technologies, some geographical distances disappeared and with them physical geography gave way to 'cognitive' geography based on knowledge networks and shared spaces. What does it mean, then, territory at the time of the algorithmic society? Are they physical places where to draw and live one's life and work project? Or archive and anchor of the memory of real life? Or maybe 'Digital Domain or Website' to draw new virtual geography that maps the 'Territories of the Mind'?

It is not crystal-clear at the moment, but we know that the concept of Territory will have to be refined again. Of course, it will no longer be linear or even two or three dimensional, but multidimensional. A fourth dimension has been added to the length, height and depth: the virtual dimension. And thanks also to new ICT technologies, artificial intelligence and machines will be able to reinterpret it.

This is the *incipit* for our research agenda. Below we will try to describe some fragments, each of which would deserve a separate discussion, waiting to be able to solve the puzzle of the new paths of culture and creativity that are starting between opportunities for exploitation and risks to face (Figure 2).

4. Culture as a resource and a digital creative capacity

The digital revolution has transformed the entire world economy and the new giants are no longer the seven 'oil sisters' but the new 'Five Sisters', the techno-giants of IT (Google,

Apple, Facebook Amazon, Microsoft). According to the DCMS Model (2001) – a leading taxonomy to frame and classify CCIs, the five sisters abovementioned could be considered as part of the creative economy. However, things have changed a lot since the beginning of the millennium, the golden age of creative economy and other models have emerged over the last 20 years, from experience economy to sharing economy, all growing under the umbrella of the digital economy. These have been classified by Lazzeretti (2013) as technologically driven creative industries, with a presence mainly in the English-speaking countries of Northern Europe, to distinguish them from the more widespread cultural-heritage driven industries in the Mediterranean area. Now, in the recent European classifications (DCMS 2019; OECD 2019) they have been considered separately: the digital sector now also includes media categories that were previously part of the creative industries. If after 2008, the creative sector was considered in Europe a priority to get out of the crisis, now the Five Sisters are among the protagonists of the new platform capitalism (Srnicek 2017) operating in services, production and venture capital. Currently, it is the digital economy, rather than the creative one, that is at the centre of many European programs and many opportunities for the economic exploitation of culture have been created.

4.1. Digital, physical and virtual ecosystems

Among the new digital ecosystems, public or private, where humans and machines interact to solve complex problems and generate products and services, there are *cyber-physical systems* such as 'smart' cities, Industry 4.0 paradigm and augmented reality environments developed in social networks, video games, virtual visits of experiential tourism. These models have rapidly replaced those developed in the creative economy. The smart city (Glaeser and Berry 2006; Caragliu, Del Bo, and Nijkamp 2011) has occluded the creative city where concepts such as creative class, cognitive cultural capitalism, the economy of creative industries had developed (Florida 2002; Pratt 2008; Scott 2008; Potts 2016). The concept of Human Capital has been transformed. The human factor is no longer just a synonym of creativity and talent, carriers for the art values even with traits of surprise, ambiguity, but also of sharing and self-expression. Everything has been simplified in a reductive vision of what is human capital and addressed to the

Opportunities	*Risks*
■ Culture as a resource and digital ability • Digital ecosystems (smart city, Industry 4.0, augmented reality, creative hubs) • Art and digital creativity • Digitization of assets (archives/repositories, digital museums) • Digital creativity and social networks • Creative sectors (video games, TV series) • Soft power cultural organizations (reputation, visibility, trust, community)	■ Culture as a tool to face risks • Alienation and second life • Depletion of natural language • Bias and hidden errors • Memory loss • Loss of fundamental rights (privacy, profiling, democracy, etc.) • Inequalities (socio-economic, digital, recognition)

Figure 2. The opportunities and risks of culture in the algorithmic society. Source: Author's elaboration.

market logic. 'Users/workers are capable of producing information not only about themselves but also about others, *for free*.

The city of the future has become more intelligent – in an engineering sense – than creative. Technologists, rather than creative people, are responsible for the reorganization of life in the city and in the house, where home automation and IoT (Internet of Things) find multiple applications. However, this model is also criticized, especially when linked to the surveillance capitalism (Zuboff, 2019) of the so-called 'Silicon Valley imperialists' (Cooke 2020).

If, on one hand, the smart city model is mainly directed towards the algorithmic society, Industry 4.0 completely reorganizes the places of production (Liao, Loues, and Ramos 2018). Industrial Internet of Things (IIoT) like Internet of Everything (IoE), proposes the maintenance and logistic components and the relationship with customers and suppliers, untying the necessity of physical presence to manage relevant aspects of the factory, radically changing the decision-making of entrepreneurs and middle managers (e.g. monitoring of production, reconfiguration of productive lines, change of business clients' needs). Industrial robots are a classic example of this transformation, along with 3D printers that have revolutionized the times and forms of prototyping, expanding the creative capacity and customization of production (Rayna and Striukova 2014).

Of course, this new paradigm, which in more structured firms has been already embraced, is impacting (and will impact) even small businesses and artisans. Along this line, Made in Italy sectors have largely benefited from this by rejuvenating the traditional production of mature industrial districts with new makers analysed by Italian and non-Italian districts (Bianchi and Labory 2018). However, the introduction of robots has not only been an industrial phenomenon but also a social one that spread first in the USA and Japan, then in Europe. Among the social robots, we remember Alexa, who assists in domestic problems and the anthropomorphous robot Sophia, with the appearance of Audrey Hepburn, designed for the entertainment of elderly people (it may assume over 60 facial expressions).

4.2. Digital art and the digitalization of assets

Creativity does not end with the applications to artefacts 4.0 or robots but also involves the world of art. Through digital technology, art has become multifaceted. From the simple animation of a painting in a digital environment, we have moved on to bio-art, net-art, or robotic art. Artists have created virtual avatars while databases have been used to produce innovative artistic content (Paul 2016). Boden (1990) in his seminal work 'The Creative Mind: Myths and Mechanisms' anticipated this scenario by claiming that creative thought can be better understood with the help of ideas from artificial intelligence. Nowadays, many people question if computers can generate art (Hertzmann 2018). The debate is open and there are interesting studies on the relationship between artists and machines in the realization of the creative process that refer to the so-called 'algorithmic art'. A school of artists uses GANs or generative antagonist network for producing their works (Elgammal et al. 2017). Two interesting examples in this regard are that of Harold Cohen, who developed his AARON program (aaronshome.com) to create his works, and Lillian Schwartz, who uses GANs for computer graphics.[3] In other cases, the computer 'makes art'. This is the case of the 'Portrait of

Edmond Belamy, a canvas print generated from an algorithm based on 15,000 paintings of the fourteenth–twentieth centuries, part of a group of 11 portraits of an imaginary family, successfully sold by the famous auction house Christie's in New York.[4] Another example is the literary novel written by AI, with the help of a human being, who passed the selection of the famous Japanese literary prize Shinichi Hoshi.[5] In the music sector, we also mention the case of MUSE which uses deep learning methodologies to compose music.[6] In the field of poetry, we remember the 'poetic portraits' of the writer engineer Ross Goodwin, who created an algorithm to create poetry, in collaboration with Google's Arts & Culture laboratory, using 25 million words written by poets of the nineteenth century.[7]

Coming back to the cultural economy, the factor that more than others has offered concrete development is the digitalization of heritage (Navarrete 2013). It has spread first in non-European countries such as Canada, Australia, the USA and, then, in Europe. The literature has then moved from the curatorial approach to the digitization of the collections that some authors analysed for instance in the Uffizi case in Florence (Lazzeretti and Sartori 2016).

The list that we could do is very long with a wide range of cases ranging from the digitization of archives and libraries to museum collections, tourism and multimedia activities. This trend has certainly increased in the post Covid-19 scenario with the explosion of distance learning and the use of technology platforms for smart working and entertainment.

4.3. Cultural and creative technology-driven sectors

If the issue of digitization is an acquired issue to be implemented, the rise of cultural and creative technology-driven sectors in the global economy is a global success story. Some examples can be found on specialized blogs that update on the top AI projects in creative industries[8]: from video game producers such as 'Angelina' to the creation of images for Neuromation or services on demand for Nike athletes. Globally, software, video games and media companies dominate the Platform Capitalism's rankings, while in Italy, luxury companies operating in fashion prevail.

A deep consideration should be done concerning the video game sector, which, in our opinion, is one of the most representative of this transformation. It is an activity that combines cultural content, media and software for entertainment, in an era marked by 'the game' as a metaphor for existence. Starting from the 1950s, from the Arcade and Space Invaders to Pokèmon Go, the videogame has redefined the concept of entertainment in continuous evolution. From Japanese manga pioneers to developers of technology platforms (Aoyama and Izushi 2003; Johns 2006), it has become a crucial global industry also important for the construction of legitimacy and reputation (Gong 2020).

However, not only the offer has changed and developed but also cultural consumption. If, on the one hand, algorithmic society in the cinema industry was represented by science fiction movies or by the new streaming platforms for entertainment such as Disney+, YouTubeRed, Netflix, which have become both distributors and producers, on the other hand, TV series are the real novelty. They give us an idea of how consumer behaviours have changed. In particular, the perception of time has changed indefinitely. The narratives have been lost in a continuum, without having a real beginning or an end.

Their duration is not more decided in advance by the producer but by the liking of the demand, continuing from season to season. The series, unlike the films, can be called an example of post-experience of this millennium, where space and time are never exactly defined and where the actors, often, grow together with the stories. Thus, life online and on life becomes a one. A similar case is that of the protagonist of a successful series on Netflix, Tiger King. Written for lovers of big cats, featured by Joe Exotic, owner of a zoo in Oklahoma, the series talked about a crime for which the protagonist was prosecuted. He was arrested during the filming of the series for the same crime.[9]

4.4. Cultural organizations between legitimacy and soft power

Cultural institutions have changed and also the roles assigned to them in the processes of competition and legitimization. Some museums can be assimilated for functions to real cultural enterprises that provide services and products to a plurality of users, such as tourists, citizens, communities and institutions, setting up real marketing departments. This is the case of the 'Museo dell' Opera del Duomo' of Florence that makes extensive use of social media for museum promotion. An example is a recent contest created for Instagram users followed by a collective exhibition of photos posted on social media at the 'Centro Arte e Cultura' in Florence (Sociometrica 2017). Education and research activities carried out by museums and, in particular, those of scientific museums also have grown. The MUSE of Trento, for example, follows the inquiry-based science education pedagogical approach to teaching science, based on an investigation process where young visitors simulate a scientific investigation like real researcher, creating contests with digital tools (MUSE 2018). The Museum of the University of Florence is also recently going in this direction. The Whale Hub project, dedicated to young people between 18 and 25 years old – a target usually few present in the museum – has promoted the creation of a contest of a multimedia prototype to promote the new 'Sala della Balena' (Oliva and Lazzeretti 2020). The transformation of museums into real creative hubs is an ongoing trend. One best practice is the case of the archaeological museum of Naples (MANN), which has been one of the first to draw up a real multi-product strategic development plan and to conceive and create a videogame[10] becoming a best practice of quadruple helix and digital social engagement (Solima 2018).

The most interesting and not yet sufficiently studied role of cultural organizations is that of the legitimacy processes in algorithmic society related to the social perception and recognition (Suchman 1995).

These aspects underline the importance of the creation of 'value' attributable to concepts/values such as reputation, trust, visibility, a sense of community, increasingly lacking in the society of digitalization. Ad hoc evaluation indices have been developed to measure reputation and trust specifically for online communities (Jøsang, Ismail, and Boyd 2005).

In the transition from the entertainment society to that of information increasingly virtual and mediated by social networks, the need for the reconstruction of real and fiduciary social networks that can act as a barrier in times of crisis or alienation returns. We have experimented with it on the occasion of pernicious and unpredictable events, such as terrorism, environmental disasters and recently in the Covid-19 pandemic, which has increased trust and social cohesion also through actions of social engagement. An example is the wide diffusion of initiatives such as the reproduction of works of art through 'Table vivant' launched on Facebook by the Ryjsmuseum in Amsterdam, then followed in 2017 by the Italian Ministry of Cultural Heritage and Activities and Tourism (MiBACT) with the social campaign 'L'arte ti somiglia', the art looks like you. It has been repeated with great success in the spring of 2020 by the Getty Museum in Los Angeles, the Pinchuk Art Center in Kiev and Instagram profile Tussen Kunst en Quarantine.[11] Cultural organizations together with other institutions, schools and universities of all levels have returned to being recognized as an important and unavoidable defense to support individuals and communities, for their role not only in physical territories but also in the virtual space of the web. They can play an important role in the reputation, trust and reconstruction of those social bonds that underpin social capital. However, these activities can be central to the development of the so-called soft power, both in positive and negative terms. Culture together with values and policies can promote the attractiveness of the territories and help build consensus and legitimacy (Nye 2004).

5. The dark side of the digital revolution

The digital revolution can also be a threat, as the historian Harari (2018) reminds us when he claims that the conflict between democracy and dictatorship is not one between different ethical system but actually between data-processing system. In this sense, culture can be an important 'shield' to contrast the 'dark side' of the digital revolution helping to develop conservation and protection policies suitable for mitigating such risk. This important and paradigmatic innovation is also characterized by an 'opacity' due, on the one hand, to the same cybernetic nature of the algorithms and the principles of the 'black box' of their operation and, on the other, to the use of data 'in the wild' and their transformation and use also for the profiling of individuals. Furthermore, data centres are energy-intensive physical structures and an increase in their use can create sustainability problems. The debate is lively and critical not only in the US but also in Europe. Some important US lawyers have drawn up a research agenda to deal with these risks and the European community is also debating the topic in Europe (Calo 2017; EC 2018).

5.1. The risk of alienation and impoverishment of natural language

The first risk is the alienation of individuals. It can be connected to the digital ecosystems that we frequent in social networks, in video games, in the daily online/on life dualism that we live. The computer is no longer just a means but an integral part of our daily and psychological life. This is the risk associated with 'second life or second self' (Turkle 1984). When the smartphone reminds us of how long we spent connected to the mobile phone, we have us a first perception of this risk, while the extractors (platforms) give us a degree of our 'addiction'. As the sociologist Turkle in *Alone Together* (2011) reminds us, technology has changed the way we communicate. The author raises concerns about the degradation of real and genuine social interactions due to the constant exposure to significant, but illusory, exchanges with AI. The web is two-faced: from one hand it gives, while by the other, it takes away. Its central argument underlines that the same technological developments that have contributed most to the rise of inter-connectivity have, at the same time, strengthened a deep sense of alienation among people. Even in this situation, culture can help react to alienation and recover the real awareness of the self.

Directly connected to this first risk there is a second one, which concerns the progressive impoverishment of natural language. A large part of the AI research has been aimed at trying to translate natural language into artificial language or in the recognition of images, making machines more and more anthropomorphic. These practices have led humans to progressively simplify their expressions to interact with machines. The example of messaging is appropriate: the reduction of the words used in messages from Facebook to Twitter, the replacement of the written word with the voice message and, then, with Instagram images, up to the use of emoticons, new hieroglyphics, to synthesize our emotions. In the name of velocity, of continuous exchange, of transmission of the emotion of the moment, with a word, an image or a sound. These examples confirm the radical change in the forms of communication, opposite to that based on the written letter, on length, on slowness. With ordinary mail, the transmission of the message dilated over time, stimulating reflection, imagination. With the SMS or the Amazon courier, everything is consumed in one click.

5.2. Biases and hidden errors

The term bias in the field of AI refers to computer systems that systematically and wrongly discriminate against certain individuals or groups in favour of others. A system unfairly discriminates if it denies an opportunity or a good or if it assigns an unwanted result to an individual or group of individuals for reasons that are unreasonable or inappropriate. Different types of bias are defined in the literature: (i) *pre-existing bias*, they are embedded in a given software because the organization determines its requirements; (ii) *technical bias*, they emerge as a consequence of constraints or technical decisions and can be on a graphical/visual, algorithmic or input level; (iii) *emergent bias*, the use of software changes over time through the addition of new users, new data sources, or for a multiplicity of other possibilities so that bias can emerge in ways that would have been difficult, if not impossible, to predict when the system was built; (iv) *measurement bias* related to the collection of data then used in machine training (Friedman and Nissenbaum 1996).

As an example, we recall a case highly debated that concerns the field of justice (Simoncini and Suweis 2019). This is the case of an American citizen who in 2013 was arrested and sentenced for not stopping at the order of a policeman while driving a vehicle without the owner's consent, thanks to the help of the Compas software. It is a program developed by a private company to evaluate the risk of recidivism and the social danger of an individual based on different statistical data, judicial records and the administration of a questionnaire. Bias, in this case, could have been caused by an error of overestimation based on previous cases. It is known that most of the American prison population is represented by Hispanics and black people.

Another interesting case of bias concerns the gender issue. Flaounas et al. (2013) have addressed the problem of gender bias by analysing 2.5 million articles from 498 online newspapers. Scholars have analysed the articles based on the subject matter, readability, linguistic subjectivity and the presence of imbalances in the gender of the people mentioned within the articles. The results have shown that, in general, of the 1000 most cited people in the data set analysed, the majority were men. Furthermore, a gender bias existed concerning the subject of the articles: sports or financial articles, for example, referred more to male subjects while articles focused on topics relating to fashion or the arts had a more equitable reference to women and men. Another example of gender bias on media coverage has been the study by Heldman, Carroll, and Olson (2005). Their analysis, although based on a sample of about 421 articles, has shown that the media coverage of the Republican presidential candidate Elizabeth Dole has been significantly lower than that of George W. Bush and John McCain, despite his status in the polls of the time.

5.3. The loss of memory and fundamental rights

A fourth risk refers to the loss of memory due to 'digital selection'. It is directly connected to the digitalization of heritages. Not all heritages are digitized but preference is on those that have a high symbolic value and can be valued economically in a second instance. On the one hand, digitalization may be a means for conservation. On the other hand, digital selection may involve the risk that what is handed down is only what is recorded, losing the memory of those invisible heritages that leave no traces on the web. Ironically, we risk having preserved archives of distant past and losing memories of the present. However, information collected on the web by digitalization and processed by algorithms can generate hidden bias and errors. The images recognized by the machines do not always correspond to what we wanted to select and archive. The greatest concern is represented by the loss of fundamental rights and ethical issues. This underlines how these technological platforms are far from neutral (Zuboff 2019). Through the collection, processing and sale of personal data, it is possible to achieve user profiling and to predict individual and collective behaviours. A famous case is that of the Britain online marketing company Cambridge Analytica, specialized in creating psychometric profiles of users through social networks to develop a 'behavioural micro-targeting' system used to create personalized advertising messages. In the spring of 2018, Cambridge Analytica was accused by the Guardian and the New York Times of having used this data to condition both the Brexit referendum and the 2016 US presidential campaign. Following the scandal, the company was forced to declare bankruptcy in May of the same year (Arbia 2018).

Cristianini and Scantamburlo (2020) discuss these risks extensively in their work on the governance of society through algorithmic regulation, also citing some concrete cases such as that of Uber, the digital platform that coordinates nearly two million drivers, and that of the Republic of Estonia. The latter is mentioned because it provides an intelligent E-Governance model in Europe, where there is a unique identifier for each citizen connected to various repositories owned by private or public institutions and tools to provide citizens and organizations with a wide range of services, from filing taxes, parking, buying tickets to the police and voting. Many criticisms have raised at the European level arguing that these innovations destroy more value than they create (Cooke 2019). Other doubts concern the ethical behaviours and principles that AI should follow in society (Floridi and Cowls 2019). DCMS (2018) has also dealt with this argument emphasizing how the spread of false or irresponsible news through social media is not only harmful to privacy but can also be used by criminal organizations. Even finance has its dark side on the web, such as the 'dark pools', the hidden deposits of huge investments made by global investment banks, pension funds and hedge funds, which are inaccessible to investors and only known to the chosen financial institutions (Patterson 2012; Cooke 2016).

5.4. Economic, digital and recognition inequalities

The last risk relates to inequality. Economic inequality has been generated by many creative companies, protagonists of the platform economy, and has contributed to increasing the gap between the wealth of the few and the poverty of the many, as reported by the latest Oxfam report (2019). However, digital inequality and recognition are particularly important for our discussion. The transformations due to digitalization have increased the differences not only between North and South of the world but also those within the industrialized countries (Rodríguez-Pose 2018). Barca (2018) has defined the inequality of recognition as that which affects a manufacturing worker in a country like Italy: it is the inequality suffered by a worker that has lost its centrality due to advanced service and automation, especially in European and American rural areas. These inequalities add up to the economic and social inequalities that emerged in suburbs and places of the excluded. Inequalities also concern the discrimination of ethnic, gender, religious as we have had the opportunity to see throughout history and that remain unsolved today. Regional economics scholars have mapped them by drawing the so-called 'geography of discontent' which many believe to be the basis for the rise in Europe of nationalisms, sovereign movements and phenomena such as Brexit (Dijkstra, Poelman, and Rodríguez-Pose 2020; Iammarino, Rodríguez-Pose, and Storper 2019). With the rise of the algorithmic society and the massive use of the web, similar things happen. Activism on social networks has tried to satisfy the need to be visible, to have a voice. The satisfaction of these needs sanctioned the success of social networks, bringing with it the spread of disinformation (fakes) that characterized that 'digital insurrection' that changed the value system of the twentieth century.

6. A final reflection for a research agenda

How can culture help defend us from all these treats? What are the conservation and protection problems that arise? What culture policies should be designed? Culture can help to get informed, to demand more truthful and responsible information, to become aware of one's rights, also stimulating a necessary digital literacy, increasing the resilience of sectors, businesses, individuals and social communities. However, it is not enough. It is necessary to rethink the policies of protection, conservation and enhancement starting from the fundamental factors, namely: the diversity of resources and the nature and functions of the territories.

This is the last point of our reflection and our proposal, for now only drafted. We should move from considering as assets to be preserved not only the tangible, intangible, artistic, cultural, human or natural heritage but also diversities that generated such heritages. Likewise, it would be useful to conserve territories as both habitats for the protection and development of diversity and as 'anchors of reality and sedimented memory' to which cling to stem the risk of excesses of digitization and to keep vital and sustainable the new digital ecosystems. Places of life and work able, together with culture, of increasing the adaptability of communities and professions as verified during the pandemic. From the reconversions of the luxury industries to the production of coats and masks; from the production of liquors converted into disinfectants to the artists who continued to perform online; to citizens and their music on the balconies. These are examples of the bottom-up 'activation of the territories', of human communities that have become communities in progress supported by the awareness of places that seemed dormant and that has found visibility thanks to the emergency, generating trust and social cohesion that seemed lost.

UNESCO in a recent report (Kulesz 2018) has stressed the importance of protecting diversity and the need to promote creative activities. In this regard, we recall some points which appear to be trajectories for the design of future policies in the enhancement and technological conservation of culture. Mention is made of the creation of spaces dedicated to digital creativity such as laboratories or incubators; the development of the copyright debate; rethinking the status of the artist in the era of artificial intelligence; the simplification of the archiving processes of digital artistic works; the creation of creative start-ups and the prevention and training of monopolies and oligopolies in the AI sector; the update of the antitrust law to regulate digital environments and monitor mergers and acquisitions, among others.

In conclusion, we should not forget that what most distinguishes humans from machines is 'imagination' and as such it should be nourished and protected. The products are crystals of imagination, as written by the physicist Hidalgo (2015) and the ability to create and maintain diversity belong to men and nature. Computers can process thousands of information in search of models and similarities to solve problems that even the collective intelligence of humans cannot solve: computers are good for finding answers and not for asking questions (Mulgan 2018).

We should reconsider that not everything can be digitized and not everything has been handed down in the same way. It has already happened in the past when historians have told us the story of the winners rather than that of the losers. However, we have been able to reconstruct it thanks to other ways of preserving the communities and territories. This is why it is important to recall the strategic role of territories for the preservation and protection of the sedimented memory in places, harbingers of sense of belonging and symbolic capital that represent the idiosyncratic values of their communities, recognized even by web surfers. In the age of social networks marked by the end of the theories where everyone has access to communications and is looking for visibility to have 'recognition', cultural factors and territories are anchors and antidotes to recognize between reality and fiction. As Giacomo Becattini, economist and scholars of industrial districts, has written: 'and in the beginning, there was the consciousness of place and then the class consciousness was born … , therefore we must build a new idea of capitalism that starts from below, preventing chalking of places and collective dismemberment' (Becattini 2015, 158–159).

Difficult to conclude something in which we are currently immersed. Each of the issues discussed deserves a necessary study. Complexity and narratives accompany us together with AI and its applications in the new ecologies of humans and machines where quality and quantity coexist in the 'era without theories' and where numbers speak for themselves. Technology has become a founding pillar of the algorithmic society but we should remember that it is only a medium in the hands of man to be used, not as *Homus Deus* as Harari said, but as *Homus Abilis*, as Sant' Agostino stated.

Notes

1. Preliminary versions of this paper have been presented in many multidisciplinary conferences from 2019. The last one was the International Workshop 'Rethinking Culture and Creativity in the Technological Era', held in Florence, 20–21 February 2020. We thank participants for comments and suggestions.
2. https://designmuseum.org/exhibitions/california-designing-freedom.
3. Harold Cohen: enquire@aaronshome.com; Lillian Schwartz: http://lillian.com.
4. https://www.christies.com/features/A-collaboration-between-two-artists-one-human-one-a-machine-9332-1.aspx.
5. https://shinichihoshi.com/whimsical_ai_project.html.
6. https://openai.com/blog/musenet/.
7. https://artsandculture.google.com/theme/%C2%A0how-ross-goodwin-uses-computers-to-generate-poetry/qgJi59vuG1tJKA.
8. https://medium.com/neuromation-blog/top5-ai-projects-in-creative-industries-7c45040265c7.
9. https://www.netflix.com/it/title/81115994.
10. www.fatherandsongame.com.
11. https://blogs.getty.edu/iris/getty-artworks-recreated-with-household-items-by-creative-geniuses-the-world-over/.

Disclosure statement

No potential conflict of interest was reported by the author(s).

ORCID

Luciana Lazzeretti http://orcid.org/0000-0002-9759-2289

References

Acemoglu, D., and P. Restrepo. 2018. "The Race Between Man and Machine: Implication of Technology for Growth, Factor Shares and Employment." *American Economic Review* 108 (6): 1488–1542. doi:10.1257/aer.20160696

Agrawal, A., J. Gans, and A. Goldfarb, eds. 2019. *The Economics of Artificial Intelligence: An Agenda*. Chicago: University of Chicago Press.

Amabile, T. 2019. "Creativity, Artificial Intelligence, and a World of Surprises. Guidepost Letter for Academy of Management Discoveries." *Academy of Management Discoveries*. doi:10.5465/amd.2019.0075

Anderson, C. 2008. "The End of Theory: The Data Deluge Makes the Scientific Method Obsolete." *Wired Magazine* 16 (7): 16–17.

Aoyama, Y., and H. Izushi. 2003. "Hardware Gimmick or Cultural Innovation? Technological, Cultural, and Social Foundations of the Japanese Video Game Industry." *Research Policy* 32 (3): 423–444. doi:10.1016/S0048-7333(02)00016-1

Arbia, G. 2018. *Statistica, società e nuovo empirismo nell'era dei Big Data*. Roma: Edizioni Nuova Cultura.

Arendt, H. 1958. *The Human Condition*. Chicago: University of Chicago Press.

Balkin, J. 2017. "The Three Laws of Robotics in the Age of Big Data." *Ohio State Law Journal* 78: 1217.
Barca, F. 2018. "Conclusioni. Immagini, sentimenti e strumenti eterodossi per una svolta radicale." In *Riabitare l'Italia. Le aree interne tra abbandoni e riconquiste*, edited by A. De Rossi, 551–566. Roma: Donzelli Editore.
Baricco, A. 2013. *The Barbarians: An Essay on the Mutation of Culture*. New York: Rizzoli International.
Bauman, Z. 2013. *Liquid Modernity*. Cambridge: Polity Press.
Becattini, G. 2015. *La coscienza dei luoghi*. Roma: Donzelli Editore.
Bernardi, L., J. Huinink, and R. Settersten Jr. 2019. "The Life Course Cube: A Tool for Studying Lives." *Advances in Life Course Research* 41: 100258. doi:10.1016/j.alcr.2018.11.004
Berners-Lee, T., and M. Fischetti. 2001. *Weaving the Web: The Original Design and Ultimate Destiny of the World Wide Web By Its Inventor*. Darby: Diane.
Bianchi, P., and S. Labory. 2018. *Industrial Policy for the Manufacturing Revolution: Perspectives on Digital Globalisation*. Cheltenham: Edward Elgar.
Boden, M. 1990. *The Creative Mind: Myths and Mechanisms*. London: Weidenfield and Nicholson.
Boschma, R. 2005. "Proximity and Innovation: A Critical Assessment." *Regional Studies* 39 (1): 61–74. doi:10.1080/0034340052000320887
Bruner, J. 1996. *The Culture of Education*. Cambridge, MA: Harvard University press.
Calo, R. 2017. "Artificial Intelligence Policy: A Primer and Roadmap." *University of California, Davis, Law Review* 51: 399. doi:10.2139/ssrn.3015350
Caragliu, A., C. Del Bo, and P. Nijkamp. 2011. "Smart Cities in Europe." *Journal of Urban Technology* 18 (2): 65–82. doi:10.1080/10630732.2011.601117
Cooke, P. 2016. "Dark and Light: Entrepreneurship and Innovation in New Technology Spaces." *Investigaciones Regionales – Journal of Regional Research* 36: 151–167.
Cooke, P. 2019. "Responsible Research and Innovation? From FinTech's 'Flash Crash'at Cermak to Digitech's Willow Campus and Quayside." *European Planning Studies* 27 (12): 2376–2393. doi:10.1080/09654313.2018.1556610
Cooke, P. 2020. "Silicon Valley Imperialists Create New Model Villages as Smart Cities in Their Own Image." *Journal of Open Innovation: Technology, Market, and Complexity* 6 (2): 24. doi:10.3390/joitmc6020024
Cooke, P. N., and L. Lazzeretti, eds. 2008. *Creative Cities, Cultural Clusters and Local Economic Development*. Cheltenham: Edward Elgar.
Cooke, P., and L. Lazzeretti, eds. 2019. *The Role of Art and Culture for Regional and Urban Resilience*. Abingdon: Routledge.
Cristianini, N. 2014. "On the Current Paradigm in Artificial Intelligence." *AI Communications* 27 (1): 37–43. doi:10.3233/AIC-130582
Cristianini, N., and T. Scantamburlo. 2020. "On Social Machines for Algorithmic Regulation." *AI & Society* 35: 645–662.
DCMS (Department of Culture, Media and Sports). 2001. *Creative Industries Mapping Document*. London: Author.
DCMS (Department of Culture, Media and Sports). 2018. *Disinformation and Fake News: Interim Report*. London: Parliamentary Select Committee on Digital, Culture, Media & Sport.
DCMS (Department of Culture, Media and Sports). 2020. *Economic Estimates 2019, Employment*. London: Author.
Dijkstra, L., H. Poelman, and A. Rodríguez-Pose. 2020. "The Geography of EU Discontent." *Regional Studies* 54 (6): 737–753. doi:10.1080/00343404.2019.1654603
Domingos, P. 2015. *The Master Algorithm: How the Quest for the Ultimate Learning Machine Will Remake Our World*. New York: Basic Books.
EC. 2018. *Ethics Guidelines for Trustworthy AI*. Brussels: European Commission.
Elgammal, A., B. Liu, M. Elhoseiny, and M. Mazzone. 2017. "CAN: Creative Adversarial Networks, Generating 'Art' by Learning About Styles and Deviating from Style Norms." arXiv preprint arXiv:1706.07068.

Espeland, W., and M. Sauder. 2007. "Rankings and Reactivity: How Public Measures Recreate Social Worlds." *American Journal of Sociology* 113 (1): 1–40. doi:10.1086/517897

Ferraris, M. 2017. *Postverità e altri enigmi*. Bologna: Il Mulino.

Flaounas, I., O. Ali, T. Lansdall-Welfare, T. De Bie, N. Mosdell, J. Lewis, and N. Cristianini. 2013. "Research Methods in the Age of Digital Journalism: Massive-Scale Automated Analysis of News-Content—Topics, Style and Gender." *Digital Journalism* 1 (1): 102–116. doi:10.1080/21670811.2012.714928

Florida, R. 2002. *The Rise of the Creative Class: And How It's Transforming Work, Leisure, Community and Everyday Life*. New York: Basic Books.

Floridi, L. 2014. *The Fourth Revolution: How the Infosphere Is Reshaping Human Reality*. Oxford: OUP.

Floridi, L. 2020. *Il verde e il blu. Idee ingenue per migliorare la politica*. Milano: Raffaello Cortina Editore.

Floridi, L., and J. Cowls. 2019. "A Unified Framework of Five Principles for AI in Society." *Harvard Data Science Review* 1 (1): 1–15. doi:10.1162/99608f92.8cd550d1

Ford, M. 2015. *Rise of the Robots: Technology and the Threat of a Jobless Future*. New York: Basic Books.

Friedman, B., and H. Nissenbaum. 1996. "Bias in Computer Systems." *ACM Transactions on Information Systems (TOIS)* 14 (3): 330–347. doi:10.1145/230538.230561

Glaeser, E., and C. Berry. 2006. "Why Are Smart Places Getting Smarter." Rappaport Institute/Taubman Center Policy Brief, 2.

Gong, H. 2020. "Multi-scalar Legitimation of a Contested Industry: A Case Study of the Hamburg Video Games Industry." *Geoforum; Journal of Physical, Human, and Regional Geosciences* 114: 1–9. doi:10.1016/j.geoforum.2020.05.005

Halevy, A., P. Norvig, and F. Pereira. 2009. "The Unreasonable Effectiveness of Data." *IEEE Intelligent Systems* 24 (2): 8–12. doi:10.1109/MIS.2009.36

Harari, Y. 2016. *Homo Deus: A Brief History of Tomorrow*. London: Random House.

Harari, Y. 2018. "Why Technology Favors Tyranny." *The Atlantic* 322 (3).

Heldman, C., S. Carroll, and S. Olson. 2005. "'She Brought Only a Skirt': Print Media Coverage of Elizabeth Dole's Bid for the Republican Presidential Nomination." *Political Communication* 22 (3): 315–335. doi:10.1080/10584600591006564

Hertzmann, A. 2018. "Can Computers Create Art?" *Arts* 7 (2): 18. doi:10.3390/arts7020018

Hidalgo, C. 2015. *Why Information Grows. The Evolution of the Order from Atom to Economies*. New York: Basic Books.

Höller, J., V. Tsiatsis, C. Mulligan, S. Karnouskos, S. Avesand, and D. Boyle. 2014. *From Machine to the Internet of Things: Introduction to a New Age of Intelligence*. Oxford: Elsevier.

Iammarino, S., A. Rodríguez-Pose, and M. Storper. 2019. "Regional Inequality in Europe: Evidence, Theory and Policy Implications." *Journal of Economic Geography* 19 (2): 273–298. doi:10.1093/jeg/lby021

Isaacson, W. 2011. *Steve Jobs*. Milano: Mondadori.

Johns, J. 2006. "Video Games Production Networks: Value Capture, Power Relations and Embeddedness." *Journal of Economic Geography* 6 (2): 151–180. doi:10.1093/jeg/lbi001

Jøsang, A., R. Ismail, and C. Boyd. 2005. "A Survey of Trust and Reputation Systems for Online Service Provision." *Decision Support Systems* 43 (2): 618–644. doi:10.1016/j.dss.2005.05.019

Kaplan, J. 2016. *Artificial Intelligence. What Everyone Needs to Know*. New York: Oxford University Press.

Kirkpatrick, D. 2011. *The Facebook Effect: The Inside Story of the Company That Is Connecting the World*. New York: Simon and Schuster.

Kulesz, M. 2018. "Culture, Platforms and Machines: The Impact of Artificial Intelligence on the Diversity of Cultural Expressions." Report UNESCO.

Lazzeretti, L. 2004. *Art Cities, Cultural Districts and Museums*. Firenze: Firenze University Press.

Lazzeretti, L. 2005. "Città d'arte e musei come 'luoghi di significati': una possibile risposta alle sfide della 'surmodernità'." *Economia e politica industriale* 1: 65–88.

Lazzeretti, L. 2012. "The Resurge of the 'Societal Function of Cultural Heritage'. An Introduction." *City, Culture and Society* 4 (3): 229–233. doi:10.1016/j.ccs.2012.12.003

Lazzeretti, L. 2013. *Creative Industries and Innovation in Europe: Concepts, Measures and Comparative Case Studies*. New York: Routledge.

Lazzeretti, L., and A. Sartori. 2016. "Digitisation of Cultural Heritage and Business Model Innovation: The Case of the Uffizi Gallery in Florence." *IL CAPITALE CULTURALE. Studies on the Value of Cultural Heritage* XIV (14): 945–970. doi:10.13138/2039-2362/1436

Lazzeretti, L., and M. Vecco, eds. 2018. *Creative Industries and Entrepreneurship: Paradigms in Transition from a Global Perspective*. Cheltenham: Edward Elgar.

Lester, R., and M. Piore. 2004. *Innovation. The Missing Dimension*. Cambridge, MA: Harvard University Press.

Liao, Y., E. Loues, and L. Ramos. 2018. "Past, Present and Future of Industry 4.0: A Systematic Literature Review and Research Agenda Proposal." *International Journal of Production Research* 55 (12): 3609–3629. doi:10.1080/00207543.2017.1308576

Mulgan, G. 2018. *Big Mind*. Torino: Codice edizioni.

MUSE. 2018. "Bilancio di Sostenibilità 2018."

Navarrete, T. 2013. "Digital Cultural Heritage." In *Handbook on the Economics of Cultural Heritage*, edited by I. Rizzo and A. Mignosa, 251–271. Cheltenham: Edward Elgar.

Nye, J., Jr. 2004. *Soft Power: The Means to Success in World Politics*. New York: Public Affairs.

OECD. 2019. *Artificial Intelligence in Society*. Paris: Author. doi:10.1787/eedfee77-en.

Oliva, S., and L. Lazzeretti. 2020. "Natural History Museums and Sustainable Development: the Role of Education for Humanistic Tourism." In *Humanistic tourism: Values, Norms and Dignity*, edited by M. Della Lucia and E. Guidici. Abingdon: Routledge.

Oxfam. 2019. "Rapporto Oxfam 2019."

Paul, C. 2016. *A Companion to Digital Art*. West Sussex: John Wiley & Sons.

Paini, G., and M. Ferraris. 2018. *Scienza nuova: ontologia della trasformazione digitale*. Torino: Rosenberg & Sellier.

Pasquale, F. 2015. *The Black Box Society*. Cambridge, MA: Harvard University Press.

Patterson, S. 2012. *Dark Pools: High-Speed Traders, A. I. Bandits, and the Threat to the Global Financial System*. New York: Random House.

Potts, J. 2016. *The Economics of Creative Industries*. Cheltenham: Edward Elgar.

Pratt, A. 2008. "Creative Cities: The Cultural Industries and the Creative Class. Geografiska Annaler, Series B." *Human Geography* 90 (2): 107–117.

Rayna, T., and L. Striukova. 2014. "The Impact of 3D Printing Technologies on Business Model Innovation." In *Digital Enterprise Design & Management*, edited by P. J. Benghozi, D. Krob, A. Lonjon, and H. Panetto, 119–132. New York: Springer.

Rodríguez-Pose, A. 2018. "The Revenge of the Places That Don't Matter (and What to Do About It)." *Cambridge Journal of Regions, Economy and Society* 11 (1): 189–209. doi:10.1093/cjres/rsx024

Russell, S., and P. Norvig. 2016. *Artificial Intelligence: A Modern Approach*. Harlow: Prentice Hall.

Sacco, P., G. Ferilli, and G. Tavano Blessi. 2018. "From Culture 1.0 to Culture 3.0: Three Socio-Technical Regimes of Social and Economic Value Creation Through Culture, and Their Impact on European Cohesion Policies." *Sustainability* 10 (11): 3923. doi:10.3390/su10113923

Scott, A. 2008. *Social Economy of the Metropolis: Cognitive-Cultural Capitalism and the Global Resurgence of Cities*. Oxford: Oxford University Press.

Shiller, R. 2017. "Narrative Economics." *American Economic Review* 107 (4): 967–1004. doi:10.1257/aer.107.4.967

Simoncini, A., and S. Suweis. 2019. "Il cambio di paradigma nell'intelligenza artificiale e il suo impatto sul diritto costituzionale." *Rivista di filosofia del diritto* 8 (1): 87–106. doi:10.4477/93368

Sociometrica. 2017. "Di più, di meglio." Report sul Grande Museo del Duomo.

Solima, L. 2018. "Il gaming per i musei. L'esperienza del Mann." *Economia della Cultura* 28 (3): 275–290. doi:10.1446/91289

Srnicek, N. 2017. *Platform Capitalism*. Cambridge: Polity Press.

Suchman, M. 1995. "Managing Legitimacy: Strategic and Institutional Approaches." *Academy of Management Review* 20 (3): 571–610. doi:10.5465/amr.1995.9508080331

Thaler, R. 2018. "From Cashews to Nudges: The Evolution of Behavioral Economics." *American Economic Review* 108 (6): 1265–1287. doi:10.1257/aer.108.6.1265

Turkle, S. 1984. *The Second Self: Computers and the Human Spirit.* New York: Simon & Schuster.

Turkle, S. 1995. *Life on the Screen: Identity in the Age of the Internet.* New York: Simon & Schuster.

Turkle, S. 2011. *Alone Together: Why We Expect More From Technology and Less From Each Other.* New York: Basic Books.

Vignoli, D., G. Bazzani, R. Guetto, A. Minello, and E. Pirani. 2020. "Uncertainty and Narratives of the Future. A Theoretical Framework for Contemporary Fertility." In *Analyzing Contemporary Fertility*, edited by R. Schoen, 25-47. Berlin: Springer.

Von Hippel, E. 2005. *Democratizing Innovation.* Boston, MA: MIT Press.

WIPO (World Intellectual Property Organization). 2019. *WIPO Technology Trends 2019: Artificial Intelligence.* Geneva: Author.

Zuboff, S. 2019. *The Age of Surveillance Capitalism: The Fight for a Human Future at the new Frontier of Power.* London: Profile Books.

Data-driven arts and cultural organizations: opportunity or chimera?

Massimiliano Nuccio and Enrico Bertacchini

ABSTRACT
Digital transformation has deeply influenced how innovation can rise in the production, distribution and consumption of cultural products. Although data-driven innovation has been proved effective in creating value across many business functions, the pace of adoption of strong data ecosystems seems slower for Arts and Cultural Organizations (ACOs). The paper theoretically explores how data analytics can affect different areas of innovation in the core cultural sectors. By integrating marketing intelligence, arts management and policy literature with illustrative evidence from secondary sources, we discuss the potential impact of data analytics for enhancing ACOs innovation. First, digitalization and connectivity have increased opportunities for customer engagement and empowerment, shifting cultural consumption from a transaction to a relationship with cultural organizations. Second, data-driven metrics allow ACOs and policy makers to match more effectively patterns of consumption and eventually to create value from harvesting and processing information. Finally, although ACOs are encouraged to review their traditional business models through this new trajectory, significant conceptual and organizational barriers question the benefits of data analytics and slow down its adoption. The paper contributes to the academic and policy debate on the role of data-driven innovation in arts management and marketing strategies for cultural organizations.

1. Introduction

Data analytics is the pursuit of extracting useful meaning from the information trapped in different forms of data with the support of computer systems. Over the past decade the notion of data analytics has become pivotal to explain the terrific impact of digital transformation on the economies and societies at the global level. Data-driven innovation has largely proved its effectiveness shaping the new business models in the digital economy (Nuccio and Guerzoni 2019) and pushing productivity and performances of firms adopting data-driven decision making (Brynjolfsson and McElheran 2016). The cultural and creative industries (CCI) have been at the core of the data revolution since most of cultural contents including books, news, videos, music, advertising, etc. have been transformed into digital products reducing the need of any material support, dropping dramatically the cost of their production and facilitating their distribution. Whether this process has broadened opportunities for cultural producers to access a wider market and for cultural consumers to satisfy their specific taste or, on the contrary, has brought even more concentration corroborating the 'winner takes it all' character of CCI (Caves 2000) is still controversial. Less questionable is the effort of small and large firms and public sector organizations in endlessly collecting and processing huge amounts of data concerning audiences and their online and offline behaviour to make better decisions about what movies to recommend, what products to market, or what tools to use to persuade their targets.

Although insights of the impact of new digital and networked technologies on the production and dissemination chain of cultural products can be found in organization theory and management literature for cultural and media industries (i.e. Hirsch and Gruber 2015), so far no specific focus has been reserved to the emerging challenges posed by the data revolution. As suggested by Handke, Stepan, and Towse (2016) and more recently by Gilmore, Arvanitis, and Albert (2018), the arts and cultural field shows a gap in comprehensively addressing the adoption and diffusion of data analytics in order to understand their effect on audiences, organizations and stakeholders. In fact, data analytics is not simply about the opportunity to access and exploit a larger quantity of information but implies a disruptive change in the mindset of organizations towards a conscious data-driven strategy.

The paper intends to evaluate the extent to which data analytics can affect innovation in arts and cultural organizations (ACOs). With this definition, we focus on the 'core arts field' (i.e. archives, heritage, museums, theatres, festivals, etc.) as defined by KEA (2006). Compared to other sectors of cultural and creative industries with distinct value chains or a stronger 'industrial' dimension, organizations in this field are characterized by the slowest change in both semiotic codes and the material base of cultural production, often focusing on preservation and transmission of cultural heritage (Jones, Lorenzen, and Sapsed 2015).

Despite the technological dimension being only one aspect of digital transformation, we apply and adapt the conceptual framework developed by Bakhshi and Throsby's (2012) to new digital technologies in ACOs to analyse the innovative potential of a data-driven strategy.

Based on this framework, we identify and discuss key areas of innovation on which data analytics can contribute to ACOs' operations, namely innovation in customer relationship, innovation in value creation and innovation in business model. We claim that implementing data analytics to build a strategic relationship with both audience and stakeholders can open opportunities for ACOs to develop new business models. At the same time, we underline the possible limitations and risks for a full implementation of data-driven strategies by ACOs identifying key challenges related to privacy concerns in the use of audience data, as well as barriers and false expectations of the ACOs in adopting data-driven strategies for decision making.

From a methodological viewpoint, we survey and integrate different strains of literature, namely arts management, marketing intelligence and cultural policy to show how data analytics represent a new wave of the digital technological trajectory influencing ACOs innovation processes. Moreover, we support our theoretical considerations by discussing key illustrative evidence drawn from secondary sources on data analytics applications in the arts and cultural sector.

It is finally worth to notice that in the last years, there has been a growing interest in understanding the opportunities that big data can offer to the arts and humanities as disciplines, with an emphasis for example on the use of digital data in artform development (Grugier 2016) and in the emerging field of digital humanities (Kaplan 2015). Differently from these perspectives, we are interested in how data analytics mediates the relationship with the audience, on the one hand, and with funders and policy makers, on the other, in order to design new business models.

The paper is organized as follows. In Section 2, we introduce the notion of data analytics and its transformational effect and we discuss how it relates with the broader area of digital technologies in the arts and cultural sector. In Section 3 we present the conceptual framework to disentangle and interpret the innovative potential of data analytics in ACOs. Section 4 discusses key illustrative applications of data analytics in three main areas of innovation, while in Section 5 illustrates the key challenges to a widespread implementation of data-driven strategies by ACOs.

2. From digital technologies to data analytics

Technological innovation has historically shaped markets of artistic and cultural products by triggering new forms of cultural production and new consumption patterns (Jones, Lorenzen, and Sapsed 2015). It is generally recognized in the literature that technological innovation contributes to the reduction of exogenous sunk costs of creations in entertainment industries (Bakker 2015) and the introduction of new technologies have multiple effects on cultural consumption, such as changes in relative prices of products, increased variety and new induced preferences (Potts 2014).

With the spread of digitization and the information and communication technologies (ICTs), digital technologies have soon attracted an increasing attention for the challenges and opportunities that such new forms of innovation have for arts and cultural institutions, influencing their organizational capabilities and audience behaviour.

Looking at the museum and heritage sector as an illustration of this research trajectory, an extensive literature across several disciplines has identified key issues and patterns in the adoption of digital technologies.

A first analytical dimension refers to the impact of digital technologies on the communication of cultural content and its implication for value creation. Production and distribution channels of digital cultural content have created new opportunities to enhance the communication of museums' collections (Bertacchini and Morando 2013), but their adoption questions traditional economic appropriation strategies of the cultural value (Navarrete 2013) or require change in the drivers of organizations' value (Camarero and Garrido 2008; Lazzeretti and Sartori 2016).

Other works have instead focused on new professions, digital literacy and the restructuring of the internal organization that digital technologies require for an effective management of these organizational capabilities (Borowiecki and Navarrete 2017; Carvalho and Matos 2018; Orlandi et al. 2018). Finally, a third analytical perspective investigates how digital technologies have shaped in recent years audience behaviour and engagement with ACOs offer, with particular reference to the type and quality of experience of online visits for audience development (Marty 2008; Bakhshi and Throsby 2012), interaction through social media and participatory practices of co-creation (Booth, Ogundipe, and Røyseng 2020; Taylor and Gibson 2017).

Given that the effects of the digital revolution on ACOs have already been widely recognized over the last decades, a key question to answer is whether data analytics, both for its features and impacts, represent a new wave of innovation relatively to the previous technological trajectory.

Data analytics is strongly tied with the big data paradigm, whose definition is still in evolution and controversial since it is the result of different disciplinary contributions. The term started circulating in the early 2000s (Chen, Chiang, and Storey 2012), making its first appearance in scholarly research from 2008, though the very first signs of its usage can be traced back to the 1970s (Ularu et al. 2012). At the dawn of e-commerce, the distinguished analyst Doug Laney (Kitchin 2014) had proposed three challenges for data management, which have since been co-opted as a key definition based on the celebrated 'three V's': volume, variety and velocity.

First, the need to gather, store and process massive quantities of data requires new ICT standards which include cloud computing and improved computational power (Lilley and Moore 2013; Chen, Chiang, and Storey 2012). Second, the multiple typologies of unstructured data call for flexible solutions which link the different sources of datasets to extract enriched profiles of clients. Third, since the speed at which data are gathered is continuously increasing (Bughin, Chui, and Manyika 2010), organizations must properly plan their capacity for knowledge management and prevent the accumulation of useless information (LaValle et al. 2011). The good news is that both the processes of adoption of digital innovations and diffusion of digital skills (Schmarzo 2013) are accelerating, while the costs for accessing data-driven technologies are steadily dropping. Finally, data scientists attach great importance also to a fourth 'V', veracity, and stress that data must be as complete and close to the observed phenomena as possible to avoid biases in the analysis and misleading outcomes for managers and policy makers (Kwon, Lee, and Shin 2014).

The existence of multiple, ambiguous and often contradictory description of the term big data led Ward and Barker (2013) to adopt the notion of *data analytics* as more appropriate to highlight the value of computational and analytical processes. Building on this perspective, we claim that a data analytics approach is potentially useful to advance knowledge and implement activities in the arts and cultural sector. Being expressly conceived to deal with complex systems, data analytics matches the distinctive combination of cultural, social and economic values generated in the arts and cultural sector (Throsby 1999; Klamer 2004; Hutter 2008). Moreover, data analytics is not merely a set of advanced quantitative techniques to analyse data but can have strong implications in shaping the attitude through which ACOs understand and improve their multidimensional impact on individuals and society.

Compared to previous innovation in the ICT, data analytics can be portrayed as a new layer of the digital revolution based on connectivity and digitization, but with greater emphasis on the potential for agents' decision-making rather than for information dissemination and interaction. Crucially, data analytics is also a prerequisite for a potential next wave of digital technological change in cultural markets represented by Artificial Intelligence (AI) systems. As noted by Peukert (2019), as creators and cultural organizations can use data to learn about product characteristics that specific types of consumers care about, it seems possible to imagine in the future machine-generated cultural products and services. The opportunity of machine-driven creation has already been exploited in the CCI, for example in writing plots of new TV series or in making pop music. However, the limit of AI in performing creative work has been stressed in many industries, where machines are adopted and become valid human substitutes especially in routine and low skilled jobs.

3. Conceptual framework

In order to better understand the impact of data analytics we propose to rely on the conceptual framework proposed by Bakhshi and Throsby (2012) to categorize and interpret how new digital technologies have been applied in the ACOs.

Their approach starts from identifying the non-profit-oriented and multiple objective function of ACOs, which partly differs from profit-oriented market logic in pursuing and adopting technological innovation. Following this approach, it is possible to identify three main dimensions of innovative practices through which digital technologies can be applied to and impact the activities of ACOs (Figure 1). Technology-driven innovation can help: (i) to produce benefits in audience outreach by enhancing the

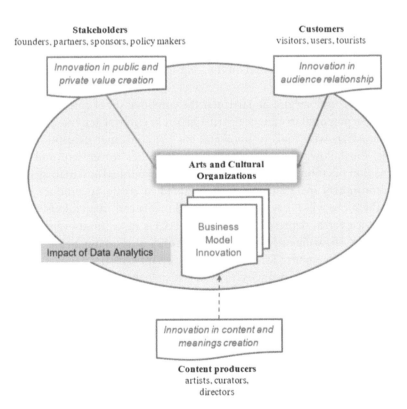

Figure 1. The effects of data analytics innovation on Arts and Cultural Organizations management and operations.
Source: Personal elaboration on Bakhshi and Throsby (2012).

relationship with customers; (ii) to develop new forms of value creation for stakeholders like policy makers, sponsors, partners and more in general funders; and (iii) to prompt artform development by cultural producers experimenting new technologies in artistic expression. The combination of the former dimensions of innovation allows ACOs to design new business models and shift away from the traditional but insufficient sources of revenues based on ticketing and donations which has often been proved not financially viable for many museums and theatres. This conceptual framework encompasses all the potential subjects related to ACOs' mission (audience, artists, managers/employees and funders/policy makers) suggesting that innovation practices arising from new technologies can trigger multifaceted effects that should be considered under a unified approach.

In our analysis we intend to show the possible impact of data analytics on three intertwined innovation processes identified in the conceptual framework (Figure 1), namely innovation in customer relations, value creation and business models. While we acknowledge the emerging contribution of data-analytics in data-driven artform development (Grugier 2016) – with artists actively and critically engaged with coding and data visualization in the field of music, dance and visual art – we consider the use of data in such innovative practices still merely instrumental to the creative process. Conversely, innovation through data-analytics in customer relations, value creation and business models have the potential to more deeply and readily influence the management structure and operation of ACOs.

First, building on the popularity of a data-driven strategy in digital marketing and business intelligence, we present its potential for audience engagement and for establishing new organizational modes based on the long-term relationship with visitors and customers (Sashi 2012).

Second, ICT technology and in particular the combination of connectivity and digitalization have the potential to enhance participation in cultural activities and, at the same time, provide ACOs with tools to track and analyse consumer perceptions, sentiments and feelings, thus allowing unprecedented opportunities to reorient and enhance the value proposition of cultural activities and their organizational and managerial practices. Nowadays, consumers are seizing the opportunity to co-create, co-produce and inoculate their own values into what they consume. Digital media can tremendously contribute to increase (or, vice versa, depress) 'buzz' around ACOs or cultural events, and enhance participation and engagement, both online and offline, spurring a new wave of brand and reputation management (Tsimonis and Dimitriadis 2014).

Finally, ACOs have often struggled to design sustainable business models which allow them to achieve their objectives and fulfil their mission, even more in times of crisis for example after the outbreak of the Covid-19 pandemic. Own sources of revenue have proved to be marginal in the overall museums and theatres income, in particular when based on ticketing. New business models should look at digital business where the main value for funders and shareholders comes from the number of affiliates, followers and fans. Since ACOs are requested to build on their attractivity and powerful symbolic value to engage their audience, this same information becomes strategic to attract both potential business funders willing to pay for accessing insights on customer behaviour and institutional stakeholders to plan and implement more effective and targeted cultural policies. Most of actual cultural policies are not informed by knowledge about users and totally incapable to target people not attending cultural activities. Predictive power of a data analytics approach is supposed to better address needs and expectations of cultural consumers and better allocate public and private resources.

Taking advantage of these opportunities does not simply imply an investment in new digital technologies. Even more than in other sectors, digital transformation in the core cultural sectors is more a managerial issue than a technical one since potentially it can bring about fundamental changes in business processes, organizational structure and capabilities, operational routines and information flows. In other words, ACO have the chance to embrace change in decision-making relying less on intuitive reckoning and more on hard evidence.

4. Data analytics and innovation in ACOs

4.1. Innovation in audience relationship

Data analytics has brought about radical changes in the understanding of consumer behaviour and, consequently, in both economic theory and marketing practice. The approach of firms in producing, distributing and marketing goods and services has undergone some remarkable changes over three major phases. In the initial mass-marketing phase firms were trying to sell the same product to all buyers, adopting a one-size-fits-all approach. Recognition of the diversity of customers' needs and desires led to the second phase, known as product-variety marketing. Firms began manufacturing products and creating services with different features, which could respond to customers' diverse tastes. Strong competition in all markets led to the third phase, known as segmentation marketing, which is marked by an effort to identify, group and satisfy different customer categories. Data-driven innovation has made this option possible by gathering and processing and then aggregating micro-data which tracks the purchasing behaviour of customers.

The extent to which this paradigm shift has been implemented by ACOs is controversial. The core arts field has progressively tried to move away from the theoretical cornerstone concerning cultural consumption: a supplier-induced demand, typically inelastic and driven by a cultural hierarchy of legitimate taste (Blaug 2001). In fact, contemporary arts marketing has witnessed a shift from a product-centric to a customer-centric perspective, where ACOs – e.g. established museums or popular festivals – now seek to create a more sophisticated offer based on their knowledge about different audience segments (Colbert and St-James 2014; Samis and Michaelson 2016). Carù and Cova (2006) have largely explored the experiential dimension of cultural consumption stressing that the quality of interaction may be more important than the cultural content and engaging with customers in the co-production of the cultural experience is very effective to empower them. Di Pietro et al. (2014) push the visitor centric perspective further suggesting that both qualitative and quantitative methods to survey customer satisfaction can enhance awareness of museums' audience and prompt outreach actions which ensure their social and economic sustainability.

The proliferation of audience studies goes together with a second major change that has marked contemporary marketing theory and practice concerning the management of customers. Namely, there has been a shift from a transaction to a relationship orientation, which pushed marketing departments to *proactively creating, developing and maintaining committed, interactive and profitable exchanges with selected customers over time* (Garrido and Camarero 2014, 95). In contrast to the transaction orientation, which centres on increasing revenues at a single purchasing occasion, the relationship orientation adopts a long-term perspective and aims at enhancing customer lifetime value (CLV), that is, the value of all profits earned from a customer during her entire relationship with a firm or organization. Data-driven organizations should be able to manage the life cycle of their customers by extracting value at each stage, for example, launching member-get-member programmes in the acquisition phase; pushing up- and cross-selling sales the development phase; and planning anti-churn campaigns in the retention phase (Ang and Buttle 2006).

The paradigm shift towards individual consumers, the enhancement of their loyalty and the desire to improve retention rates have finally led to the emergence of customer relationship management (CRM) in marketing and management practice also in the CCI. Although the attempts to precisely define CRM have proved to be more difficult than it may seem, its implementation is pivotal in a data-driven organization. Audience-related data is used for segmentation and develop targeted offers for different segments or even individual customers. Because of the different digital channels available, customized offers can be communicated directly to clients and stakeholders at a very low cost and, unlike traditional advertising, allows for two-way communication with requests of feedback and interactions.

The museum sector is a helpful example to show how this framework applies to other ACOs. There are a number of studies examining loyalty in museums that have found several factors to be equally as important as satisfaction to retain visitors. To be more specific, staff services, perceived organizational efforts, organizational identification, and existing visitor loyalty have emerged as the four key factors. The accessibility and friendliness of museum personnel has a positive impact on visitors' decisions to renew their membership (e.g. Harrison and Shaw 2004; Maher, Clark, and Gambill Motley 2011). High-quality customer service in museums consists of paying attention to each visitor and being able to respond to their needs and interests as well as to provide accurate and relevant information about buildings, collections and exhibits. As shown in a study carried out by Siu et al. (2013), visitors respond positively to perceived efforts in relationship investment by ACOs, valuing a museum's attempt to provide new and innovative services more than tangible rewards. Garrido and Camarero (2014) conducted an extensive analysis of museums from four European countries – France, Italy, Spain, and the UK – and observed that organizational learning, namely an organization's effort to learn more about customers and use that insight for development of new products and processes, has a positive impact on visitor loyalty and community involvement.

Festivals seem also at the forefront in the adoption of such innovations. Established in 1999, the Coachella Valley Music and Arts Festival animates for some days a remote area in the desert of Colorado. The success of the festival (250.000 tickets sold and $114 millions of revenues in 2017) is also based on a data-driven strategy which helped to determine which artists to select on the following season studying audience preferences of the former performers.[1] IBM, one of the largest player in the market for integrated data analytics and AI solutions, has partnered two popular festivals in Denmark – Roskilde and Smuck – and track the movements of hundreds of thousands people onsite across the different stages and stalls not only to predict music preferences, but to manage complex logistical issues related to the distribution of food and beverage and to prevent possible risky gatherings.[2]

4.2. Innovation in public and private value creation

The advantages that data analytics provides in terms of tools to track and analyse cultural consumption offer unprecedented opportunities to reorient and enhance the value proposition of cultural activities and their organizational and managerial practices.

A first channel is through data-driven metrics for measuring artistic quality or the economic and cultural value created by ACOs and use them for refining their strategies. It is commonly recognized that adequate metrics are lacking to capture the complex set of direct, indirect, instrumental and intrinsic benefits created by the activities and services provided by ACOs (McCarthy et al. 2001). So far, value generation has relied on few quantifiable indicators, such as figures about audience attendance, revenues, number of educational programmes, donors, friends, funds and sponsors attracted.

However, as the transition to digitization has enabled tracking in more systematic ways how different groups of audience access and use the services provided by ACOs, data analytics may be used to develop novel metrics of value creation. As noted by Bertacchini and Morando (2013) for museums' digital collections, collecting and crunching data about how museum content is utilized is an important asset for an organization in assessing the social impact and success of its activities or the fulfilment of its inherent public mission. In this context, some pioneering open access initiatives suggest that digital image metadata make it possible to track how audiences are integrating and connecting knowledge and information about museum artworks using Web 2.0 tools (Bray 2009).

Similarly, cultural institutions can draw relevant information about impacts on the audience by tracking and measuring visitors' sentiment or audience mobility and attention. The former strategy is usually implemented through social media analytics and can be helpful to capture and monitor the social value of cultural experiences and visitor engagement (Gerrard, Sykora, and Jackson 2017). The latter usually requires technological infrastructure such as Bluetooth proximity detection systems and is apt to improve on site visiting conditions and the quality of a visitor's experience in the museum. For example, through this technique, Yoshimura et al. (2014) have examined visitors' mobility styles at Louvre Museums and found that the behaviour of short-stay and long-stay visitors is not substantially different in terms of path length or number of unique nodes visited.

Data analytics may also potentially foster public value creation by improving the design and monitoring of cultural policies. In this case, the same data analytics strategies to enhance the audience reach or to improve the measurement of the values created by individual cultural institutions may be equally used at a larger and more systemic urban or regional scale to coordinate policies in different cultural sectors, given the heterogeneity of ACOs and their audiences, and relate them more closely to local dynamics. A parallel may be considered here with the digital realm, where tracking individuals' online cultural consumption patterns has already provided a better understanding of individuals' behaviour and informed providers of cultural content in their marketing strategies.

For example, the 'superstars vs the long tail' debate (Anderson 2006; Brynjolfsson, Hu, and Smith 2006; Elberse 2008) has shown that it is more likely that cultural omnivores sustain both the consumption of popular and niche products rather than having a more tailored and distributed consumption across diversified products, based on individual tastes. Piccialli et al. (2020) suggest that data analytics could be systematically adopted to understand and monitor the use of cultural spaces also highlighting hidden behaviours and visiting styles.

In a similar vein, we contend that by pooling and analysing information about ACOs' activities and individual audience profile and behaviour for different cultural services, data analytics may provide new tools to achieve some crucial goals in cultural policy:

- enhancing the planning of the local cultural offer, which is traditionally poorly coordinated across several cultural, heritage and arts institutions in a region;
- integrating and facilitating different cultural consumption patterns;
- addressing socio-economic barriers to the access of cultural activities.

One of the most illustrative examples to reach these goals is Audience Finder, a free audience data and development tool managed by the UK Audience Agency (Ellerton 2018). Audience Finder exploits the aggregation of ticketing data and data collected using a standardized audience survey by individual organizations which have joined the project. The data collected can then be used by the same organizations to understand, compare, and apply audience insight.

Similarly, another promising application of linked shared data across cultural organizations may come from an improved use of data generated by users' passes to networks of museums and other art and cultural institutions. These schemes are usually designed as a marketing solution for cultural tourists or, in few cases, for local residents, such as the Dutch Museum pass or the Carta Musei Piemonte (Werff, Koopmans, and Boyer 2014; Bertacchini, Nuccio, and Durio 2021). So far, The academic and policy interest for these schemes has been mainly relegated to understanding the effect that a bundling pricing strategy, coupled with unlimited or extended accessibility, have on the aggregate demand for the involved cultural services and their implication in terms of financial sustainability. By contrast, the potential of analysing data related to individual passholders to devise a more customized cultural offer at the local level and to coordinate cultural policies has been far less explored.

4.3. Innovation in business models

While data-driven metrics are so far the clearest application of data analytics to ACOs' strategies for enhancing audience relationship and expanding their value creation processes, a less evident, but equally promising trajectory is the development in the arts and cultural field of new data-driven business models that go beyond standard digital strategies. Professionals in museums, theatres, festivals and other ACOs have long recognized the advantages of nurturing long-term relationships with their audience and enhancing customer loyalty and commitment. In order to encourage repeat attendance, organizations resort to the creation of membership schemes and the organization of special events. If membership programmes are well designed, i.e. able to attract an audience and donors, they have several advantages and potentially a higher ROI than doing special events (Maher, Clark, and Gambill Motley 2011). This is because members join such schemes for a number of intangible benefits, whose symbolic value often exceeds that of tangible benefits, especially at higher tiers (Paswan and Troy 2004). In addition, ACOs can count on revenues from membership fees whether members actually attend events or not.

Subscription models developed in the digital economy for streaming services of cultural content have been applied successfully across a range of cultural and creative industries (Peukert 2019) and they should be considered when implementing digital strategies into ACOs' membership schemes, in particular with the objective to offer extended or customized experience and commercial services in exchange for information about their subscribers.

Subscription models will continue to depend on the benefits offered. While this requires further programming and scheduling of events and activities that spread equally across a year and cover the wide range of public interests, it will encourage staff to become more creative when programming. It would also require long term strategic planning, yet this could produce lasting benefits for any ACOs.

Less explored by ACOs is the adoption of a digital advertising business model, where a content provider offers free services to customers to ensure a large enough audience to advertise third parties' products. It is difficult to imagine a museum or a library as digital platforms able to attract advertisers, but many ACOs have pushed the borders of their merchandizing well beyond the traditional gift shop we are used to in many museums. For example, the National Museum of China in Beijing, probably the leading institution of Chinese traditional and material culture, has set a partnership with TaoBao, the online shopping website controlled by Alibaba, to distribute any sort of artifact or product related to the collection. The museum website created a dedicated page which works both as a search engine and ecommerce and where anyone can buy not only books, replicas and jewellery, but also lamps and mobile accessories.

The museum sector can show that in most of CCI there is a huge potential for organizational change to adapt to evolving taste and to personalize and tailor experiences and products. One illustrative example of such an emerging approach comes from the pioneering experience run by the Dallas Museum of Art (DMA) – one of the prominent art museums in America, located in the nation's largest arts district in downtown Dallas (Anderson 2019). In 2012 the value of the admission tickets and entry-level membership (18.000 paid members) corresponds to only 7% of the budget. In January 2013 the museum introduced a programme of free membership in order to expand the customer base among non-visitors.

The key features of the new DMA membership scheme clearly illustrate the attempt to leverage on subscribers' data to enhance the museum experience by innovating a traditional museum marketing tool:

- At the time of enrolment, new DMA Friends receive a card that allows them to chart their engagement with the Museum.
- The programme allows members to earn badges and points to unlock special rewards when visiting the DMA.
- Members can link their mobile phone to their DMA Friends account.

- The new membership scheme encourages the sharing of your museum experience on social media sites.

The DMA has found that due to the amount of data one participant can produce, approximately 1,000 records in one visit, the database and analysis of data has required extensive work as well as greater cross departmental collaboration. This was also due to the unexpected high volume of interest in the programme, originally thought to be 20,000 members in one year and found to be five times larger. The number of staff needed, 25-35 people just working on the DMA Friends programme, was larger than anticipated.

The vision behind this marketing tool is a broader vision for the data-driven museum. The museum can be a multiplier of urban areas related to cultural consumption thanks to a coalition loyalty programme (Breugelmans et al. 2015). A loyalty card scheme can involve a wide network of retail and commercial activities at urban, regional and national level. The consumer can take advantage of discounts and promotions, earn points, enjoy preferential access and much more. Benefits to the coalition partners range from the acquisition of new customers by sharing with other partners to the reduction in operating costs and increase of ROI by decreasing churn. Most important, such an approach offers the opportunity to know the consumption habits of and enables coalition partners to seize new business opportunities by crossing data provided by the business intelligence system.

Also, from an organizational design perspective, the adoption of a data-driven strategy shall favour the integration of small and medium organizations to build a common standard infrastructure able to perform data analytics. The best practices of loyalty programmes and museum cards suggest the advantages of sharing information about consumer behaviour in the whole range of cultural consumption. Centralization of data technologies and management is not only cost saving but can improve real cooperation across ACOs and implementation of local decentralized networks catering for their ordinary audience.

5. Challenges in data analytics adoption

While a data-driven strategy has the potential to radically innovate ACOs' practices in both audience relationship and value creation, it is worth to notice how such an evolution of the technological trajectory also poses some key challenges for its wide adoption in the arts and cultural sector.

A first potential drawback to the widespread and optimistic adoption of data analytics in the ACOs stems from privacy concerns related to audience behaviour. This concern is not specific to the cultural domain but has already been clearly identified as one of the main social challenges and potential unintended negative consequences of the rise of big data. According to Boyd and Crawford (2012), data analytics as a radical socio-technical phenomenon may lead to new waves of privacy incursions and invasive marketing which can eventually reduce consumers' welfare or even arbitrarily deter alleged deviant behaviour.

From an economic viewpoint, privacy in the age of algorithms poses to consumers and organizations newer trade-offs. Individuals benefit from sharing more and more information about themselves with firms and providers to enhance customization and usability of services. At the same time, the decline in the cost of storing and manipulating information has led organizations to a growing incentive to price discriminate, coupled with the increasing ability to price discriminate (Odlyzko 2003). On the opposite side, consumers want to avoid misuse of the information they pass along to others, while organizations are leveraging more and more from the value of aggregated data and don't want to alienate their data with policies deemed as intrusive (Acquisti, Taylor, and Wagman 2016).

The optimal solution to these trade-offs mainly depends on the value that individuals and society attach to private information about identity and behaviour in different realms of human action. The main challenge is therefore to understand whether the adoption of data analytics in the core arts field, where cultural values and preferences are particularly relevant not only in driving consumers choice but also in revealing individuals' identities, will lead to larger concerns or not.

From an empirical viewpoint, data analytics might not be the panacea for addressing all the questions instrumental for ACOs to understanding their audience and markets. This can be clearly illustrated by comparing the analysis of information collected through transactional data generated by audience's activity with respect to more traditional survey-based approaches.

Transactional data generated by audience activity in general may be flawed by a self-selection bias as no information regarding non-participants or prospective audience is collected (Gilmore, Arvanitis, and Albert 2018). Additionally, compared to surveys, transactional data usually collect less sensitive information about the sociodemographic characteristics and preferences of the individuals observed. Yet transactional data also offer remarkable advantages as compared to survey-based approaches because they enable ACOs to monitor any past choice of cultural consumption precisely, and researchers do not have to rely on self-reported accounts of past behaviour (Bertacchini, Nuccio, and Durio 2021). As a result, transactional data is better suited for the analysis of behavioural patterns, while other analytical aspects concerning audience's attitudes and preferences can be better explored through other empirical approaches.

More generally, data analytics implies a resurgence of inductive over deductive research aimed at discovering hidden or latent patterns in data and therefore formulating some theoretical hypothesis. Provocatively labelled as the 'end of theory' (Anderson 2008), the fear of the return to empiricism has been criticized by Kitchin (2014) who instead calls for a new paradigm of 'data-driven science' combining prediction and causation. According to the author, social sciences and humanities can only benefit from leaving behind neo-positivistic approaches to attain more breadth, depth and reliability in current understanding of human behaviour.

A final critical aspect of data analytics concerns its actual diffusion and application in ACOs. According to the Digital Culture Report (NESTA 2019), only about 20% of the surveyed cultural organizations in the UK have adopted a strategic perspective for data collection and analysis (e.g. Using audience data for creating a CRM system) and data driven decision-making. The same report points out that there have been no increases in any data-related area since 2013 and that there have been significant falls in a number of data-related activities, such as using audience data to personalize marketing and fundraising campaigns or develop new commercial products and services. Moreover, more sophisticated uses of data remain the exception rather than the rule, with 41% of organizations using data to develop online strategy, 38% using data to inform their broader, strategic direction and just 14% using data to model future audience. These findings suggest that the promise of advancement in business intelligence and improvement in market comprehension seems to be not enough to prompt a change that could transform the daily work of ACOs if some relevant barriers are not overcome.

Three major hindering factors to adoption of data analytics can be identified. First, the management aspiration to transform museums, theatres and festivals into data-driven organizations must imply an explicit financial commitment able to equip them with new capabilities and infrastructures. Yet, the availability of financial resources to invest in such technological trajectory often represents an economic barrier for many ACOs. According to the previously cited UK Digital Culture Report, both lack of internal funding and access to external funding ranked at the top of the major obstacles to achieving digital aspirations, with performing arts organizations reporting to be more negatively affected by such constraints than museums and galleries. One of the reasons for such a barrier is that investing in data-analytics infrastructure would often require an explicit financial commitment in the medium and long-term to avoid the obsolescence in the use of these new digital tools and strategies. Moreover, such a commitment might be seen by many ACOs as a sunk investment, whose return is still too uncertain. While policies aimed at supporting or incentivizing funding in data-analytics solutions can partly solve this problem, these programmes should also foster partnerships between ACOs and tech companies to ensure the sustainability of the investments in the long-term.

The search and integration of new technological skills is a second major challenge for organizations which are primarily aimed at delivering cultural services. Many ACOs are locked-in with pre-existent organizational routines and still believe that the impact of digitalization is related to social media and its use as a marketing tool to promote cultural events and products on the web. On the contrary, data management should be pervasive and affect any level of the organization with the creation of mixed teams and interaction between domain-specific knowledge in the cultural fields, managerial and marketing skills and new data analytics competency.

Finally, another significant barrier in adopting a data analytics approach within ACOs is cultural and attitudinal. As pointed out by Ellerton (2018), data analytics and more broadly data-driven decision-making can be off-putting to many leaders and managers in ACOs, as they could believe that the use of such language and techniques is the top of a slippery slope leading to a purely commercial, transactional relationship with audiences and the cultural sector becoming just another part of consumer society. In this context, the history of the DMA case previously described is quite instructive. The data-driven free loyalty programme ended in December 2017 following the change of the museum director who developed the initiative. This suggests that, without a cultural change and long-term vision, the adoption of data-driven strategies by ACOs might be strongly sensitive to change of single managers and directors with different attitudes toward this innovative approach.

6. Conclusion

The paper has proposed a changing perspective in the arts and cultural sector offered by the rise of data analytics. The relatively limited and dispersed literature on data-driven strategies shares the idea that digitization and connectivity have issued the whole potential of information whose value is still to be captured. Applying this framework to ACOs, we claim that data analytics are useful for more than just optimizing business-as-usual processes. The innovative potential of data analytics spurs from the conjoint effect of innovating the relationship with the audience and enhancing public/private value for patrons and funders, which eventually shall lead to updating business models even in traditional organizations like museums, theatres, festivals and heritage sites.

Using illustrative examples, we have shown that data-driven strategies offer promising avenues to enhance cultural consumption and value creation for both customers and stakeholders of ACOs. On the demand side, a new source of value can emerge not simply from the substitution of the traditional 'physical' experience of arts and culture with new forms of digital exploration and engagement, but from the integration of online and offline practices. On the supply side, data-driven ACOs can build new partnerships with stakeholders on the basis of a more informed evaluation and monitoring of activities and can reconsider their organizational design to become locally more responsive.

Yet, the adoption of data analytics currently poses significant challenges to ACOs. Although data-driven decision-making requires conspicuous financial and technological resources, preventing cultural distrust and organizational inertia is the major hurdle to adoption. Only if every organizational level from board and directors down to educational and customer services will embrace digital transformation, the effect of data analytics can positively affect the management of ACOs and contribute to their long-term sustainability.

Notes

1. For more details: https://channels.theinnovationenterprise.com/articles/predictive-modeling-around-music-festivals Last accessed 28.12.2020.
2. For more details: https://www.ibm.com/blogs/nordic-msp/smukfest-2019 Last accessed 28.12.2020.

Disclosure statement

No potential conflict of interest was reported by the author(s).

ORCID

Massimiliano Nuccio http://orcid.org/0000-0002-0751-2143
Enrico Bertacchini http://orcid.org/0000-0003-4832-5798

References

Acquisti, A., C. Taylor, and L. Wagman. 2016. "The Economics of Privacy." *Journal of Economic Literature* 54 (2): 442–492. doi:10.1257/jel.54.2.442

Anderson, C. 2006. *The Long Tail: Why the Future of Business is Selling Less of More.* New York, NY: Hyperion.

Anderson, C. 2008. "The End of Theory: The Data Deluge Makes the Scientific Method Obsolete." *Wired Magazine* 16 (7): 16–07.

Anderson, S. 2019. "Visitor and Audience Research in Museums." In *The Routledge Handbook of Museums, Media and Communication*, edited by K. Drotner, V. Dziekan, R. Parry, and K. Schrøder, 80–95. Abingdon, Oxon: Routledge.

Ang, L., and F. Buttle. 2006. "Customer Retention Management Processes: A Quantitative Study." *European Journal of Marketing* 40 (1/2): 83–99. doi:10.1108/03090560610637329

Bakhshi, H., and D. Throsby. 2012. "New Technologies in Cultural Institutions: Theory, Evidence and Policy Implications." *International Journal of Cultural Policy* 18 (2): 205–222. doi:10.1080/10286632.2011.587878

Bakker, G. 2015. "Sunk Costs and the Dynamics of Creative Industries." In *The Oxford Handbook of the Creative and Cultural Industries*, edited by C. Jones, M. Lorenzen, y J. Sapsed, 351–386. Oxford: Oxford University Press.

Bertacchini, E., and F. Morando. 2013. "The Future of Museums in the Digital Age: New Models for Access to and Use of Digital Collections." *International Journal of Arts Management* 15 (2): 60–72.

Bertacchini, E., M. Nuccio, and A. Durio. 2021. "Proximity Tourism and Cultural Amenities: Evidence from a Regional Museum Card." *Tourism Economics* 27 (1): 187–204. doi:10.1177/1354816619890230

Blaug, M. 2001. "Where are We Now on Cultural Economics." *Journal of Economic Surveys* 15 (2): 123–143. doi:10.1111/1467-6419.00134

Booth, P., A. Ogundipe, and S. Røyseng. 2020. "Museum Leaders' Perspectives on Social Media." *Museum Management and Curatorship* 35 (4): 373–391. doi:10.1080/09647775.2019.1638819

Borowiecki, K., and T. Navarrete. 2017. "Digitization of Heritage Collections as Indicator of Innovation." *Economics of Innovation and New Technology* 26 (3): 227–246. doi:10.1080/10438599.2016.1164488

Boyd, D., and K. Crawford. 2012. "Critical Questions for big Data: Provocations for a Cultural, Technological, and Scholarly Phenomenon." *Information, Communication and Society* 15 (5): 662–679. doi:10.1080/1369118X.2012.678878

Bray, P. 2009. "Open Licensing and the Future for Collections." In *Museums and the Web 2009: Proceedings*, edited by J. Trant and D. Bearman. Toronto Archives and Museum Informatics. Accessed November 16, 2020. https://www.archimuse.com/mw2009/papers/bray/bray.html

Breugelmans, E., T. Bijmolt, J. Zhang, L. Basso, M. Dorotic, P. Kopalle, and N. Wünderlich. 2015. "Advancing Research on Loyalty Programs: A Future Research Agenda." *Marketing Letters* 26 (2): 127–139. doi:10.1007/s11002-014-9311-4

Brynjolfsson, E., Y. Hu, and M. Smith. 2006. "From Niches to Riches: Anatomy of the Long Tail." *Sloan Management Review* 47 (4): 67–71.

Brynjolfsson, E., and K. McElheran. 2016. "The Rapid Adoption of Data-Driven Decision-Making." *American Economic Review* 106 (5): 133–139. doi:10.1257/aer.p20161016

Bughin, J., M. Chui, and J. Manyika. 2010. "Clouds, Big Data, and Smart Assets: Ten Tech-Enabled Business Trends to Watch." *McKinsey Quarterly* 56 (1): 75–86.

Camarero, C., and J. Garrido. 2008. "The Role of Technological and Organizational Innovation in the Relation Between Market Orientation and Performance in Cultural Organizations." *European Journal of Innovation Management* 11 (3): 413–434. doi:10.1108/14601060810889035

Carù, A., and B. Cova. 2006. "How to Facilitate Immersion in a Consumption Experience: Appropriation Operations and Service Elements." *Journal of Consumer Behavior* 5 (1): 4–14. doi:10.1002/cb.30

Carvalho, A., and A. Matos. 2018. "Museum Professionals in a Digital World: Insights from a Case Study in Portugal." *Museum International* 70 (1–2): 34–47. doi:10.1111/muse.12191

Caves, R. 2000. *Creative Industries: Contracts Between Art and Commerce.* Cambridge, MA: Harvard University Press.

Chen, H., R. Chiang, and V. Storey. 2012. "Business Intelligence and Analytics: From Big Data to Big Impact." *MIS Quarterly* 36 (4): 1165–1188. doi:10.2307/41703503

Colbert, F., and Y. St-James. 2014. "Research in Arts Marketing: Evolution and Future Directions." *Psychology and Marketing* 31 (8): 566–575. doi:10.1002/mar.20718

Di Pietro, L., R. Guglielmetti Mugion, M. Renzi, and M. Toni. 2014. "An Audience-Centric Approach for Museums Sustainability." *Sustainability* 6 (9): 5745–5762. doi:10.3390/su6095745

Elberse, A. 2008. "Should You Invest in the Long Tail?" *Harvard Business Review* 86 (7/8): 88–98.

Ellerton, C. 2018. "Toward a Data Culture in the Cultural and Creative Industries." In *Big Data in the Arts and Humanities: Theory and Practice*, edited by G. Schiuma and D. Carlucci, 117–127. Boca Raton, FL: CRC Press.

Garrido, M., and C. Camarero. 2014. "Learning and Relationship Orientation: An Empirical Examination in European Museums." *International Journal of Nonprofit and Voluntary Sector Marketing* 19 (2): 92–109. doi:10.1002/nvsm.1490

Gerrard, D., M. Sykora, and T. Jackson. 2017. "Social Media Analytics in Museums: Extracting Expressions of Inspiration." *Museum Management and Curatorship* 32 (3): 232–250. doi:10.1080/09647775.2017.1302815

Gilmore, A., K. Arvanitis, and A. Albert. 2018. "Never Mind the Quality, Feel the Width": Big Data for Quality and Performance Evaluation in the Arts and Cultural Sector and the Case of "Culture Metrics." In *Big Data in the Arts and Humanities: Theory and Practice*, edited by G. Schiuma and D. Carlucci, 27–39. Boca Raton, FL: CRC Press.

Grugier, M. 2016. "The Digital Age of Data Art." TechCrunch. https://techcrunch.com/2016/05/08/the-digital-age-of-data-art

Handke, C., P. Stepan, and R. Towse. 2016. *Cultural Economics and the Internet. Handbook on the Economics of the Internet*. Cheltenham: Edward Elgar Publishing.

Harrison, P., and R. Shaw. 2004. "Consumer Satisfaction and Post-Purchase Intentions: An Exploratory Study of Museum Visitors." *International Journal of Art Management* 6 (2): 23–32.

Hirsch, P., and D. Gruber. 2015. "Digitizing Fads and Fashions." In *The Oxford Handbook of the Creative and Cultural Industries*, edited by C. Jones, M. Lorenzen, y J. Sapsed, 421–448. Oxford: Oxford University Press.

Hutter, M. 2008. *Beyond Price: Value in Culture, Economics, and the Arts*. Cambridge: Cambridge University Press.

Jones, C., M. Lorenzen, and J. Sapsed, eds. 2015. *The Oxford Handbook of Creative Industries*. Oxford: Oxford University Press.

Kaplan, F. 2015. " A Map for Big Data Research in Digital Humanities." *Frontiers in Digital Humanities* 2: 1. doi:10.3389/fdigh.2015.00001

KEA European Affairs. 2006. *The Economy of Culture in Europe: A Study Prepared for the European Commission (Directorate-General for Education and Culture)*. Brussels: EC.

Kitchin, R. 2014. "Big Data, New Epistemologies and Paradigm Shifts." *Big Data and Society* 1 (1): 1–12. doi:10.1177/2053951714528481

Klamer, A. 2004. "Cultural Goods are Good for More Than Their Economic Value." In *Culture and Public Action*, edited by V. Rao and M. Walton, 138–162. Washington, DC: World Bank.

Kwon, O., N. Lee, and B. Shin. 2014. "Data Quality Management, Data Usage Experience and Acquisition Intention of Big Data Analytics." *International Journal of Information Management* 34 (3): 387–394. doi:10.1016/j.ijinfomgt.2014.02.002

LaValle, S., E. Lesser, R. Shockley, M. Hopkins, and N. Kruschwitz. 2011. "Big Data, Analytics and the Path from Insights to Value." *MIT Sloan Management Review* 52 (2): 20–32.

Lazzeretti, L., and A. Sartori. 2016. "Digitisation of Cultural Heritage and Business Model Innovation: The Case of the Uffizi Gallery in Florence." *IL CAPITALE CULTURALE. Studies on the Value of Cultural Heritage* 14: 945–970.

Lilley, A., and P. Moore. 2013. *Counting What Counts. What Big Data Can Do for the Cultural Sector*. London: NESTA, Magic Lantern.

Maher, J., J. Clark, and D. Gambill Motley. 2011. "Measuring Museum Service Quality in Relationship to Visitor Membership: The Case of a Children's Museum." *International Journal of Arts Management* 13 (2): 29–42.

Marty, P. 2008. "Museum Websites and Museum Visitors: Digital Museum Resources and Their use." *Museum Management and Curatorship* 23 (1): 81–99. doi:10.1080/09647770701865410

McCarthy, K., E. Ondaatje, L. Zakaras, and A. Brooks. 2001. *Gifts of the Muse: Reframing the Debate About the Benefits of the Arts*. Santa Monica, CA: Rand Corporation.

Navarrete, T. 2013. "Digital Cultural Heritage." In *Handbook on the Economics of Cultural Heritage*, edited by I. Rizzo and A. Mignosa, 251–271. Cheltenham: Edward Elgar Publishing.

NESTA. 2019. *Digital Culture 2019*. London: NESTA.

Nuccio, M., and M. Guerzoni. 2019. "Big Data: Hell or Heaven? Digital Platforms and Market Power in the Data-Driven Economy." *Competition and Change* 23 (3): 312–328. doi:10.1177/1024529418816525

Odlyzko, A. 2003. "Privacy, Economics, and Price Discrimination on the Internet." In *Economics of Information Security*, edited by L. Jean Camp and S. Lewis, 187–212. Norwell, MA: Kluwer Academic Publishers.

Orlandi, S., G. Calandra, V. Ferrara, A. Marras, S. Radice, E. Bertacchini, and T. Maffei. 2018. "Web Strategy in Museums: An Italian Survey Stimulates New Visions." *Museum International* 70 (1–2): 78–89. doi:10.1111/muse.12194

Paswan, A., and L. Troy. 2004. "Non-Profit Organization and Membership Motivation: An Exploration in the Museum Industry." *Journal of Marketing Theory and Practice* 12 (2): 1–15. doi:10.1080/10696679.2004.11658515

Peukert, C. 2019. "The Next Wave of Digital Technological Change and the Cultural Industries." *Journal of Cultural Economics* 43 (2): 189–210. doi:10.1007/s10824-018-9336-2

Piccialli, F., P. Benedusi, L. Carratore, and G. Colecchia. 2020. "An IoT Data Analytics Approach for Cultural Heritage." *Personal and Ubiquitous Computing* 24: 429–436. doi:10.1007/s00779-019-01323-z

Potts, J. 2014. "New Technologies and Cultural Consumption." In *Handbook of the Economics of Art and Culture*, edited by V. Ginsburg and D. Throsby, Vol. 2, 215–231. Amsterdam: Elsevier.

Samis, P., and M. Michaelson. 2016. *Creating the Visitor-Centered Museum*. Routledge. Abingdon: Oxon.

Sashi, C. 2012. "Customer Engagement, Buyer-Seller Relationships, and Social Media." *Management Decision* 50 (2): 253–272. doi:10.1108/00251741211203551

Schmarzo, B. 2013. *Big Data: Understanding How Data Powers Big Business*. New York: John Wiley and Sons.

Siu, N., T. Zhang, P. Dong, and H. Kwan. 2013. "New Service Bonds and Customer Value in Customer Relationship Management: The Case of Museum Visitors." *Tourism Management* 36: 293–303. doi:10.1016/j.tourman.2012.12.001

Taylor, J., and L. Gibson. 2017. "Digitisation, Digital Interaction and Social Media: Embedded Barriers to Democratic Heritage." *International Journal of Heritage Studies* 23 (5): 408–420. doi:10.1080/13527258.2016.1171245

Throsby, D. 1999. "Cultural Capital." *Journal of Cultural Economics* 23 (1-2): 3–12. doi:10.1023/A:1007543313370

Tsimonis, G., and S. Dimitriadis. 2014. "Brand Strategies in Social Media." *Marketing Intelligence and Planning* 32 (3): 328–344. doi:10.1108/MIP-04-2013-0056

Ularu, E., F. Puican, A. Apostu, and M. Velicanu. 2012. "Perspectives on Big Data and Big Data Analytics." *Database Systems Journal* 3 (4): 3–14.

Ward, J., and A. Barker. 2013. Undefined by Data: A Survey of Big Data Definitions. arXiv preprint arXiv:1309.5821.

Werff, S., C. Koopmans, and C. Boyer. 2014. "The Effects of the Dutch Museum Pass on Museum Visits and Museum Revenues." SEO Discussion Paper, 79. SEO Economisch Onderzoek.

Yoshimura, Y., S. Sobolevsky, C. Ratti, F. Girardin, J. Carrascal, J. Blat, and R. Sinatra. 2014. "An Analysis of Visitors' Behavior in the Louvre Museum: A Study Using Bluetooth Data." *Environment and Planning B: Planning and Design* 41 (6): 1113–1131. doi:10.1068/b130047p

Valuing culture and creativity impacts in a global technological era: reshaping the analytical framework

Pedro Costa

ABSTRACT

In a global world, increasingly mediated by new technologies, but where place, communities and territories assume even more importance, the valuing of culture and creativity faces new conceptual and operational challenges. This paper addresses these challenges in order to question the measurement tools usually applied in valuing the impact of culture in society, proposing a new conceptual grid to assess the impacts of creative and cultural activities, in all their diversity and multidimensionality. This results from an intense co-construction process, over the few past years, involving a variety of cultural agents, both in Portuguese and European contexts, in the scope of several research projects. This analytical framework helps disentangling the increasing complexity of the mechanisms underlying value creation in cultural activities, enabling self-assessment of its diverse impacts, in a particular territory or community. A specific grid is presented, comprising five main dimensions (cultural, economic, social, environmental; citizenship and participation), for assessing the territorial impacts of cultural activities. These are subdivided into 15 subdimensions and operationalized in 75 different indicators. This analytical framework is being transposed to a digital application that allows the systematization, self-assessment and self-awareness of value creation and their impacts by the agents of the cultural/creative sector.

1. Introduction: valuing culture and creativity in a global technological era

In a global world, increasingly mediated by new technologies, but where place, communities and territories assume even more importance, the valuing of culture and creativity faces new conceptual and operational challenges. The very role of creative activities and culture is being challenged by the current digital transition (Lazzeretti 2020).

A diversity of anchoring mechanisms link global economic, social and cultural processes to the specificities of each territory. Cultural activities and creativity, which are central in these processes, are increasingly challenged by technologic mediation and by new forms of production and consumption. New intangible added values are generated, based on symbolic value and identity, where creativity, technology transfer, intangible heritage or craftsmanship are crucial components. All the traditional functions associated to cultural activities and creative processes (and the way they produced value and this value was recognized and appropriated, by minor or larger spheres of the society) are facing new opportunities and threats, and the way the diverse (cultural, economic, social, etc.) value(s) of culture is perceived and measured require new conceptualizations and operative tools.

This paper addresses these challenges in order to question the measurement tools usually applied in valuing the impact of culture in society, drawing upon a research programme that mobilizes and crosses work developed in the scope of four different research projects ongoing at DINAMIA'CET-ISCTE in recent years (RESHAPE, ARTSBANK, IMPACTOS-AR, CREATOUR), which contribute to this discussion in several ways – working with artists, cultural promoters, creative tourism agents and public authorities, in several territorial contexts, both at Portuguese and European levels, assessing the impact of their activities in their communities. Combining the work developed (and still ongoing) in these four research projects, and assuming the co-construction of knowledge with all the agents involved in those projects, we aim to propose a new analytical framework and a toolkit to help disentangling the increasing complexity and diversity of these mechanisms of creation of value and to facilitate the assessment of its social impacts in any particular territory or community, in all their diversity and multidimensionality.

In a world marked by deep change, the cultural field is no exception. All the intervenient in the creative (and reputation-building) processes see their traditional roles blur: they are all increasingly 'prosumers', as the distinctions between creators/producers/consumers often disappear; they become all gatekeepers, as their role in the intermediation and reputation process change, and all share increasingly, voluntarily or inadvertently, a diversity of kinds of symbolic, aesthetic and tacit knowledge about the contents they experience or they create. The circuits and processes of intermediation clearly are changing, not just in the more global and tech mediated cultural and creative industries, but in all kinds of artistic products and in heritage goods. The fruition and consumption modes, the way creation and production is made, all these are in profound reconfiguration, and naturally this brings challenges to the mechanisms of creation of value.

The formation of value seems to be a much more decentralized process, compared to the past, despite the very strong concentration of distribution channels, in particular the big globalized platforms for distribution and experiencing of contents. As always, power relations (fuelled by technological, economic, social and cultural disparities) play a crucial role in this game. The opinion of any blogger or influencer seems to have sometimes a larger reach than the one of an expert or those of the traditional cultural intermediaries and gatekeepers. In this supposed flattened world, which are the voices to be heard? And which ones are effectively heard? It is fundamental to understand the new mechanisms of dissemination of information in creative activities, as this is always the key-factor to the organization of these markets. The processes of spreading knowledge and the diversity of kinds of cultural capital, in a much less hierarchical cultural field, should be under scrutiny. In other words, it is fundamental to acknowledge the diversity of interests, motivations and expectations (and therefore, also the diversity of 'value grids') that are inherent to these processes and that are assumed by the various agents intervenient in the cultural and creative processes.

Therefore, it is essential for an effective assumption of the multidimensionality of the value created by cultural and creative production/consumption, comprising several layers of social, artistic, economic, environmental, participative dimensions of value. It requires new frameworks for that analysis, with the development of more flexible (and adaptative) 'grids' as well as new procedures for collecting, treating and analysing data, both quantitative and qualitative, that could be used to assess the importance and impacts that these activities bring to the well-being of the persons involved in these processes, to the society as a whole, and to the community and territories where these processes take place.

The recognition of the importance of the link to the territories and the communities where these processes are embedded is essential, assuring the understanding of the creative dynamics as the product of the territorial anchoring of global (cultural, economic and social) processes in specific contexts, outside which they cannot be analysed (nor their value understood).

In line with Pier Luigi Sacco's notion of paradigm 'Culture 3.0' (based on a regime enhanced by open communities of practice, rather than the patronage relations, or the weight of cultural and creative industries that marked the predecessor paradigms), culture is here assumed as one of the most important platforms for behavioural change, at the most diverse levels of society, and that is not naturally compatible with the conventional tools normally used to measure the social and economic impacts of creative and cultural activities (quite often merely reduced to the assessment of quantitative and economic dimension-oriented aspects). Being artistic and cultural practices assumed as increasingly 'sense making' and 'sense giving' for the ones involved in all creative and productive process, the effective production of meaning, that results of these, in each particular case, cannot be perceived in such a simplistic manner.

In order to address these profound changes, an effective perception of the mechanisms underlying value creation requires innovative methodologies and processes. Therefore, this paper discusses and proposes a general grid to assess the multidimensionality of value, drawing upon preceding work of co-creation of knowledge with creative and cultural agents, developed in the scope of the above-mentioned research programme, delivering a new analytical framework to do it. Being the delivering of this grid is the main purpose of this paper, we do not enter here in detail in the inherent and precedent conceptual debates on impact assessment processes, and on its methodological challenges, neither in the discussion on specific results arising from operationalization and the application of this grid to specific cultural agents, which are both done elsewhere (Tomaz et al. 2020; Gato et al. 2021; Costa et al. 2021).

The paper organizes as follows. Next section will address the need for reshaping the analytical framework for impacts measurement in cultural activities, acknowledging its multidimensionality and drawing attention to the identification of some particular challenges that need to be addressed considering the current digital shift. In Section 3, our research framework and the process of co-construction of a new assessment framework are briefly explained. In Section 4, the typologies are presented, with the description of the analytical grid that results from this research, and the paper finishes with a brief concluding note.

2. Cultural activities, multidimensionality of value and measurement of their territorial impacts: the need for reshaping the analytical framework

The issue of value and its measurability have been naturally a fundamental question in the history of economic thought and particularly in the history of cultural economics (e.g. Throsby 2001). In face of the deep transformations of contemporary societies, and the rise of what Alan Scott (2008) labels as cognitive-cultural capitalism, particular challenges are raised to the analysis of value creation in general, and in the activities intensive in symbolic and aesthetic knowledge (such as cultural and artistic ones), which have their particular mechanisms of value creation, linked to specific intermediation and gatekeeping processes, as well as strong asymmetries in the information and in the cultural and social capital required for the complexities or particularities of the codification and de-codification processes of meaning in these activities (cf. Caves 2002; Becker 1984; Costa 2007).

Recent dynamics in cultural and creative activities (which Pier Luigi Sacco 2011, labels as culture 3.0) unveil a new paradigm, based on open communities of practice, where consumption and production are increasingly blurred, and culture is seen as network organized, in the way of construction of diversified forms of collective sense making (contrary to the previous 'regimes', of Culture 1.0, based on patronage, and culture 2.0, fuelled by cultural and creative industries).

Being marked by the centrality of aesthetic-symbolic knowledge (compared to the other components of knowledge essential for innovative dynamics – technical and analytical knowledge), cultural and creative activities are particularly central for the enlightenment of creation of value processes, at this stage of cultural-cognitive capitalism. The understanding of the territorial expression of cultural activities, the study of the creative milieus and the enlightenment of the territorial dynamics that embed cultural activities' development are essential components for this (cf. Camagni, Maillat, and Matteaccioli 2004; Kebir et al. 2017). Basically, the disentangling of the value of arts and culture in social fabric can only be seen from this perspective, understanding fully the relation of creative processes and cultural dynamics with the local communities and their territories, even if these processes are anchored in globally structured economic, social and symbolic mechanisms (Kebir et al. 2017).

In fact, territorialized production complexes based on cultural activities became increasingly important, as these activities distinguished as central in the promotion of regional development and urban competitiveness. Drawing upon the broad literature developed in recent decades in several scientific fields (Scott 2000, 2014; Camagni, Maillat, and Matteaccioli 2004; Costa 2007; Cooke and Lazzeretti 2008; Lazzeretti and Vecco 2018), we assume its importance, penetrating into the mechanisms that are underneath those creative dynamics and how they can be mobilized to promote territorial development, taking the co-creation of knowledge between artists, stakeholders and local communities as a privileged point of view.

Recognizing that the territory may be able to access and introduce present knowledge in other locations and scales, and to jointly (re)contextualize and spread it in a sustained manner between the various actors and sectors present in that place, and thus foster its development, vitality and competitiveness (Crevoisier and Jeannerat 2009; Vale 2012), we assume the fundamental relevance of these creative milieus, linked to specific governance mechanisms, for urban competitiveness and territorial vitalization.

Therefore, the disentangling of the value of arts and culture in social fabric can only be seen in this light, understanding fully the relation of creative processes and cultural dynamics with the local communities and their territories, even if these processes are anchored in global processes or even globally structured economic, social and symbolic mechanisms.

As it is pointed out in the scope of RESHAPE project

> for the lack of a more effective method, the value of contemporary art is often reduced just to visible results or products. Processes developed by artistic practices mainly end up to be invisible or unrecognized so the audiences and decision-makers often don't recognize the importance and the value of arts in society.[1]

It is important to understand the influence of the artists and their work in the local context, urban or rural, the way it is embedded in the territory, as well as perceive practices which create intangible value for society and discuss the pertinence of the support to it. Therefore, it is also essential to recognize the relativity of value.

New understandings and dynamics in culture require new methodological approaches and operative tools to examine, communicate and sensitize cultural actors, policymakers and the public about the various values associated with the specific and multifaceted nature of these activities and the impacts on local territories and communities at the economic, social, environmental, cultural-artistic and participatory level. Traditional impact assessment methods are usually quite unsatisfactory, tending to focus on short-term indicators, often quantitative, and on easily collectible data, not contemplating the multiple effects on local territories and communities. In the name of comparability, these exercises tend to be often quite reductionist and simplistic, merely focused on the assessment of the most quantifiable dimensions and, above all, on the economic impacts of these activities (both direct or indirect). To this end, indicators that are readily available, based on available empirical data or on the conduct of brief questionnaire surveys, are privileged, reinforcing the trend towards an overvaluation of the economic aspects, easily quantifiable, in these processes.[2] In addition, these impact assessment exercises typically have several other problems, such as the fact that they focus predominantly on more commodified cultural provision, on larger events, on activities carried out in more formal/institutional contexts, or provided in urban centres (neglecting or not being adapted to other realities). Thus, most of these exercises fail in not responding to the complexity of reality, the multidimensionality, multiplicity and time-range of impacts, and the specificity of each situation (UNESCO 2009, 2012, 2019; Tomaz et al. 2020). On the other hand, merely qualitative case studies, based on in-depth fieldwork with cultural agents and the communities, despite its frequently interesting results, end up always facing the barriers related to the difficulties of generalization, extrapolation and non-comparability with different realities.

Despite the huge debates on impact assessment conceptual challenges, which we will not address here in detail (cf. Tomaz et al. 2020; and Gato et al. 2021, for the roots of our conceptual approach and for our discussion on this, as well as, e.g. Belfiore and Bennett 2010; Galloway 2009; CHCfE Consortium 2015; CAE 2018; Dessein et al. 2015; Soini and Dessein, 2016), it is important to refer a diversity of methodological approaches and technique used in this field, at several levels and scales, including the toolbox approach, quantitative valuation methodologies (including market and non-market-based techniques, in line with traditional cultural economics approaches), as well as a diversity of qualitative methods, mostly used for assessing socio-cultural values (CHCfE Consortium 2015).

It is important to notice that an academic response to this demand, assuming the aforementioned challenges faced by these activities in contemporaneity, must also consider the tensions between research and policy advocacy around the impact of arts and culture and the development of methodologies for their measurement and evaluation, and how they influence the decision-making processes (e.g. Belfiore and Bennett 2010; Galloway 2009). The pragmatic need of operative answers must always be balanced with a quality that helps not just to justify funding and advocate the activity, but is useful for a self-awareness of the diverse impacts of each activity and the way it influences individuals' and community lives.

Summing up, to evaluate the effects of a specific cultural project in a territory, we must assume that its effects (multiple, subjective, perceived both collectively and individually, etc.), have to be seen in the light of the (different kinds of) value they create for the actors in the community/society – that is, the value(s) that is recognized by them, in their diversity. Therefore, this value has to be assumed as (i) multidimensional; (ii) relative and contextual (e.g. varying depending on the individual, social or territorial context) and (iii) always referring to the subjectivities of the agents involved in the activity (carrying different perceptions, motivations and interests), both at supply and demand sides.

That is, to understand the importance and impacts of creative activities in territories/communities, we must move from (or combine with) the general ambition of (more immediate) measurability to the perception (and self-awareness) of the multidimensionality of the value, finding innovative ways to capture it (and, at the limit, to confront it with other comparable contexts).

In order to address that complexity in a more effective way, we have been developing a framework for analysis that encompasses a diversity of dimensions related to the creation of this value (and to the measurement of its impacts). For instance, in the field of creative tourism, in low-density areas, we've been able to co-create and test with pilot-projects new instruments to assess and to allow self-assessment and self-awareness of the diversity of quantitative and qualitative impacts of territorially embedded creative projects (e.g. Tomaz et al. 2020; Gato et al. 2021[3]). By the same token, we've been working with artists, producers and other cultural agents in understanding the impacts of cultural activities in social fabric and in the territories/communities, within the diversity of the above-mentioned projects (RESHAPE; IMPACTS_AR; ARTSBANK).

Several other research projects, at international level, have been also recently trying to develop new tools (some of them based on interesting participatory practices) to help the measurement of these multiple impacts, at different levels, and raise the awareness of the cultural agents and policy makers to this issue (e.g. Sacco's methodology for measuring the impact of cultural heritage activities; the 'Impact Playbook' developed by Europeana to support cultural heritage organisations,[4] the works of Flanders Arts Institute; the research of Paul Heritage and Leandro Valiati on the 'Relative Value' for Arts and Humanities Research Council, and their work on the currency of cultural exchange). Drawing upon the broad contemporary debates on the social value of the art (e.g. Belfiore and Bennett 2010; Galloway 2009; CHCfE Consortium 2015; CAE 2018), and European initiatives aiming to develop new perspectives and improved methodologies for capturing the wider societal value of culture, including but also beyond its economic impact, interesting research is being conducted Europe-wide, such as UNCHARTED (Understanding, Capturing and Fostering the Societal Value of Culture) project[5] or MESOC (Measuring the Social Dimension of Culture) project.[6]

All these interesting examples, with several variants, relate to the strong social need that is felt around the world in order to develop new forms of measuring the value and impacts of cultural and creative activities, and overcome many of the blockages that have been crucial to the frequent instrumentalization of these activities in relation to other economic, social or political objectives. In this sense, all these projects – and our research programme in particular – correspond to a social need that has been recurrently identified in the contact with the stakeholders, the policy makers and the communities and creative actors that structure this field.

This need of an academic response to this social demand is amplified by the responsibility of giving answer to some specific challenges that stem from the current digital shift in our societies, which undoubtedly conditions the functioning of cultural activities and the perception of their value(s). The digital transition requires us to draw attention, among other factors, to (i) the new challenges for understanding value creation with much more decentralized gatekeeping mechanisms and mediation processes, and evolving attitudes towards originality and creativity; (ii) the questionings on the resilience of much more flexible and informally network-based business models; (iii) the importance of the participatory turn in culture and the role of new forms of participation in the co-production of meaning and value in these activities; (iv) the increasing challenges in the management of the relation between personal life, leisure and work; (v) the development of experiences of fair(er) governance models in the sector or (vi) the increasing role of the negative externalities induced by these activities and all the problems related to their regulation, just to cite some fundamental areas.

3. The process: co-constructing a pragmatic self-assessment framework

A multidisciplinary research team[7] has been developing at DINAMIA'CET-iscte an investigation that mobilizes and crosses the work produced in different action-research projects carried out in recent years (CREATOUR, RESHAPE, IMPACTOS-AR, ARTSBANK[8]), co-producing knowledge with artists, cultural promoters, creative tourism agents and public authorities, in several territorial contexts, both at European and Portuguese levels (cf. Costa, Lopes, and Bassani 2019; Tomaz et al. 2020; Gato et al. 2021).

This broad research programme aims to deepen knowledge about the mechanisms of creation and sharing of value in cultural and creative activities in contemporaneity, about the impacts (on all their economic, social, artistic and environmental diversity) of these activities on the social fabric, and about the role of culture in the transformation of behaviours (and in the renegotiation of identities). In parallel, it intends to deepen knowledge about the importance of the territorialized logics of cultural and creative dynamics in this creation of value and the importance of the local anchoring on globalized (cultural, economic and social) processes as a factor of value creation, disentangling the symbolic mediation mechanisms behind these processes.

In practice, this presupposes to develop a pragmatic analytical grid that allows and enhances the awareness and the perception about the multidimensionality of value creation by cultural and creative activities (and operationalization of its measurement, for each concrete agent), which implies to test and apply, from a perspective of co-creation of knowledge with cultural and creative agents, this grid to a diversity of empirical situations that are provided by parallel research projects. The aim is to develop a toolkit that can be used autonomously by cultural agents and policymakers to perceive the diversity of factors underlying value creation and the multiplicity of impacts of cultural and creative activity on society and on their specific communities.

These broad objectives have been pursued, in the framework of the four research projects mentioned above, in multiple but complementary ways.

At the national level, the CREATOUR project[9] allowed to co-design and test with a diversity of stakeholders a conceptual and analytical framework designed to measure the impacts of 40 pilot initiatives of creative tourism in the particular context of small cities and rural areas in Portugal. The experience revealed the challenges, opportunities and constraints in the diversity of situations found and the necessity to develop a qualitative self-assessment tool that could be adaptable to a diversity of contexts.

The development and adaptation of this analytical grid to other contexts, and particularly, to 'independent' cultural and creative activities, was possible with the collaboration of eight 'Reshapers' (artists, curators and cultural managers), from all Europe, that reunited in the scope of RESHAPE project[10] to discuss the value of art in the social fabric.

In parallel to these projects, ARTEMREDE, a network of 15 municipalities in Portugal, which combines programming with cultural training and community-oriented work, is working with DINAMIA'CET-iscte on a project[11] to assess the impact of the activities of their associated city-councils on their respective communities, being open to testing new approaches and methodologies tools.

In addition to this, the use of exploratory methodologies, and particularly urban artistic interventions, to work with the communities has been used in the disentangling of the effects of these activities in the territories, in the scope of ARTSBANK project.[12] This has been another way of exploring, in practice, new tools to try to question the notions of value and the evolving perceptions that the cultural agents and policymakers have about it, and the way they measure the impacts of cultural and creative activities.

The work carried out in the projects mentioned above, with a diversity of stakeholders, exposed some vulnerabilities of usual impact assessment procedures, in public and private entities, given the nature of the culture and the specific circumstances of each project, location or scale intervention. At the same time, these projects confirmed the difficulties of stakeholders in providing and communicating evidence on some qualitative effects and their value in achieving more sustainable development in these territories and communities. In addition, they highlighted the need to integrate these evaluation exercises into their internal processes of the definition of objectives and reflection on possible gaps, challenges and opportunities that may arise from the identification of multiple effects of their activities (Gato et al. 2021; Costa et al. 2021).

There is a general awareness of the scope of the impacts of these activities and their multidimensionality for everyone involved. This is generally complemented with the clear perception of the individual/institutional diversity of motivations and expected impacts. Additionally, it is also often clear the perception of discrepancies between the (intrinsic) motivations of the actors and their discourses (mostly based on extrinsic motivations, particularly related to funding issues).

The mobilization of the knowledge from these stakeholders was important in the development of an integrative and multidimensional approach to impact assessment, crossing these different streams of research and allowing a co-construction of the broad analytical framework that is presented in the next section (after that operationalized in a toolkit accessible in a digital application/platform allowing the systematization, self-assessment and self-awareness of value creation and its impacts by actors in the cultural/creative sector).

4. Reshaping the analytical framework: an operative typology

Considering this conceptual and methodological context, we've been operationalizing an operative framework, through a step by step process (cf. Tomaz et al. 2020; Gato et al. 2021) which assumed the assessment of the impacts of the creative activities through the lens of the territorial development perspective. This implied to assume five main dimensions to embody the multidimensionality of sustainable development (Ferrão 1995; Costa 2007, 2015), drawing upon the vast discussions on the dimensions of sustainability and the debate on 'culture' as the 4th pillar of sustainable development. Naturally, this took into account the contemporary debates on the shifts in cultural policies and cultural participation and their role in territorial development (Bonet et al. 2018; Dupin-Meynard and Négrier (2020); Costa 2015). Still, it was also particularly grounded on the discussions on how to assess sustainability and sustainable development (Singh et al. 2009; Waas et al. 2014; Sala, Ciuffo, and Nijkamp 2015), and on the debates how to bring this evaluation and its measurement to the fields of culture (Bianchini 1999; Dessein et al. 2015; Duxbury 2011; Duxbury and Gillette, 2007; Duxbury and Jeannotte, 2012; Duxbury et al, 2016; Meireis and Rippl 2018; Hawkes 2001; Nurse 2006; CAE 2018; CHCfE Consortium 2015) and creative tourism (Korez-Vide 2013; Richards 2018; Duxbury and Richards 2019; Tomaz et al. 2020; Gato et al. 2021); as well as in its discussion and adoption on multiple international organization agendas (e.g. WTO 2004; UNEP/WTO 2005; UN 2015; UCLG 2015; EC 2018; EU 2018; UNESCO 2015, 2019).

Naturally, this was inspired by several previous exercises and proposals that can be found in many of these references, as well as in the scope of the aforementioned contemporary debates on the social value of the art and in the diverse projects that are being internationally developed on this topic. All those were inspiring and important to this work, as well as the tacit empirical knowledge brought by all our co-creator cultural agents, who worked with us in this research.

But some main innovative aspects can be highlighted, that distinguish this proposal from other frameworks:

– The structuring around five main sustainable development 'pillars' (instead of the more frequent assumption of culture as the 4th pillar by cultural actors – e.g. CHCfE Consortium (2015) – or the assumption of citizenship, participation and governance issues as this 4th pillar, by several international institutions);

- The fact of being the result of debate and co-construction with a diversity of cultural agents, with different roles, in several cultural fields and contexts;
- The fact of assuming its worth essentially as a self-assessment tool and a self-reflective instrument, that can be used for different contexts and different kind of actors, rather than have extensive comparative ambitions;
- But, at the same time, the fact that the assumption of this natural relativeness, does not prevent comparability, which is possible – for specific purposes and in certain conditions – due to its scale implementation (for details on the toolkit implementation see Costa et al. 2021);
- Not having the ambition to reach a composite index or a single number (just envisaged at the level of each dimension, eventually);
- And the fact of being applicable to a diversity of contexts and situations, particularly the ones less 'covered' by conventional assessment methodologies (such as informal activities, or low-density territories).

The final results are presented below and detailed in the respective figures.

Regarding the first of the five main dimensions (Cultural Value), we assume three sub-dimensions (cf. Figure 1 for details and indicators):

(i) Artistic/cultural relevance (related to the intrinsic artistic and creative value of the projects and its subjective importance);
(ii) Cultural richness (including cultural enrichment and heritage safeguard as well as creating and reinventing sustainable cultural heritage);
(iii) Creative embeddedness in the community/territory (associated to the artistic/creative rooting in community, territorial embeddedness and the relations with community well-being).

Concerning the second dimension (Economic value), we propose three assessment subdimensions (cf. Figure 2 for details and indicators):

(iv) Economic viability (referring to the direct generation of economic activity and vitality of the promoters, the 'direct economic boost' resulting from the activity itself);
(v) Economic growth and local prosperity (assuming here all the indirect economic effects in the community and the externalities affecting the agents in that territory);
(vi) Structural change (relating to other induced economic effects, the transformations in the structural context or changes in economic structure).

The third dimension (Social Value) is operationalized through the following subdimensions (cf. Figure 3 for details and indicators):

(vii) Social cohesion and equity (assuring a degree of equity and inclusion in the access, and enhancing community cohesion, internally and externally);
(viii) Participants fulfilment (providing fruitful and meaningful experiences, knowledge improvement and opening mentalities);
(ix) Engagement with social fabric (related to the involvement of local community in the activities).

Dimension	Subdimension	Indicators	Question to rate (1-7 scale): Concerning the development of the community/territory, your activity/project allowed/contributed to:	Rationale (Culture -> Territorial Development)
1. Cultural	1. Artistic/cultural relevance	1.1. Intrinsic cultural value and artistic "quality"	- Develop an artwork/creation/experience with quality and artistic/cultural relevance	Intrinsic cultural value and artistic quality of the activity developed; increasing artistic/cultural quality
		1.2. Empowerment of artists/creators	- Empower artists/creators and strengthen their artistic skills and reflective ability	Artists' empowerment and enhancement of artistic skills; foster cultural knowledge and artists' reflexivity
		1.3. Contribution to a (more) creative society	- Promote human creativity, and a more creative society, recognizing and integrating different (formal and informal) cultural expressions	Promotion of creation and human creativity, both individually and collectively; developing a (more) creative society, recognizing and integrating different cultural expressions
		1.4. Social recognition of creative value	- The recognition, by peers and/or the community, of the artistic value of the work/activity carried out and of its creators	Reputation; recognition of value (by peers / community); Legitimation of artistic value of the artworks / heritage / author / place / milieu
		1.5. (Degree of) novelty and artistic innovation	- Do something innovative and/or bring something new, original, different, in artistic terms	Bringing novelty, innovation, a certain degree of creativity, even if relative
	2. Cultural richness	2.1. Preservation and safeguarding of cultural heritage	- Ensure the identification, valorization and/or conservation of tangible/intangible cultural heritage	Safeguard of heritage, traditions, etc.; including Intangible heritage value creation
		2.2. Accumulation, valorization and intergenerational transmission of locally-based know-how	- Value and transmit local know-how (and/or its intersections with external knowledge/cultures)	Intergenerational knowledge transmission
		2.3. Differentiation and uniqueness	- Integrate local heritage and distinctiveness features to promote/create unique and innovative cultural experiences	Cultural differentiation
		2.4. Reinvention of tradition	- Reinterpret local traditions and ways of doing, to bridge cultural gaps	Reinterpretation of ancestral traditions; modernization and adaptation of traditional knowledge
		2.5. Cultural diversity	- Value and promote cultural and social diversity in your activity (representation of different cultural perspectives in the events/activity)	Promotion, valorization (and preservation) of local cultural and social diversity; Ensuring representation of different cultural perspectives in the activities
	3. Creative embeddedness (in the community)	3.1. Articulation of creation with the community and its daily life	- Develop artistic/cultural experiences focused on the community and/or increase the relevance of art and culture in the daily life of the community	Creative anchoring in the community
		3.2. Rooting in the local creative environment and consolidation of the creative ecosystem	- Develop a creative activity embedded in the local creative milieu, and/or collaborate with the local creative ecosystem	Improvement of collaboration amongst local artistic scene; densification of a cultural milieu; embeddedness of creative ecosystem in the community
		3.3. Strengthening local cultural identity (and appropriation of activities by the community)	- Strengthen local cultural identity (with the appropriation of the activities by the community)	Local appropriation of artistic activities; Identity enhancement (appropriation by the community - cultural and social identification)
		3.4. Openness and hybridization of local identities	- Encourage behaviours oriented towards sustainability, tolerance and acknowledgement of diversity, opening mindsets and enhancing cosmopolitanism	Evolution / transformation of identities (recognizing multiplicity of identity belongings); nurturing the opening of mindsets; stimulating cosmopolitanism and cultural diversity; opening the "local" to the "world")
		3.5. Personal conditions for creation	- Create conditions in the personal lives of artists and cultural workers that facilitate their activity (e.g., individual time management, work-life balance, work/leisure relationship, ...)	Management of personal conditions that allow artistic creation; "quality time"; possibility of individual time management; personal/family life compatibility; balance with leisure and living conditions

Figure 1. Operationalization of the 'Cultural' dimension.
Source: Own elaboration.

Dimension	Subdimension	Indicators	Question to rate (1-7 scale): *Concerning the development of the community/territory, your activity/project allowed/contributed to:*	Rationale (Culture -> Territorial Development)
2. Economic	4. Economic Viability	4.1. Revenue/income creation with the activity developed (for the promoter and its partners)	- Generate (new sources of) income for your organization and its partners	Direct economic impact of this activity to the promoter/partners
		4.2. Market expansion and generation of new markets	- Reach new (or larger) audiences/markets	Development of audiences / loyalty relations
		4.3. Enhancement of autonomy and enabling economic self-sustainment (and resilience of the "business model")	- To ensure your economic sustainability and some long-term financial independence for your activity/organization	Project's self sufficiency and improvement of economic resilience for the promoter institution
		4.4. Notoriety and appreciation of the promoter's (/creator/author) brand	- Generate notoriety and recognition for your activity and promote your brand/name	Notoriety and reputation value generated for the promoters.
		4.5. Creation of new organizational/institutional solutions	- Improve the practices and logics of your organization's operation, internally and externally	New logics of operation and practices; creation of innovative institutional tools or solutions; create/adapt governance models (e.g. public/market support) for more efficient operation
	5. Economic growth and local prosperity	5.1. Value creation in other economic sectors (accommodation, transport, catering, traditional local products, tour operators,...)	- Create market for other businesses (e.g, transport, restaurants, accommodations) or add value to other local traditional/cultural products and local commerce	Indirect economic effects on other activities and local businesses.
		5.2. Contribution to the development (and visibility) of a local creative cluster/milieu/scene	- Contribute to the development of a local creative cluster and the external awareness of your creative product/activity (increasing the visibility as a creative place)	Cross-fertilization and positive externalities within local creative milieu
		5.3. Incorporation of creative content (aesthetic and symbolic) in other sectors' value chains	- Aggregate creative contents/products and experiences in other economic value chains (e.g. tourism, design, traditional product brands, etc.)	Indirect/induced economic effects in non-related value-chains
		5.4. Increase in local control and autonomy	- Expand the local control to a larger part of the value chain, within the scope of globalized production/creation processes	Ensuring larger control of parts of the global value chain, maximizing local-global anchoring opportunities in the territory
		5.5. Negative economic implications on the community (negative externalities) (*)	- Cause additional economic losses or costs to other economic agents or residents in the community (e.g. increased costs in accessing infrastructures, with the maintenance of heritage, increase in land prices, gentrification, displacement, devaluation of land prices,...)	Negative externalities (e.g. negative economic impacts to other actors in the community; increased costs in access to infrastructures; in upholding heritage, positive and negative impacts in land prices; gentrification; displacement)
	6. Structural change	6.1. Quality of jobs offered	- Improve the quality of employment generated by your organization generates (e.g. stability in contracts, overcoming jobs seasonality,...)	Structural employment creation in the promoter (e.g. ensure job stability, extend the season for creative products and services,...)
		6.2. Generation/preservation of employment in the territory/community	- Raise work opportunities in the cultural/creative sector (or in maintaining traditional crafts)	Structural employment creation in the community / creative milieu
		6.3. Stimulation to investment in the territory/community	- Encourage other/new investments in the cultural/creative sector and related activities	Demonstration effect; inducing new "followers" in the activity
		6.4. Promotion of collaboration and networking	- Enhance collaboration with other agents and networks, internally and externally to local community	Deepening of collaboration among actors and accumulation of relational capital, endogenously and exogenously to the territory
		6.5. Development of business/management skills and soft skills for access to finance	- Support the development of entrepreneurial skills (marketing, management, funding programs, etc) and experience in applying for funding opportunities	Development of soft skills as well as specialized codified and tactical knowledge

Figure 2. Operationalization of the 'Economic' dimension.
Source: Own elaboration / (*) Reverse scale.

Dimension	Subdimension	Indicators	Question to rate (1-7 scale): *Concerning the development of the community/territory, your activity/project allowed/contributed to:*	Rationale (Culture -> Territorial Development)
3. Social	7. Social cohesion and equity	7.1. Promoting equity in access to culture and expansion of cultural capital	- Increase (more equative) access to cultural knowledge and creative experiences	Creation of "cultural habits" and generic cultural capital in the population (e.g. traditional role of educational services)
		7.2. Fight to exclusion and promotion of inclusion (and access conditions) of minorities or specific population segments	- Promote the access and inclusion for social excluded and/or economically disadvantaged people (as well as affected by digital illiteracy)	Increasing access for specific segments (less accustomed to cultural consumption), e.g., vulnerable populations, the elderly, disabled, prisoners, ethnic minorities, digitally excluded,...
		7.3. Promotion of social cohesion	- Promote social cohesion and its "values"	Enhancing social cohesion (integration of different sectors/actors) as well as promoting the values of cohesion and equity also in the creative "content" itself
		7.4. Contribution to territorial attractiveness and population retention	- Encourage the retention and/or establishment of new residents in the community (particularly younger generations)	Demographic vitality; contributing to combat desertification and retain population; enhance territorial attractiveness and fix population (particularly young adults in low density and rural areas); promote territorial cohesion.
		7.5. Promotion of social innovation and community development	- Stimulate social innovation ideas in the cultural/creative sector and community development	Support social innovation projects and social entrepreneurship in the creative/cultural field
	8. Participants fulfilment	8.1. Personal fulfilment of the participants (enjoying the creative experience)	- Satisfy and culturally enrich participants through aesthetic pleasure and artistic fulfillment during the creative experience	Satisfaction of cultural "needs" of audiences/tourists visiting the event/destination; aesthetic enjoyment; "feel"; construction of meaning; realization of cultural/religious/historical value
		8.2. Creation of cultural habits and recurrence of participants	- Increase participants' availability to enjoy creative goods and develop their cultural habits	Improvement of cultural capital and loyalty of participants; enhancing the recurrence of visits; increasing cultural habits; creation and qualification of audiences
		8.3. Opening mentalities and changing behaviours	- Confront participants with themselves and contribute to change mindsets and behaviors	"Open horizons" and allow individual empowerment; promotion/production of new narratives, worldviews and subjectivities
		8.4. Learning, knowledge and understanding of the world	- Stimulate participants' interest in learning and promote their knowledge	Art as education, providing participants with new tools for knowledge; art as an educational tool; art as a platform for knowing and understanding the world
		8.5. Wellness and personal development	- Promote the physical and psychological well-being of participants and their personal development	Physical and psychological well-being, and personal development of all actors; Participants' wellness; Healthy living for residents; Relation with leisure, sports and recreation.
	9. Engagement with social fabric	9.1. Suitability and adaptation to community	- Foster experiences that meet the needs of local population and the expectations of the participants	Cultural negotiation with the community
		9.2. Social participation	- Sustain an active community participation in your activities	Social participation (active audience participation in the events)
		9.3. Involvement and social appropriation	- Engage different (local) stakeholders in the planning and development of activities	Enabling social appropriation; individual/group formal/informal taking of ownerships; community involvement
		9.4. Negative impacts on residents' quality of life and conflict in the community (*)	- Cause disturbances in the daily lives of residents (e.g., noise, traffic or parking congestion, saturation of collection systems, pollution, etc.) and/or conflicts in the community	Negative externalities: social external impacts
		9.5. Community awareness of the importance of creative activities	- Raise awareness among audiences and the community about the benefits of promoting/experiencing cultural/creative activities	Public and community awareness of the benefits of culture and creative tourism

Figure 3. Operationalization of the 'Social' dimension.
Source: Own elaboration / (*) Reverse scale.

For the fourth dimension (Environmental Value), we assume the following subdimensions (cf. Figure 4 for details and indicators):

(a) Valorization and protection of the physical environment (assuming physical integrity and reliable valorization of physical resources);

(b) Responsible use of resources (addressing an efficient management of resources);
(c) Environmental quality and biodiversity (ensuring the minimization of negative environmental externalities and ecosystems protection).

And finally, for the fifth dimension (Citizenship and Participation Value), we propose these three subdimensions (cf. Figure 5 for details and indicators):

(xiii) Identity expression (assuming the potential for the expression of identities and the freedom – and empowerment – for identity affirmation);
(xiv) Civic participation (including participation and access issues, citizenship rights, as well as citizens' cultural expression as means for inclusion);
(xv) Governance and quality of processes and policies (ensuring quality formal and informal regulating mechanisms in the creative sector, as well as democratic and transparent structures).

In order to shed additional light, in this necessarily summarized and schematic presentation, to the contents of each subdimension and the way they are being operationalized, it is provided, in the 4th column of the table, an example of operationalization in the form of a question to rate (in a 1–7 scale)[13] by the respondent, and in the 5th column a brief rationale of the mechanisms inherent to the contribution of each indicator used to territorial sustainable development.

5. Conclusive note

In this paper, we propose a new analytical framework to help disentangling the increasing complexity and diversity of the mechanisms of creation of value in cultural activities and to facilitate the assessment of its social impacts in a particular territory or community, in all their diversity.

This is particularly important considering the current digital transition, as the organization of the creative sector is confronted with wide challenges, including, among others, (i) the new challenges for understanding value creation with much more decentralized gatekeeping mechanisms and mediation processes, and evolving attitudes towards originality and creativity; (ii) the questionings on the resilience of much more flexible and informally network-based business models; (iii) the importance of the participatory turn in culture and the role of new forms of participation in the co-production of meaning and value in these activities; (iv) the increasing challenges in the management of the relation between personal life, leisure and work; (v) the development of experiences of fair(er) governance models in the sector or (vi) the increasing role of the negative externalities induced by these activities and all the problems related to their regulation. The assumption of the relativity and multidimensionality of value by the cultural agents,

Dimension	Subdimension	Indicators	Question to rate (1-7 scale): Concerning the development of the community/territory, your activity/project allowed/contributed to:	Rationale (Culture -> Territorial Development)
4. Environmental	10. Valorization and protection of the physical environment	10.1. Generation of alternatives to massification and management of carrying capacities	- Control the negative impacts of your activity in physical environment, respect carrying capacities, and combat massification	Considering the scale of activities, reduce impacts in physical environment; resistance to high-impact activities and massification
		10.2. Appreciation and protection of the landscape	- Value the landscape in the creative experience and maintain the integrity and quality of rural and/or urban landscapes	Valuing and protecting the landscape; Seizing visual landscape; Using integrity of rural and urban landscapes as resources for creative experiences
		10.3. Use and valorization of existing physical and natural resources and infrastructures	- Create or (re)use local physical/natural structures/resources for creative experiences	Adequate use and valorisation of existing physical resources
		10.4. Vitality and appropriation of public space	- Transform (regenerate/appropriate) public spaces through cultural/creative experiences	Revitalize public spaces (through creativity) and promote urban regeneration/revitalization
		10.5. Physical integrity (*)	- Contribute to affect or destroy the physical characteristics of the local system and/or the physical environment (and natural resources) where your activity takes place	Negative impacts on the physical environment; irreversible (or hardly reversible) changes; depredation of natural resources
	11. Responsible use of resources	11.1. Efficient planning of resource use in activities, encouraging the use of local resources	- Promote the efficient use of resources in your activity, encouraging their reduction, recycling and reuse (and enhancing the use of local resources)	Reduce emissions and ecological footprint (from the supply side); reduce travelling and flows of goods; encouraging reduction, reuse, recycling
		11.2. Reduction of the carbon footprint of audiences/visitors	- Minimize the carbon footprint of participants, and encourage greener forms of travel (e.g soft mobilities or collective transport)	Reduce carbon emissions and ecological footprint (from the audiences/visitors side)
		11.3. Management of scarce natural resources	- Reduce the use of scarce or threatened natural resources (e.g., water)	Decrease in the use of scarce / non-renewable resources; water conservation
		11.4. Energy efficiency	- Promote energy efficiency in your activity (including use of equipment and facilities), in face of the possibilities available	Enhancement of energy efficiency in the activity; energy conservation
		11.5. Taking advantage of the small scale	- Take advantage of the small scale to reduce the externalities and negative impacts (physical and social) of your activity	Valuing the small scale as a way to reduce the externalities of cultural/creative activity; exploring the benefits of small-scale creative tourism projects; plan to reduce waste, noise, congestion
	12. Environmental quality and biodiversity	12.1. Pressure on traffic and parking infrastructure and transport systems (*)	- Further overload traffic and parking infrastructure and/or transport systems, as a result of your activity	Negative externalities arising from cultural / creative tourism projects in environmental terms (e.g., congestion of road infrastructure, parking, transport system)
		12.2. Pressure on supply and sanitation systems and waste collection/treatment systems (*)	- Further overload the infrastructure of supply systems (water / energy), sanitation or waste collection and treatment, due to your activity.	Negative externalities arising from cultural / creative tourism projects in environmental terms (e.g., pressure on collection and treatment systems (waste, sewers, etc.).
		12.3. Pollution and degradation of natural resources (*)	- Generate a significant increment of noise and other types of pollution (water, air, ground, sound, visual), or contribute to the degradation of local natural resources	Negative externalities arising from cultural / creative tourism projects in environmental terms (e.g., air pollution, water quality, noise, species and biodiversity loss, etc.).
		12.4. Protection of local ecosystem	- Ensure the protection of local ecosystems	Ecosystem protection, by the activity itself, or by the content/message conveyed
		12.5. Awareness of environmental quality values, biodiversity and ecological footprint reduction	- Raise awareness on the need to reduce ecological footprints and integrate biodiversity and environmental values into the planning and implementation of the cultural/creative projects	Awareness on the need to reduce the ecological footprint; general environmental awareness

Figure 4. Operationalization of the 'Environmental' dimension.
Source: Own elaboration / (*) Reverse scale.

and their capacitation with tools that enable them to self-assessing the impacts they have in increasingly wider fields is therefore crucial.

Dimension	Subdimension	Indicators	Question to rate (1-7 scale): *Concerning the development of the community/territory, your activity/project allowed/contributed to:*	Rationale (Culture -> Territorial Development)
5. Citizenship and Participation	13. Identity expression	13.1. Recognition and provision of place for the expression of diversity and identity multiplicity	- Make room for diversity and for the affirmation of the multiplicity of identities and identity belongings	Acknowledge / allow / represent / give space for the expression of diversity and multiple identities
		13.2. Empowerment (of individuals and groups) for the expression of (their) identities	- Empower for the personal, free and open expression of the "self" for everyone, safeguarding in particular the rights of minorities (e.g., gender, ethnic, religious, cultural identities).	Empower individuals and groups for the expression of subjectivities, and their multiple identities
		13.3. Provision of a safe space	- Provide a safe space for individuals or populations at risk (e.g., stigmatized minorities, refugees, people in situations of war or conflict, victims of domestic violence, marginality)	Provide security through culture and art by providing safe space for populations at risk (and promoting the respective risk management); Enhance culture as "safe space (e.g., welcoming gender or religious minorities, refugees, or victims of war, conflict, marginality, domestic violence, etc)
		13.4. Promotion of intercultural and cross-cultural intersections	- Promote intercultural and transcultural intersections	Enhancing cross cultural dialogue as enabler of the transformation of local identities
		13.5. Promotion of tolerance and openness to difference	- Promote tolerance and openness to difference	Encourage tolerance, open mindsets and enhance cosmopolitanism
	14. Civic Participation	14.1. Enabling of citizenship and individuals' involvement in social life	- Foster involvement in collective social life and active citizenship	Culture as promoter of citizenship; exploring all relations between arts and citizenship
		14.2. Furthering of cultural audiences engagement and participation in the artistic processes	- Engage audiences and allow their participation in decision making processes	Enable cultural participation, in a diversity of ways: active spectatorship, participatory programming, involvement in creative processes, participatory cultural management, etc.
		14.3. Creative freedom	- Enable artistic freedom and free creative expression	Promote/assure artistic freedom
		14.4. Empowerment in the access to culture	- Empower citizens with tools and skills, in order to facilitate accessibility(ies) to creative production and cultural enjoyment (e.g. cultural barriers, language, skills to overcome digital shift)	Promoting accessibility to culture, from the perspective of audiences' skills development / cultural capital
		14.5. Promotion of questioning and critical thinking	- Make room for questioning, reflexivity, and critical thinking	Provide "space for struggle"; enable critical thinking; promote reflexivity within the artistic field
	15. Governance and quality of processes and policies	15.1. Development of fair, supportive and efficient governance models	- Develop/improve fairer, supportive and efficient governance models (internally and externally to the institution) that allow the sustainability of creative projects	Improvement of fairer, more solidary and efficient governance models; potentially assuming multiple and diverse governance logics (based on market, public support, networks, untraded interdependencies, etc.), aiming resilience of the activity (including visibility/reputation within the institution - in hierarchical structures); solidarity funding
		15.2. Solidification of the (formal and informal) mechanisms for regulating the creative ecosystem	- Enhance capacity building and institutional structuring of local cultural/creative ecosystem, developing space for collective or collaborative projects, and creating collaborations between local actors and/or with external actors.	Community empowerment through capacity building and collaboration between stakeholders; promotion of spaces for collaboration and collaborative practices in collective processes; coordination through associations, networks, alliances
		15.3. Influence in the development of public policies	- Have a demonstration effect for public policies and/or contribute to the development of new policies, plans and measures	Contribution to new policy developments; inductive effect on public policies; evolution of open governance standards and procedures
		15.4. Transparency in governance structures	- Ensure transparent governance mechanisms	Guarantee of transparency and accountability in the functioning
		15.5. Democracy	- Promote democracy and cultural democratization in the community, assuming culture as an universal right	Promotion of democracy and cultural democratization, as well as development of culture as a right

Figure 5. Operationalization of the 'Citizenship and participation' dimension.
Source: Own elaboration.

In this sense, we followed an assessment approach based on the notion of value, assuming that the value produced by culture activity is necessarily multidimensional, contextual and relative, dealing with different perceptions, motivations and interests of all those involved in these activities. Therefore, we assume that the fundamental would be to provide the cultural agents with a toolkit that would provide them with the awareness of the diversity of impacts and the multidimensionality of the value generated by their activity, as well as the diversity of valuations (individual and social) and different interests/motivations at stake. The focus is on the importance of the (self)monitoring of the value generated, both for extrinsic reasons (e.g. to influence access to finance or definition of public policies) and intrinsic motivations (for the development and resilience of the activity itself).

Our departing point was the work developed in the scope of diverse research projects held in DINAMIA'CET-iscte in recent years (RESHAPE, ARTSBANK, IMPACTOS-ARTEMREDE, CREATOUR), which have been working with artists, cultural promoters, creative tourism agents and public authorities, in several territorial contexts, both at Portuguese and European levels, in the assessment of the impacts of their activities in their communities.

Combining the work developed (and still ongoing) in these four research projects, we propose an analytical assessment framework that expresses the diversity and multidimensionality in value creation, focused in the impacts of creative activities in their territories and communities. The specific grid that is presented in this paper comprises five main dimensions for assessing the territorial impacts of cultural activities: cultural, economic, social, environmental; citizenship and participation. These are subdivided into 15 subdimensions, and operationalized in 75 different indicators. This impacts self-assessment toolkit has been developed and tested with cultural and creative actors in some of these projects, and is being transposed to a digital application/platform that allows the systematization, self-assessment and self-awareness of value creation and their impacts by the agents of the cultural/creative sector.

Notes

1. RESHAPE Webpage https://reshape.network/trajectory/value-of-art-in-social-fabric.
2. And these are often the ones already expected in an unquestionable or uncritical way by the institutions on which projects or promoters depend, financially or institutionally, for the development of these activities.
3. Previous versions of our analytical framework, directed for the specific case of creative tourism initiatives, can be consulted in these references.
4. Cf. Verwayen et al. (2017); https://pro.europeana.eu/page/impact#impact-playbook.
5. https://uncharted-culture.eu/.
6. https://www.mesoc-project.eu/.
7. We naturally acknowledge the important contributions of all colleagues involved—in a 'variable geometry'—in all these projects, particularly Elisabete Tomaz, Margarida Perestrelo, Maria Assunção Gato, Ana Rita Cruz and Ricardo Lopes, as well as the partners and community members involved in all of them. We also appreciate the discussions held with the eight Reshapers engaged on trajectory three of RESHAPE ('Value of art in social fabric'): Bojan Krištofić, Caroline Melon, Jean-Lorin Sterian, Margarita Pita, Marina Urruticoechea, Minipogon, Tewa Barnosa and Zoe Lafferty.

8. And more recently, also a 5th project— 'STRONGER PERIPHERIES—a Southern Coalition' (funded by Creative Europe program)—in the testing and application of the framework presented in this paper.
9. CREATOUR—Creative Tourism Destination Development in Small Cities and Rural Areas (SAICTPAC/0003/2015) (project No. 16437), funded by the Portuguese Foundation for Science and Technology (FCT/MEC) through national funds and co-funded by FEDER through the Joint Activities Programme of COMPETE 2020 and the Regional Operational Programmes of Lisbon and Algarve.
10. RESHAPE—Reflect, Share, Practice Experiment, funded by EC, Creative Europe Program.
11. IMPACTOS-AR—Study on the impacts of the activities of ARTEMREDE, funded by ARTEMREDE municipalities network.
12. ARTSBANK—Creative milieus at "Margem Sul": triggering territorial development through co-creation of knowledge in the contemporary metropolis (several sources of funding).
13. As it is being applied in practice. Please note that in parallel to this scale questions, we envisage to apply, in certain research cases, additional quantitative and qualitative questions for each sub-dimension.

Disclosure statement

No potential conflict of interest was reported by the author(s).

ORCID

Pedro Costa http://orcid.org/0000-0001-9106-463X

References

Becker, H. 1984. *Art Worlds*. London: University of California Press.
Bianchini, F. 1999. "Cultural Planning for Urban Sustainability." In *City and Culture. Cultural Processes and Urban Sustainability*, edited by L. Nyström. Karlskrona: Swedish Urban Environment Council.
Belfiore, E., and O. Bennett. 2010. "Beyond the 'Toolkit Approach': Arts Impact Evaluation Research and the Realities of Cultural Policy-Making." *Journal for Cultural Research* 14 (2): 121–142. doi:10.1080/14797580903481280
Bonet, L., G. Calvano, L. Carnelli, F. Dupin-Meynard, and E. Négrier. 2018. *Be SpectACTive! Challenging Participation in Performing Arts*. Spoleto: Editoria & Spettacolo.
CAE. 2018. *The Value and Values of Culture*. Brussels: Culture Action Europe.
Camagni, R., D. Maillat, and E. Matteaccioli. 2004. *Ressources naturelles et culturelles, milieux et développement local*. Neuchâtel: EDES.
Caves, R. 2002. *Creative Industries: Contracts Between Art and Commerce*. Cambridge, MA: Harvard University Press.
CHCfE Consortium. 2015. *Cultural Heritage Counts for Europe*. , England: Europa Nostra, ENCATC, Heritage Europe, International Cultural Centre, Krakow, Raymond Lemaire International Centre for Conservation at KU Leuven, The Heritage Alliance.
Cooke, P., and L. Lazzeretti (eds.) 2008. *Creative Cities, Cultural Clusters and Local Development*. Cheltenham: Edward Elgar.
Costa, P. 2007. *A Cultura em Lisboa: Competitividade e desenvolvimento territorial*. Lisboa: Imprensa de Ciências Sociais.
Costa, P. (ed.) 2015. *Políticas Culturais para o Desenvolvimento: Conferência ARTEMREDE*. Santarém: Artemrede.
Costa, P., R. Lopes, and J. Bassani. 2019. *BRR2018: Quando a periferia se torna trendy*. Lisboa: DINAMIA'CET-IUL/FAU-USP.

Costa, P., E. Tomaz, M. Perestrelo, R. Lopes, et al. 2021. "Acknowledging the Multidimensionality of Value Creation in Cultural Activities: An Impact Self-Assessment Toolkit." In *Entre Transições: Retrospetivas, Transversalidades, Perspetivas*, edited by M. Gato and P. Guibentif. (org.) Lisboa: DINAMIA'CET-Iscte.

Crevoisier, O., and H. Jeannerat. 2009. "Territorial Knowledge Dynamics: From the Proximity Paradigm to Multi-Location Milieus." *European Planning Studies* 17 (8): 1223–1241. doi:10.1080/09654310902978231

Dessein, J., K. Soini, G. Fairclough, and L. Horlings. 2015. *Culture in, for and as Sustainable Development. Conclusions from the COST Action IS!007 Investigating Cultural Sustainability.* Jyvaskyla: Jyvaskyla University Press.

Dupin-Meynard, F., and E. Négrier, (eds. with L. Bonet, G. Calvano, L. Carnelli, and E. Zuliani). 2020. *Cultural Policies in Europe: A Participatory Turn?* Éditions de L'Attribut et Occitanie en scène: Toulouse.

Duxbury, N. 2011. "Shifting Strategies and Contexts for Culture in Small City Planning: Interlinking Quality of Life, Economic Development, Downtown Vitality and Community Sustainability." In *Cultural Political Economy of Small Cities*, edited by A. Lorentzen, and B. van Heur, 161–178. London: Routledge.

Duxbury, N., J. Baltà, J. Hosagrahar, and J. Pascual. 2016. "Culture in Urban Development Policies: An Agenda for Local Governments." In UNESCO (org.), *Culture: Urban Future – Global Report on Culture for Sustainable Urban Development*, 204–211. Paris: UNESCO.

Duxbury, N., and E. Gillette. 2007. *Culture as a Key Dimension of Sustainability: Exploring Concepts, Themes, and Models.* Vancouver, British Columbia: Creative City Network of Canada. Centre of Expertise on Culture and Communities.

Duxbury, N., and M. Jeannotte. 2012. "Including Culture in Sustainability: An Assessment of Canada's Integrated Community Sustainability Plans." *International Journal of Urban Sustainable Development* 4 (1): 1–19. doi:10.1080/19463138.2012.670116

Duxbury, N., and G. Richards. 2019. *A Research Agenda for Creative Tourism.* Cheltenham: Edward Elgar.

EC. 2018. *A New European Agenda for Culture, Communication from the Commission to the European Parliament, the European Council, the Council, the European Economic and Social Committee and the Committee of the Regions, COM(2018) 267 Final, 22.5.2018.* Brussels: European Commission.

EU. 2018. *Draft Council Conclusions on the Work Plan for Culture 2019-2022, 13886/18 CULT 132.* Brussels: Council of the European Union.

Ferrão, J. 1995. "Colectividades Territoriais e Globalização: Contributos para uma Nova Acção Estratégica de Emancipação." *INFORGEO, Lisboa*, n° 9/10: 65–75.

Galloway, S. 2009. "Theory-based Evaluation and the Social Impact of the Arts." *Cultural Trends* 18 (2): 125–148. doi:10.1080/09548960902826143

Gato, M., E. Tomaz, P. Costa, A. Cruz, and M. Perestrelo. 2021. "An Impact Assessment Tool for Creative Tourism: Insights from its Application to CREATOUR Project." In *Creative Tourism: Activating Cultural Resources and Engaging Creative Travellers*, edited by N. Duxbury, S. Albino, and C. P. Carvalho, 439–456, Egham: CABI.

Hawkes, J. 2001. *The Fourth Pillar of Sustainability: Culture's Essential Role in Public Planning.* Victoria: Common Ground Publishing / Cultural Development Network.

Kebir, L., O. Crevoisier, P. Costa, and V. Peyrache-Gadeau. 2017. *Sustainable Innovation and Regional Development: Rethinking Innovative Milieus.* Cheltenham: Edward Elgar.

Korez-Vide, R. 2013. "Promoting Sustainability of Tourism by Creative Tourism Development: How far is Slovenia." *Innovative Issues and Approaches in Social Sciences* 6 (1): 77–102. doi:10.12959/issn.1855-0541.IIASS-2013-no1-art05

Lazzeretti, L. 2020. "What is the Role of Culture Facing the Digital Revolution Challenge? Some Reflections for a Research Agenda." *European Planning Studies*, doi:10.1080/09654313.2020.1836133.

Lazzeretti, L., and M. Vecco. (orgs). 2018. *Creative Industries and Entrepreneurship: Paradigms in Transition from a Global Perspective.* Cheltenham: Edward Elgar.

Meireis, T., and G. Rippl. 2018. *Cultural Sustainability: Perspectives from the Humanities and Social Sciences.* London: Routledge.

Nurse, K. 2006. "Culture as the Fourth Pillar of Sustainable Development. Prepared for: Commonwealth Secretariat." *Small States: Economic Review and Basic Statistics* 11: 28–40.

Richards, G. 2018. "The Experience Footprint: A Tool to Measure Leisure and Event Experiences." *Uncover* 2018 (2): 8–9.

Sacco, P. 2011. "Culture 3.0: A New Perspective for the EU 2014-2020 Structural Funds Programming." EENC (European Expert Network on Culture) Paper, April 2011.

Sala, S., B. Ciuffo, and P. Nijkamp. 2015. "A Systemic Framework for Sustainability Assessment." *Ecological Economics* 119 (November): 314–325. doi:10.1016/j.ecolecon.2015.09.015

Scott, A. 2000. *The Cultural Economy of Cities.* New Delhi: Sage.

Scott, A. 2008. *Social Economy of the Metropolis: Cognitive-Cultural Capitalism and the Global Resurgence of Cities.* Oxford: Oxford University Press.

Scott, A. 2014. "Beyond the Creative City: Cognitive–Cultural Capitalism and the new Urbanism." *Regional Studies* 48 (4): 565–578. doi:10.1080/00343404.2014.891010

Singh, R., R. Murty, A. Gupta, and A. Dikshit. 2009. "An Overview of Sustainability Assessment Methodologies." *Ecological Indicators* 9 (2): 189–212. doi:10.1016/j.ecolind.2008.05.011

Soini, K., and J. Dessein. 2016. "Culture-Sustainability Relation: Towards a Conceptual Framework." *Sustainability* 8 (2): 167. doi:10.3390/su8020167

Throsby, D. 2001. *Economics and Culture.* Cambridge: Cambridge University Press.

Tomaz, E., P. Costa, M. Gato, A. Cruz, and M. Perestrelo. 2020. *Discussing Impact Assessment on Creative Tourism: A Theoretical and Analytical Model, DINAMIA'CET Working Papers, WP 2020/5, Setembro 2020.* Lisboa: Dinamia'CET_iscte.

Vale, M. 2012. *Conhecimento Inovação e Território.* Lisboa: Edições Colibri.

Verwayen, H., J. Fallon, J. Schellenberg, and P. Kyrou. 2017. *Impact Playbook for Museums, Libraries, Archives and Galleries.* Den Haag: Europeana Foundation.

UCLG. 2015. *Culture 21: Actions. Commitments on the Role of Culture in Sustainable Cities.* Barcelona: United Cities and Local Governments / Agenda 21 for culture.

UN. 2015. *Transforming our World: The 2030 Agenda for Sustainable Development.* New York: United Nations.

UNEP and WTO. 2005. *Making Tourism More Sustainable – A Guide for Policy Makers.* Paris: UNEP, Division of Technology, Industry and Economics.

UNESCO. 2009. *The 2009 UNESCO Framework for Cultural Statistics.* Montreal: UNESCO Institute for Statistics.

UNESCO. 2012. *Measuring the Economic Contribution of Cultural Industries: A Review and Assessment of Current Methodological Approaches.* Montreal: UNESCO Institute for Statistics.

UNESCO. 2015. "UNESCO's Work on Culture and Sustainable Development: Evaluation of a Policy Theme." Final Report. Nov 2015. UNESCO.

UNESCO. 2019. *Culture | 2030 Indicators.* Paris: UNESCO.

Waas, T., J. Hugé, T. Block, T. Wright, F. Benitez-Capistros, and A. Verbruggen. 2014. "Sustainability Assessment and Indicators: Tools in a Decision-Making Strategy for Sustainable Development." *Sustainability* 6 (9): 5512–5534. doi:10.3390/su6095512

WTO. 2004. *Indicators of Sustainable Development for Tourism Destinations: A Guidebook.* Madrid: World Tourism Organization.

Museums and digital technology: a literature review on organizational issues

Francesca Taormina and Sara Bonini Baraldi

ABSTRACT
In the past 20 years, museums have made digital technologies key resources for accomplishing and innovating their functions. The current pandemic affirms museums' dependence on digital tools, which have become the only means to reach the public during lockdowns. While the scientific community generally examines information and communication technology as a tool to provide innovative museum functions, it rarely seeks to understand how digital solutions permeate daily organization and management. Through an extensive literature review, this paper aims to consolidate a pre-pandemic body of knowledge from which further investigations and useful suggestions can be developed. By benchmarking heterogeneous literature sources, the study identifies three core topics (business models, digital professions and digital strategy), questioning whether changes driven by digital technology within museums follow radical innovation or gradual adaptation. In the conclusions, the paper underlines major implications for museums, policy makers and scholars.

1. Introduction[1]

On top of their traditional duties and competencies (McGovern 2013), museums are today increasingly invested with new responsibilities (Dubuc 2011). More and more they are considered powerful institutions that indirectly benefit the surrounding environment: as drivers for tourism, as sources of creative capital and as means for social inclusion (Knell 2009; Badalotti, De Biase, and Greenaway 2011; Hatton 2012; Della Corte, Aria, and Del Gaudio 2017; OECD and ICOM 2019; Li and Ghirardi 2019). Moreover, museums belong to wider systems of relationships as nodes of cultural ecosystems (Borin and Donato 2015).

Digital technologies are increasingly essential to how museums, and cultural organizations more generally, accomplish their mission (Parry 2005, 2007, 2013; Bakhshi and Throsby 2010; Accenture, 2017). Technological innovation affects several fields of museum activity: conservation and management of collections (Borowiecki and Navarrete 2017; Dragoni, Tonelli, and Moretti 2017), display of objects (vom Lehn and Heath 2005), customer service (Camarero and Garrido 2012; Schettino 2016), media and communication (Badalotti, De Biase, and Greenaway 2011; Rivera 2013) and collaboration (Li and Ghirardi 2019). The ongoing digital transformation seems to be so pervasive that the notion of a 'virtual museum' is increasingly debated (Münster 2019; Bonacini 2011).

Digital technology is also claimed to revolutionizing museums' relationship with the public, which now comprise both physical visitors and virtual followers (Waterton 2010; Cassidy et al. 2018; Hancock 2018). By leveraging new digital interactive methods (Pallud and Monod 2010; vom Lehn and Heath 2005), visitors are also increasingly active in the production of cultural content (Karp 2014), shifting from mere consumers to co-producers of museum offerings (Pulh and Mencarelli 2015). In Europe, the diffusion of digital technology is turning so much audience engagement to the extent of drawing policy attention (Tomka 2013).

Scholars widely acknowledge the role of ICT as a powerful resource to strengthen the adaptive and competitive ability of museums (Knell 2009; Hamma 2004; Bonacini 2011; Camarero and Garrido 2012; Vicente, Camarero, and Garrido 2012; Schettino 2016; Hossaini and Blankenberg 2017). Much attention focuses on the positive effects of ICT for museums' primary functions: documenting and preserving, displaying and interpreting, researching and fostering social participation (Lord and Lord 2009; Gombault et al. 2018). However, the way in which the adoption of digital solutions 'diffuses across organizational work processes and becomes routinized in the activities associated with those processes' has been rarely investigated (Parry 2013, 3). This question is fundamental, as sustainable digital innovation cannot be ensured without adequately considering its organizational implications (Markus and Robey 1988; Hanelt et al. 2021).

Currently, the COVID-19 pandemic is significantly accelerating digital transformations within museums, which suddenly end up interacting only with digital audiences for long periods (Agostino, Arnaboldi, and Lampis 2020). Due to prolonged closures, museums are increasingly forced to reinvent their business models to cleverly exploit digital technologies. An increasingly targeted digital offering may change physical interaction between museums and the public, leading to pioneering digital strategies like those based on the use of artificial intelligence (Agostino, Arnaboldi, and Lampis 2020). Sudden lockdowns are also negatively affecting museums' workforces, to the extent they are influencing national cultural policies (Betzler et al. 2021).

As museums continue to struggle with their role in an 'increasingly pervasive information society' (Knell 2009, 133), investigating organizational transformations resulting from the ubiquitous use of digital technology (Tsai and Chiang 2012) is crucial to critically rethink the 'missing links' (Peacock 2008, 346) between museums' operations and ICT. As theorized by Parry (2013), museums are entering the post-digital era, where the use of digital is considered an integral component of museums' articulation and function. It is legitimated through the emergence of new job profiles and workflows, and it influences strategic decisions, for example, via budget allocations for digital projects. Yet, the post-digital condition fosters novel research perspectives whereby digital technology is a 'normative presence' (Parry 2013, 2) regardless of the degree of assimilation, and requires an integrated analytical approach concerning several dimensions: operational, organizational and strategic.

Grounding these reflections, our paper questions how the pre-pandemic knowledge concerning museum organization and digital innovation can contribute to addressing emerging challenges, in a context that is already seeking new research perspectives (Koslow 2019). Adopting an organizational and managerial approach (Abraham, Griffin, and Crawford 1999; Hamma 2004; Peacock 2008), the paper examines how and whether digital technologies permeate museums' structures and organization and what are the major implications for the museum, policy making and academic communities. Its central aim is to identify macro strands of change by benchmarking heterogeneous literature sources in the past 20 years: academic articles, project reports, conference proceedings and books. Embracing this holistic perspective, it grasps both opportunities and challenges for museums in achieving a good level of 'digital maturity' in the near future (McKenzie and Poole 2011, 4; Hatton 2012; Gombault et al. 2018).

The paper is structured as follows. Section two presents the methodological approach adopted to identify and interpret heterogeneous literature sources on the relationship between museums and digital technology. Section three explores and articulates this literature according to three interweaved domains: business models, emerging professionals and digital strategy. Finally, section four summarizes our major remarks and addresses novel inputs for future research.

2. Research design and methodology

This review aims to understand how the diffusion of ICT affects the organization and management of museums and what the implications of these transformations are for museum life. It includes both retrospective and prospective aspects (Taylor and Spicer 2007), covering a 20-year time frame. The retrospective view emerges from the collection and correlation of multidisciplinary studies, reducing the considerable fragmentation of the topic. Although the issue has been recognized for many years (Hamma 2004), currently, there is no systematic review. This review seeks to define the most relevant themes, to outline trends of transformations and to understand how they occur (whether radical or gradual).

The prospective view looks at the current pandemic scenario. The pandemic has accelerated digital transformation: digital technology is the only way museums can interact with the public during lockdown periods. Uncertainty about the pandemic's duration and its cultural repercussions suggest an increasingly digital-centric future scenario for museums. This review seeks to foster new threads of research on managerial and organizational issues, questioning the pervasive use of digital technology in post- pandemic museums.

Aligned with other reviews, this study adopts a systematic approach (Ankrah and AL-Tabbaa 2015; Weinfurtner and Seidl 2019) for the following reasons. First, the review is driven by a specific research question: how is the management and organization of museums influenced by the increasingly pervasive use of digital technology? Second, the study is designed through a robust review process, reducing the risk of overlooking publications crucial to the topic (Ankrah and AL-Tabbaa 2015). It specifies criteria for exclusion and inclusion of sources. Finally, it strives to assemble multidisciplinary contributions in a coherent plot and yield suggestions for future studies (Hammersley 2001). The review is articulated into two macro phases, to identify primary and additional sources.

- Phase 1 – Primary sources

The first phase focuses on the identification and analysis of academic papers published in scientific journals. Papers are considered primary sources since their content is approved after a peer-review process and therefore validated in terms of quality and relevance. Given the interdisciplinary nature of the topic, scientific papers are expected to cover the central contributions in each discipline involved in our research question (culture and humanities, management, ICT; Ankrah and AL-Tabbaa 2015; Weinfurtner and Seidl 2019). A specific timeframe covering the past 20 years (2000–2019)[2] is set to focus on studies of current relevance. To grasp the first reflections emerging from the outbreak of the pandemic, the review also includes five articles published in 2020, when the emergency was already underway.

First, we use keywords to identify the journals to be searched. The search was carried out on the Scimago Journal & Country Rank (SJR) platform, given it only includes citations from peer-reviewed journals on Scopus. Furthermore, the Scimago platform provides information about journals' relevance and subject categories. This latter element is particularly relevant, as it suggests the possible content of the articles in each journal. We developed a set of 178 journals, containing single and combined keywords in the title (Lindqvist 2012).[3] From these, we exclude 63 journals because they refer to disciplines unrelated to the research question (medicine, agriculture, etc.). We thus select 115 journals belonging to three categories (arts, humanities and cultural studies; general business management; and computer science) to search for papers published between 2000 and 2019 on our research topic.

Second, to select papers in the journals, we search for keywords in titles and then screen the contents of the abstracts. Our screening was sharply selective on a subjective basis: only topical papers were considered, excluding those that treated digitization in museums in a more technical and applicative way. For example, papers describing the operation of digital devices have been left out (Emery, Toth, and Noel 2009; Vavoula and Mason 2017). Following this method, we select 33 articles from 8 journals in the following categories: arts, humanities and cultural studies (24); general business management (5); and computer science (4) (see Table 1).

Third, we analyze the selected papers for a preliminary understanding. Eleven led to the identification of three thematic domains (business models, emerging professionals, and digital strategy), which we use to build the results.[4] The three domains are aligned with broader literature analyzing the impact of digital innovation on firms' competitive advantage (Yoo, Henfridsson, and Lyytinen 2010; Lyytinen, Yoo, and Boland 2016; Yunis, El-Kassar, and Tarhini 2017). The remaining 22 papers are also used to frame and discuss the topic.

Finally, we add 33 further papers to the 33 detected through keywords and abstract analysis. These are chosen because four papers we knew are relevant to the topic did not surface in keyword searches; six papers from 2020 examine some pivotal contemporary contributions; one paper has been recommended by one of the reviewers; two papers focus on the relationship between organizational transformation and information technology and 20 papers deepen specific themes.[5] As a result, our analysis examines 66 papers.

- Phase 2 – Additional sources

Table 1. Phase 1: Selected journals and papers (primary sources).

Journal categories (from Scimago)	Journals	Papers
• Art, humanities and cultural studies (24)	International Journal of Arts Management	Bertacchini and Morando (2011); Gombault et al. (2018); Pulh and Mencarelli (2015); vom Lehn and Heath (2005)
	Museum International	Carvalho and Matos (2018); Cassidy et al. (2018); Hess, Colson, and Hindmarch (2018); Karp (2014); Orlandi et al. (2018); Rivera (2013); Schettino (2016)
	Museum Management and Curatorship	Della Corte, Aria, and Del Gaudio (2017); Dubuc (2011); Greffe, Krebs, and Pflieger (2017); Griffin (2008); Hatton (2012); Jensen (2019); Koslow (2019); Li and Ghirardi (2019); Marty (2006); Parry (2005); Peacock (2008); Waterton (2010)
	Cultural Trend	Tomka (2013)
• Business, management and cultural economics (5)	International Studies of Management & Organization	Coblence and Sabatier (2014); Lyubareva, Benghozi, and Fidele (2014); Moyon and Lecocq (2014)
	Journal of Cultural Economics.	Peukert (2019)
	Il Capitale Culturale	Lazzeretti and Sartori (2016)
• Computer science (4)	Journal on Computing and Cultural Heritage	Damala, Ruthven, and Hornecker (2019); Dragoni, Tonelli, and Moretti (2017); Münster (2019); Seifert et al. (2017)

Source: authors' own work.

To add empirical evidence and integrate knowledge from scientific papers, we consult three additional sources: project reports, books and papers in conference proceedings. To do so, we use a set of keywords on several browsers (i.e. Google Chrome, Scholar and Book) and websites (i.e. Worldcat, OPAC, ICOM).[6] We select only relevant contributions, based on the three identified themes and the core topics. We search quickly but purposefully for abstracts, introductions and book chapters concerning each topic. This process results in the selection of 10 project reports, seven books and six papers in conference proceedings. Furthermore, we add two books and three papers in conference proceedings, thanks to advice from the reviewers. As a result, we collect a total of additional 28 sources. In total, primary and additional sources amount to 94 elements.[7]

Table 2. Primary and additional sources in each thematic domain.

Thematic domains	Sources
1. Business models (23)	**Papers:** Baden-Fuller and Morgan 2010; Berman 2012; Bertacchini and Morando 2011; Bonini Baraldi and Ferri 2019; Borin and Donato 2015; Coblence and Sabatier 2014; Gombault 2003; Lazzeretti and Sartori 2016; Li 2015; Lyubareva, Benghozi, and Fidele 2014; Moyon and Lecocq 2014; Seetharaman 2020; Senyo, Liu, and Effah 2019; Parry 2013 **Books:** Borin 2017; McKeever 2017; Navarrete 2013; Blankenberg 2017 **Project reports:** European Commission 2002; Nesta and MTM London (2017) **Conferences:** Borin, Donato, and Badia 2015; Borin and Paunovic 2016; Koseki, Shimizu, and Iio 2010
2. Emerging professionals (11)	**Papers:** Carvalho and Matos 2018; Marty 2006; Jensen 2019; Peacock 2008; Lacedelli, Tamma, and Fazzi 2019; van Laar et al. 2020 **Books:** Blankenberg 2017 **Project Reports:** Silvaggi 2017; European Commission 2002 **Conferences:** Parry et al. 2018; Price and Dafydd 2018
3. Digital strategy (7)	**Papers:** Orlandi et al. 2018; Damala, Ruthven, and Hornecker 2019; Orlandi 2020 **Books**: Rumelt 2011; Hossaini and Blankenberg 2017 **Project Reports:** Morrison 2019 **Conferences:** Price and Dafydd 2018

Source: authors' own work

Among them, 41 are grouped according to the three thematic domains and are used to build the next section (see Table 2).[8] The remaining are used throughout the overall paper.

3. Results

The move towards 'an economy and society increasingly shaped by digital information and communications technology' (Peacock, Swatman, and Lu 2009, 52) leads museums to reconcile digital assets and traditional features, optimizing available resources to address the requirements of managing both physical and digital spaces. Indeed, the fast-evolving nature of technology (Hamma 2004; Badalotti, De Biase, and Greenaway 2011) provides challenges for museums in terms of managing digital items and collections, nurturing digital skills and creating new workflows (McGovern 2013; Hossaini and Blankenberg 2017).

These challenges add to the already high level of the complexity characterizing the operations of contemporary museums. This complexity is due to a range of pressures such as operating with inadequate resources, counting on underpaid staff or volunteers (Sandell and Janes 2007) and a growing decline in public funding (Greffe, Krebs, and Pflieger 2017). The pervasive dissemination of digital technologies in the cultural field (Peukert 2019) is further affecting the dynamics of production and distribution of museums' products and services, meaning museums are more likely to adopt business attitudes and be subjected to market requirements, especially in the areas of audience development and commercial services (Griffin 2008). Piecing together the state of the art of new business models, emerging professionals and digital strategy are thus crucial to reflect on how and whether the intersection of digital technologies, museums' public function and market forces can lead to suitable conditions for the development of the sector. In the following pages, we examine these three issues in detail.

- *New business models*

Our literature review shows a significantly high number of contributions dealing with the impact of digital technology on museums' business models. Business models relate to how organizations coordinate internal activities to create value for external parties such as users, partners and suppliers, etc. (Baden-Fuller and Morgan 2010; Seetharaman 2020; Berman 2012). Unlike business plans – formal documents envisioning the financial and marketing strategy of a company (McKeever 2017) – the business model is an analytical tool developed in managerial literature to explain and define the value proposition characterizing organizations (profit and not-for-profit, including museums). Indeed, while an organization can exist without a business plan, any organization has an implicit business model. Research on business models is becoming increasingly relevant for heritage management (Bonini Baraldi and Ferri 2019), especially in light of the digital transformations under way in both creative industries (Lyubareva, Benghozi, and Fidele 2014; Moyon and Lecocq 2014) and museums (Gombault 2003; Navarrete 2013; Parry 2013; Coblence and Sabatier 2014; Lazzeretti and Sartori 2016; Pop and Borza 2016; Blankenberg 2017).

Our literature review pinpoints three areas of interest to analyze the effects of ICT on museums' business models. Pioneer studies, such as the DigiCult report (European

Commission 2002), provide an overview of widespread e-business models in cultural institutions based on existing taxonomies. Later researches differentiate business models looking at digital transformations first 'within' museums (Bertacchini and Morando 2011), such as for digital collections and online sales, and then 'between' museums and the external environment (Lazzeretti and Sartori 2016), as in the case of partnerships and ecosystems.

The first stream concerns the influence of digital technology on museum revenue, with a focus on online sales processes, as examined by the DigiCULT study (European Commission 2002). In the 'Handbook of the Economics of Cultural Heritage', Navarrete (2013) points out five business models concerning the online offering of cultural institutions: selling online spaces to advertizers, selling physical products online, digital commerce, online subscriptions and programmes for donations. More generally, the available literature suggests that cultural organizations confidently rely on the effects of ICT on business models sustainability. In this regard, the Digital Culture report (Nesta and MTM London 2017), published as a follow-up to a longitudinal investigation carried out by the Arts Council England and Nesta on approximately one thousand cultural organizations in England, reveals that a growing percentage of organizations (from 34 per cent in 2013 to 53 per cent in 2017) consider digital assets 'important or essential' to their financial health and operational functions (Nesta and MTM London 2017, 5). Positive perceptions are related to increased opportunities to boost revenues through the implementation of additional activities (such as donations) and the development of specific agreements with third-party platforms to sell cultural content (YouTube, Eventbrite, etc.). However, despite the increasing confidence in digital value for business models sustainability, the majority of the organizations analyzed claim a lack of adequate competencies in digital tools compared with their peers (Nesta and MTM London 2017).

A second emerging perspective refers to the production and distribution of digital collections. To this purpose, Bertacchini and Morando (2011) question how the economic properties of a museum's digital collections can affect its business models through online access and distribution. The authors identify four main models. The 'proprietary image-licensing' model is one of the most traditional, as museums, at the specific request of publishers, release digital artwork images under licensing agreements that which limit use and price mechanisms that benefit direct revenue. The 'online and display' model allows free access and use of digital artwork images on online platforms (as in the case of the Google Art Project) to decrease transaction costs for a wide range of users. Images are protected from illicit reproduction by technical means such as low resolution and visible watermarks. Finally, the 'open licensing' and the 'user-generated digital content' models (Bertacchini and Morando 2011, 6) share both the principle of allowing fast use, reuse and redistributions of digital images by web users through open access platforms. Both systems give priority to the role of the museum's online communities but are characterized by different legal control systems.

The third area of interest is the relationship between business model innovation and partnership enhancement. This strand is extrapolated from two iconic cases: the Louvre Museum in France (Gombault 2003; Coblence and Sabatier 2014) and the Uffizi Gallery in Italy (Lazzeretti and Sartori 2016). Concerning the Louvre, Coblence and Sabatier (2014) use six analytical factors – technology, competition, users, profitability, and organizational architecture – and identify a trajectory of change from a 'growth-oriented' business model to a 'global and innovative' one. The 'growth-oriented' model was adopted by the museum in the mid-1980s. Its core value proposition points to the exhibition quality of the permanent collection, the diversification of cultural projects and the strengthening of merchandizing activities. The 'global and innovative' business model refers to a further phase of the museum's reorganization commencing in the early 2000s. Its core value proposition focuses on ICT technologies as a means to strengthen the processes of 'digitization, networking, and user-generated content' (Coblence and Sabatier 2014, 17), and to foster the establishment of national and international partnerships that increase both the visibility and competitiveness of the museum. The case of the Louvre Lens museum reveals the importance of partnerships for digital innovation in museums (Borin and Paunovic 2016; Borin 2017; Borin, Donato, and Badia 2015). Opened in 2012, the Louvre Lens invested in digital technologies to socially and culturally revitalize a depressed mining region in the north of France. Through a long-term partnership with 'Orange', the museum is equipped with a digital research centre that is constantly experimenting with digital mediation projects to engage the public and triggering know-how exchange between public and private stakeholders. This case illustrates how developing and/or exploiting digital skills outside the organizational boundaries might be an effective strategy to overcome the lack of competences and resources of museums in the digital sphere.

In the Uffizi Museum, the digital innovation process has been implemented in two macro phases. From the late 1980s to the 2000s, the Uffizi museum focused on digitizing the collections through several research projects and scientific experimentation. The second phase, which lasts approximately until 2013, aimed to improve 'public access and commercial use of such collections (mobile apps, virtual exhibitions)' (Lazzeretti and Sartori 2016, 961). In this case, the reluctance to invest in human resources dedicated to digital strategy, along with the 'organizational rigidity of the Italian administrative system that would hardly admit hybrid figures like social media managers' (Lazzeretti and Sartori 2016, 961), led the museum to consider long-term partnerships with 'local research bodies, creative companies in the field of ICT and technical partners' (Lazzeretti and Sartori 2016, 949), one of the key value propositions for reviewing its business model. In line with the dynamics of cultural ecosystems (Borin and Donato 2015), both the Louvre Lens and the Uffizi case highlight how value co-creation by several stakeholders is a core aspect of museum's business models. Flexible partnerships are vital to keep digital innovation responsive to time-changing circumstances (Borin 2017). As a result, participation in new digital business ecosystems (DBEs) – defined as 'collaborative environments made up of different entities that co-create value through ICT' (Senyo et al., 2019, 52; see also Koseki, Shimizu, and Iio 2010) – is fundamental to ensure a sustainable digital functioning of museums.

In conclusion, the three streams demonstrate how ICT and digital business practices demand flexibility in reconfiguring museums' traditional business models according to museum-specific features (as demonstrated in the Louvre and in the Uffizi case). However, digital transformation rarely implies 'radically new' models (Li 2015, 1273), as this would require long validation periods, an appetite for risky experimentation incompatible with institutions like museums, together with high availability of resources to invest. Rather, business models that use ICT seek to strengthen some crucial assets for museums: higher direct profits, public involvement, visibility and position in national and international networks.

Although cultural institutions are increasingly confident in business models involving digital innovation, they complain about a lack of adequate expertise in the sector compared to their peers (Nesta and MTM London 2017), causing digital innovation to remain an unfamiliar theme for museums (Peacock, Swatman, and Lu 2009). Modes of online distribution, access, use, and reuse of digital collections are crucial nodes for the innovation of museum business models, where the major challenge is to find a trade-off between the economic benefit derived from the commercial use of digital collections and the right to free access to fulfil museums' public functions (Bertacchini and Morando 2011; Lazzeretti and Sartori 2016).

- *Emerging professional and organizational issues*

Another stream in our literature review involves emerging professional and organizational issues. Indeed, the sorts of digital transformations affecting business models go hand-in-hand with human resources changes. This includes both the rise of new digital professions that are now part of museums' staff, and the development of external relationships with research groups, consultants and service providers (Marty 2006; Blankenberg 2017; Silvaggi 2017; Carvalho and Matos 2018; Parry et al. 2018; Jensen 2019; Lacedelli, Tamma, and Fazzi 2019; van Laar et al. 2020; Sturabotti and Surace, 2017).

Based on these considerations, our literature review highlights two main topics, which seem to follow an evolving perspective: while early research projects sought to identify the most common museums' e-profiles (Silvaggi 2017), later studies aimed to clarify how the inclusion of such new professionals transformed museum teams, both in terms of organizational models and behavioural practices (Price and Dafydd 2018; Lacedelli, Tamma, and Fazzi 2019).

Going more into detail, the first topic concerns the phenomenon of emerging digital professionals in the museum sector. The Museum Sector Alliance project, approved in the framework of the European Erasmus Plus programme and implemented between 2013 and 2015, points out four crucial profiles crucial to the development of digital skills among employees of Portuguese, Italian and Greek museums (Silvaggi 2017; Blankenberg 2017). These profiles are: digital strategy manager, with the 'responsibility to plan the development of a museum's digital innovation strategy, inform the staff about new digital products and mediate relations with external actors'; digital collections curator, 'expert in the conservation and maintenance of digital collections and in charge of organizing online and offline exhibitions'; digital interactive experience developer, dedicated to the 'development and innovation of experiential and interactive products for the public'; online community manager, responsible for 'marketing and audience development and for managing activities and communication on interactive platforms and social media' (Carvalho and Matos 2018, 44). These roles are intertwined with further technical profiles in ICT, IT (Silvaggi 2017), and commercial fields (Blankenberg 2017). Many of the tasks undertaken by digital professionals focus on the public. This confirms the omnichannel museum vision recently theorized by Hossaini and Blankenberg (2017), according to which museums are increasingly taking an audience-centric approach (customer centrism), geared toward meeting visitors' demands where, when and how they want with every possible channel. Digital technologies play a key role in this, in addition to enabling a dematerialization of museum content and services.

The second topic questions how emerging digital professions can impact on museum organization and environment. The DigiCULT report already noticed that digital technologies lead museums to develop a more marked level of 'interoperability' between various working groups internal to the organization (European Commission 2002, 79) in order to facilitate the transmission of data and knowledge across multiple departments (Blankenberg 2017).

To this regard, Price and Dafydd (2018) find a correlation between the degree of digital maturity and organizational structures, following a survey of 56 galleries, libraries, archives and museums worldwide. They develop four organizational models, depending on different digital transformation processes. The 'decentralized model' is poorly structured and consists of individuals or small groups with digital skills, spread across multiple departments. It is characterized by a sceptical attitude towards the adoption of new technologies (sceptics). On the other hand, the 'centralized model' consists of one multidisciplinary department that manages all digital activities. It is marked by a predisposition to use digital technologies, although still in an embryonic phase and slow in progress (adopters). The 'hub and spoke model' is based on a small central unit that coordinates and delegates digital activities to multiple teams in different sectors. It is marked by greater openness and trust in digital technologies and by at least partial investment in new digital business models (collaborators). The 'holistic model' occurs when digital skills and activities are spread among various departments, and a digital leader has the task of coordinating them. In this (ideal) case, digital technology is imbued with all museum functions and programmed for the long-term (differentiators) (Price and Dafydd 2018). The authors also reveal that museums' digital transformation is not only hampered by scarce economic resources but also by a lack of long-term vision to stimulate motivation and proactive attitudes toward change among museum's employees.

As well as the advent of new digital professions, training practices and 'digital literacy' within museums support sustainable long-term transformations. For example, the 'One by One' project in Britain mapped the level of digital literacy of staff and demonstrated that a widespread mastery of digital skills can create a climate of greater confidence in organizational change and can imply a consequent propensity to share knowledge, triggering informal learning processes (Parry et al. 2018).

The literature on emerging professionals offers reflections on three main issues. The first relates to professional hybridization, referring to the ability of introducing specific digital skills while preserving the museum's traditional know-how. In this regard, some authors stress a viable strategy would gradually integrate pre-existing roles with digital knowledge, as in the case of the digital collection curator.

The second factor concerns the capability to foster digital literacy among museum units to instil greater trust in digital transformations among employees (Parry et al. 2018). Indeed, digital knowledge must be prevented from being isolated in compartments. A crucial issue remains how to address educational needs required by the fast-evolving nature of the digital sphere, consistent with museum resources and operations (Lacedelli, Tamma, and Fazzi 2019).

The third factor refers to the way in which museums aim to achieve digital maturity. The digital turn indeed can be perceived as an 'external force to resist' (reactive model), as a process to be managed to reach specific objectives (proactive model) or as a set of continuously evolving dynamics based on actors' interactions (emerging model) (Peacock 2008, 336–337). However, little has been done to investigate how and why such different organizational processes occur (Peacock 2008; Parry et al. 2018).

- *Digital strategy*

The theme relating to digital strategy appears to be less outlined in the literature than the previous two, but it is still significant. As the concept of digital strategy is quite recent in museum studies, a longitudinal perspective does not yet emerge from the literature. As part of strategic management studies, Rumelt defines the concept of strategy as a 'coherent response to a crucial challenge. Unlike a stand-alone decision or a single goal, a strategy is a coherent set of analyzes, concepts, policies, arguments and actions that respond to a high-risk challenge' (Rumelt 2011, 16). The author identifies three factors that distinguish a good strategy: diagnosis to identify the obstacles; policy guidance to overcome such obstacles; and coherent actions with policy content. If these phases are implemented consistently, the strategy can guide the organization in advancing its interests. In museum studies, digital strategy refers to a museum's capability to achieve a certain degree of digital success. Price and Dafydd (2018) define digital success as a set of often random and discretionary factors that depend on a museum's organization and the context in which it operates: audience engagement, strengthening business processes, achieving commercial goals, enhancing digital knowledge and infrastructure are all crucial elements to define the digital success of a cultural organization. In this study, strategy is understood as an 'orientation' towards the integration of different factors. The European Mu.SA project (Carvalho and Matos 2018) stresses some of the factors that might positively or negatively influence the achievement of museums' digital success and that have to be included in the planning of a digital strategy: availability of financial resources, awareness of the museum's functions, enhancement of digital skills, investment in market research and infrastructure.

In line with Rumlet's definition, in the manual Digital Strategy for 'Museums', Morrison (2019) defines digital strategy as a 'statement of vision with objectives for the organization's digital programmes, based on evidence, owned by leadership, backed up by adequate resources and used as a guide by management and operations' (Morrison 2019, 15). The author correlates the concept of museum digital strategy with the ability to optimize the use of limited resources.

To support museums in developing a digital strategy, the literature provides some analytical frameworks, such as the Web Strategy Scheme (WSS) (Orlandi 2020; Orlandi et al. 2018) and the Musetech model (Damala, Ruthven, and Hornecker 2019). The first gathers 17 useful dimensions to monitor the strategic orientation of museums' websites. The second aims at evaluating the effects of museum technology on three correlated dimensions: cultural heritage professionals, cultural heritage institutions and museum visitors. Both frameworks highlight the multidimensional nature of a digital strategy.

Indeed, whether a museum's digital strategy strives to integrate multiple domains (communication, research, promotion, etc.), each domain should ground its operability in a digital vision (Hossaini and Blankenberg 2017). As stated by Lawler, digital director of Tate (UK), 'The [digital] vision should ultimately support the vision/mission for the organization. A digital strategy should never be separated from the overall strategy, but a means to achieve' (Price and Dafydd 2018, 32). In other words, this mutual correlation will avoid digital failure, whereby technological innovation dominates the overall vision of museums. As such, a successful digital strategy is most likely to be introduced gradually, to better adapt its approach to the overall organizational culture.

4. Concluding remarks

In the past two decades, digital technology has transformed museums' traditional ways of operating, impacting their activities and services and challenging their organizational and managerial structures. In line with a wider literature that analyzes the impact of digital innovation on the competitive advantage of firms (Yoo, Henfridsson, and Lyytinen 2010; Lyytinen, Yoo, and Boland 2016; Yunis, El-Kassar, and Tarhini 2017), this study identifies three macro areas of change that the digital revolution produced within museums' organization: new business models, emerging professionals and digital strategy. By examining these three macro strands, some general considerations are drawn.

Firstly, while it is true that museums can benefit from opportunities fostered by digital technologies, they also face important managerial challenges: the need to develop in-house capacity for deploying an effective digital strategy (Hess, Colson, and Hindmarch 2018); the employees' perception that they do not possess appropriate digital skills (Nesta and MTM London 2017); and the difficulty of integrating digital functions into daily activities, due to limited resources (Gombault et al. 2018). Our starting consideration is that the digital transformation of museums brings in major challenges not only from the technical and cultural points of view but also for the organization.

This brings us to a second point. While the development of digital tools is truly revolutionary from a technological point of view (Hossaini and Blankenberg 2017), our sources show that organisational change driven by technological innovation seems to take place gradually rather than through radical innovation. Business models, for example, are subjected to partial changes, as in the case of the Louvre and Uffizi museums. Regarding emerging professionals, the tendency is to integrate traditional know-how with innovative digital skills. A successful digital strategy is also gradually integrated within the museum's overall vision. Indeed, while digital tools evolve rapidly (Hossaini and Blankenberg 2017), digital-driven changes in museum organization are less disruptive (Peacock 2008). This supports a well-known argument in the organizational literature, whereby organizational change usually follows long and non-linear paths to become operative (Hannan and Freeman 1984).

A third consideration develops as a consequence. Management scholars have widely acknowledged the implications of digital transformation for strategy and organizational change (see Hanelt et al. 2021). While the ongoing pandemic is accelerating the introduction of digital technology in many fields, our literature review shows there is still no extensive knowledge on how these transformations take place in museums (Peacock 2008). Yet, understanding such changes is relevant to ensure a strengthened role of museums in the future, enabling them to cope with fast-changing technologies and renewed societal demands (Agostino, Arnaboldi, and Lampis 2020). Indeed, technical, cultural and organizational transformations are closely linked to each other. Acknowledging organizational inertia is also crucial to effectively plan for investments, manage resources and address challenges, guiding museums into the post-digital era.

Major implications of these considerations for both museums, policy makers and the academic community are discussed below.

- *Implications for museums*

The outbreak of the pandemic is opening up a scenario of significant European investments in cultural digitization. In order to maximize returns from investments and steer current digital transformations towards a promising future, a considered balance among museums' social mandate and digital innovation is needed. Otherwise there is the risk of plunging into digital failure or of digital infrastructures overriding museums' missions. The organizational implications of digital innovation is crucial to adequately pursuing a sustainable balance. For instance, new business models are essential to reorganize museums' resources and strengthen their value proposition through more inclusive and accessible digital offers (Lazzeretti and Sartori 2016). Investing in cultural digital ecosystems can enhance museums' partnerships and involve business and civil society in museums' missions. Also, a forward-looking digital strategy might help in aligning technological innovation with the contemporary museums' role of tackling societal requests and interests. Through the use of cutting-edge languages and online content, museums can increasingly democratize their content and draw up new imagery on relevant societal issues, such as environmental sustainability and climate change.

- *Implication for policy makers*

The acceleration of digitization processes in museums is resulting in asymmetric and heterogeneous transformations in need of targeted policies. Indeed, our sources suggest that the relationship between digital technologies and museums should always be considered in relation to context specificities: factors such as the size of a museum, its available resources, administrative system and territorial governance strongly influence strategy and goals attainable in the short and long-term (Price and Dafydd 2018). In a context of rapid digital transformation accelerated by the epidemic, smaller museums seem to suffer the most as they often lack adequate competence and resources to cope with the rapid technological progress. Policymakers should foster fairer and systemic digital transformations, supporting small and medium-size museums in the change.

- *Implications for scholars*

Although overall knowledge on organizational changes and digital innovation in museums is already widespread, the longitudinal perspective adopted in this study reveals a progressive enlargement of the research focus. While early studies tend to analyze circumscribed issues such as digital skills or new online markets, later studies adopt a wider approach, eventually recognizing the transversal character of digital technologies within (and outside) organizational boundaries. The lens of time also reveals the novelty and paucity of studies on this topic, suggesting that there is still ample room for scholars in the field of management and organization to explore the subject further. Future research could focus on the role that policymakers and public administrators play in supporting an organizational change consistent with the fast-changing digital environment. It could also deepen hitherto little-researched dynamics at the micro level of digital transformation, clarifying, for example, how the obsolescence and maintenance of digital devices can alter museums' business models.

Notes

1. This article was conceived within the DAHMUSE research project and was further developed within the MNEMONIC research project. Both projects were co-funded by the Interuniversity Department of Regional and Urban Studies and Planning – Polytechnic of Turin and University of Turin.
2. Only three papers were published before the year 2000, included because of their centrality to the research topic.
3. Single keywords: museum; heritage; cultural; digital. Combined keywords: art management; management and organization; museum organization; and digital heritage management.
4. The remaining 22 out of 33 papers selected through keywords were then used in other parts of the paper.
5. Business models (4), methodology (5), firms (3), heritage and innovation (3); museums in general (4); digital business ecosystem (1).
6. Some keyword combinations: digital professionals, digital strategy museums, digital technology museums, digital business models and museums, etc.
7. The reference list contains 97 sources, since it includes the two papers referred to in the excluded topics, and the book by Hossaini and Blankenberg (2017) is cited twice (as a whole contribution and as a single chapter).
8. One source is shared across multiple themes.

Disclosure statement

No potential conflict of interest was reported by the author(s).

Funding

This work was supported by DIST – Interuniversity Department of Regional and Urban Studies and Planning – Polytechnic of Turin, University of Turin.

ORCID

Sara Bonini Baraldi http://orcid.org/0000-0001-6853-8075

References

Abraham, M., D. Griffin, and J. Crawford. 1999. "Organisation Change and Management Decision in Museums." *Management Decision* 37 (10): 736–751. doi:10.1108/00251749910302827

Accenture. 2017. "Digital adoption: How workforce development nonprofits can accelerate employment and entrepreneurship outcomes at scale." Accessed 26 November 2021. https://

www.accenture.com/t20170206T201908Z__w__/us-en/_acnmedia/PDF-42/Accenture-Digital-Adoption-Report.pdf

Agostino, D., M. Arnaboldi, and A. Lampis. 2020. "Italian State Museums During the COVID-19 Crisis: From Onsite Closure to Online Openness." *Museum Management and Curatorship* 35 (4): 362–372. doi:10.1080/09647775.2020.1790029

Ankrah, S., and O. AL-Tabbaa. 2015. "Universities–Industry Collaboration: A Systematic Review." *Scandinavian Journal of Management* 31 (3): 387–408. doi:10.1016/j.scaman.2015.02.003

Badalotti, E., L. De Biase, and P. Greenaway. 2011. "The Future Museum." *Procedia Computer Science* 7: 114–116. doi:10.1016/j.procs.2011.12.034

Baden-Fuller, C., and M. Morgan. 2010. "Business Models as Models." *Long Range Planning* 43 (2-3): 156–171. doi:10.1016/j.lrp.2010.02.005

Bakhshi, H., and D. Throsby. 2010. *Culture of Innovation: An Economic Analysis of Innovation*. London: Nesta.

Berman, S. 2012. "Digital Transformation: Opportunities to Create new Business Models." *Strategy & Leadership* 40 (2): 16–24. doi:10.1108/10878571211209314

Bertacchini, E., and F. Morando. 2011. "The Future of Museums in the Digital Age: New Models of Access and Use of Digital Collections." *International Journal of Arts Management* 15 (2): 60–72.

Betzler, D., E. Loots, M. Prokůpek, L. Marques, and P. Grafenauer. 2021. "COVID-19 and the Arts and Cultural Sectors: Investigating Countries' Contextual Factors and Early Policy Measures." *International Journal of Cultural Policy*, 27 (6), 796–814. doi: 10.1080/10286632.2020.1842383

Blankenberg, N. 2017. "Museum Organization for the Future." In *Manual of Digital Museum Planning*, edited by A. Hossaini and N. Blankenberg, 271–287. London: Rowman and Littlefield.

Bonacini, E. 2011. *Il museo Contemporaneo. Fra tradizione, marketing e nuove tecnologie*. Roma: Aracne.

Bonini Baraldi, S., and P. Ferri. 2019. "From Communism to Market: Business Models and Governance in Heritage Conservation in Poland." *Journal of Management and Governance* 23 (3): 787–812. doi:10.1007/s10997-018-09448-8

Borin, E. 2017. *Public-private Partnership in the Cultural Sector: A Comparative Analysis of European Models*. Bruxelles: Peter Lang Verlag.

Borin, E., and F. Donato. 2015. "Unlocking the Potential of IC in Italian Cultural Ecosystems." *Journal of Intellectual Capital* 16 (2): 285–304. doi:10.1108/JIC-12-2014-0131

Borin, E., F. Donato, and F. Badia. 2015. "How the Financial Crisis Affected Models of Public-Private Partnership in the Cultural Sector: Empirical Evidence from France, Germany and Italy." International Conference on Arts and Cultural Management 2015, 26 June - 01 July, 2015, Aix-en Provence, France. Accessed 26 November 2021. http://aimac2015-aix-marseille.univ-amu.fr/themes/aimac/papers/PS2_track6/256.pdf

Borin, E., and I. Paunovic. 2016. "The Case of Louvre-Lens: Regional Regeneration Through Cultural Innovation." In *Innovazione, sostenibilità e competitività. Teoria ed evidenze empiriche*, edited by H. Pechlaner, M. Hon and M. Valeri, 67–76. Italia: Giappichelli Editore.

Borowiecki, K., and T. Navarrete. 2017. "Digitization of Heritage Collections as Indicator of Innovation." *Economics of Innovation and New Technology* 26 (3): 227–246. doi:10.1080/10438599.2016.1164488

Camarero, C., and M. Garrido. 2012. "Fostering Innovation in Cultural Contexts: Market Orientation, Service Orientation, and Innovations in Museums." *Journal of Service Research* 15 (1): 39–58. doi:10.1177/1094670511419648

Carvalho, A., and A. Matos. 2018. "Museum Professionals in a Digital World: Insights from a Case Study in Portugal." *Museum International* 70 (1–2): 34–47. doi:10.1111/muse.12191

Cassidy, C., A. Fabola, A. Miller, K. Weil, S. Urbina, M. Anta, and A. Cummins. 2018. "Digital Pathways in Community Museums." *Museum International* 70 (1–2): 126–139. doi:10.1111/muse.12198

Coblence, E., and V. Sabatier. 2014. "Articulating Growth and Cultural Innovation in Art Museums." *International Studies of Management & Organization* 44 (4): 9–25. doi:10.2753/IMO0020-8825440401

Damala, A., I. Ruthven, and E. Hornecker. 2019. "The MUSETECH Model." *Journal on Computing and Cultural Heritage* 12 (1): 1–22. doi:10.1145/3297717

Della Corte, V., M. Aria, and G. Del Gaudio. 2017. "Smart, Open, User Innovation and Competitive Advantage: A Model for Museums and Heritage Sites." *Museum Management and Curatorship* 32 (1): 50–79. doi:10.1080/09647775.2016.1247380

Dragoni, M., S. Tonelli, and G. Moretti. 2017. "A Knowledge Management Architecture for Digital Cultural Heritage." *Journal on Computing and Cultural Heritage* 10 (3): 1–18. doi:10.1145/3012289

Dubuc, É. 2011. "Museum and University Mutations: The Relationship Between Museum Practices and Museum Studies in the Era of Interdisciplinarity, Professionalisation, Globalisation and New Technologies." *Museum Management and Curatorship* 26 (5): 497–508. doi:10.1080/09647775.2011.621734

Emery, D., M. Toth, and W. Noel. 2009. "The Convergence of Information Technology and Data Management for Digital Imaging in Museums." *Museum Management and Curatorship* 24 (4): 337–356. doi:10.1080/09647770903314712

European Commission. 2002. "The DigiCULT report: Technological landscapes for tomorrow's cultural economy." Unlocking the value of cultural heritage. Accessed 23 November 2021. https://www.digicult.info/downloads/html/6/6.html

Gombault, A. 2003. "La nouvelle identité organisationnelle des Musées. Le cas du Louvre." *Revue française de gestion* 29 (142): 189–204. doi:10.3166/rfg.142.189-204

Gombault, A., O. Allal-Chérif, A. Décamps, and C. Grellier. 2018. "ICT Adoption Behaviours of Heritage Organizations in South West Europe: Conservative." *Pragmatist and Pioneering. International Journal of Arts Management* 21 (1): 4–16.

Greffe, X., A. Krebs, and S. Pflieger. 2017. "The Future of the Museum in the Twenty-first Century: Recent Clues from France." *Museum Management and Curatorship* 32 (4): 319–334. doi:10.1080/09647775.2017.1313126

Griffin, D. 2008. "Advancing Museums." *Museum Management and Curatorship* 23 (1): 43–61. doi:10.1080/09647770701757716

Hamma, K. 2004. "Becoming Digital." *Bulletin of the American Society for Information Science and Technology* 30 (5): 11–13. doi:10.1002/bult.322

Hammersley, M. 2001. "On "Systematic" Reviews of Research Literatures: A "Narrative" Response to Evans & Benefield." *British Educational Research Journal* 27 (5): 543–554. doi:10.1080/01411920120095726

Hancock, M. 2018. "Culture is digital." UK Dept. for Digital, Culture, Media & Sport. Accessed 29 November 2021. https://assets.publishing.service.gov.uk/government/uploads/system/uploads/attachment_data/file/687519/TT_v4.pdf

Hanelt, A., R. Bohnsack, D. Marz, and C. Antunes Marante. 2021. "A Systematic Review of the Literature on Digital Transformation: Insights and Implications for Strategy and Organizational Change." *Journal of Management Studies* 58 (5): 1159–1197. doi:10.1111/joms.12639

Hannan, M. T., and J. Freeman. 1984. "Structural Inertia and Organizational Change." *American Sociological Review* 49: 149–164. doi:10.2307/2095567

Hatton, A. 2012. "The Conceptual Roots of Modern Museum Management Dilemmas." *Museum Management and Curatorship* 27 (2): 129–147. doi:10.1080/09647775.2012.674319

Hess, M., A. Colson, and J. Hindmarch. 2018. "Capacity Building and Knowledge Exchange of Digital Technologies in Cultural Heritage Institutions." *Museum International* 70 (1–2): 48–61. doi:10.1111/muse.12192

Hossaini, A., and N. Blankenberg. 2017. *Manual of Digital Museum Planning*. London: Rowman and Littlefield.

Jensen, S. 2019. "What a Curator Needs to Know – the Development of Professional Museum Work and the Skills Required in Danish Museums 1964–2018." *Museum Management and Curatorship* 34 (5): 468–485. doi:10.1080/09647775.2019.1641832

Karp, C. 2014. "Digital Heritage in Digital Museums." *Museum International* 66 (1–4): 157–162. doi:10.1111/muse.12069

Knell, S. J. 2009. "The Shape of Things to Come: Museum in the Technological Landscape." *Museum & Society* (pp. 443–461). in Parry, R. (Ed.). (2009). Museums in a Digital Age (1st ed.). Routledge. doi: 10.4324/9780203716083

Koseki, Y., H. Shimizu, and J. Iio. 2010. "Business Ecosystem for Digital Museums." 16th International Conference on Virtual Systems and Multimedia, 20–23 October 2010, Seoul, South Korea. pp. 382–385.

Koslow, J. 2019. "Museums and Digital Culture: New Perspectives and Research." *Museum Management and Curatorship* 34 (5): 537–539. doi:10.1080/09647775.2019.1661098

Lacedelli, S., M. Tamma, and F. Fazzi. 2019. "Digital Education as a Catalyst for Museum Transformation: The Case of the "Museums and New Digital Cultures" Course." *European Journal of Cultural Management and Policy* 9 (2): 47–65. https://www.encatc.org/media/5148-european-journal-of-cultural-management-policy-vol.9issue2.pdf#page=47

Lazzeretti, L., and A. Sartori. 2016. "Digitization of Cultural Heritage and Business Model Innovation: The Case of the Uffizi Gallery in Florence." *Il Capitale Culturale. Studies on the Value of Cultural Heritage* 14: 945–970. doi:10.13138/2039-2362/1436

Li, F. 2015. "Digital Technologies and the Changing Business Models in Creative Industries." 48th Hawaii International Conference on System Sciences, 5-6- January 2015, Hawaii, USA. pp. 1265–1274.

Li, C., and S. Ghirardi. 2019. "The Role of Collaboration in Innovation at Cultural and Creative Organisations. The Case of the Museum." *Museum Management and Curatorship* 34 (3): 273–289. doi:10.1080/09647775.2018.1520142

Lindqvist, K. 2012. "Effects of Public Sector Reforms on the Management of Cultural Organizations in Europe." *International Studies of Management & Organization* 42 (2): 9–28. doi:10.2753/IMO0020-8825420201

Lord, G., and B. Lord. 2009. *The Manual of Museum Management*. Plymouth: AltaMira Press.

Lyubareva, I., P. Benghozi, and T. Fidele. 2014. "Online Business Models in Creative Industries: Diversity and Structure." *International Studies of Management & Organization* 44 (4): 43–62. doi:10.2753/IMO0020-8825440403

Lyytinen, K., Y. Yoo, and R. Boland. 2016. "Digital Product Innovation Within Four Classes of Innovation Networks." *Information Systems Journal* 26 (1): 47–75. doi:10.1111/isj.12093

Markus, M., and D. Robey. 1988. "Information Technology and Organizational Change: Causal Structure in Theory and Research." *Management Science* 34 (5): 583–598. doi:10.1287/mnsc.34.5.583

Marty, P. 2006. "Finding the Skills for Tomorrow: Information Literacy and Museum Information Professionals." *Museum Management and Curatorship* 21 (4): 317–335. doi:10.1080/09647770600702104

McGovern, M. 2013. "Digital Asset Management: Where to Start." *Curator: The Museum Journal* 56 (2): 237–254. doi:10.1111/cura.12022

McKeever, M. 2017. *How to Write a Business Plan*. Berkeley: Nolo.

McKenzie, B., and N. Poole. 2011. "Mapping the use of digital technologies in the heritage sector." Flow Associates and the Collections Trust for the Heritage Lottery Fund.

Morrison, A. 2019. "Digital strategy for museums." Cogapp agency for digital projects. Accessed 26 November 2021. https://www.cogapp.com/museum-digital-strategy-examples-resources

Moyon, E., and X. Lecocq. 2014. "Rethinking Business Models in Creative Industries." *International Studies of Management & Organization* 44 (4): 83–101. doi:10.2753/IMO0020-8825440405

Münster, S. 2019. "Digital Heritage as a Scholarly Field—Topics, Researchers, and Perspectives from a Bibliometric Point of View." *Journal on Computing and Cultural Heritage* 12 (3): 1–27. doi:10.1145/3310012

Navarrete, T. 2013. "Digital Cultural Heritage." In *Handbook on the Economics of Cultural Heritage*, edited by I. Rizzo and A. Mignosa, 251–271. Cheltenham: Edward Elgar Publishing Limited.

Nesta and MTM London. 2017. "Digital culture." Arts Council England. Accessed 15 October 2021. https://media.nesta.org.uk/documents/digital_culture_2017.pdf

OECD & ICOM. 2019. "Culture and local development: maximising the impact. A guide for local governments, communities and museums." Accessed 10 Febraury 2021. https://www.oecd-ilibrary.org/docserver/9a855be5en.pdf?expires=1622548790&id=id&accname=guest&checksum=8A23265F89DD5868523A26CE75595409

Orlandi, S. 2020. "Museums Web Strategy at the Covid-19 Emergency Times." *Scientific Journal on Digital Cultures* 5: 57–66.

Orlandi, S., G. Calandra, V. Ferrara, A. Marras, S. Radice, E. Bertacchini, V. Nizzo, and T. Maffei. 2018. "Web Strategy in Museums: An Italian Survey Stimulates New Visions." *Museum International* 70 (1–2): 78–89. doi:10.1111/muse.12194

Pallud, J., and E. Monod. 2010. "User Experience of Museum Technologies: The Phenomenological Scales." *European Journal of Information Systems* 19 (5): 562–580. doi:10.1057/ejis.2010.37

Parry, R. 2005. "Digital Heritage and the Rise of Theory in Museum Computing." *Museum Management and Curatorship* 20 (4): 333–348. doi:10.1080/09647770500802004

Parry, R. 2007. *Recoding the Museum Digital Heritage and the Technologies of Change.* London: Routledge.

Parry, R. (2013) The End of the Beginning. *Museum Worlds.* 1(1), 24–39. doi:10.3167/armw.2013.010103

Parry, R., D. Eikhof, S. Barnes, and E. Kispeter. 2018. "Development, supply, deployment, demand: Balancing the museum digital skills ecosystem: First findings. MW18: Museums and the Web 2018, 18-21 April 2018, Vancouver, Canada." Accessed 18 February 2019. https://mw18.mwconf.org/paper/development-supply-deployment-demand-balancing-the-museum-digital-skills-ecosystem-first-findings-of-the-one-by-one-national-digital-lit

Peacock, D. 2008. "Making Ways for Change: Museums, Disruptive Technologies and Organisational Change." *Museum Management and Curatorship* 23 (4): 333–351. doi:10.1080/09647770802517324

Peacock, D., P. Swatman, and N. Lu. 2009. "Supporting SME Collecting Organisations: A Business Model Framework for Digital Heritage Collections." *Australasian Journal of Information Systems* 16 (1): 51–75. doi:10.3127/ajis.v16i1.558

Peukert, C. 2019. "The Next Wave of Digital Technological Change and the Cultural Industries." *Journal of Cultural Economics* 43 (2): 189–210. doi:10.1007/s10824-018-9336-2

Pop, I., and A. Borza. 2016. "Technological Innovations in Museums as a Source of Competitive Advantage." The 2nd International Scientific Conference SAMRO, 14–16 October 2016, Păltiniş, Romania.

Price, K., and J. Dafydd. 2018. "Structuring for digital success: A global survey of how museums and other cultural organizations resource, fund, and structure their digital teams and activity. MW18: Museums and the Web 2018, 18-21 April 2018, Vancouver, Canada." Accessed 18 February 2019. https://mw18.mwconf.org/paper/development-supply-deployment-demand-balancing-the-museum-digital-skills-ecosystem-first-findings-of-the-one-by-one-national-digital-lit

Pulh, M., and R. Mencarelli. 2015. "Web 2.0: Is the Museum-Visitor Relationship Being Redefined ?" *International Journal of Arts Management* 18 (1): 43–51.

Rivera, L. 2013. "The Museum 2.0 Divide: Approaches to Digitisation and New Media." *Museum International* 65 (1–4): e1–e8. doi:10.1111/muse.12042

Rumelt, R. 2011. *Good Strategy/Bad Strategy The Difference and Why it Matters.* London: Profile Books.

Sandell, R., and R. Janes. 2007. *Museum Management and Marketing.* London: Routledge.

Schettino, P. 2016. "Successful Strategies for Dealing With New Technology in Museums: A Case Study of Immersive Technology at the Immigration Museum, Melbourne." *Museum International* 68 (1–2): 130–135. doi:10.1111/muse.12091

Seetharaman, P. 2020. "Business Models Shifts: Impact of Covid-19." *International Journal of Information Management* 54: 102173–4. doi:10.1016/j.ijinfomgt.2020.102173

Seifert, C., W. Bailer, T. Orgel, L. Gantner, R. Kern, H. Ziak, A. Petit, J. Schlötterer, S. Zwicklbauer, and M. Granitzer. 2017. "Ubiquitous Access to Digital Cultural Heritage." *Journal on Computing and Cultural Heritage* 10 (1): 1–27. doi:10.1145/3012384

Senyo, P., K. Liu, and J. Effah. 2019. "Digital Business Ecosystem: Literature Review and a Framework for Future Research." *International Journal of Information Management* 47: 52–64. doi:10.1016/j.ijinfomgt.2019.01.002

Silvaggi, A. 2017. "Museum professional in the digital era. Agents of change and innovation." Accessed 4 May 2021. http://www.project-musa.eu/wp-content/uploads/2017/03/MuSA-Museum-professionals-in-the-digital-era-full-version.pdf

Sturabotti, D., and R. Surace. 2017. "Museum of the future insights and reflections from 10 international museums." Accessed 15 February 2020. http://www.project-musa.eu/wp-content/uploads/2017/03/MuSA-Museum-of-the-future.pdf

Taylor, S., and A. Spicer. 2007. "Time for Space: A Narrative Review of Research on Organizational Spaces." *International Journal of Management Reviews* 9 (4): 325–346. doi:10.1111/j.1468-2370.2007.00214.x

Tomka, G. 2013. "Reconceptualizing Cultural Participation in Europe: Grey Literature Review." *Cultural Trends* 22 (3-4): 259–264. doi:10.1080/09548963.2013.819657

Tsai, I., and J. Chiang. 2012. "The Study of Ubiquitous Computing and Business Process Management Convergence: A Case of National Palace Museum." 6th International Conference on New Trends in Information Science, Service Science and Data Mining, 23–25 October 2021, Taipei, Taiwan. pp. 57–62.

van Laar, E., A. van Deursen, J. van Dijk, and J. de Haan. 2020. "Measuring the Levels of 21st-Century Digital Skills among Professionals Working Within the Creative Industries: A Performance-Based Approach." *Poetics* 81: 1–14. https://doi.org/10.1016/j.poetic.2020.101434

Vavoula, G., and M. Mason. 2017. "Digital Exhibition Design: Boundary Crossing, Intermediary Design Deliverables and Processes of Consent." *Museum Management and Curatorship* 32 (3): 251–271. doi:10.1080/09647775.2017.1282323

Vicente, E., C. Camarero, and M. Garrido. 2012. "Insights Into Innovation in European Museums." *Public Management Review* 14 (5): 649–679. doi:10.1080/14719037.2011.642566

vom Lehn, D., and C. Heath. 2005. "Accounting for New Technology in Museum Exhibitions." *International Journal of Arts Management* 7 (3): 11–21.

Waterton, E. 2010. "The Advent of Digital Technologies and the Idea of Community." *Museum Management and Curatorship* 25 (1): 5–11. doi:10.1080/09647770903529038

Weinfurtner, T., and D. Seidl. 2019. "Towards a Spatial Perspective: An Integrative Review of Research on Organisational Space." *Scandinavian Journal of Management* 35 (2): 101009–30. doi:10.1016/j.scaman.2018.02.003

Yoo, Y., O. Henfridsson, and K. Lyytinen. 2010. "Research Commentary —The New Organizing Logic of Digital Innovation: An Agenda for Information Systems Research." *Information Systems Research* 21 (4): 724–735. doi:10.1287/isre.1100.0322

Yunis, M., A. El-Kassar, and A. Tarhini. 2017. "Impact of ICT-Based Innovations on Organizational Performance." *Journal of Enterprise Information Management* 30 (1): 122–141. doi:10.1108/JEIM-01-2016-0040

Is innovation in ICT valuable for the efficiency of Italian museums?

Calogero Guccio ⓘ, Marco Ferdinando Martorana ⓘ, Isidoro Mazza ⓘ, Giacomo Pignataro ⓘ and Ilde Rizzo ⓘ

ABSTRACT
This paper investigates the influence of information and communication technologies (ICT) on the efficiency in attracting visitors of Italian museums. Notwithstanding the extensive literature on museum performance measurement, the analysis of the role of technological innovation is relatively neglected. As a first attempt to fill this lacuna, this study presents a two-stage analysis of a novel sample of Italian state-owned museums built by merging information drawn from different sources. In the first stage, we use bootstrapped Data Envelopment Analysis (DEA) to measure the efficiency of museums. In the second stage, we use a bootstrap truncated regression approach to test the extent to which different forms of ICT affect museum efficiency. We distinguish the ICT investments into 'in situ' and online services, since the former improve the visitors' experience on site, while the latter can prepare for the visit or, even, be a substitute of the visit. The results reveal that the use of ICT is generally associated with better performances but 'in situ' services show to play a major role.

1. Introduction

The continuous improvements and the increasing diffusion of information and communication technology (ICT) have recently contributed to promote innovation in the cultural sector (Borowiecki and Navarrete, 2017). It is generally acknowledged that ICT not only affects supply and demand of cultural goods (Rizzo, 2016) but also modifies the scope and mission of cultural organizations: new sources of economic and cultural value and new business models emerge, while education as well as cultural appreciation and participation are enhanced (Bakhshi and Throsby, 2012). Such aspects are fundamental for museums, which have progressively embraced the use of ICT, though with significant differences across institutions and countries. An interesting issue yet to see is whether the diffusion of technological innovation in museums has indeed contributed to improve their efficiency.

The analysis of technical efficiency of museums has developed remarkably in recent years and is characterized by a growing use of the frontier techniques (for recent reviews, see Basso et al, 2018; Guccio et al., 2020a). However, this literature mostly neglects the relationship between ICT advancement and efficiency of cultural institutions (Guccio et al., 2020b). This study aims at contributing to fill this gap by investigating the effects of ICT applications on the technical efficiency of Italian state-owned museums using a two-stage approach: in the first stage, the analysis assesses the ability of museums to utilize resources efficiently for the production of outputs via a bootstrapped DEA (Simar and Wilson, 2000); in the second stage, it evaluates the impact of technological innovation on the estimated technical efficiency, using a boostrap truncated approach (Simar and Wilson, 2007). The study is based on a novel dataset, built by merging information drawn from the statistical office of the Ministry for Heritage, Cultural Activities and Tourism (MIBACT) and from a survey run in 2015 by the Italian National Statistical Office (ISTAT) (ISTAT, 2017). The latter contains over 100 questions, and we focus on those investigating whether and how museums use ICT in the provision of their services, to improve both the accessibility and quality. Results show that ICT services are positively associated with the performances of museums in attracting visitors. In particular, making a distinction between 'in situ' and online services, the former play a major role in obtaining this outcome.

The remainder of the paper is structured as follows. Section 2 positions our contribution in the context of the relevant literature. Section 3 presents the methodology, offers a concise description of the institutional setting and describes the data. Section 4 gathers estimates and results. Finally, Section 5 summarizes the main conclusions.

2. Literature review

Museums are cultural institutions devoted to conserve, interpret, research and display heritage (Mairesse and Vanden Eeckaut, 2002). This study refers to two different strands of literature, one investigating the relationship between technological innovation and museums, and another one evaluating the efficiency of museums.

2.1. ICT and museums

Technologies can be used in museums in many ways: apart from standard utilization for administrative purposes (such as word processing, computerized accounting methods and so on), applications range from diagnostics, conservation and restoration to Information and Communication Technology (ICT). Focusing on the latter, it is worth noting that museums use ICT for a number of functions both 'in situ' and online, such as websites, online ticketing and service information, online access to collections and databases, online exhibitions, mobile applications, virtual reconstructions, interactive kiosks, social media networks or online shopping.

The influence of ICT on museum management has been explored from different disciplinary perspectives, both theoretically and empirically. A common tenet is that ICT and digitization affect the scope and the mission of museums and impact transversally on their activities, modifying conservation and exhibition practices, widening cultural participation and appreciation (Fernandez-Blanco and Prieto-Rodriguez, 2020), and reshaping their role as producers and distributors of cultural content.[1]

Because of technological interactivity, terms such as 'produsers', 'prosumption' and 'produsage' have become popular to describe the evolution in producer/consumer relationships (Bruns, 2013) with implications for museums demand and supply.[2] Moreover, web statistics may offer new opportunities to address the old problem of the revelation of preferences and to orientate museums to meet future users' needs (Giardina et al., 2016).

It is worth noticing, however, that, notwithstanding the claimed beneficial impact of ICT, the empirical evidence of ICT effects on performance is rather scarce. The implementation of websites is the first and most widespread use of ICT in museums, with different functions, ranging from functional tasks to creations of new cultural experiences. Providing information and facilities for potential visitors to physical museums appears to be prevailing in line with the strategic goal of maintaining a link between the web and the physical site (Pallud and Straub, 2014). The effectiveness of museums websites in being attractive for visitors with different knowledge about collections cannot be taken for granted and an extensive literature deals with evaluation methods (for a review of evaluation studies, see Kabassi, 2017).

In such a perspective, digitization plays a crucial role because it potentially increases the fruition of collections and involves users actively by allowing the online access to collections. However, museums seem to have a limited attention to the adoption of digital technology. According to the figures provided by Enumerate Core Survey 4 in Europe,[3] in 2017, on average, only 22% of the heritage collections were digital (31% in museums), 54% still needed to be reproduced (57% in museums) and only 36% of digital collections was accessible on line (Nauta et al., 2017),[4] with national libraries being 'front runners' (58%) and museums being quite behind (28%).[5] These figures have to be interpreted with great caution since the sample is not representative and suffers of self-selection bias. Nonetheless, the main findings suggest that cultural heritage institutions are still lagging behind in adopting digital technologies.

Different explanations can be put forward for the partial use of digitization by museums. A political economy explanation might apply when considering that the government has a prominent role in the cultural heritage field and most of the major heritage organizations are somehow publicly funded (Holler and Mazza, 2013). In such a context, the conventional wisdom about the behaviour of heritage experts, such as museum directors, highlights a potential bias in favour of an 'elitist' curatorial approach, due to their educational background and peers' scrutiny. Consistently with this view, communication methods such as ICT and virtual reality may not be adequately appreciated as a tool for the promotion of museum's collections and considered to downgrade the 'high' character of heritage (Peacock and Rizzo, 2008). Paolini et al. (2013) outline that when museums rely on public funding, the relationship with the audience may not be considered a priority and, therefore, the investment in ICT may be limited: one major effect would be the occurrence of a digital divide across countries and institutions, with the consequence that culturally important institutions that are not visible on Internet may be dominated by less relevant ones.[6]

Another possible explanation for the apparently scarce interest of museums toward the online publication of collections may be due to 'the fear of cannibalization' and the related risk of losing onsite visitors because of their availability online (Navarrete, 2013).[7] However, this does not seem to be the case. Empirical evidence, although scant, would suggest that complementarity – rather than substitution – prevails both with respect to single museums (for Tate Modern, see Bakhshi and Throsby, 2010; for Louvre, see Evrard and Krebs, 2018) and at country level (for US, see Ateca-Amestoy and Castiglione, 2014). At the same time, while there is no evidence at European level that digitization has extended audiences (Ateca-Amestoy, 2018) it is widely agreed that cultural online access enhances inequalities between socio-economic groups (Krebs, 2012; Mihelj et al., 2019).

The adoption of technological innovation in museums and its effects are likely to depend on their specific features, such as size, governance and degree of autonomy. For example, Camarero et al. (2011) find that larger museums are more likely to engage in technological innovation than small ones. Bertacchini et al. (2018) show that, in Italy, private museums as well as public ones – autonomous, or outsourced – perform better than public museums directly managed by government bodies, as far as web visibility is concerned; similarly, Leva et al. (2019) show that among state museums, the autonomous ones are more active in implementing policies aimed at enhancing accessibility (including ticket on line and facilities through websites), attractiveness (including on-site audio visual equipment for visitors) and relations with the local context (including web advertising).

2.2. Efficiency of museums

The measurement of the efficiency of museums has attracted a growing interest in the last decades. The early works on this topic usually adopted productivity and performance indicators (Weil, 1995) that however have many limitations (Pignataro, 2011). In recent times, the application of non-parametric frontier estimation techniques (mainly the Data Envelopment Analysis – DEA) has become more common. Their use is now well-established due to their flexibility and the fact that they allow for handling production processes involving multiple inputs and outputs. The latter is a critical advantage, given the multifaced nature of museums and the wide range of activities they carry out. Not surprisingly, works in this strand of literature remarkably differ in the set of inputs and outputs chosen as well as in the way museums' 'production' process is modelled. In general, among other aspects, museums can be regarded as cultural institutions that preserve and provide access to pieces of art and items of cultural interest, using their staff and physical endowment. Thus the number of workers and the size of the exhibition area is customarily included among inputs, and the number of visitors among outputs in the large majority of works since the very first applications of non-parametric techniques, and DEA especially, to evaluate museums' efficiency (Pignataro, 2002, Del Barrio et al. 2009). Nevertheless, scholars have tried to deepen the investigation of museums' activities and performance often using a richer set of inputs and outputs as well as more advanced techniques. Among them, Basso and Funari (2004) disentangle visitors according to whether they pay a full-fee or a reduced-fee and consider also temporary exhibitions and other activities among outputs, in their analysis of the efficiency of Italian museums. Similarly, Del Barrio and Herrero (2014) construct indexes related to dissemination and impact of collection as outputs.

A more complex framework to evaluate the efficiency of museums in different activities is the one proposed by Mairesse and Vanden Eeckaut (2002) that uses the Free

Disposal Hull (FDH) to run three models, using different sets of outputs to account for preservation, research and communication. Among the inputs they use the opening hours that conversely is included in the output set by Carvalho et al. (2014). On a different perspective, the recent works by Del Barrio-Tellado and Herrero-Prieto (2019) and Guccio et al. (2020a) have exploited the idea that museums activity can be disentangled in two stages and the related distinction between outputs that are under the direct control of the museum's management and those which depend on the operational environment. While the latter paper focuses on the efficiency in the provision of the service potential of museums and estimate the frontier conditional to the environmental factors, Del Barrio-Tellado and Herrero-Prieto (2019) use a network two-stage DEA to study the overall efficiency of museums.

With the only exception of Taheri and Ansari (2013), including ICT to construct a set of input indexes (which also include information on the size of exhibition area, opening times, different types of workers, facilities and promotion activities), the link between the diffusion of ICT and museums' efficiency in attracting visitors has been so far neglected, to the best of our knowledge. This is particularly surprising considering the remarkable debate about the use of digital technologies in the field of cultural heritage preservation and promotion.

3. Methods, data and model specification

3.1. Methods

We employ a two-stage non-parametric method to evaluate museums' efficiency and assess the impact of ICT. Specifically, we use a bootstrapped Data Envelopment Analysis (DEA) in the first step to estimate the best-practice frontier and measure museums' efficiency levels (Simar and Wilson, 2000). DEA (Charnes et al., 1978) is a widely used method to assess efficiency of a sample of Decision-Making Units (DMUs). From a technical point of view, DEA allows to compute an efficiency score by solving a linear programming problem for every DMU to identify the nonparametric production frontier; this score represents a radial measure of efficiency computed with respect to the estimated efficient frontier.

As mentioned, a growing number of researchers have adopted DEA to assess the relative performance of museums. There are few reasons for this choice that we follow here. First, non-parametric methods can handle multiple inputs and outputs in a simple manner, while most stochastic approaches require choosing a single output variable. Second, non-parametric approaches do not require assumptions about the functional form or specification of the error term, in contrast to stochastic methods. Furthermore, DEA provides an overall measure of performance that takes the multidimensional nature of museum's performance into account.

Using DEA, the sources of inefficiency can be analysed and quantified for every evaluated unit. We employ an output-oriented model, assuming that museums maximize outputs for given inputs. This choice is rather common in the literature and also preferable in our specification as, in fact, inputs such as the exhibition space and, to some extent, the number of workers are generally fixed, at least in the short run. DEA uses linear programming techniques to identify the (empirical) efficient frontier or best-practice frontier for a sample of n observations. In formal terms, any efficiency score θ_i, for $i = 1, 2, \ldots, n$ DMUs, is derived by solving the following linear program, assuming Constant Returns of Scale (CRS) and output orientation:

$$\max_{\theta_i, \lambda} \theta_i \qquad (1)$$

$$\text{subject to } x_i - X\lambda \geq 0$$
$$\theta_i y_i - Y\lambda \leq 0$$
$$\lambda \geq 0$$

where λ is an $n \times 1$ vector of non-negative scalars λ_i, X is the matrix of inputs, Y is the matrix of outputs, x_i and y_i are the non-negative inputs and outputs of ith DMU. The efficiency score θ_i is comprised between 0 and 1. The value 1 characterizes the efficient museums, while the lower the efficiency score, the more inefficient is the museum. For an inefficient museum (with $\theta_i < 1$) the value of the variables λ_i allows you to identify a set of efficient museums that constitutes a 'best practice' benchmark. Such a museum could improve its efficiency by simultaneously increasing the value of its outputs while using the same amount of inputs, or even less. To account for variable returns to scale (VRS) Banker et al. (1984) add to (1) the convexity constraint $e\lambda = 1$, where e is a row vector with all elements at unity, which allows to distinguish between Technical Efficiency (TE) and Scale Efficiency (SE).

As the deterministic frontier models does not allow for any statistical inference and measurement error, we employ the Simar and Wilson (1998, 2000) bootstrapping procedure, developed to determine statistical properties of DEA estimators, which allows to derive unbiased efficiency scores. The use of bootstrapping techniques is recommended in order to consider a random error model and correct biases and inconsistencies in DEA estimates (Simar and Wilson, 1998; 2000). Furthermore, as the deterministic frontier models are sensitive to outlying and atypical observations, we employ the procedure proposed by Simar (2003). Finally, to improve the robustness of our efficiency assessment, we perform a sensitivity analysis using different nonparametric model specifications and a different subsample.

In addition to knowing the efficiency with which the museums operate, it is interesting for the present study to explain if the use of ICT affects the productive process positively or negatively. Thus, in the second step, we assess the impact of ICT by regressing the efficiency scores θ_i on a vector of explanatory variables (z_i) based on different extent of ICT. The general model in cross-sectional setting is the following:

$$\theta_i = f(z_i) + \varepsilon_i \qquad (2)$$

where ε_i is the error term.

Given that OLS and Tobit estimators would be biased due to the violation of independence between z_i and ε_i, we follow the two-step bias-corrected semi-parametric estimator proposed by Simar and Wilson (2007)[8] that ensures a feasible, consistent inference on the parameters for estimation in the second stage.

3.2. Italian institutional background

We conduct our empirical analysis on a sample of Italian state-owned museums. Italy has a wide and heterogeneous set of museums, which differ as far as institutional features, type of collection, geographical location, and number of visitors are concerned.

According to the survey run by ISTAT (2017) on Italian Museums and Cultural Institutions (Indagine sui musei e le istituzioni similari), in Italy there are 4158 museums, galleries or collections (out of 4976 total cultural institutions). Among them, 64.1% are public: 43% belongs to Municipalities while those belonging to the state are only 8.8% of the total.

Museums are dispersed all over the country and are located even in very small Municipalities. Italian museums are also very heterogeneous in terms of type of collection and number of visitors. State museums and similar institutions play a major role, attracting 42.6% of total visitors.

Institutional responsibilities are shared between the state – through the MIBACT – and the decentralized levels. A detailed analysis of the institutional setting is beyond the scope of this paper Bodo and Bodo (2016). Focusing on state museums, it is worth noting that in the last 20 years, as a result of major reforms, some institutions have been granted autonomy. In 1998, four National Museum Poles (Poli Museali Nazionali) including the national art galleries and museums in Rome, Venice, Florence and Naples were created, with an autonomous status and a budget. In 2014, a national museum system was established: autonomy and full responsibility for the management of collections was gradually granted, first to 20 top museums, monuments and archaeological sites and, 2 years after, to additional 10 museums. On the other hand, all the other less important national non-autonomous museums and heritage sites have been gathered in seventeen regional museum poles (Poli museali regionali), under the responsibility of Regional secretariats.

The reform of state museums has been widely debated: while recognizing positive changes in terms of increasing financial autonomy (Unioncamere, 2018), it is also widely agreed that the new organizational model is weak from a managerial perspective. In fact, the management of human resources is still under the control of the ministerial administration (Zan et al., 2018) hindering, therefore, the effective autonomy of museums.

3.3. Data description

We draw data for our empirical excise on Italian state-owned museums from two sources. Data on the relevant inputs and outputs as well as on the use and extent of ICT are taken from ISTAT (2017), which collects information on all Italian museums and similar institutions for a wide range of topics, including the services provided to visitors, the number of exhibitions and standard proxies for capital and labour, all regarding the year 2015. The survey however does not contain information on the number of visitors that we take from a data set provided by the statistical office of the MIBACT.[9]

Given the sensibility of our methodology to the outliers we restrict the full sample originally containing 487 observations on Italian state-owned museums, in order to provide a fair efficiency evaluation and avoid problems due to museums' heterogeneity.

Specifically, we first exclude monuments and archaeological sites (which have specific characteristics making them hardly comparable to museums) as well as museums included in parks (since the number of visitors cannot be clearly identified) and those museums presenting missing or incomplete data on input and output variables. This first set of checks reduced our initial sample to 172 museums.

Moreover, observations that, due to errors in the data, are placed on the efficient border could lead to incorrect assessments. Therefore, it is important to detect outliers and treat them properly to avoid increasing sampling noise and distort the results when performing any efficiency assessment. To do so, we apply the semiautomatic procedure developed by Simar (2003).[10] The resulting final sample of 107 observations is, therefore, quite homogenous for institutional characteristics and features of service provision and virtually free from outliers.[11]

Even if we are aware that the selection of a subset of state-owned museums may give some problems to the estimates of efficiency, should the institutional nature of museums have an empirical significant impact on the incentives to innovation, still the selected museums represent a specific and homogeneous set of small museums. The estimates of efficiency based on this sample, therefore, allow to draw some insights on the management of innovation of a crucial segment of museums in the Italian context, i.e. 'minor' museums, which are widespread all over the country, with close links with local communities. For what said, however, the results of our analysis cannot necessarily and immediately be extended to the universe of Italian museums and, consequently, our empirical choice comes at a price of losing some information, related to the potential variability of the efficiency behaviour of museums characterized by a different institutional nature.

For the first stage analysis of museums efficiency, we have followed the main literature in the field that indicates the relevant inputs and outputs characterizing museums' 'production' process (Guccio et al., 2020a). Among the different purposes of museums, we focus on the access to the public; thus we evaluate the efficiency of museums in attracting visitors. To provide more robustness of our efficiency assessment we employ four specifications, differing in the definition of outputs. Table 1 summarizes the input and output variables employed in the models whereas the relative descriptive statistics are gathered in Table 2.

For inputs, we use in all models the number of workers (Personnel) and the available space for exhibitions (Exhibition_space), which are widely used in the literature as proxies for capital and labour. Outputs include the total number of visitors (Visitors)

Table 1. Estimated efficiency models.

Variable name	Description	MOD_1	MOD_2	MOD_3	MOD_4
Inputs					
Personnel	No. of workers	X	X	X	X
Exhibition space	Available space for exhibitions in square meters	X	X	X	X
Outputs					
Visitors	No. of total visitors	X	X		
Visitors_paying	No. of visitors paying entrance fee			X	X
Visitors_free	No. of visitors with free entrance			X	X
Temp_ex	No. of temporary exhibitions	X		X	
W_temp_ex	No. of visitors of temporary exhibitions		X		X

Source: Our elaboration on data provided by ISTAT and by MIBACT.

Table 2. Sample statistics of inputs and outputs variables.

Variable	Obs.	Mean	Std. Dev.	Min	Max
Personnel	107	18.64	17.58	1.00	90.00
Exhibition space	107	1227.11	1480.03	90.00	10000.00
Visitors	107	14731.53	14769.25	1282.00	74406.00
Visitors_paying	107	4894.88	8043.28	0.00	41424.00
Visitors_free	107	9836.65	8400.64	1282.00	42512.00
Temp_ex	107	1.90	3.86	0.00	30.00
W_temp_ex	107	4661.34	10439.02	0.00	74406.00

Source: Our elaboration on data provided by ISTAT and by MIBACT.

and the number of temporary exhibitions (Temp_ex) in MOD_1. The latter variable is used also in MOD_3 while the number of visitors at the exhibitions is used in MOD_2 and MOD_4. Museums differ in their ticket policies: some have free entrance and others combine it with entrance fee. We therefore distinguish them on whether visitors pay (Visitors_paying) or not (Visitors_free) in MOD_3 and MOD_4. Furthermore, to provide robustness to our results we also estimate all our models on the subsample of museums with a mixed entrance policy (free entrance and entrance fee).[12]

Regarding the second stage analysis, we mainly use data derived from the survey run by ISTAT (2017) that we merge with data provided by the MIBACT. The survey run by ISTAT (2017) provides a number of items referring to the services that museums supply, including those related to the use of ICT.

We present the descriptive statistics of ICT services in our sample in Table 3, distinguishing between services provided 'in situ', i.e. during the visit, which are aimed at improving the overall cultural experience, and services provided in the website, which are generally accessed before (or independently of) the visit.[13]

The first type of services includes smartphone and tablet apps, multimedia devices, QRcodes and PC/tablet devices. 'In situ' services are active in a percentage of museums not greater than 17.48%, for the availability of multimedia devices, which goes down to about 6.9%, for the availability of PC and tablet devices. Online services

Table 3. Sample statistics of second stage analysis.

Variable	Answer	Mean	Std. Dev.	Min.	Max.
In situ services					
Smartphone and tablet apps	102	0.1078	0.3102	0.0000	1.0000
Multimedia devices	103	0.1748	0.3798	0.0000	1.0000
QRcode	102	0.1176	0.3222	0.0000	1.0000
PC and tablet devices	102	0.0686	0.2528	0.0000	1.0000
Online services					
Website	101	0.6436	0.4813	0.0000	1.0000
Online catalogue	99	0.1010	0.3013	0.0000	1.0000
Online ticket office	98	0.0714	0.2575	0.0000	1.0000
Virtual visit	98	0.1224	0.3278	0.0000	1.0000
Social media	99	0.5253	0.4994	0.0000	1.0000
Photo and prints shop	96	0.1667	0.3727	0.0000	1.0000
Merchandizing	95	0.0632	0.2432	0.0000	1.0000
Newsletter	97	0.0515	0.2211	0.0000	1.0000
Web community	96	0.1146	0.3185	0.0000	1.0000
Composite index					
In situ services index	102	0.4608	0.8043	0.0000	3.0000
Online services index	92	1.1630	1.3850	0.0000	8.0000

Source: Our elaboration on data provided by ISTAT and by MIBACT.

are: website, online catalogue, online ticket office, virtual visit, social media accounts, online selling of photos and prints, merchandising, newsletter and community. Services provision ranges from about 64% of museums declaring to have a website, and 52% to have a social media account, to less than 20% for advanced services such as online ticket office, shops and catalogue and virtual visit as well as for the more traditional newsletter and community. A marked variability emerges among museums in the website content and in the implementation of the different ICT services. In order to estimate the impact of ICT, we build for both types of services composite indexes based on the sum of provided services by each museum (see, infra, 4.2.).

4. Empirical results

4.1. First stage efficiency estimates

Table 4 shows the main descriptive statistics of estimates for the four efficiency models, under both assumptions of constant (CRS) and variable returns to scale (VRS)[14] in the output-oriented case. The VRS approach assumes that the size of the museums is flexible and that they are able to improve the performance not only by increasing technical efficiency but also by exploiting scale economies. From the bootstrapped results, we can observe that bias-corrected estimates are strictly close to the uncorrected estimates and the estimated bias is quite small indicating the consistency of our efficiency assessment.

The results in Table 4 show that the average value of efficiency is rather low (depending on the model and scale assumption, in a range between 0.34 and 0.50). A note of caution is in order when making a comparison with results of other studies, both for Italy and for other countries, because of differences in the sample, time period, inputs and outputs considered, but it is quite common to find low values of efficiency of museums.[15] Moreover, the high value of the standard deviation indicates high variability of scores, probably resulting from the residual heterogeneity of museums in the sample, primarily in terms of collection and location and, consequently, of attractivity of visitors.

Additionally, there is some limited variability across the different models, in terms of average efficiency. As expected, MOD_2 and MOD_4 provide, on average, higher efficiency scores, due to the higher number of outputs. In general, however, the efficiency estimates of all the models are highly correlated, as shown by the correlation

Table 4. Efficiency estimates – full sample.

Model	Obs	Uncorrected efficiency scores		Bias-corrected efficiency scores		
		Mean	Std. Dev.	Mean	Std. Dev.	Bias
MOD_1 (CRS)	107	0.3440	0.2825	0.3369	0.2791	0.0071
MOD_1 (VRS)	107	0.4335	0.2910	0.4283	0.2875	0.0052
MOD_2 (CRS)	107	0.4331	0.2942	0.4279	0.2907	0.0052
MOD_2 (VRS)	107	0.5014	0.2974	0.4813	0.2855	0.0201
MOD_3 (CRS)	107	0.3476	0.2885	0.3434	0.2850	0.0042
MOD_3 (VRS)	107	0.4400	0.2968	0.4347	0.2932	0.0053
MOD_4 (CRS)	107	0.4337	0.2958	0.4207	0.2922	0.0130
MOD_4 (VRS)	107	0.4963	0.3014	0.4913	0.2978	0.0050

Source: Our elaboration on data provided by ISTAT and by MIBACT.

Table 5. Correlation between efficiency estimates in the employed models – full sample.

		(1)	(2)	(3)	(4)	(5)	(6)	(7)	(8)
(1)	MOD_1 (CRS)	1.0000							
(2)	MOD_1 (VRS)	0.8479	1.0000						
(3)	MOD_2 (CRS)	0.9211	0.7986	1.0000					
(4)	MOD_2 (VRS)	0.8228	0.9336	0.8859	1.0000				
(5)	MOD_3 (CRS)	0.9168	0.8155	0.8503	0.8028	1.0000			
(6)	MOD_3 (VRS)	0.8264	0.9881	0.7941	0.9372	0.8392	1.0000		
(7)	MOD_4 (CRS)	0.8680	0.7999	0.9326	0.8744	0.9368	0.8285	1.0000	
(8)	MOD_4 (VRS)	0.8107	0.9347	0.8597	0.9898	0.8279	0.9519	0.8872	1.0000

Source: Our elaboration on data provided by ISTAT and by MIBACT.

estimates in Table 5. Thus, in conclusion, the different specification of the production function as well as the assumption on returns to scale do not change the relative performance assessment of museums with respect to the efficiency frontier. In light of the above result, we choose to focus on MOD_4 in the following analysis, because it provides a more refined and comprehensive definition of museums' outputs.

It is worth mentioning that efficiency estimates are robust also when we perform the analysis on subsample of museums with a mixed entrance policy (free entrance and entrance fee).[16]

We use the bootstrap approach to test the returns to scale characteristics of our sample (Simar and Wilson, 2000). Specifically, we test whether the returns to scale are constant and museums operate under optimal size, using 2000 replications. Results indicate the presence of scale inefficiency and also that the majority of DMUs in the sample are not operating at an optimal scale.[17] Thus the VRS estimates are used in the analysis reported hereafter.

4.2. Second stage analysis: the estimation of the impact of ICT on museums' efficiency

We will now explore the issue of whether and to what extent the ICT services provided by museums have an impact on the differences in their efficiency, as estimated in the previous sections. In particular, we will regress the efficiency scores of each museum on a set of variables representing the different ICT services.[18]

Following the questions included in ISTAT (2017), we can study the ICT 'effort' of Italian museums along different dimensions. We differentiate the ICT investment on 'in situ' services from the realization of online services since the former mainly aim to improve visitors' experience on site, while the latter prepare for – or stimulate – the visit or, is a substitute of the visit. In addition, we further ascertain whether a museum has implemented different services for each category of services.[19]

We also build up a summary index for each category of ICT services, as the sum of values recorded for each dummy variable, within each of the two categories of services, on the basis of the YES/NO answers to the survey questions. The maximum potential value of the index for the 'in situ' services is, therefore, equal to 4 (even if, in the sample, the maximum number of recorded services reached is 3 for one missing answer), while, for the online services, the maximum potential value is 9 (8 in the sample).[20] As a consequence of the low values recorded for each single service, the average values of the composite indices are low and, again, with a high variability across museums.

Turning, now, to the research question about whether the ICT effort of museums affects their efficiency, we consider the efficiency values estimated according to MOD_4, under the assumption of variable returns to scale.[21] We estimate the impact of the different ICT variables, according to different models. In particular, we estimate three different sets of models. The first one considers, as regressors, all the single ICT variables: we run two separate regressions, one with all the variables for the 'in situ' services and the other with all the variables for the online services. Moreover, for each of these two estimates, we also run an additional regression with the same set of variables and controlling for whether museums allow for free entrance. In such a way, we can take into account the potential effect of free entrance on the number of visitors of a museums and its efficiency (since the number of visitors is regarded as a measure of its outputs), avoiding in this way improper attributions of this effect to the existence of the different ICT services.

The second set of estimates include models where the impact of ICT services is considered separate for each single service. Since the ICT services are generally provided jointly, and their measures are highly correlated, these set of estimates, in which the variables representing the ICT services are introduced one by one, may avoid the estimation bias potentially arising from the correlation of the variables.

Finally, the third set of estimates include the ICT variables through the composite indices: we run an estimate of the impact of the composite index of only 'in situ' services, one with the index of only the 'online' services and another one with both. Moreover, as before, we run three additional estimates, controlling for free entrance.

In general, we expect that the existence of 'in situ' services, improving the quality of the experience at a museum, will attract more visitors and, therefore, can potentially improve the efficiency of a museum. As for the online services, the expected potential effect on efficiency may be ambiguous since these services can either stimulate or be a substitute for the visits to a museum.[22]

Table 6 reports the results of the first set of estimates, including the regressions with all the variables representing the ICT services (separately for the 'in situ' and for the online services).

Results show that, independently of the model estimated, the only significant effect is observed for the applications for tablets and smartphones, among the 'in situ' services, and for the online catalogue, among the online services. The variables representing the website and the photo and print shop are weakly significant. For all the significant variables, the observed coefficient is positive. While this is the expected outcome for the 'in situ' services, this result for the online services show that they are reinforcing the number of visitors and are not to be interpreted as a substitute for the visit.

Very similar results are obtained when regressions are run, introducing the ICT variables one by one, as shown in Table 7.[23]

Finally, Table 8 reports the results for the third set of estimates, the one with the ICT services represented by the composite indices.

When the ICT services are represented with a summary index of each category, the only significant category is the one of the 'in situ' services. This result complements the previous ones considering a more 'analytical' impact of ICT and provides a test of

Table 6. Results for Bootstrap Truncated Two-Stage Estimates – all ICT services.

Variables	(1)	(2)	(3)	(4)
In situ services				
Smartphone and tablet apps	0.205*		0.291***	
	(0.120)		(0.112)	
Multimedia devices	0.014		0.074	
	(0.092)		(0.077)	
QRcode	−0.004		0.009	
	(0.103)		(0.086)	
PC/tablet devices	−0.080		0.042	
	(0.139)		(0.127)	
Online services				
Website		0.128*		0.125*
		(0.068)		(0.066)
Online catalogue		0.298**		0.345**
		(0.148)		(0.147)
Online ticket office		0.288		0.236
		(0.196)		(0.189)
Virtual visit		0.171		0.174
		(0.147)		(0.145)
Social media		−0.025		−0.034
		(0.095)		(0.096)
Photo and prints shop		0.242*		0.245*
		(0.145)		(0.145)
Merchandizing		−0.155		−0.156
		(0.301)		(0.301)
Newsletter		0.041		0.026
		(0.312)		(0.309)
Community		0.031		0.037
		(0.202)		(0.199)
Entrance policy				
Free entrance dummy			−0.116	−0.049
			(0.072)	(0.069)
Constant	0.375***	0.338***	0.388***	0.356***
	(0.069)	(0.039)	(0.062)	(0.041)
Obs	102	94	102	94

* Significant at 10 %; ** Significant at 5 %; *** Significant at 1 %. Standard errors are reported in parenthesis.
Notes: Table report double bootstrap truncated estimates ($n = 2000$, Algorithm 2), proposed by Simar and Wilson (2007).
Source: Our elaboration on data provided by ISTAT and by MIBACT.

the relative strength of the two categories of services, in terms of their ability to improve the efficiency of museums in attracting visitors.

5. Concluding remarks

There are several reasons why ICT services, here described, can be useful to increase the performance of museums in attracting visitors. Information available on the website can provide useful information to prepare or stimulate the visit. Other ICT services, provided in the museum itself, can improve the experience of the visitor. The recent pandemic has put an important spotlight on ICT showing the crucial importance of technology – unforeseen to this extent – as source of remedies for keeping alive the activity of the institutions as well as the attention of the visitors.

Several studies have investigated the adoption of new ICT services by museums, addressing how these can affect management and demand, and even determine new forms of interaction between suppliers and consumers. However, they have neglected the relationship between ICT and museum efficiency. This is further remarkable because there is a growing literature investigating the efficiency of museums.

Table 7. Second stage estimates including variables on ICT services one by one.

Variables	Estimated coefficient	Constant	Obs
In situ services			
Smartphone and tablet apps	0. 192*	0.346***	102
	(0.106)	(0.040)	
Multimedia devices	0.067	0.354***	103
	(0.087)	(0.042)	
QRcode	0.030	0.359***	102
	(0.106)	(0.042)	
PC/tablet devices	0.020	0.362***	102
	(0.133)	(0.041)	
Online services			
Website	0.135*	0.371***	101
	(0.074)	(0.041)	
Online catalogue	0.351**	0.356***	99
	(0.154)	(0.057)	
Online ticket office	0.327*	0.370***	98
	(0.201)	(0.050)	
Virtual visit	0.112	0.349***	98
	(0.119)	(0.037)	
Social media	0.019	0.352***	99
	(0.067)	(0.033)	
Photo and prints shop	0.037	0.353***	96
	(0.099)	(0.034)	
Merchandizing	0.087	0.352***	95
	(0.162)	(0.035)	
Newsletter	0.169	0.372***	97
	(0.195)	(0.051)	
Community	0.082	0.374***	96
	(0.142)	(0.045)	

* Significant at 10 %; ** significant at 5 %; *** significant at 1 %. Standard errors are reported in parenthesis.
Notes: Table report double bootstrap truncated estimates (*n* = 2000, Algorithm 2), proposed by Simar and Wilson (2007). Each row in the table represents a different estimate. Source: Our elaboration on data provided by ISTAT and by MIBACT.

Table 8. Second stage estimates – composite indexes.

Variables	(1)	(2)	(3)	(4)	(5)	(6)
'In situ' services index	0.086*		0.076*	0.081**		0.077**
	(0.045)		(0.040)	(0.034)		(0.035)
Online services index		0.007	0.016		0.011	0.015
		(0.032)	(0.031)		(0.032)	(0.033)
Entrance policy						
Free entrance dummy				−0.030	−0.049	−0.096
				(0.104)	(0.069)	(0.076)
Constant	0.397***	0.339***	0.323***	0.396***	0.340***	0.324***
	(0.093)	(0.056)	(0.067)	(0.093)	(0.055)	(0.066)
Obs	102	94	92	102	94	92

* Significant at 10 %; ** significant at 5 %; *** significant at 1 %. Standard errors are reported in parenthesis.
Notes: Table report double bootstrap truncated estimates (*n* = 2000, Algorithm 2), proposed by Simar and Wilson (2007). Source: Our elaboration on data provided by ISTAT and by MIBACT.

This study is the first attempt to bridge the gap between the investigation on ICT applications and efficiency analysis. It investigates efficiency in terms of the ability of museums to attract visitors, using a novel data set, merging recent information on supply and demand concerning provided by two main Italian sources, ISTAT and MIBACT. Due to the wide heterogeneity of the museums regarding, among others, their ownership, management, size, type of collection, we have been very cautious and reduced the original data set to a rather homogeneous sample of Italian state-owned museums. The empirical analysis shows that the presence of ICT services – both 'in situ' and online – is associated with higher efficiency of museums, but that is true for a limited number of services. This outcome contradicts the claim that information on the web is a substitute for physical visits. It also shows that ICT services are not 'the' solution to the problem of improving efficiency. Some services do not show to have significant effect. Moreover, among those that do have a positive relationship with efficiency, 'in situ' services are relative more influent on efficiency.

However, the conclusions made in this study are still partial, and several issues remain open to scrutiny. First, due to data limitation and differences in the institutional setting (such as those regarding the degree of autonomy of museum management and the specific incentives in place to enhance the application of ICT), we have been forced to restrict the analysis to state-owned museums to have a complete and homogenous sample; as a consequence, our results can hardly be generalized to the universe of Italian museums.

Second, future research is needed to ascertain why some services are more successful than others in attracting visitors. This is a broad problem that requires a multidisciplinary approach. For example, it would be interesting to investigate if private management can be more innovative than the public one in improving efficiency through the adoption of ICT services and whether there can be political economic reasons, probably connected to a specific institutional framework of a country. In such a perspective, it might be also interesting to investigate whether the size of museums and/or the type of collections (for instance, archaeological, fine arts, ethnographical, etc.) matter. From the demand side, the study of visitors' behaviour could be helpful in guiding the selection and implementation of ICT services to the purpose of improving efficiency. Useful research insights might also derive by the use of Web Analytics and users generated content. Finally, since the implementation of ICT constitutes a type of investment from the museum's management perspective, there is room to study the impact of ICT as a frontier shifter in a dynamic perspective, using panel data methods.

Notes

1. The different options for managing the access to and the re-use of digital images of museum collections are explored by Bertacchini and Morando (2013).
2. Contributing content raises questions of authority, as far as the responsibility of the information provided by the public is concerned. Different approaches can be adopted by museums such as, for instance, reviewing the information before incorporating it or presenting the different sources of information (public, curators, etc.) separately on the website (Navarrete, 2013).
3. Enumerate Core Survey 4 is the fourth edition of a survey monitoring the status of cultural heritage in Europe. 983 institutions belonging to 28 European countries participated to this fourth round. The dataset includes information for each institution in 2017 on: the state of digitisation activity, the dimension and characteristics of collections, digital access, preservation strategy and expenditure. For more information, see Nauta et al. (2017).
4. These figures are not weighted. Therefore, the actual percentage of the digitization for cultural heritage in Europe is likely to be even lower than what is shown, since institutions with small collections have the same weight as institutions with large collections.
5. Online access of metadata is higher but with similar differences: 76% of libraries and 33% of museums have metadata available online for general use.

6. The issue is quite important for countries like Italy with outstanding heritage distributed across a huge number of sites and museums/institutions.
7. Digital content from museums can be found at the museum websites, but also in the Google Art Project, Wikipedia, image banks, iTunes and Europeana, as well as in a number of video games, blogs and software applications.
8. How to deal with this issue is still an open question in the literature. See, for instance, Simar & Wilson (2007; 2011) Banker & Natarajan (2008), McDonald (2009), Daraio et al. (2018) and Banker et al. (2019).
9. The statistical office of MIBACT provides detailed information regarding museums only for those which are state-owned.
10. This procedure makes use of the order-m partial frontier estimator by Cazals et al. (2002) that allows for identifying superefficient units and is based on an iterative procedure. In a few words, at each iteration, the *order-m* score for each observation is computed (for a set of values of *m*) leaving out the observation from the reference set. Potential outliers are identified as those superefficient units reporting an output-oriented *order-m* score lower than 1−α and an input-oriented score higher than 1+α (where α is a parameter and 1±α are thresholds defined for both the orientations) and then further investigated and possibly removed. Once that *m* and *α* have been chosen through sensitivity analysis, a potential outlier is removed if the number of observations outperforming it is relatively low. Then the process is iterated until outliers are no longer identified (see Simar, 2003 for details).
11. The list of museums in the final sample is available in the online Table A.5.
12. For descriptive statistics of the variable in the subsample see Table A.1.
13. The values of the ICT variables reflect the museums' answers to the relevant questions of the ISTAT survey. Since all these questions are about the implementation of each service, we build up a set of dummy variables, consistently with the possible answers: YES (we attribute a value of 1) or NO (we attribute a value of 0). A museum could also choose not to answer a question and, therefore, the differences in the number of observations for each variable reflect the different response rates for the different questions. Table A.4 details the distribution of answers for each question.
14. The estimates reported in this Section are obtained using the Stata package developed by Badunenko and Mozharovskyi (2016).
15. A recent study (del Barrio-Tellado and Herrero-Prieto, 2019) on some Spanish museums finds similar average scores.
16. See Tables A.2 and A.3.
17. Results are available from the authors upon request.
18. The descriptive statistics of the employed second stage variables are reported in Table 3.
19. Their features and distribution have been described in detail *supra*, at the end of 3.3.
20. For the *online* services the number of observations for which the composite index is computed drops to 92, since this is the number of museums that have filed a YES/NO answer to each of the 9 relevant questions.
21. The other estimated models with results largely overlapping those reported here. The results of these additional exercises are available upon request.
22. All estimates are obtained with the bootstrap truncated algorithm proposed by Simar and Wilson (2007). We computed 2000 bootstrap iterations, showing here the mean, the standard deviation and the significance of the coefficients for each variable. The estimates are obtained using the Stata package developed by Badunenko and Tauchmann (2019).
23. The different specifications employed in the estimates shown in Tables 6 and 7 and the use of a robust semiparametric estimator (Simar and Wilson, 2007) make us confident about the impact of the variables used on the boundary of frontier efficiency. Moreover, Simar and Wilson (2011) show that the estimator developed by Simar and Wilson (2007) used here is less sensitive to the problem of the omitted variable bias. However, given the limited

availability of data and, in particular, the unavailability of panel data, the reported estimates should be taken with some caution.

Disclosure statement

No potential conflict of interest was reported by the authors.

ORCID

Calogero Guccio http://orcid.org/0000-0002-1053-4968
Marco Ferdinando Martorana http://orcid.org/0000-0003-2616-4460
Isidoro Mazza http://orcid.org/0000-0001-7182-3619
Giacomo Pignataro http://orcid.org/0000-0002-1972-0572
Ilde Rizzo http://orcid.org/0000-0002-7978-4957

References

Ateca-Amestoy, V. 2018. "Cultural Heritage Participation. Engagement Models, Evidence for the EU." *Economia Della Cultura* 28 (4): 419–432.
Ateca-Amestoy, V., and C. Castiglione. 2014. "*Live and Digital Engagement with the Visual Arts.*" Paper presented at the 18th International Conference on cultural Economics. Université du Québec, Montreal.
Badunenko, O., and H. Tauchmann. 2019. "Simar and Wilson Two-Stage Efficiency Analysis for Stata." *The Stata Journal* 19 (4): 950–988.
Badunenko, O., and P. Mozharovskyi. 2016. "Nonparametric Frontier Analysis Using Stata." *The Stata Journal* 16 (3): 550–589.
Bakhshi, H., and D. Throsby. 2010. *Culture of Innovation. An Economic Analysis of Innovation in Arts and Cultural Organisations*. London: Nesta Report.
Bakhshi, H., and D. Throsby. 2012. "New Technologies in Cultural Institutions: Theory, Evidence and Policy Implications." *International Journal of Cultural Policy* 18 (2): 205–222.
Banker, R., A. Charnes, and W. Cooper. 1984. "Some Models for Estimating Technical and Scale Inefficiencies in Data Envelopment Analysis." *Management Science* 30: 1078–1092.
Banker, R., and R. Natarajan. 2008. "Evaluating Contextual Variables Affecting Productivity Using Data Envelopment Analysis." *International Journal of Operational Research* 56 (1): 48–58.
Banker, R., R. Natarajan, and D. Zhang. 2019. "Two-Stage Estimation of the Impact of Contextual Variables in Stochastic Frontier Production Function Models Using Data Envelopment Analysis: Second Stage OLS Versus Bootstrap Approaches." *European Journal of Operational Research* 278 (2): 368–384.
Basso, A., and S. Funari. 2004. "A Quantitative Approach to Evaluate the Relative Efficiency of Museums." *Journal of Cultural Economics* 28 (3): 195–216.
Basso, A., F. Casarin, and S. Funari. 2018. "How Well Is the Museum Performing? A Joint Use of DEA and BSC to Measure the Performance of Museums." *Omega* 81: 67–84.
Bertacchini, E., and F. Morando. 2013. "The Future of Museums in the Digital age: New Models for Access to and Use of Digital Collections." *International Journal of Arts Management* 15 (2): 60–72.
Bertacchini, E., C. Dalle Nogare, and R. Scuderi. 2018. "Ownership, Organization Structure and Public Service Provision: the Case of Museums." *Journal of Cultural Economics* 42 (4): 619–643.
Bodo, C., and S. Bodo. 2016. Country profile: Italy. In Council of Europe/ERICarts, Compendium of Cultural Policies and Trends in Europe", 18th edition. http://www.culturalpolicies.net. ISSN: 2222-7334
Borowiecki, K., and T. Navarrete. 2017. "Digitization of Heritage Collections as Indicator of Innovation." *Economics of Innovation and New Technology* 26 (3): 227–246.

Bruns, A. 2013. "From Prosumption to Produsage." In *Handbook on the Digital Creative Economy*, edited by R. Towse, and C. Handke, 67–78. Cheltenham: Edward Elgar Publishing.

Camarero, C., M. Garrido, and E. Vicente. 2011. "How Cultural Organizations' Size and Funding Influence Innovation and Performance: the Case of Museums." *Journal of Cultural Economics* 35 (4): 247.

Carvalho, P., J. Costa, and A. Carvalho. 2014. "The Economic Performance of Portuguese Museums." *Urban Public Economics Review* 20: 12–37.

Cazals, C., J. Florens, and L. Simar. 2002. "Nonparametric Frontier Estimation: a Robust Approach." *Journal of Econometrics* 106 (1): 1–25.

Charnes, A., W. Cooper, and E. Rhodes. 1978. "Measuring the Efficiency of Decision Making Units." *European Journal of Operational Research* 2 (6): 429–444.

Daraio, C., L. Simar, and P. Wilson. 2018. "Central Limit Theorems for Conditional Efficiency Measures and Tests of the 'Separability' Condition in Non-Parametric, Two-Stage Models of Production." *The Econometrics Journal* 21 (2): 170–191.

Del Barrio, M., and L. Herrero. 2014. "Evaluating the Efficiency of Museums Using Multiple Outputs: Evidence from a Regional System of Museums in Spain." *International Journal of Cultural Policy* 20 (2): 221–238.

Del Barrio, M., L. Herrero, and J. Sanz. 2009. "Measuring the Efficiency of Heritage Institutions: a Case Study of a Regional System of Museums in Spain." *Journal of Cultural Heritage* 10 (2): 258–268.

Del Barrio-Tellado, M., and L. Herrero-Prieto. 2019. "Modelling Museum Efficiency in Producing Inter-Reliant Outputs." *Journal of Cultural Economics* 43 (3): 485–512.

Evrard, Y., and A. Krebs. 2018. "The Authenticity of the Museum Experience in the Digital age: the Case of the Louvre." *Journal of Cultural Economics* 42 (3): 353–363.

Fernandez-Blanco, V., and J. Prieto-Rodríguez. 2020. "Museums." In *Handbook of Cultural Economics*, 3rd ed., edited by R. Towse, and T. Navarrete-Hernández, 349–357. Cheltenham: Edward Elgar Publishing.

Giardina, E., I. Mazza, G. Pignataro, and I. Rizzo. 2016. "Voluntary Provision of Public Goods and Technology." *International Advances in Economic Research* 22: 321–332.

Guccio, C., M. Martorana, I. Mazza, G. Pignataro, and I. Rizzo. 2020a. "An Analysis of the Managerial Performance of Italian Museums Using a Generalised Conditional Efficiency Model." *Socio-economic Planning Sciences*. doi:10.1016/j.seps.2020.100891.

Guccio, C., M. Martorana, I. Mazza, and I. Rizzo. 2020b. "Back to the Future: Does the use of Information and Communication Technology Enhance the Performance of Public Historical Archives?" *Journal of Cultural Economics*. doi:10.1007/s10824-020-09385-1.

Holler, M., and I. Mazza. 2013. "Cultural Heritage: Public Decision-Making and Implementation." In *Handbook on the Economics of Cultural Heritage*, edited by I. Rizzo, and A. Mignosa, 17–36. Cheltenham: Edward Elgar.

ISTAT. 2017. *Indagine sui Musei e le Istituzioni Similari: Microdati ad uso Pubblico*. Roma: ISTAT. https://www.istat.it/it/archivio/167566

Kabassi, K. 2017. "Evaluating Websites of Museums: State of the art." *Journal of Cultural Heritage* 24: 184–196.

Krebs, A. 2012. *Education and access to digital culture: the current situation and future directions for European culture*. http://www.houseforculture.eu/upload/Docs%20ACP/581educationdigitalencatcannekrebsENGL.pdf

Leva, L., V. Menicucci, G. Roma, and D. Ruggeri. 2019. *Innovazioni nella governance dei musei statali e gestione del patrimonio culturale: alcune evidenze da un'indagine della Banca d'Italia*, Questioni di Economia e Finanza, n. 525.

Mairesse, F., and P. Vanden Eeckaut. 2002. "Museum Assessment and FDH Technology: Towards a Global Approach." *Journal of Cultural Economics* 26 (4): 261–286.

McDonald, J. 2009. "Using Least Squares and Tobit in Second Stage dea Efficiency Analyses." *European Journal of Operational Research* 197 (2): 792–798.

Mihelj, S., A. Leguina, and J. Downey. 2019. "Culture is Digital: Cultural Participation, Diversity and the Digital Divide." *New Media & Society* 21 (7): 1465–1485.

Nauta, G., W. van den Heuvel, and S. Teunisse. 2017. *Report on ENUMERATE Core Survey 4*, Europeana. https://pro.europeana.eu/files/Europeana_Professional/Projects/Project_list/ENUMERATE/deliverables/DSI-2_Deliverable%20D4.4_Europeana_Report%20on%20ENUMERATE%20Core%20Survey%204.pdf

Navarrete, T. 2013. "Museums." In *Handbook on the Digital Creative Economy*, edited by R. Towse, and C. Handke, 330–343. Cheltenham: Edward Elgar Publishing.

Pallud, J., and D. Straub. 2014. "Effective Website Design for Experience-Influenced Environments: The Case of High Culture Museums." *Information & Management* 51 (3): 359–373.

Paolini, P., D. Mitroff Silvers, and N. Proctor. 2013. "Technologies for Cultural Heritage." In *Handbook on the Economics of Cultural Heritage*, edited by I. Rizzo, and A. Mignosa, 272–289. Cheltenham: Edward Elgar Publishing.

Peacock, A., and I. Rizzo. 2008. *The Heritage Game. Economics, Policy and Practices*. Oxford: Oxford University Press.

Pignataro, G. 2002. "Measuring the Efficiency of Museums: a Case Study in Sicily." In *The Economics of Heritage: a Study in the Political Economy of Culture in Sicily*, edited by I. Rizzo, and R. Towse, 65–78. Cheltenham: Edward Elgar Publishing.

Pignataro, G. 2011. "Performance Indicators." In *A Handbook of Cultural Economics. Second Edition*, edited by R. Towse, 332–338. Cheltenham: Edward Elgar Publishing.

Rizzo, I. 2016. "Technological Perspectives for Cultural Heritage." In *The Artful Economist*, edited by I. Rizzo, and R. Towse, 197–214. Cham: Springer International Publishing.

Simar, L. 2003. "Detecting Outliers in Frontier Models: A Simple Approach." *Journal of Productivity Analysis* 20: 391–424.

Simar, L., and P. Wilson. 1998. "Sensitivity Analysis of Efficiency Scores: How to Bootstrap in Nonparametric Frontier Models." *Management Science* 44 (1): 49–61.

Simar, L., and P. Wilson. 2000. "Statistical Inference in Nonparametric Frontier Models: the State of the art." *Journal of Productivity Analysis* 13 (1): 49–78.

Simar, L., and P. Wilson. 2011. "Two-stage DEA: Caveat Emptor." *Journal of Productivity Analysis* 36 (2): 205.

Simar, L., and P. Wilson. 2007. "Estimation and Inference in Two-Stage, Semi-Parametric Models of Production Processes." *Journal of Econometrics* 136 (1): 31–64.

Taheri, H., and S. Ansari. 2013. "Measuring the Relative Efficiency of Cultural-Historical Museums in Teheran: DEA Approach." *Journal of Cultural Heritage* 14 (5): 431–438.

Unioncamere. 2018. *Io Sono Cultura*. Rome: Quaderni di Symbola.

Weil, S. 1995. "Performance Indicators for Museums: Progress Report from Wintergreen." *The Journal of Arts Management, Law, and Society* 23 (4): 341–351.

Zan, L., S. Bonini Baraldi, and M. Santagati. 2018. "Missing HRM: the Original sin of Museum Reforms in Italy." *Museum Management and Curatorship* 33 (6): 530–545.

APPENDIX A

Table A.1. Sample statistics of inputs and outputs variables in subsample with mixed entrance (with and without fee).

Variable	Obs	Mean	Std. Dev.	Min	Max
Personnel	58	23.38	18.85	1.00	90.00
Exhibition space	58	1644.50	1823.14	115.00	10000.00
Visitors	58	20079.55	17239.30	2514.00	74406.00
Visitors_paying	58	9030.21	9072.53	663.00	41424.00
Free visitors	58	11049.34	9114.12	1445.00	42512.00
Temp_ex	58	2.16	4.77	0.00	30.00
W_temp_ex	58	7278.97	13477.09	0.00	74406.00

Source: our elaboration on data provided by ISTAT and by MIBACT.

Table A.2 Efficiency estimates – subsample with mixed entrance (with and without fee).

		Uncorrected efficiency scores		Bias-corrected efficiency scores		
Variable	Obs.	Mean	Std. Dev.	Mean	Std. Dev.	Bias
MOD_1 (CRS)	58	0.3589	0.2936	0.3481	0.2930	0.0108
MOD_1 (VRS)	58	0.5095	0.3084	0.4993	0.3078	0.0102
MOD_2 (CRS)	58	0.4052	0.3048	0.3971	0.3042	0.0081
MOD_2 (VRS)	58	0.5356	0.3144	0.5302	0.3138	0.0054
MOD_3 (CRS)	58	0.3770	0.3025	0.3582	0.3019	0.0189
MOD_3 (VRS)	58	0.5188	0.3153	0.4877	0.3147	0.0311
MOD_4 (CRS)	58	0.4215	0.3099	0.4046	0.3093	0.0169
MOD_4 (VRS)	58	0.5424	0.3181	0.5153	0.3175	0.0271

Source: our elaboration on data provided by ISTAT and by MIBACT.

Table A.3 Correlation between efficiency estimates in full and subsample – Model 4.

		(1)	(2)	(3)	(4)
(1)	MOD4_CRS	1.0000			
(2)	MOD4_CRS_S	0.9851	1.0000		
(3)	MOD4_VRS	0.8393	0.8174	1.0000	
(4)	MOD4_VRS_S	0.7998	0.8053	0.9547	1.0000

Source: our elaboration on data provided by ISTAT and by MIBACT.

Table A.4. Extent of ICT services.

Service	Obs	Yes	Answer No	No answer
In situ services				
Smartphone and tablet apps	107	11	91	5
Multimedia devices	107	18	85	4
QRcode	107	12	90	5
PC/tablet devices	107	7	95	5
Online services				
Website	107	65	36	6
Online catalogue	107	10	89	8
Online ticket office	107	7	91	9
Virtual visit	107	12	86	9
Social media	107	52	47	8
Photo and prints shop	107	16	80	11
Merchandising	107	6	89	12
Newsletter	107	5	92	10
Community	107	11	85	11

Source: our elaboration on data provided by ISTAT.

Table A.5 List of museums in the final sample.

Museums	Province	Municipality
MUSEO ARCHEOLOGICO STATALE	Ancona	Arcevia
ANTIQUARIUM STATALE DI NUMANA	Ancona	Numana
MUSEO ARCHEOLOGICO NAZIONALE DELLE MARCHE	Ancona	Ancona
MUSEO TATTILE STATALE 'OMERO'	Ancona	Ancona
MUSEO DELLE ARTI E TRADIZIONI POPOLARI DELL'ALTA VALLE DEL TEVERE	Arezzo	Anghiari
MUSEO ARCHEOLOGICO STATALE – ASCOLI PICENO	Ascoli piceno	Ascoli Piceno
MUSEO ANTIQUARIUM DI AVELLA	Avellino	Avella
MUSEO ANTIQUARIUM DI ARIANO IRPINO	Avellino	Ariano Irpino
MUSEO DI SAN FRANCESCO A FOLLONI	Avellino	Montella
MUSEO NAZIONALE ARCHEOLOGICO	Bari	Altamura
MUSEO NAZIONALE JATTA	Bari	Ruvo di Puglia
GALLERIA NAZIONALE DELLA PUGLIA 'GIROLAMO E ROSARIA DEVANNA'	Bari	Bitonto
MUSEO ARCHEOLOGICO DI PALAZZO SINESI	Barletta-Andria-Trani	Canosa di Puglia
MUSEO ARCHEOLOGICO NAZIONALE DEL SANNIO CAUDINO	Benevento	Montesarchio
PINACOTECA NAZIONALE DI BOLOGNA	Bologna	Bologna
MUSEO ARCHEOLOGICO DELLA VAL CAMONICA	Brescia	Cividate Camuno
PINACOTECA NAZIONALE DI CAGLIARI	Cagliari	Cagliari
MUSEO ARCHEOLOGICO DI SEPINO – ALTILIA	Campobasso	Sepino
MUSEO ARCHEOLOGICO NAZIONALE DELL'ANTICA ALLIFAE	Caserta	Alife
MUSEO ARCHEOLOGICO DELL'AGRO ATELLANO	Caserta	Succivo
MUSEO ARCHEOLOGICO DI CALATIA	Caserta	Maddaloni
MUSEO ARCHEOLOGICO DI TEANUM SIDICINUM	Caserta	Teano
MUSEO ARCHEOLOGICO NAZIONALE D'ABRUZZO – VILLA FRIGERJ	Chieti	Chieti
MUSEO ARCHEOLOGICO NAZIONALE	Cosenza	Amendolara
ANTIQUARIUM DI TORRE CIMALONGA	Cosenza	Scalea
MUSEO ARCHEOLOGICO NAZIONALE DELLA SIBARITIDE	Cosenza	Cassano all'Ionio
GALLERIA NAZIONALE DI COSENZA	Cosenza	Cosenza
MUSEO ARCHEOLOGICO NAZIONALE	Crotone	Crotone
MUSEO E PARCO ARCHEOLOGICO NAZIONALE DI CAPO COLONNA	Crotone	Crotone
MUSEO DI CASA ROMEI	Ferrara	Ferrara
MUSEO ARCHEOLOGICO NAZIONALE DI FERRARA	Ferrara	Ferrara
PINACOTECA NAZIONALE DI FERRARA	Ferrara	Ferrara
MUSEO DI CASA MARTELLI	Firenze	Firenze
CENACOLO DI ANDREA DEL SARTO	Firenze	Firenze
MUSEO DELL'OPIFICIO DELLE PIETRE DURE	Firenze	Firenze
CENACOLO DEL FULIGNO	Firenze	Firenze
CENACOLO DI SANT'APOLLONIA	Firenze	Firenze
MUSEO STORICO DELLA CACCIA E DEL TERRITORIO – VILLA MEDICEA DI CERRETO GUIDI	Firenze	Firenze
MUSEO DI PALAZZO DAVANZATI O DELLA CASA FIORENTINA ANTICA	Firenze	Firenze
MUSEO ARCHEOLOGICO NAZIONALE DI FIRENZE	Firenze	Firenze
MUSEO ARCHEOLOGICO NAZIONALE DI SARSINA	Forlì-Cesena	Sarsina
MUSEO CASA PASCOLI	Forlì-Cesena	San Mauro Pascoli
MUSEO ARCHEOLOGICO NAZIONALE 'G. CARETTONI'	Frosinone	Cassino
MUSEO ARCHEOLOGICO NAZIONALE PALAZZO ROCCA	Genova	Chiavari
MUSEO ARCHEOLOGICO NAZIONALE DI COSA	Grosseto	Orbetello
MUSEO NAZIONALE DEL PALEOLITICO D'ISERNIA	Isernia	Isernia
MUSEO D'ARTE SACRA DELLA MARSICA	L'aquila	Celano
MUSEO ARCHEOLOGICO NAZIONALE DI FORMIA	Latina	Formia
MUSEO ARCHEOLOGICO NAZIONALE DI SPERLONGA E VILLA DI TIBERIO	Latina	Sperlonga
MUSEO ARCHEOLOGICO STATALE DI CINGOLI MOSCOSI	Macerata	Cingoli
MUSEO ARCHEOLOGICO STATALE	Macerata	Urbisaglia
MUSEO ARCHEOLOGICO NAZIONALE DI MANTOVA	Mantova	Mantova
MUSEO ARCHEOLOGICO NAZIONALE DI METAPONTO	Matera	Bernalda
MUSEO ARCHEOLOGICO NAZIONALE 'DOMENICO RIDOLA'	Matera	Matera
MUSEO NAZIONALE D'ARTE MEDIEVALE E MODERNA DELLA BASILICATA	Matera	Matera
GALLERIA ESTENSE	Modena	Modena
MUSEO LAPIDARIO ESTENSE	Modena	Modena
MUSEO NAZIONALE DELLA CERAMICA 'DUCA DI MARTINA'	Napoli	Napoli

(Continued)

Table A.5 Continued.

Museums	Province	Municipality
MUSEO STORICO ARCHEOLOGICO	Napoli	Nola
MUSEO ARCHEOLOGICO NAZIONALE G. ASPRONI	Nuoro	Nuoro
MUSEO ANTICA SPEZIERIA DI SAN GIOVANNI EVANGELISTA	Parma	Parma
MUSEO ARCHEOLOGICO DELLA LOMELLINA	Pavia	Vigevano
MUSEO DEL CASTELLO BUFALINI	Perugia	San Giustino
MUSEO DEL PALAZZO DUCALE DI GUBBIO	Perugia	Gubbio
MUSEO ARCHEOLOGICO NAZIONALE	Perugia	Perugia
MUSEO ARCHEOLOGICO STATALE E TEATRO ROMANO	Perugia	Spoleto
MUSEO NAZIONALE DEL DUCATO DI SPOLETO	Perugia	Spoleto
GALLERIA NAZIONALE DELL'UMBRIA	Perugia	Perugia
MUSEO 'CASA NATALE DI GABRIELE D'ANNUNZIO'	Pescara	Pescara
MUSEO DI CASA GIUSTI	Pistoia	Monsummano Terme
MUSEO ARCHEOLOGICO NAZIONALE DI MURO LUCANO	Potenza	Muro Lucano
MUSEO ARCHEOLOGICO NAZIONALE DELLA BASILICATA 'DINU ADAMESTEANU'	Potenza	Potenza
MUSEO NAZIONALE DELL'ETÀ NEOCLASSICA IN ROMAGNA IN PALAZZO MILZETTI	Ravenna	Faenza
MUSEO E PARCO ARCHEOLOGICO DI ROSARNO	Reggio di Calabria	Rosarno
MUSEO E PARCO ARCHEOLOGICO DELL'ANTICA CAULONIA	Reggio di Calabria	Monasterace
MUSEO E PARCO ARCHEOLOGICO NAZIONALE	Reggio di Calabria	Locri
MUSEO GIACOMO MANZU'	Roma	Ardea
MUSEO MARIO PRAZ	Roma	Roma
ANTIQUARIUM DI PYRGI	Roma	Santa Marinella
MUSEO BONCOMPAGNI LUDOVISI PER LE ARTI DECORATIVE, COSTUME E MODA	Roma	Roma
MUSEO HENDRIK CHRISTIAN ANDERSEN	Roma	Roma
MUSEO NAZIONALE DEGLI STRUMENTI MUSICALI	Roma	Roma
MUSEO DELL'ISTITUTO CENTRALE PER LA GRAFICA	Roma	Roma
MUSEO DELLA VIA OSTIENSE	Roma	Roma
MUSEO ARCHEOLOGICO NAZIONALE	Roma	Civitavecchia
MUSEO DELLE NAVI ROMANE DI NEMI E SANTUARIO DI DIANA NEMORENSE	Roma	Nemi
MUSEO ARCHEOLOGICO NAZIONALE DI PALESTRINA	Roma	Palestrina
MUSEO NAZIONALE DEL PALAZZO DI VENEZIA	Roma	Roma
GALLERIA SPADA	Roma	Roma
MUSEO NAZIONALE ETRUSCO DI VILLA GIULIA	Roma	Roma
MUSEO ARCHEOLOGICO NAZIONALE (BARCHESSA DI VILLA BADOER)	Rovigo	Fratta Polesine
MUSEO ARCHEOLOGICO NAZIONALE DELLA VALLE DEL SARNO	Salerno	Sarno
MUSEO ARCHEOLOGICO DI EBOLI E DELLA MEDIA VALLE DEL SELE	Salerno	Eboli
MUSEO ARCHEOLOGICO NAZIONALE DI PONTECAGNANO'GLI ETRUSCHI DI FRONTIERA'	Salerno	Pontecagnano Faiano
PINACOTECA MUS'A AL CANOPOLENO	Sassari	Sassari
MUSEO NAZIONALE ARCHEOLOGICO – ETNOGRAFICO 'GIOVANNI ANTONIO SANNA'	Sassari	Sassari
PINACOTECA NAZIONALE DI SIENA	Siena	Siena
MUSEO ARCHEOLOGICO NAZIONALE	Taranto	Taranto
MUSEO NAZIONALE ARCHEOLOGICO D'ABRUZZO SEZIONE DI CAMPLI	Teramo	Campli
MUSEO PALEOCRISTIANO	Udine	Aquileia
MUSEO ARCHEOLOGICO NAZIONALE	Udine	Cividale del Friuli
MUSEO ARCHEOLOGICO DI QUARTO D'ALTINO	Venezia	Quarto d'Altino
MUSEO STATALE DI SASSARI	Vibo valentia	Mileto
MUSEO ARCHEOLOGICO DELL'AGRO FALISCO E FORTE SANGALLO	Viterbo	Civita Castellana
MUSEO ARCHEOLOGICO NAZIONALE	Viterbo	Tuscania
MUSEO NAZIONALE ETRUSCO DI ROCCA ALBORNOZ	Viterbo	Viterbo
MUSEO ARCHEOLOGICO DI VULCI	Viterbo	Canino

Exploring the marriage between fashion and 'Made in Italy' and the key role of G.B. Giorgini

Luciana Lazzeretti and Stefania Oliva

ABSTRACT
The first high fashion show organized in Florence in 1951 represented an important event for the development of the Italian fashion sector, increasing the importance of the fashion industry in international trade. Research in economic business history has identified this period as crucial for the advent of the 'Made in Italy' label. The article aims to understand if and how the high fashion shows organized in Florence between 1951 and 1967 influenced the emergence of the Italian fashion industry and the concept of 'Made in Italy'. Supported by data collected from the historical archive 'Italian Fashion Archive of Giovanni Battista Giorgini' and three online archives of digitalized books and newspapers, the analysis sheds light on the perception of the national and international press on the cultural phenomena of Italian fashion and 'Made in Italy'. Results reveal an increasing trend in the frequency of terms related to the Italian fashion industry coinciding with the years of the Florentine events. The analysis evidences the crucial role of the entrepreneurial activity of Giovanni Battista Giorgini, buyer and organizer of the first Italian high fashion show in Florence, for the emergence of the Italian fashion industry and 'Made in Italy'.

1. Introduction

Over the last few years, a wide literature has investigated the characteristics and evolution of the fashion industry and the 'Made in Italy' label (Santagata 2009, 2010; Belfanti 2015; Reinach 2015; Lazzeretti and Capone 2020). The topic has been studied from several points of view. Part of the literature has analysed the fashion industry according to its geographical dimension, investigating the relationship between the fashion system and exemplary cities (D'Ovidio 2015; Bellini and Pasquinelli 2016; Capone and Lazzeretti 2016; Casadei 2018). Other studies have focused on the cultural dimension of the Italian fashion industry and its relationship with artistic and cultural heritage (Paulicelli 2014; Calanca and Capalbo 2018; Lazzeretti and Oliva 2018). Finally, a further part of the literature has explored the industrial dynamics of the fashion industry and 'Made in Italy' concerning the process of globalization (Amighini and Rabellotti 2006; Corbellini and Saviolo 2004; Fortis 2016).

Despite the results of research in these fields of study, further empirical investigation is required concerning the origins of the development of the sector, which elements fostered its emergence and how this is related to the concept of 'Made in Italy'. The article focuses on the establishment and evolution of the Italian fashion industry and 'Made in Italy'. It aims to investigate if and how the emergence of the Italian fashion industry and the concept of 'Made in Italy' was influenced by the Italian high fashion shows organized in Florence from its origin in 1951 to 1967 by Giovanni Battista Giorgini.

Following these considerations, the article has developed two different analyses. First, textual analysis is applied to the titles of 199 fashion articles published by Italian, British and US newspapers and magazines between 1953 and 1965. The articles are collected from the 'Italian Fashion Archive of Giovanni Battista Giorgini', from here GBG Archive. The textual analysis sought to identify the most cited terms in the national and international press for describing the advent of the Italian fashion industry in the period considered. The second analysis has been an N-grams analysis focused on the frequency of some key terms, extrapolated from the documents of the GBG Archive, in international digitalized periodicals, magazines and books published from 1920 to 2000. The analysis was carried out using three different online archives: The British Newspaper Archive, Newspapers.com and Google Books.

This approach rests on the idea that the digital revolution has influenced knowledge production, making access to a huge amount of information through digital means such as online databases easier (Wenzel and Will 2019). Moreover, the use of large datasets, such as databases of historical books and periodicals, has affected the study of macro-trends of cultural, economic and social change (Lansdall-Welfare et al. 2017). Specialist scholars have defined this discipline as 'Culturomics', the high-throughput data collection and analysis for the study of human culture. In other words, the use of large digital archives to investigate cultural trends as interpreted in language and word usage (Michel et al. 2011). Concerning the fashion industry, moreover, scholars have used the 'Big Data' approach and textual analysis in marketing studies as support tools to analyse the value and perception of a brand by consumers (Ranfagni, Camiciottoli, and Faraoni 2016; Acuti et al. 2018).

The proposed analysis highlights the relationship between the establishment of the fashion industry, the affirmation of 'Made in Italy' and the organization of the Italian high fashion shows in Florence starting from 1951. Results show an increasing trend in the frequency of terms related to the Italian fashion industry starting in the years coinciding with the Florentine events, underlining the crucial role of entrepreneurial activity by Giovanni Battista Giorgini, buyer and organizer of the first Italian high fashion show.

The article is structured as follows. Section 2 explores the 'Made in Italy' concept and its relationship with the fashion industry. Section 3 describes the methodology applied and explains in detail the sources for the data collection. Section 4 presents the results of the analyses. The final section presents conclusions and gives insights into further research on the topic.

2. The 'Made in Italy' concept and the relationship with the fashion industry

2.1. Exploring the 'Made in Italy' concept

The literature on 'Made in Italy' can be traced back to different strands of research. Some studies focused on the 'country-of-origin' effect mainly related to brand research associated with marketing studies (Bertoli 2013; Aiello et al. 2015). This strand of the literature has its roots in studies devoted to investigating the possible advantage coming from a 'country-of-origin' label to influence consumers' behaviour in global markets (Agrawal and Kamakura 1999). Other research, moreover, has focused on studies of specific sectors to understand the dynamics and characteristics of the different specializations belonging to Made in Italy sectors (Fortis 2016). Many studies have investigated 'Made in Italy' focusing on the fashion sector with different aims (Belfanti 2015).

Defining 'Made in Italy' is a controversial issue. It represents the aggregation of heterogeneous sectors, characterized by a certain degree of specialization (Curzio and Fortis 2000). Fortis (2016, 87) defines the sectors belonging to 'Made in Italy' as *the 4F's of Italian excellence: Fashion and cosmetics; Food and wine; Furniture and ceramic tiles; Fabricated metal products, machinery and transport equipment*. As underlined by Brusco and Paba (2014), despite differences from a merceological (merchandizing) point of view, products of 'Made in Italy' present some crucial common features. They are responsible for a large part of Italian exports and their production is mostly located in Italy's industrial districts (Becattini 1998). They have roots in the artisan tradition and employ highly skilled human capital (Brusco and Paba 2014). Their production may be horizontally diversified or vertically disintegrated (Asheim, Cooke, and Martin 2006). However, 'Made in Italy' production is not just related to tradition but presents a high degree of innovative capacity and creativity. If, on the one hand, innovative capability is intrinsic to craft activities, studies of 'Made in Italy' show, on the other, that consumer communities contribute to feeding the innovativeness of products and give them symbolic value and identity (Di Maria and Finotto 2008). Finally, products of 'Made in Italy' have a common feature represented by the country of origin, namely Italy. However, 'Made in Italy' is more than a country-of-origin label. It represents a vehicle for the symbolic value of Italian culture and its artistic heritage (Corbellini and Saviolo 2004). Considering these characteristics, 'Made in Italy' is configured as a group of sectors closely connected to Italian culture. It involves not only the quality of the products but the brand's ability to transmit and communicate values and meanings related to the *Italian way of living* (Paulicelli 2014; Giumelli 2016).

In addition to the industrial components under study, another part of the literature underlines the cultural value of 'Made in Italy' and its close relationship with cultural heritage. Starting from this reflection, sectors belonging to 'Made in Italy' present some interesting overlaps with the cultural and creative industries (CCIs) in a 'broad' definition (Lazzeretti and Capone 2015). Santagata (2010) defines the cultural and creative sectors as broad and heterogeneous, also including those sectors in which cultural value is linked to the quality, tradition and material culture of products. He includes among these sectors *Fashion, Industrial design and crafts, Food and the wine industry*. 'Made in Italy' represents a group of products with a high degree of cultural content that reflects the values and heritage of a specific territory (Reinach 2015). It expresses the beautiful and high quality of Italian products, designed for a large global market but not standardized (Balicco 2015). According to Anna Zegna, entrepreneurship and president of the Foundation Zegna, the success of Made in Italy in the international market depends on its strict relationship with Italian creativity and cultural heritage:

the elegance of the taste and landscape in which we are immersed, the talent for solving problems, the individual impetus, being sons of the most important artisan tradition in the world; all these premises make Made in Italy a very particular phenomenon of success that still arouses so much admiration. (Zegna 2015, 87)

Although the 'Made in Italy' sectors continue to represent the quality and style of Italian culture in the world, the effects of globalization have produced important changes both in the perception of the concept and in its production structure. Again, the economic and cultural dimensions are strongly interconnected.

The entry into the market of new competitor countries has led to a revision of the policies and strategies of 'Made in Italy' companies (Pucci, Simoni, and Zanni 2013). The consequence has been the relocation of production in countries with lower labour costs (Fortis 2016). This has led to a shift from the advantage deriving from producing in a specific place to the importance of the brand of large companies (Pucci, Simoni, and Zanni 2013). This is clearly evident in the fashion industry where 'Made in Italy' is dominated by the leading brands in the luxury industry guided by large international groups (Reinach 2014). If, on the one hand, the challenges of globalization require a change of strategies, on the other, the loss of importance of places brings with it a decrease in the value of the identity, culture and heritage of a place. In this regard, some critics wonder if 'Made in Italy' still exists or if it can rather be replaced by 'Made by Italy' (Giumelli 2016).

Moreover, national brands like 'Made in Italy' have been generally associated with stereotypes or have been created mobilizing narratives that mix reality and fiction in order to produce a credible symbolic meaning for foreign consumers (Pinchera and Rinallo 2020). This has raised questions about the authenticity of the values that these types of brands can communicate to the international market. Such criticisms may be also applied to the case of 'Made in Italy' and the rise of Italian fashion in the 1950s when the emerging national label was promoted through a conscious branding strategy associated with the 'Italian Renaissance', the period when Italian artistic culture excelled in Europe (Belfanti 2015).

Finally, despite the 'Made in Italy' label as a vehicle for Italian culture, traditions and art, its relationship with cultural heritage should also be recognized as controversial. The literature recognizes the role played by cultural heritage as a source of inspiration for creatives and designers working in 'Made in Italy' sectors. In a simplistic vision, this can lead to the belief that the mere physical presence of cultural heritage is the key element for feeding creativity (Muzzarelli 2011). However, the birth of 'Made in Italy' was the result of specific economic 'miracle' and cultural conditions that occurred in post-war Italy. These conditions involved the presence of skilled labour, small and medium-sized enterprises and industrial districts and a precise promotional strategy implemented by knowledge key actors during the 1950s (Belfanti 2015).

2.2. The birth of Made in Italy and the first Italian fashion show

According to the literature concerning the history of Italian fashion, the concept of 'Made in Italy' was established in the post-war era and its importance became crucial in the 1970s–1980s (Paulicelli 2014). This period coincided with the affirmation of fashion as a production system and the invention of the *fashion boutique* (Reinach 2014). As pointed out by Belfanti (2015), although capabilities already existed, it was developmental to build a national identity for Italian fashion, in order to create an image capable of competing with French *Haute Couture*.

An event recognized as important for the establishment of the fashion industry, and in general to the affirmation of 'Made in Italy', was the organization of the first Italian high fashion shows in Florence in 1951 by the Tuscan entrepreneur Giovanni Battista Giorgini (Paris 2010; Lazzeretti and Oliva 2018). Many pieces of research on fashion in business economic history have underlined the crucial role played by Giorgini and the Florentine fashion shows in building a national identity in fashion (Pinchera and Rinallo 2020).

Giorgini was a promoter of the excellence of Italian products abroad. In 1923 he opened his buying office in Florence where he acted as an independent mediator between the demand of the foreign market, especially the American, and the Italian offer. In 1924 he left for the United States intending to enhance the quality of the products to make Italian craftsmanship, tradition and culture known abroad (Pagliai 2011). The clients of Giorgini's buying office ranged across the US from San Francisco to New York, Chicago, St. Louis and Dallas, including important companies such as the James McCutcheon department store in New York or Tiffany jewelry emporium (Fadigati 2018).

The knowledge gained concerning the US market made it clear to Giorgini the great interest of American buyers in fashion products. After a first attempt to organize a fashion show at the Brooklyn Museum of New York to present some models of Italian High Fashion, Giorgini understood that the best way to promote Italian fashion and make it competitive with that of the French, was to move American buyers to the places where production occurred. In a short time, Giorgini decided to organize such an event in Florence by inviting the most important exponents of Italian fashion. On 12 February 1951, the 'First Italian High Fashion Show' was organized in Florence, at Villa Torrigiani, Giorgini's residence. He created a unique show, where he combined the presence of large fashion houses and minor sartorial fashion 'boutiques' (Vergani 1992).

This event is symbolically considered as the birth of Italian fashion (Belfanti 2015). However, it is unlikely that a competitive and complex structure such as that of the Italian fashion industry was developed in such a short time. Moreover, the activities of Italian fashion designers such as Salvatore Ferragamo and Emilio Pucci were already well known on foreign markets (Pagliai 2011). Before 1951, although the textile industry already performed on the international market, the Italian fashion industry was still at an early stage (White 2000) in which the Italian design was usually sold and labelled as a French product.

Thanks to the quality, innovativeness and creativity of the collections combined with a relatively low price, the event was such a success that a second edition was repeated in July of the same year and, in 1952, the show was organized in the prestigious Sala Bianca in the Medici palace of Palazzo Pitti in Florence. It became an international event that recalled important names in the specialized American press (Belfanti 2015).

Giorgini played a crucial role in the affirmation of an Italian fashion and 'Made in Italy' as highlighted by the international press: '*the growth of the Italian fashion industry is in good part the work of Giorgini, known throughout Italy as 'Il Papa' of fashion*'.[1] However, other elements also contribute to explanation of the success of the Italian fashion industry and 'Made in Italy'.

A further element was the structure and organization of the fashion shows. On the one hand, they combined different lines of products (High Fashion, Fashion *Boutique* and Accessories) differentiating the offer and prices for clients. In particular, fashion *boutiques* affirmed a new line of products of luxury ready-to-wear goods, differentiating the Italian product from the French one (Lazzeretti and Oliva, 2018). On the other hand, the choice of concentrating fashion companies, sartorialists (tailors), designers and artisans in a unique location allowed consumers to appreciate collections and acknowledge the quality of the products, without the necessity to move from one fashion *atelier* (workshop) to another (Pinchera and Rinallo 2020).

Moreover, the relationship between the textile industry and fashion companies played an important role in promoting the establishment of a national fashion industry. This relationship contributed to reducing production costs and increasing production levels, bringing benefits not only to the foreign market but also for the domestic market (Garrison 2012).

Finally, a crucial role was played by the promotional activity of collective fashion shows organized by Giorgini. On the one hand, the Italian fashion shows recalled the increasing interest of the international press: from 1951 to 1961 the presence of an international press increased by about 50%, counting the participation of almost 200 representatives of the most important international newspapers. The international press created a positive overseas image of the Florentine collections reflecting the growing interest and recognition of the foreign public towards fashion and 'Made in Italy'.[2] Moreover, during the period of the fashion events, Giorgini entertained buyers and international press, organizing grand balls and performances attended also by the Italian aristocracy (Lavanga 2018). Italian fashion promotion was also characterized by the organization of particular commercial experiences. This was, for example, the case of the organization of a two-week journey to New York City on the cruise ship Cristoforo Colombo to present the latest Italian fashion models (Pinchera and Rinallo 2020).

Such event promotion, public relations and organizational strategy combined with the positive evolution of intra-sectorial fashion industry relationships and an innovative line of products worked. A key consequence was the diffusion of Italian production and an increase in the export of textile and clothing products. From 1950 to 1957 total exports in the textiles, clothing and costume jewelry sector had gone from 81 billion lire in 1950 to around 208 billion lire in 1957, with an increase of almost 127 billion, of which almost 18% was made between 1956 and 1957. Exports increased by another 30% in the next two years (1957–1959).[3]

Key factors that have contributed to the success of Italian Fashion and Made in Italy are summarized in Table 1.

Despite the great success of these Florentine events, they did not lead to the creation of modern industrial businesses. Production was still at the tailoring level more than being factory produced (Merlo and Polese 2006). In the decade between 1960 and 1970 Florence lost its supremacy because it lacked the infrastructure to support production on an industrial scale while the increasingly close relationship between the textile industry and service sectors remained insufficient (Reinach 2015). Accordingly, increasing competition for fashion supremacy between Italian cities, particularly Florence, Rome and Milan, led to a change in Italian fashion geography. Fashion shows gradually moved from Florence to Rome and the last high fashion event held in Florence was organized

Table 1. Determinants influencing the establishment of the Italian fashion industry path.

Determinant	Key elements
Industrial and business structure	• Entrepreneurship: the entrepreneurial capabilities of Giovanni Battista Giorgini and his knowledge of the international market • Intra-sectoral relationships: strict collaboration between textile and fashion industries
Innovation capacity	• Events: the innovative formula of 'Florentine high fashion shows' to promote the quality of Italian production • Product categories: presentation of the products of fashion boutiques and high-quality ready-to-wear productions
Promotional and marketing activity	• International press: the presence of the Florentine initiatives in the international press, particularly British and American • Collateral activities: differentiation of the marketing strategy through collateral promotional events for exporting the Italian fashion image abroad

Source: Our elaboration.

in 1967. In the following years, Rome became confirmed as the capital of *haute couture*, while Milan emerged as the centre for womens' *prêt-à-porter* and designer collections (Lavanga 2018; Pinchera and Rinallo 2020).

Considering the importance of the entrepreneurial activity of Giovanni Battista Giorgini and the collective fashion shows organized in Florence between 1951 and 1967, the article wants empirically to test the following hypothesis, which is largely recognized in the literature. This is that this period signals the advent of the fashion industry and 'Made in Italy', with new international recognition of the quality of Italian production abroad. Despite this being a topic largely discussed in the literature of 'Made in Italy' and fashion, to the best of our knowledge, no such empirical tests or investigations exist. Moreover, some scholars based their analysis mainly on the contents of the GBG Archive (Vergani 1992; Pinchera 2009; Pagliai 2011, 2018; Fadigati 2018), meaning such analyses have been mostly descriptive. In order to fill this gap, the article aims at investigating the relationships among the establishment of the Italian fashion industry, the advent of 'Made in Italy' and the organization of the first high fashion shows in Florence.

3. Data and methodology

Over the last few years, an emerging strand of the literature has tried to apply the 'Big Data' approach to the study of economic, cultural and social phenomena. In particular, some studies observe that macroscopic patterns of cultural change over time may be found by analysing large textual time series, such as digitized books and periodicals (Lansdall-Welfare et al. 2017). Following this idea, several studies have been conducted to study different phenomena in the social sciences. Michel et al. (2011) analysed a corpus of more than 5 million books to identify both linguistic changes, such as variation in the lexicon, grammar and cultural phenomena. A similar approach was applied by Roth et al. (2017) to the exploration of the idea of the 'global brain' analyzing word frequency time-series plots of key social concepts.

The analysis starts with the idea that large-scale content analysis of historical periodicals and books may reveal '*the statistical traces of events and ideas that shaped a remarkable place and period*' (Cristianini, Lansdall-Welfare, and Dato 2018, 139). Following this approach, the source of data is twofold: a physical historical archive, the 'Italian Fashion Archive of Giovanni Battista Giorgini' (GBG Archive), that contains documents of the activity of Giovanni Battista Giorgini for promoting and developing the Italian fashion industry from the first years of the twentieth century; second, three massive online archives which collect digitalized newspapers and books in a long-time span of more than a century. Despite many studies reconstructing the development trajectories of the fashion industry in Italy in the post-war era (Pinchera and Rinallo 2020; Stanfill 2020), there remain few empirical analyses on the topic in existence. In order to develop the research objective, this analysis followed two steps.

In the first step, primary data was collected from the GBG Archive from April 2019 to November 2019. The archive is located at the State Archives of Florence and consists of different documents collected by Giovanni Battista Giorgini – entrepreneur and promoter of the Italian fashion during the 1950s – and his family, from the first decade of the twentieth century to 2001. These documents concern Giorgini's entrepreneurial activities and, in particular, the promotional activities of the Italian fashion industry developed in Italy and around the world. The inventory material consists of over 12,000 records and has been classified in (a) press articles of US and Italian newspapers and magazines, (b) organizational and promotional material, (c) correspondence and (d) graphic material (Gallai 2007).

The first analysis focuses on 199 articles in national and international newspapers published between 1953-1965, belonging to the GBG Archive. The period coincides with the years recognized by literature as crucial for the advent of Made in Italy and the establishment of the Italian fashion industry (Belfanti 2015). Data collected have been useful to trace back events that led toward the establishment of the Italian fashion industry and 'Made in Italy', identifying the factors that contributed most to the official launch of the industry. The titles of the articles have been analyzed through text mining tools in order to identify terms that have the highest frequency. Analysis of word frequency is useful to extract meaningful information from text data (Welbers, Van Atteveldt, and Benoit 2017). Text analysis has been carried out using the *tm package* for text mining of R statistical software. The *tm package* allows the management of textual data importing data from text, handling the corpus and preprocessing the textual records (Abascal-Mena, Lema, and Sèdes 2015; Choi et al. 2015). The most frequently cited term has been visualized through the *Wordcould* package of R software.

The second step involves an N-grams analysis of the frequency of terms related to the fashion industry. An 'N-gram' represents a string used for automated data retrieval (Richey and Taylor 2020). A uni-gram is a string of characters uninterrupted by a space. A 1-gram is represented by one word, a 2-grams is a sequence of two words, and so on (Michel et al. 2011). We have selected four keywords by analyzing the contents of the articles collected from the GBG Archive and the most frequent terms: Italian Fashion, Fashion Show, High Fashion, Buying Offices. For each of N-grams, we have generated a time series of term frequencies from the following online databases:

(1) *The British Newspaper Archive*, that counts 35 million pages of newspapers collected in the British Library collection from 1700 to 2020 (https://www.britishnewspaperarchive.co.uk);

(2) *Newspapers.com*, a large dataset of over 16 thousand historical newspapers from 1700 to 2020 related to 9 countries, United States, England, Ireland, Northern Ireland, Scotland, Wales, Australia, Canada and Panama (https://www.newspapers.com/search);

(3) *Google Books N-gram Viewer*, a search engine based on Google Books that allows us to find out how often a word or more words appear in the set of books published between 1500 and 2008 (https://books.google.com/ngrams);

The databases were chosen according to the possibility to consult a large time-span of the published documentation and our interest in British and US press, the main ones present at the high fashion shows organized by Giorgini. The analysis explores the distribution of the terms over time (1920–2000) in order to identify the peak of the highest frequency of the selected key terms.

4. Results of the analysis

As underlined in the theoretical section, the promotional activities of Giorgini played a central role in supporting the emergence of the fashion industry in the Italian post-war era. National and international press, particularly British and American outlets, significantly contributed to developing a positive image of the emerging sector and realizing a first idea of 'Made in Italy'. This was strictly related to the key narrative of the Italian Renaissance tradition characterized by the key elements of its cultural heritage, artisanal tradition and good taste of the Italian aristocracy (Belfanti 2015).

Considering the importance of the national and international press in promoting the emergence of the fashion industry and Made in Italy, we have analysed the contents of a part of the press materials belonging to the GBG. Archive. Table 2 shows the composition of the collected material present in the Archive and classified by the typology of the document.

Our analysis has focused on Italian and British/US articles representing 79% of the consulted material. These have been analysed through textual analysis in order to identify the words which have the highest frequency within the selected articles.

The textual analysis has involved 132 Italian articles and 67 English articles for a total amount of 199 collected records from 1953 and 1965. Concerning the Italian articles, the total number of analysed words was 1484 while, for English articles, it was 480 words.

Moreover, articles were distinguished between those published by the specialized press and those published by the non-specialised press. Table 3 shows the percentage of articles distinguished based on their publication in specialized or non-specialised magazines.

The non-fashion magazines were the most numerous (about 86%), among the main ones: 'La Nazione', 'The Daily American' and 'Los Angeles Times'. Among the most important sector magazines (about 14%) were: 'Women's Wear Daily (WWD)' and 'Vogue'.

Table 2. Typologies of the analyzed documents in the G.B.G. Archive.

Italian articles	British/US articles	CFMI reports	Press releases	Other	Total
50%	29%	10%	6%	5%	100%

Source: Our elaboration.

Table 3. The percentage of magazines divided between specialized and not specialized.

Magazines	Specialized	Non-specialised
Italian	58%	4%
International	28%	10%
% of Tot.	86%	14%

Source: Our elaboration.

The body under analysis was processed using *tm* package. First, we created a *corpus* from the collected text in order to have a structure on which to make elaborations. Second, the *corpus* was processed in order to eliminate numbers, punctuation, additional spaces and *stopwords*, such as conjunctions, adverbs and articles. We created a 'documents x terms' matrix from which we analysed the frequency of the terms. Finally, the matrix of terms and documents was transformed into a data frame from which a word cloud was generated through the *Wordcould* package. Figures 1 and 2 show the results of the analysis.

Figure 1 shows the textual analysis of the words contained in the articles published by Italian newspapers and magazines. After the cleaning of the *corpus*, the terms analysed were 463.

What emerges from the textual analysis is that the words most used by the Italian press are 'Moda' (fashion), with 12.5% of frequency, followed by 'Firenze' (Florence), with a frequency of 11.2%. It is possible to note that, among the most cited terms, there are 'Palazzo' and 'Pitti', both with a frequency of 4.7% highlighting the relationship with the historical places in which the high fashion shows took place. The textual analysis of Italian articles reveals the relationship between the events of the Italian high fashion shows and the geographical dimension of the city of Florence.

Figure 2 shows the results obtained from the analysis of the titles of the articles published by British and US articles. In the case of the articles in English, after the cleaning of the *corpus*, terms analysed amounted to 216. The word most used by the international press was 'Florence' repeated 26 times and with a frequency of 12.5%, followed by the word 'Fashion' with a frequency percentage equal to 8.8%. It is interesting to note

Words	Number	Frequency
Moda	104	22.4%
Firenze	52	11.2%
Italiana	43	9.3%
Alta	31	6.7%
Palazzo	22	4.7%
Pitti	22	4.7%
Modelli	11	2.4%
Mostra	11	2.4%
Rassegna	10	2.1%
Centro	7	1.1%
Mondo	7	1.1%

Figure 1. Visualization of the most frequent terms in Italian articles.

Words	Number	Frequency
Florence	27	12.5%
Fashion	19	8.8%
Italian	17	7.9%
Italy	14	6.5%
Style	8	3.7%
Fashions	6	2.8%
Rome	6	2.6%
Buyers	5	2.3%
Show	5	2.3%
World	5	2.3%

Figure 2. Visualization of the most frequent terms in British/US articles.

that, in the analysis of the most frequent terms used by international press, 'Rome' had a frequency of 2.6%. This may be due to the importance that the city of Rome had at that time for fashion, due to the presence of important fashion ateliers such as Fabiani, Simonetta, Fontana sisters, etc.

The textual analysis gives some interesting results to analyse the main topic discussed by the national and international press concerning the emergence of the Italian fashion industry and the advent of Made in Italy. However, the analysis has some limitations. First, due to the number of words analysed, the frequency of words is not very high because the analysis was not conducted on the entire text of the articles. Moreover, the material collected in the GBG Archive concerns the articles that the press had produced on Florentine events. Therefore, the centrality of the topics identified is closely related to the content of the archive material.

Precisely for this reason, starting from the analysis of the documents of the GBG Archive, some key terms have been identified and, through an N-grams analysis, the frequency of citations of these terms was observed in international journals, periodicals and books.

Figures 3–6 show the results of the Bi-Gram analysis devoted to identifying the time series of the frequency of four keywords identified by a content analysis of the articles collected by the Giorgini Archive. The keywords analyzed were: 'Italian Fashion', 'Fashion Show', 'High Fashion' and 'Buying Offices'. The timespan reached from 1920, when Giorgini started his entrepreneurial activities, and 2000 to evaluate the possible development of the related aspects to the Italian fashion industry from a long-term perspective. The analysis reveals an increasing debate by the Italian and international press after the 1950s.

Figures 3 and 4 show the time series of the frequency of the keywords 'Italian Fashion' and 'High fashion' within the three selected databases.

The analysis shows an increasing trend starting from the end of 40s and the beginning of 50s for both terms in all the publications stored in the databases. This suggests the growth of the interest of public opinion in the years immediately preceding the launch of the first Italian fashion show in Florence.

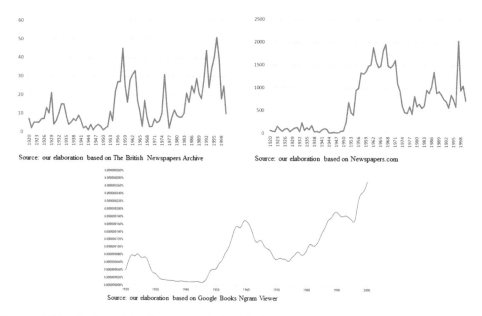

Figure 3. Visualization of the N-grams analysis of 'Italian Fashion'.

Those years coincided with a post-war era that placed the relationship between Europe and the United States at the centre of the reconstruction. Furthermore, in previous years, some Italian designers had already started their careers and were appreciated internationally (Muzzarelli 2011). This is the case of the Gucci brand founded in Florence in 1921 where it opened its first stores, soon to expand to the rest of Italy with the opening of the first Gucci boutique in Rome in 1938 and, subsequently, abroad in New York in 1953 and

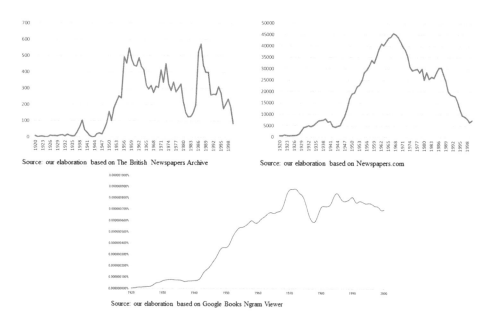

Figure 4. Visualization of the N-grams analysis of 'High fashion'.

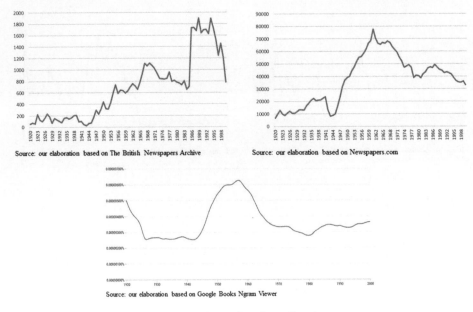

Figure 5. Visualization of the N-grams analysis of 'Fashion Show'.

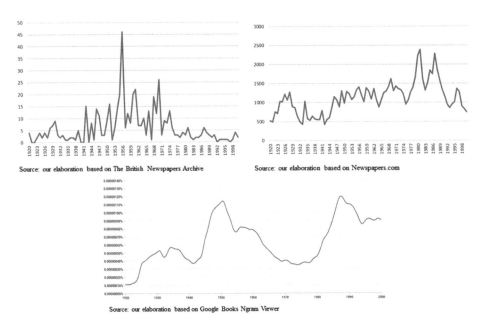

Figure 6. Visualization of the N-grams analysis of 'Buying Offices'.

London in 1961 (Oh and Rugman 2006). A further case was the shoe designer Salvatore Ferragamo who founded his company in Florence in 1927, opening his first boutique in 1938. However, its artisanal capabilities and style were already known by American buyers (Som and Blanckaert 2015). Other designers were Emilio Pucci, who opened his first boutique in Capri in 1949 but who had already been noticed by the American press when the ski suit he designed was photographed by a *Harper's Bazaar* magazine reporter (Muzzarelli 2011). Some Italian tailoring companies were also highly appreciated for the production of high fashion garments. Among these, the Fontana sisters, who opened an atelier in Rome in 1943 and dressed the wedding of Hollywood celebrities in 1949 (Gundle 2002).

Figure 5, instead, shows the trend of the key term 'Fashion Show'. Even in this case, despite the word already being a topic in the international debate, it is possible to observe an increasing trend starting from around 1945. In those years, Giorgini had consolidated his activities. It was in those years, precisely in 1947, that he contributed to the organization of the 'Italy at Work' exhibition, at the Museum of Modern Art in Chicago. The events of those years would form the background for the organization of high fashion shows in Italy (Fadigati 2018).

Finally, Figure 6 shows the distribution of the term 'Buying Offices' among newspapers, magazines and books from 1920 to 2000. Although the activity of the buying offices began in the 1920s, an increasing frequency of this term is recorded around the 1950s. In particular, data of The British Newspaper Archive show a peak of publications containing the term between 1953 and 1959 and data from Google Books Ngram a peak in 1950. In those years, the buying offices played a crucial role in the development of the Italian fashion industry and its internationalization being the mediators between the fashion houses and foreign buyers.

5. Conclusions

This article focused on the establishment and evolution of the Italian fashion industry and 'Made in Italy'. It aimed to investigate if and how the emergence of the Italian fashion industry and the concept of 'Made in Italy' was influenced by the Italian high fashion shows organized in Florence in 1951–1967 by Giovanni Battista Giorgini.

After an exploration of the concept of 'Made in Italy' and its relationship with the fashion industry through an analysis of the literature, the article described the context and the events that led to the organization of the first Italian high fashion show in Florence, on 12 February 1951. Such an event is largely recognized by scholars of the history of fashion as a crucial event for the establishment of the Italian fashion industry and the development of the identity of 'Made in Italy'. Based on this hypothesis, the analysis developed in the article tested if a relationship existed between the organization of high fashion shows in Florence and the establishment of Italian fashion and 'Made in Italy'.

In order to do that, two different analyses were developed. First, the titles of 199 articles published by Italian, British and US newspapers and magazines between 1953 and 1965 and collected from the GBG Archive were analysed to find the most cited terms by the national and international press for describing the advent of the Italian fashion industry in the period considered. Second, a Bi-gram analysis of four key terms showed their frequency in international digitalized periodicals, magazines and books published from 1920 to 2000.

The theoretical contribution of the article is multiple. First, it has empirically tested a hypothesis debated in the literature of fashion history showing an existing correlation between the promotional strategy operated by Giovanni Battista Giorgini for enhancing the Italian fashion industry, 'Made in Italy' and, more in general,

Italian culture, and its recognition and appreciation abroad. The textual and N-gram analyses confirm the importance of Giovanni Battista Giorgini as a key actor for the emergence of a unitary identity for fashion and for establishing the foundations of what would be a highly internationalized and competitive sector in the future.

Second, the analyses highlight the centrality of the role of the city of Florence in those years. This is mainly due to the presence of the textile industry, with which the nascent fashion industry had relationships, the artisan tradition and the emergence of the fashion *boutique*. However, a crucial role was also played by the cultural heritage that acted as an attractor for foreign buyers and a vehicle for promoting Italian history and beauty. Although the geography of fashion has changed in Italy and new fashion capitals have subsequently emerged, in particular, with the strategic role of Milan (D'Ovidio 2015), some features still make the city of Florence attractive both for the localization of important fashion houses, skilled workers and designers and for the tourist flows related to fashion (Lazzeretti, Capone, and Casadei 2017). This suggests that the characteristics of places together with locally embedded resources played a crucial role in the development of the fashion sector and in the affirmation of the idea of 'Made in Italy'.

Third, a further contribution from the analysis is represented by the proposed methodology and the original data sources. On the one hand, the contents of the GBG Archive have been poorly explored. A large part of the documents still needs to be cataloged. This may represent a source of precious information for tracing back origins and development trajectories of the Italian fashion sector and for reconstructing the international commercial dynamics developed in those years. On the other hand, large databases containing texts covering such a large time, as Google Books and others, can be valuable sources of data for original analyses. Data of this kind have been used in the context of language studies, however, their potential in economic studies is still unexplored. On this front, the large datasets of textual corpora can give insights into exploring economic dynamics and language but also in the study of economic actors and decision-making processes. An added value of textual analysis is represented by the possibility of applying new quantitative approaches to issues that were previously tackled merely through descriptive methodologies (Gutmann, Merchant, and Roberts 2018).

The case analysed shows that through documents from the past it is possible to contribute to reconstructing interrelationships between places, actors, assets and the development of economic trajectories. Concerning 'Made in Italy' sectors, these dynamics of the past should be kept in mind and carefully considered also in current studies to avoid the moving from 'Made in Italy' to 'Made by Italy' (Giumelli 2016). Interesting future research is to understand how the values, identity and cultural heritage associated with the idea of 'Made in Italy' have evolved and transformed with the entry into international markets and the emergence of the new competitors of *fast fashion* (*pronto moda*) within a global scenario.

Notes

1. Documentation of the Italian Fashion Archive of Giovanni Battista Giorgini, State Archives of Florence, Album 42 n. 82, article by Mattina N., Florence new capital of world thanks to G.B. Giorgini, The Italian News, 1959.

2. Documentation of the Italian Fashion Archive of Giovanni Battista Giorgini, State Archive of Florence, Album 44, correspondence to the Italian Embassy, addressed to the Italian Fashion Authority of Turin, to the Roman High Fashion Center in Rome and to the Center for Italian Fashion in Florence, January 25, 1961.
3. Documentation of the Italian Fashion Archive of Giovanni Battista Giorgini, State Archives of Florence, Album 30, article by Austin J., interview with Giovanni Battista Giorgini, The father of fashion, February, 1960.

Acknowledgment

Authors express their gratitude to Dr. Neri Fadigati for the concession to consult and collect the data from 'Italian Fashion Archive of Giovanni Battista Giorgini', held in the State Archive of Florence, and to Dr. Federica Pennacchio for the collection of the data and some data elaboration.

Disclosure statement

No potential conflict of interest was reported by the authors.

ORCID

Luciana Lazzeretti http://orcid.org/0000-0002-9759-2289
Stefania Oliva http://orcid.org/0000-0003-2933-4795

References

Abascal-Mena, R., R. Lema, and F. Sèdes. 2015. "Detecting Sociosemantic Communities by Applying Social Network Analysis in Tweets." *Social Network Analysis and Mining* 5 (1): 38. doi:10.1007/s13278-015-0280-2.
Acuti, D., V. Mazzoli, R. Donvito, and P. Chan. 2018. "An Instagram Content Analysis for City Branding in London and Florence." *Journal of Global Fashion Marketing* 9 (3): 185–204. doi:10.1080/20932685.2018.1463859.
Agrawal, J., and W. Kamakura. 1999. "Country of Origin: A Competitive Advantage?" *International Journal of Research in Marketing* 16 (4): 255–267. doi:10.1016/S0167-8116 (99)00017-8.
Aiello, G., R. Donvito, L. Grazzini, C. Halliburton, B. Wagner, J. Wilson, B. Godey, D. Pederzoli, and I. Shokola. 2015. "An International Comparison of 'Made in Italy' in the Fashion, Furniture and Food Sectors: An Observational Research Study in France, Russia and The United Kingdom." *Journal of Global Fashion Marketing* 6 (2): 136–149. doi:10.1080/20932685.2015. 984822.
Amighini, A., and R. Rabellotti. 2006. "How Do Italian Footwear Industrial Districts Face Globalization?" *European Planning Studies* 14 (4): 485–502. doi:10.1080/09654310500421105.
Asheim, B., P. Cooke, and R. Martin. 2006. "The Rise of the Cluster Concept in Regional Analysis and Policy." In *Clusters and Regional Development: Critical Reflections and Explorations*, edited by Björn Asheim, Philip Cooke, and Ron Martin, 1–29. London: Routledge.
Balicco, D. 2015. "Introduzione. Il Made in Italy e la cultura italiana contemporanea." In *Made in Italy e cultura. Indagine sull'identità italiana contemporanea*, edited by D. Balicco, 7–15. Palermo: G. B. Palumbo & C. Editore.
Becattini, G. 1998. *Distretti industriali e made in Italy: le basi socioculturali del nostro sviluppo economico*. Torino: Bollati Boringhieri.
Belfanti, C. 2015. "Renaissance and 'Made in Italy': Marketing Italian Fashion Through History (1949–1952)." *Journal of Modern Italian Studies* 20 (1): 53–66. doi:10.1080/1354571X.2014. 973154.

Bellini, N., and C. Pasquinelli. 2016. "Urban Brandscape as Value Ecosystem: The Cultural Destination Strategy of Fashion Brands." *Place Branding and Public Diplomacy* 12 (1): 5–16. doi:10.1057/pb.2015.21.

Bertoli, G. 2013. *International Marketing and the Country of Origin Effect: the Global Impact of 'Made in Italy'*. Cheltenham: Edward Elgar Publishing.

Brusco, S., and S. Paba. 2014. *Towards a History of the Italian Industrial Districts from the End of World War II to the Nineties*. DEMB Working Paper Series (N. 37). University of Modena and Reggio Emilia.

Calanca, D., and C. Capalbo. 2018. "Introductory Essay. Fashion and Cultural Heritage." *ZoneModa Journal* 8 (1): V–XXVII. doi:10.6092/issn.2611-0563/8420.

Capone, F., and L. Lazzeretti. 2016. "Fashion and City Branding: An Analysis of the Perception of Florence as a Fashion City." *Journal of Global Fashion Marketing* 7 (3): 166–180. doi:10.1080/20932685.2016.1166715.

Casadei, P. 2018. "Unpicking the Fashion City: Theoretical Issues and Ideal Types. An Empirical Analysis of London." PhD thesis., University of Trento.

Choi, J., D. Jang, S. Jun, and S. Park. 2015. "A Predictive Model of Technology Transfer Using Patent Analysis." *Sustainability* 7 (12): 16175–16195. doi:10.3390/su71215809.

Corbellini, E., and S. Saviolo. 2004. *La scommessa del made in Italy: e il futuro della moda italiana*. Milano: Etas.

Cristianini, N., T. Lansdall-Welfare, and G. Dato. 2018. "Large-Scale Content Analysis of Historical Newspapers in the Town of Gorizia 1873–1914." *Historical Methods: A Journal of Quantitative and Interdisciplinary History* 51 (3): 139–164. doi:10.1080/01615440.2018.1443862.

Curzio, A. Q., and M. Fortis, eds. 2000. *Made in Italy oltre il duemila*. (Vol. 1). Bologna: Il Mulino.

D'Ovidio, M. 2015. "The Field of Fashion Production in Milan: A Theoretical Discussion and an Empirical Investigation." *City, Culture and Society* 6 (2): 1–8. doi:10.1016/j.ccs.2015.02.002.

Di Maria, E., and V. Finotto. 2008. "Communities of Consumption and Made in Italy." *Industry and Innovation* 15 (2): 179–197. doi:10.1080/13662710801954583.

Fadigati, N. 2018. "Giovanni Battista Giorgini, la famiglia, il contributo alla nascita del Made in Italy, le fonti archivistiche." *ZoneModa Journal* 8 (1): 1–15. doi:10.6092/issn.2611-0563/8385.

Fortis, M. 2016. *Pillars of the Italian Economy*. Cham: Springer International Publishing Switzerland.

Gallai, M. 2007. *Il riordinamento e l'inventariazione dell'Archivio della Moda Italiana di Giovan Battista Giorgini: resoconto del primo anno di lavoro*. Firenze: Archivio di Stato di Firenze.

Garrison, E. 2012. "The Italian Reconstruction and Post-War Fashions." *Young Historians Conference, Paper 8*.

Giumelli, E. 2016. "The Meaning of the Made in Italy Changes in a Changing World." *Italian Sociological Review* 6 (2): 241–263. doi:10.13136/isr.v6i2.133.

Gundle, S. 2002. "Hollywood Glamour and Mass Consumption in Postwar Italy." *Journal of Cold War Studies* 4 (3): 95–118. doi:10.1162/152039702320201085.

Gutmann, M., E. Merchant, and E. Roberts. 2018. "'Big Data' in Economic History." *The Journal of Economic History* 78 (1): 268. doi:10.1017/S0022050718000177.

Lansdall-Welfare, T., S. Sudhahar, J. Thompson, J. Lewis, F. Team, and N. Cristianini. 2017. "Content Analysis of 150 Years of British Periodicals." *Proceedings of the National Academy of Sciences* 114 (4): E457–E465. doi:10.1073/pnas.1606380114.

Lavanga, M. 2018. "The Role of Pitti Uomo Trade Fair in the Menswear Fashion Industry." In *The Fashion Forecasters: A Hidden History of Color and Trend Prediction*, edited by R. Blaszczyk, and B. Wubs, 191–209. London: Bloomsbury Academic Publishing.

Lazzeretti, L., and F. Capone. 2015. "Narrow or Broad Definition of Cultural and Creative Industries: Evidence From Tuscany, Italy." *International Journal of Cultural and Creative Industries* 2 (2): 4–19.

Lazzeretti, L., and F. Capone. 2020. "The Role of Education in the Entrepreneurial Ecosystem: The Case of 'Made in Italy Tuscany Academy' in the Florence Fashion City." *International Journal of Entrepreneurship and Small Business* 40 (2): 270–290. doi:10.1504/IJESB.2020.107753.

Lazzeretti, L., F. Capone, and P. Casadei. 2017. "The Role of Fashion for Tourism: An Analysis of Florence as a Manufacturing Fashion City and Beyond." In *Tourism in the City*, edited by Nicola Bellini, and Cecilia Pasquinelli, 207–220. Cham: Springer.

Lazzeretti, L., and S. Oliva. 2018. "Rethinking City Transformation: Florence From Art City to Creative Fashion City." *European Planning Studies* 26 (9): 1856–1873. doi:10.1080/09654313.2018.1478951.

Merlo, E., and F. Polese. 2006. "Turning Fashion Into Business: The Emergence of Milan as an International Fashion Hub." *Business History Review*, 415–447. doi:10.1017/S0007680500035856.

Michel, J., Y. Shen, A. Aiden, A. Veres, M. Gray, J. Pickett, D. Hoiberg, et al. 2011. "Quantitative Analysis of Culture Using Millions of Digitized Books." *Science* 331 (6014): 176–182. doi:10.1126/science.1199644.

Muzzarelli, M. 2011. *Breve Storia Della Moda in Italia*. Bologna: il Mulino.

Oh, C., and A. Rugman. 2006. "Regional Sales of Multinationals in the World Cosmetics Industry." *European Management Journal* 24 (2-3): 163–173. doi:10.1016/j.emj.2006.03.006.

Pagliai, L. 2011. *Florence at the Time of Giovanni Battista Giorgini, Arts, Craft and Fashion in Italy and the United States*. Firenze: Edifir.

Pagliai, L. 2018. "Febbraio 1951: Giovanni Battista Giorgini Creatore a Firenze dell'Alta Moda e del Made in Italy." *Portale Storia di Firenze*, 1–3.

Paris, I. 2010. "Fashion as a System: Changes in Demand as the Basis for the Establishment of the Italian Fashion System (1960—1970)." *Enterprise & Society* 11 (3): 524–559. doi:10.1017/S1467222700009289.

Paulicelli, E. 2014. "Fashion: The Cultural Economy of Made in Italy." *Fashion Practice* 6 (2): 155–174. doi:10.2752/175693814X14035303880597.

Pinchera, V. 2009. *La moda in Italia e in Toscana. Dalle origini alla globalizzazione*. Venezia: Marsilio Editori.

Pinchera, V., and D. Rinallo. 2020. "The Emergence of Italy as a Fashion Country: Nation Branding and Collective Meaning Creation at Florence's Fashion Shows (1951–1965)." *Business History* 62 (1): 151–178. doi:10.1080/00076791.2017.1332593.

Pucci, T., C. Simoni, and L. Zanni. 2013. "Country of Origin Effect, Brand Image and Retail Management for the Exploitation of 'Made in Italy'in China." In *International Marketing and the Country of Origin Effect*, edited by Giuseppe Bertoli, and Riccardo Resciniti, 154–178. Cheltenham: Edward Elgar Publishing.

Ranfagni, S., B. Camiciottoli, and M. Faraoni. 2016. "How to Measure Alignment in Perceptions of Brand Personality Within Online Communities: Interdisciplinary Insights." *Journal of Interactive Marketing* 35: 70–85. doi:10.1016/j.intmar.2015.12.004.

Reinach, S. 2014. "Italian Fashion: The Metamorphosis of a Cultural Industry." In *Made in Italy: Re-Thinking a Century of Italian Design*, edited by G. Lees-Maffei, and K. Fallan, 239–251. London: Bloomsbury.

Reinach, S. 2015. "The Meaning of 'Made in Italy' in Fashion." *Craft+ Design Enquiry* 7: 135–150.

Richey, S., and J. Taylor. 2020. "Google Books Ngrams and Political Science: Two Validity Tests for a Novel Data Source." *PS: Political Science & Politics* 53 (1): 72–77. doi:10.1017/S1049096519001318.

Roth, S., C. Clark, N. Trofimov, A. Mkrtichyan, M. Heidingsfelder, L. Appignanesi, M. Pérez-Valls, J. Berkel, and J. Kaivo-oja. 2017. "Futures of a Distributed Memory. A Global Brain Wave Measurement (1800–2000)." *Technological Forecasting and Social Change* 118: 307–323. doi:10.1016/j.techfore.2017.02.031.

Santagata, W. 2009. *White Paper on Creativity. Towards an Italian Model of Development*. San Francisco: Creative Commons Attribution.

Santagata, W. 2010. *The Culture Factory: Creativity and the Production of Culture*. Verlag Berlin Heidelberg: Springer Science & Business Media.

Som, A., and C. Blanckaert. 2015. *The Road to Luxury: The Evolution, Markets, and Strategies of Luxury Brand Management*. Singapore: John Wiley & Sons.

Stanfill, S. 2020. "Anonymous Tastemakers: The Role of American Buyers in Establishing an Italian Fashion Industry, 1950–55." In *European Fashion*, edited by Regina Lee Blaszczyk, and Véronique Pouillard, 146–170. Manchester: Manchester University Press.

Vergani, G. 1992. *La Sala Bianca: nascita della Moda italiana*. Milano: Electa.

Welbers, K., W. Van Atteveldt, and K. Benoit. 2017. "Text Analysis in R." *Communication Methods and Measures* 11 (4): 245–265. doi:10.1080/19312458.2017.1387238.

Wenzel, M., and M. Will. 2019. "The Communicative Constitution of Academic Fields in the Digital Age: The Case of CSR." *Technological Forecasting and Social Change* 146: 517–533. doi:10.1016/j.techfore.2019.05.006.

White, N. 2000. *Reconstructing Italian Fashion: America and the Development of the Italian Fashion Industry*. Oxford: Berg Pub Limited.

Zegna, A. 2015. "Stile italiano e mercato internazionale. Il caso Zegna (interview by Balicco D.)." In *Made in Italy e cultura. Indagine sull'identità italiana contemporanea*, edited by D. Balicco, 86–91. Palermo: G. B. Palumbo, and C. Editore.

Path renewal dynamics in the Kyoto kimono cluster: how to revitalize cultural heritage through digitalization

Silvia Rita Sedita and Tamane Ozeki

ABSTRACT
The digitalization of cultural heritage is crucial for revamping the creative and cultural sectors during a period of stagnation. This work is about the revitalization of the Kyoto kimono cluster through digitalization, which initiated a new exaptive development path for a declining cluster. A growing community of economic geographers and regional scientists has begun to discuss regional path development beyond related and unrelated diversification. We focus on path renewal, which involves major change of a path into a new direction based on new technologies or organizational innovations. Existing knowledge and skills in a region are combined in new ways and may be linked to relevant extra-regional knowledge to provide new knowledge, enabling innovation and entrepreneurship in the region. The process encompasses the intentional and serendipitous actions of individual entrepreneurs (firm-level) and networks of systemic configurations (system-level). A narrative approach is used to capture the path renewal dynamics in the Kyoto kimono cluster.

1. Introduction

This work explores how the digitalization of cultural heritage might be a way to revitalize a declining manufacturing cluster through path renewal processes based on exaptive patterns. Overall, our study provides food for thought for entrepreneurs and policy makers struggling to find ways to improve the economic performance of places that suffer from market stagnation and offers a novel contribution to the literature on territorial resilience.

The resilience of places has recently become a hot topic for research (Sedita, De Noni, and Pilotti 2017; Hassink 2017; Rocchetta et al. 2021). Natural disasters, pandemic diseases, and financial crises have undermined the economic development of territories and revealed the need for new growth models. Accordingly, new path development (MacKinnon et al. 2019; Martin 2010; Martin and Sunley 2006; Pike et al. 2016), city transformation (Glaeser 2011; Cooke, Parrilli, and Curbelo 2012; Sunley, Martin, and Tyler 2017; Simmie 2017), and cluster evolution (Menzel and Fornahl 2010; Belussi and Sedita 2009) have become important subjects of analysis. In particular, a stream of literature on culture-driven economic development and the resilience capacity of culture has emerged (Lazzeretti 2009; Lazzeretti and Oliva 2018).

This work offers a new perspective on the digitalization of cultural heritage and its potential for creating new regional path development trajectories (Tödtling and Trippl 2013; Isaksen 2015; Isaksen and Trippl 2016; Grillitsch, Asheim, and Trippl 2018; Isaksen, Tödtling, and Trippl 2018). It draws on previous research on regional development and exaptation to offer a possible way forward to renew localized traditional industries through cross-fertilization (Lazzeretti 2009) and exaptive pathways (Sedita 2012). Knowledge recombination is at the heart of the renewal process presented in this article. As Nelson and Winter (1982, 130) put it, 'the creation of any sort of novelty in art, science, or practical life [...] consists to a substantial extent of a recombination of conceptual and physical materials that were previously in existence.' In this work, we focus mainly on the recombination of symbolic knowledge, which is often embedded in local culture, and synthetic knowledge, which is embodied in local handcrafters (Asheim and Gertler 2005; Asheim 2007; Asheim, Boschma, and Cooke 2011). The medium through which the renewal process occurs is digital technology.

The object of our analysis is the kimono cluster in Kyoto, Japan. Our exploration of the modalities and effects of the digitalization of cultural heritage in the development of the Kyoto kimono cluster stimulates reflection on the preconditions for path renewal processes driven by the creative capacity of culture (Lazzeretti 2009) and suggests ways of revitalizing declining clusters in other regions, including regions outside Japan. A narrative research method was used for this study, which involved collecting information from both primary and secondary sources (Andrews, Squire, and Tamboukou 2013). The storytelling is guided by theories of regional development and exaptation, the combination of which enables us to explain the present transformation of the kimono cluster in Kyoto. The analysis has the potential for replication in other contexts, where cultural heritage is at risk of extinction and traditional industries are suffering due to a lack of action to restructure local production systems that are trapped in lock-in processes.

The work is structured as follows. Section 2 presents the theoretical background, Section 3 introduces the research design, Section 4 presents the empirical setting of the analysis, Section 5, after illustrating three case studies, provides a synthesis of the lessons learned and an interpretative framework of key drivers for path transformation. Section 6 offers some concluding remarks.

2. Theoretical background

This work departs, on the one hand, from the theoretical debate on regional path development and how existing industries, capabilities, and resources can influence path renewal and, on the other hand, from the concept of exaptation, which is here considered a specific driver of regional path renewal. It addresses the following research question: How does exaptation favour path renewal in cultural industries?

A growing community of economic geographers and regional scientists has become interested in regional development based on related variety and regional branching (Frenken and Boschma 2007; Frenken and Boschma 2007), focusing mainly on regional diversification patterns (Boschma 2015). There is general agreement that diversity is an important driver of regional development and that related variety is the optimal industrial structure for enabling regions not only to perform better but also to develop more resilience capacities (Boschma 2015). Regional branching is a preferred strategy for stimulating regional growth through smart specialization development policies (Foray 2015). According to the theory of regional branching, new industries and technologies emerge more easily in regions where they are related to preexisting ones (Frenken and Boschma 2007; Boschma and Frenken 2011a, 2011b; Neffke, Henning, and Boschma 2011).

A coherent pool of scholarly contributions has emerged on different types of path development (Tödtling and Trippl 2013; Simmie 2013; Isaksen 2015; Isaksen and Trippl 2016; Grillitsch, Asheim, and Trippl 2018; Isaksen, Tödtling, and Trippl 2018; Chen and Hassink 2020). These contributions stem from the notion of regional path dependence, discussed in detail by Martin and Sunley (2006). In their seminal contribution, the authors suggested the existence of alternative path-dependent regional development trajectories that may be based on positive lock-in phenomena, whereby regions are able to adapt and change over time by drawing on their resource endowments. The adoption of new technologies or new specializations can also generate new paths to move the region forward. Grillitsch, Asheim, and Trippl (2018) provide a systemic conceptualization of types and mechanisms of regional industrial path development, distinguishing between path extension, path upgrading, path importation, path branching, path diversification, and path creation.

Path renewal is a subcategory of path upgrading, which points to development processes triggered by the infusion of new technologies or major organizational changes. Path renewal might involve the growth of new activities and new industries from recombination of existing knowledge and skills in a region, but also from insertion of extra-regional knowledge. Both patterns create new knowledge that enables innovation and entrepreneurship within the region. The process encompasses both intentional and serendipitous actions of individual entrepreneurs (firm-level), as well as networks of systemic configurations (cluster-level) (Isaksen and Jakobsen 2017). Among the local resources responsible for fostering new path development trajectories, culture and creative resources are growing exponentially in importance (Lazzeretti 2009). Lazzeretti and Oliva (2018) offered a clear example of how a city of art (Florence) engaged in path creation by developing new industrial trajectories based on its cultural and creative resources.

The analysis of the microfoundations of new path development trajectories is still in its infancy and deserves scholarly attention (Hassink, Isaksen, and Trippl 2019). Here, we discuss how the concept of exaptation can be considered as a modality through which existing knowledge recombination gives rise to novelty and opportunities for path renewal.

Exaptation is defined as 'characters, evolved for other usages (or for no function at all), and later 'co-opted' for their current role' (Gould and Vrba 1982). A typical example from the field of evolutionary biology is feathers, which likely evolved in baby dinosaurs for thermal insulation and were later co-opted first for camouflage, then for sexual display, and finally for flight (Stettenheim 1976). Exaptation is characterized by a logic of diversification whereby new applications are discovered for existing knowledge or technology (Dew, Sarasvathy, and Venkataraman 2004). We can distinguish between 'technology-based' and 'use-based' exaptations. According to Sedita (2012), technology-based exaptation occurs when a scientific or technological phenomenon is applied in a new context, which may be far from the knowledge domain in which it was discovered; use-based exaptation occurs when the function of artifacts changes as they are used in new contexts. When a technology or an artifact moves from one context to the other, a shift takes place in the knowledge domain of application. By adopting the renowned knowledge bases approach (Asheim and Gertler 2005; Asheim 2007), it is possible to distinguish between three types of knowledge domains: synthetic, analytical, and symbolic. Exaptation patterns reflect the movement of knowledge and technology from one domain to the other. Our work draws on Sedita's (2012) idea of exaptive patterns of creativity through knowledge reuse. She distinguishes between four types of exaptive processes (Figure 1): 1) intra-domain technology-based; 2) intra-domain use-based; 3) inter-domain technology-based; and 4) inter-domain use-based processes. She also illustrates how intangible cultural heritage can be leveraged to realize inter-domain technology-based and use-based exaptations. These exaptations are made possible by the recombination of symbolic knowledge (from cultural heritage) with synthetic or analytical knowledge. Sedita's framework for interpreting regional development aligns with recent reflections by Boschma et al. (2017) on the importance of exaptation as a specific driver of regional development and finds support in the literature on cross-fertilization (Lazzeretti 2009; Lazzeretti, Capone, and Cinti 2010). It is also supported by Asheim, Grillitsch, and Trippl (2017), who argue that the knowledge bases approach is particularly useful for capturing unrelated knowledge combinations.

3. Research design

Our work takes the cluster as the unit of analysis to explore path development processes that combine traditional and modern industries by recombining different knowledge bases. Inspired by Lazzeretti and Oliva (2018), we combine an actor-based approach with a systems approach to investigate how path renewal might occur in a geographical area characterized by an abundance of embedded cultural resources.

		Knowledge base	
		Intra-domain	Inter-domain
Nature of exaptation	Technology-based	Intra-domain technology-based exaptations ▪synthetic ▪analytical	Inter-domain technology-based exaptations ▪synthetic-analytical ▪synthetic-symbolic ▪analytical-symbolic
	Use-based	Intra-domain use-based exaptations ▪synthetic ▪analytical ▪symbolic	Inter-domain use-based exaptations ▪synthetic-analytical ▪synthetic-symbolic ▪analytical-symbolic

Figure 1. Exaptation taxonomy. Source: Sedita (2012).

From a methodological point of view, our goal is that of theory building from an in-depth qualitative case study (Eisenhardt 1989; Eisenhardt and Graebner 2007). In particular, we adopt a narrative approach to case study research (Andrews, Squire, and Tamboukou 2013; Lewis and Adeney 2014). In recent decades, narrative approaches to analysis have attracted interest among scholars in the human and social sciences (Moen 2006). One of the main characteristics of narrative research is the process of collaboration between the researcher and her or his research subjects. With this approach, the research subject is regarded as a collaborator rather than an informant guided by the agenda of the researcher (Altork 1998). Following the case study tradition, we collected relevant information from multiple data sources, including primary and secondary data (Yin 2009). The primary data are from in-depth interviews conducted by one of the authors between February 2019 and April 2021 with qualified informants operating in Kyoto's kimono cluster and who are involved in the digitalization of cultural heritage. In the interest of privacy protection, their names are not disclosed. Interviews were conducted face to face when possible and through digital media during the COVID-19 pandemic period. We contacted informants multiple times to obtain adequate responses to new questions raised during the theory-building process. The secondary data are from the websites of companies and professional associations, relevant television programmes, the 2020 kimono industry yearbook, the Teikoku Databank, the Imperial Data Bank, and relevant books and reports on digital archives and traditional craftworks in Japan.

We decided to analyze in detail three family businesses that key informants had identified as exemplifying the transformation of the kimono cluster: Chiso, Yunosuke Kawabe, and Hosoo. When discussing the kimono industry in Kyoto, it is impossible not to mention Chiso, a multigenerational family business and one of the most famous kimono manufacturers, which dates back to the Muromachi period (1336–1573). Traditionally, the prestige of a kimono is linked to the name of the artisan and the designer rather than the final producer; the only successful exception is Chiso. Today, Chiso uses digital technology to keep the business alive and to reduce its production costs. The stories of Yunosuke Kawabe and Hosoo are intertwined due to their participation in the digital archive initiative, which was launched by the Kyoto City Government in 2000. They represent two cases where digital technologies have been adopted to create artifacts inspired by the kimono tradition in different sectors.

4. The rise and decline of the Kyoto kimono cluster

Over time, the kimono became the recognized symbol of Japanese apparel and one of the most powerful vehicles for communicating traditional Japanese values. Kyoto had maintained its leading position as a kimono production centre by producing the latest fashion patterns and refining certain finishing skills, particularly dyeing, painting, and embroidery. Kyoto is the home of innovation in *yuzen*-dyed kimonos, which are hand-painted kimonos dyed with resist paste.[1]

Kyoto's link to textiles can be traced back to the Kofun period (250–538 CE), when a Korean named Hata and his clan of silk weavers settled on the Kyoto plain. Kimono businesses are typically traditional manufacturers. Most factories are small and run by families because special techniques are needed to weave and draw unique designs on the kimonos (Fujitsuka 2005). Practice is crucial in the transmission of Japanese culture. The traditional method of teaching traditional arts is through mimicry and repetition. This ritualistic training process is referred to as kata (Hall 2020). The master artisan transfers tacit knowledge to the learner through practice, which is learned by repeated trial and error mechanisms. In Western terms, this form of learning is known as 'vicarious learning' (Manz and Sims Jr 1981). This form of imitative learning is typical of industrial districts (Belussi 1999).

In the inner city of Kyoto, kimono factories are concentrated in two areas: the Nishijin[2] district (a historical weaving centre) and the western part of the central area (where *yuzen* dyeing factories are located). Both areas are integrated industrial-residential areas, where small factories have accumulated in accordance with the typical Marshallian industrial district (Becattini 2017). There is a substantial division of labour, since it is unusual for one company to complete all aspects of the production process. The kimono manufacturing process consists of around 20 steps leading to the completion of the final product, and this process is divided among many artisans. Thus, the complex system of kimono production is populated by a variety of actors: industry associations, wholesalers, weavers, dyers, finishers, and retailers. The first weavers' guild was established in the city during the Heian period (794–1185). Later, thanks to the patronage of shoguns such as Toyotomi Hideyoshi (1536–1598) and the increasing wealth of the merchant class in the Edo period (1600–1868), textile production experienced a boom in production and sales. At the beginning of the eighteenth century, the Kyoto kimono industry had an estimated 7,000 weaving machines and 10,000 employees (Nakaoka et al. 1988).

In the 1970s, Japanese women began to wear more European-style garments for daily and casual wear. Kimonos began to be worn more as ceremonial or formal wear (Franck 2015). The market for kimonos was worth 296 billion yen in 2012 (Yano Research Institute 2013, 15), having fallen from a peak of 1,800 billion yen in 1981 (METI-Kansai Bureau of Economy, Trade and Industry 2009, 3). Yoshida (2013) argued that kimono and kimono-related industries declined not only because of consumer lifestyle changes but also because producers decided to shift production to the higher price range in the market. This strategy resulted in a reduced demand for kimonos, which began to be worn only by wealthier people for special occasions (Yoshida 2013, 435). In the face of demands for Western-style clothes, the kimono weaving industry shifted its production from the popular kimono to the luxury kimono and obi for women (Hashino 2015). As the socio-economic landscape of Japanese society changed, the domestic market for luxury kimonos has steadily shrunk, causing many factories to close. The number of firms in the cluster decreased dramatically, and kimono companies facing financial difficulties began to sell properties. Many young people and white collar workers moved to the district from inner city areas to live in new condominiums built where the kimono factories had previously stood, and the district became gentrified (Fujitsuka 1992) Figure 2.

5. Mapping the transition from tradition to modernity

5.1 Revisiting tradition for the next generation: the case of Chiso

Chiso Co., Ltd. is a traditional Japanese textile producer. Founded in 1555, it is one of the oldest *yuzen* dyeing companies in the Nishijin district of Kyoto. It produces many styles of kimono, and its customers include members of the royal family. The company has

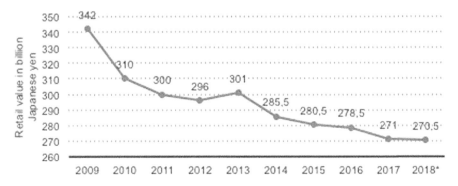

Figure 2. Retail value of the domestic kimono market in Japan from 2009 to 2018 (in billion Japanese yen). Our elaboration from Yano Research; ID 696682.

demonstrated a clear capacity for resilience by investing in marketing activities to reach customers more effectively and tap into new market segments, such as the critical millennial market.

All around Japan, kimonos are sold in department stores, and Kyoto is no exception. Customers considering the purchase of a kimono will most likely go to their local department store. However, the display capacity of department stores is limited, making it difficult to communicate the true value of Chiso's products. To increase its brand awareness and loyalty through more effective marketing of the Chiso heritage, Chiso decided to open a spectacular flagship store in Kyoto. A renowned architect was commissioned to devise a display of Chiso's kimonos that not only presented the kimonos but also conveyed the beauty of kimonos. The shopping experience was then improved by giving customers the option of customizing kimonos. A pool of artisans, who are not trained artists but are trained on the job to reproduce the styles and models typical of the Chiso tradition, guarantees the company's production capacity, and all its products are labelled 'Made in Kyoto'. Moreover, each year the company launches a theme for its kimono designs. In 2020, the theme was 'View from the Window,' representing garden scenery (including not only traditional Japanese views, but also Western landscapes) seen from window frames. The theme for 2021 is 'Kyou Ka Sui Getsu' (Mirror Flower Water Moon). New products are launched every six months, but the theme holds for a year. Notwithstanding the quality of the products and the investment in increasing the value of the brand, Chiso, like other producers, has suffered due to a decline in domestic demand for kimonos, which are largely limited to purchases for special occasions, such as weddings, Shichi-Go-San[3], and Kanreki celebrations (60th birthday celebrations). The COVID-19 pandemic has worsened the situation due to limitations on wedding ceremonies. To overcome the declining demand for kimonos, Chiso oriented some of its production toward younger generations, implementing more affordable designs, with items ranging from around 400,000 yen to 1,000,000 yen. The company digitalized their designs (although digital design accounts for just a fraction of the numerous weaving and dyeing techniques used) to increase its differentiation ability in terms of colours and patterns and its capacity to customize products and reduce prices. Recently, Chiso has been experimenting with colours associated with the Pokemon character Pikachu to attract millennials. Despite its efforts to attract younger generations, the company does not intend to create mass-produced products through digitalization, and this reflects the ethos of the Kyoto kimono industry, which does not favour mass production. In addition, in 2016, the company created a spin-off, S.Nishimura, which is dedicated to the creative business of Chiso. As its motto, 'innovate tradition,' suggests, the mission of the spin-off is to preserve Japanese historical tradition while supporting a wide range of product development – from textiles to fashion accessories – based on the culture, technique, and designs of kimonos aimed at younger generations.

The case illustrates that substantial investment in marketing and the creation of a dedicated showroom museum have enabled Chiso to preserve its leading position as a kimono maker. At the same time, the creation of a spin-off dedicated to younger generations has extended the product portfolio beyond luxury garments to include digitally manufactured high-quality clothes and accessories.

5.2 From handcraft to digital design: the case of Yunosuke Kawabe

Yunosuke, whose family had been *yuzen* dyers for generations, had been around his father's craftsmanship since birth, learning the orthodox hand-dyed *yuzen*. Learning the technology of hand-dyed is a tacit form of learning, which occurs through observation and practice (*kata*). In essence, Yunosuke absorbed that knowledge from his father in a very natural way. Nevertheless, his dream was to become a graphic designer. His first job was at a graphic design office, where he created content for the advertising industry using Adobe Illustrator software.

However, around 1997, Yunosuke decided to start his own business, and drawing upon the skills and knowledge he had inherited from the family business, he began to produce digital content inspired by the *yuzen* style. Kawabe set up a graphic design studio in his *yuzen* workshop and started creating new *yuzen* patterns using computer graphics. The digitalization process that enables the kimono patterns to be reproduced is based on a sketch drawn on paper, which is scanned and the lines converted into data. This process is similar to that of creating outlines for animations except that digital dyeing with a paintbrush creates uniform colours and combinations of colour arrangements can be changed easily through a single command. Therefore, each pattern can instantly be reproduced in multiple combinations of colours. Digitalization allows for the codification of tacit knowledge that is difficult to replicate and thus contributes to the preservation of cultural heritage.

This process was made possible because Kawabe was born into a family who had been using *yuzen* technology for many generations and had memories and experience of his father's work. Thus, Kawabe's CG Yuzen (computer graphics *yuzen*) is the product of his life experience, and would be difficult for a CG designer without hand-dyed *yuzen* skills to imitate. The combination of a symbolic knowledge base (handcraft) and a synthetic knowledge base (CG) allowed Kawabe to create a completely new product, which, while rooted in tradition, can be used in a multitude of applications in different contexts. In this way, the original artifact is modernized through an exaptive process.

Kawabe's business idea found the support of the Kyoto Digital Archive Research Center (KDARC), which was established in 2000 under the auspices of Kyoto City and the Kyoto Chamber of Commerce and Industry and was aimed at creating new industries through digitalization. Located in the Kyoto City University Town Center, the KDARC has a dedicated area of 880 square metres and includes laboratories, presentation rooms, a salon for industry – academic exchange, and a digital archive studio. Kazuo Inamori, president of the Kyoto Chamber of Commerce and Industry and director and honorary chairman of Kyocera (the global leading manufacturer of advanced ceramics), was appointed chairman of the board. However, the promotion of the digital archive project dates to 1997. It was started in accordance with the Kyoto City Action Plan for the Promotion of Advanced Information Technology established by Kyoto City. In 1998, the Kyoto Digital Archive Promotion Organization was established with the strong cooperation of Kyoto City and the Kyoto Chamber of Commerce and Industry. In December of the same year, the city hosted the Digital Archive Big Bang Kyoto '98 Session V at the Kyoto International Conference Center and vigorously promoted the digital archive business.

Yunosuke developed various products using digital archive technology. For example, in partnership with the Japanese sportswear manufacturer Mizuno, he developed a swimsuit with kimono patterns, which the Japanese synchronized swimming team wore at the 2004 Olympics in Athens. The design was based on a kabuki[4] motif. The Japanese swimmers won silver medals in both the team and duet events. Television broadcasts of the team wearing the swimsuit brought worldwide recognition to *yuzen*. The first encounter between Yunosuke and Mizuno happened during an exhibition funded by the Ministry of International Trade to promote the digital archiving business. As a key actor involved in the protection of the cultural heritage of *yuzen*, Yunosuke received a subsidy of 5 million yen for the development of digital *yuzen*, and Mizuno assigned him the task of releasing a *yuzen*-patterned swimwear design.

Yunosuke brought great visibility to the project due to his knowledge of the advertising industry and his social media presence. He received recognition from both the world of craftsmen (thanks to the reputation of his father, who was certified by the Ministry of Economy, Trade and Industry, as a 'traditional craftsman' and from Kyoto Prefecture as a 'Kyoto master craftsman') and that of CG. His reputation grew to the point that he began to be invited to give lectures for universities and governments, and, increasingly, companies and authorities reverted to him for advice on applying digital *yuzen* in a variety of contexts.

In the Japanese Confucianist worldview, novelty is considered an evolution of tradition. Accordingly, new digital technology exhibitions were held alongside demonstration workshops (factory tours) of Yunosuke's father's *yuzen* dye techniques. This process has also been supported by initiatives promoted by Mr. Isao Kitabayashi, the president of COS Kyoto, a knowledge-intensive business service in charge of revitalizing ancient craftworks, and the founder of Kyoto Design Week, which first took place in 2016 with the objective of empowering creativity in Kyoto through diverse interactions between craftspeople, manufacturing industries, and new technologies. 'Open Factory' is the main highlight of the event-filled week, when factories and studios throughout Kyoto are opened to the public, and anyone who is interested can visit and talk directly with the *Shokunin* ('artisan', in English) to learn about his or her work.

The swimsuit experience signaled a turning point for the *yuzen* design and its cultural heritage; younger generations began wearing not only swimsuits but also kimonos. This resulted in younger Japanese people beginning to recognize the value of their culture. The dissemination of these Japanese-style products is only beginning. In the future, it is expected to yield added value by enriching existing regional resources, lifestyles, and economic activities (Bolstanski and Esquerre, 2017). Unlike a revival of antique products in the form of a collection, this activity has the potential to create a brand-new market.

Kawabe launched *yuzen* on a new stage, that of technology, and is in the process of extending its possibilities to a range of other areas, such as interiors and bookbinding. He also designed a 3-meter tall standing lantern, which was lit on December 31, 2000 for the Lantern Festival commemorating the beginning of the twenty-first century. Oike Street was lined with 250 of these lanterns, which made for an impressive sight.

Kawabe's work can be described as an outstanding embodiment of the combination of a traditional cultural inheritance and new business innovations. It was made possible by the original intuitions of a graphic designer who moved beyond the family business and paved the way for the creation of a new market for symbolic products and by the constant support of local institutions.

5.2 From kimonos to contemporary fabrics: the case of Hosoo

Hosoo is a Kyoto-based textile company, founded in 1688, which specializes in superior quality fabrics for high-end interior and fashion design. Hosoo's history can be traced back to the Kyoto silk industry of the 6th century. Today, the company is renowned for its exceptional skills in traditional Japanese three-dimensional weaving techniques and for applying richly textured Nishijin weaving to contemporary design.

When kimono manufacturing started to decline as a core business of textile companies in Kyoto, Hosoo Masao, whose family ran a business that produced and traded in kimonos and obis in Kyoto, wanted to collect some international experience. As his first job, he joined ITOCHU[5] and was assigned to the textile trade. In 1975, he established a joint venture spanning Italy and Japan, which he managed in Milan, where he lived for four years. However, he never forgot the family business and the Nishijin tradition. In his fourth year in Italy, he was asked to take over the family business, and he decided to promote Nishijin across the world. He maintained his relationship with Italy, and especially with Italian artisans, whose skills in handcrafts he admired and with whom he shared his passion and experience for craft.

When he became president of the Hosoo company in 2000, the business model and the concept of the kimono itself was collapsing. Hosoo Masao believed that something had to be done about the kimono industry. He was among the promoters of a project launched by the Kyoto Chamber of Commerce in 2005 called 'Kyoto Premium,' the objective of which was to enhance the Hosoo brand value and develop new markets for traditional Kyoto crafts. At the same time, Hosoo Masao turned his attention to overseas markets and intensified his presence in markets other than the kimono market, including through collaboration with Italian artisans.

To open up a luxury market using Nishijin-ori technology, Hosoo also exhibited interior design products, including chairs, tapestries, and futon-like beds, every year from 2006 onward at the Maison et Objet, an international trade fair for lifestyle and furniture in Paris. However, sales were not as expected. There were three main reasons for this. The first relates to the capacity to differentiate the original Nishijin product from cheaper imitations. The second, which is connected to the first, is that prices were too high. The third reason is that the width of the kimono was traditionally 38 cm, while the standard fabric width overseas was 150 cm. Therefore, it was technically difficult to satisfy requests from clients abroad. It took two years to develop machines to please the clients, and the market started to expand only a few years after that. Since Nishijin-ori was supplied to the upper class of the time, changing the modalities of kimono production was a risk because it might have resulted in the products being regarded as inferior, which, in Japanese culture, would correspond to an offense against the family honour. Despite the difficulties, beautiful Nishijin textiles have been used for the production of casual clothing.

Peter Marino, an American architect who has designed luxury flagships across the world, discovered the fabrics of Nishijin-ori in 2008 and asked Hosoo to produce their original shaped cloths for interior design, bringing a radical change in the business. This was the origin of Hosoo's fabrics used for Western-style designs and the start of a vast process of product extension and differentiation.

It was in this spirit that Hosoo supplied the luxury fabrics for cushions in the suite rooms and interior fabrics for the restaurants of the luxury Ritz Carlton hotels in Tokyo and Kyoto, which are furnished using elements of Japanese traditional culture and crafts. Hosoo also created the textiles for a new model of the Lexus LS car, launched in November 2020. After four years of trial and error, Hosoo was able to create a special textile for the LS that brilliantly depicted the path of the moon in Nishijin-ori weave, using silver thread and the glittering platinum foil to recreate a band of light floating on the surface of water illuminated by moonlight. Hosoo also began a collaboration with the premium camera brand Leica, creating handmade camera bags and covers that reflected a respect for tradition and craftsmanship.

Since 2020, Hosoo has been conducting research and development in collaboration with the University of Tokyo Graduate School's Interfaculty Initiative in Information Studies, the Yasuaki Kakehi Laboratory, and ZOZO Technologies Inc. to create new textiles that combine beauty with functionality and traditional crafts with cutting-edge technologies. This led to the creation woven textile using artificial intelligence (AI), which allowed the technique of warp-and-weft weaving to be learning through deep learning. Furthermore, by analyzing the genes of silkworms, jellyfish, and other organisms, the research team came up with the idea of using green fluorescence to revolutionize materials. An exemplary case is that of the collaboration with the artist Sputniko, responsible for the installation Transflora, created by simulating a reinterpretation of the kimono made of a fabric created using transgenic luminous silk (obtained by injecting the genes of a coral and luminous jellyfish into silkworm eggs), which was tested in the laboratories of the National Institute of Agrobiological Sciences (NIAS) in Tokyo. In recent years, Panasonic has become interested in developing sophisticated products with traditional designs created by artisans. In 2015, Hosoo collaborated with Panasonic to create a speaker made of Nishijin textile, which is highly conductive and plays sound only when in contact with a stereoscopic fabric. The gold and silver foils embedded into the texture trigger the sensors. It was exhibited at the Milano Salone.

Hosoo believes that technology can be developed as an extension of human physical capabilities and is interested in the relationship between the world of beauty and the world of technology, which are often considered in isolation. His idea is to use textiles as medium to connect humans and technologies, whereby AI and biotechnology discoveries guide new path developments in textile production, and humans lend additional value to the products by leveraging cultural heritage. In accordance with this 'credo,' the Hosoo Gallery on the third floor of the company's flagship store in Kyoto is a kimono showroom. Although it is not open to the public, it preserves the beauty of Japan and houses a vast collection that includes masterpieces of living national treasures and from members of the Japan Crafts Association. The building itself is an artistic product, combining the finest craft architecture with innovative technologies.

Hosoo fabrics are now globally available to furniture manufacturers, architects, interior designers, and fashion designers through the House of Hosoo, the company's showroom and office located in Kyoto, Japan. The list of clients includes Dior; Chanel; Louis Vuitton; Bulgari; Peter Marino's Graff luxury stores around the world; the Hyatt Regency Kyoto Hotel by the Japanese design firm Super Potato; Leica Gion Store; Mikimoto Stores in Japan and China; the fashion brands Thome Brown, Mihara Yasuhiro, Tatras and Noir Kei Ninomiya; and artists Teresita Fernández and Moon Kyungwon. Hosoo has also partnered with the fashion designer Masaya Kushino to produce stage shoes for Lady Gaga.

The case of Hosoo demonstrates the powerful creative capacity of culture in generating new regional path development thanks to the actions of an open-minded entrepreneur, who was able to keep his family business alive through a rejuvenation process. The international experience of the entrepreneur and his international collaborations were crucial for sustaining the process.

5.4 Lessons learned

Kyoto is that rare place, a city in which heritage industries and cutting-edge high-tech industries coexist. On the one hand, there is the ancient Kyoto of Nishijin brocade, *yuzen* dyeing, Kiyomizu pottery, and Kyoto dolls. On the other hand, there is the new Kyoto in which corporations such as Kyocera, Omron, Rohm, and Nintendo are at the leading edge of technology. In the twenty-first century, Japan's strengths and presence might be encapsulated by the twin realms of culture and technology. Japan's immense potential lies in the integration of both of these. The path transformation of the Kyoto kimono cluster has resulted from deliberate and serendipitous actions and situational factors that operate at the firm and system levels, both within and outside the cluster (see Figure 3).

Regarding firm-level agency, the cases presented in this article show that the co-existence in a cluster of visionary entrepreneurs (kimono designers and producers, companies operating in other sectors), start-up founders (specialized in computer graphics), artisans, and artists creates a fertile ground for rethinking regional path development thanks to the innovative matching of different knowledge bases (synthetic and symbolic). At present, 85 traditional companies and 71 ICT companies operate in the arts and crafts industry in Kyoto (source: TEIKOKU DATABANK), which may give rise to future creative projects extending the work already done by Yunosuke Kawabe.

In addition to the mobilization of local resources, the global brands that are customers of Kyoto-based companies represent a strong stimulus for offering new products and solutions derived from the hybridization of Western and Eastern culture. This cultural mix

Firm-level agency	System-level agency
• **Local firm-level agency:** home-grown incumbents (traditional kimono producers, ICT companies, swimwear companies) start-up companies in the ICT and in the design sector • **Non-local firm-level agency:** inflows of MNCs or individuals (skilled experts)	activity undertaken by multiple actors with the aim to transform the (functioning of) cluster • **Local system-level agency:** local actors (design institutes, government) • **Non-local system-level agency:** non-local actors (low-cost competition from China)

Figure 3. Key drivers for path transformation. Source: Our elaboration inspired by Trippl et al. (2020).

results in innovative products that are highly valued in the market, as the case of Hosoo demonstrates.

Research centres located in Tokyo that specialize in AI and advanced materials constitute an external source of analytical knowledge, which is embodied in artistic productions that revitalize the kimono culture, as evidenced by the collaboration between Sputniko, Hosoo, and the NIAS laboratories in Tokyo. Some local entrepreneurs have benefited from professional experience abroad, especially in countries renowned for being leaders in the fashion and cultural industries, such as Italy and France. The absorptive capacity of visionary entrepreneurs has allowed for a cross-fertilization between different concepts of beauty and the creation of innovative products that represent a synthesis between European and Japanese cultures, as in the case of Masao Hosoo.

The transformation process presented in this article is heavily sustained by the institutional setting, where governmental actors, in collaboration with innovative minds such as Yunosuke Kawabe and Masao Hosoo, have supported the digitalization of cultural heritage. In addition, an emergent domestic market composed of millennials who are deeply rooted in tradition but oriented toward a future of digital technologies and low-cost purchasing preferences has motivated companies to create new products and new shopping experiences to fit the tastes of this new market, as in the case of Chiso. In general, considerable public research and development expenses have constantly nurtured the university system, creating opportunities for new discoveries, which have been quickly applied to manufactured products thanks to the strong commitment of academics to technology transfer activities and the establishment of efficient technology transfer offices by a government that firmly believes in the importance of university – industry relationships. At the systems level, as Masao Hosoo noted, the low-cost competition of foreign production, mainly Chinese, has stimulated a rethinking of traditional products, with the consistent maintenance of high-quality standards and a resistance to mass production as a reaction to the market crisis. The risk of conveying the idea that Chinese and Japanese products were equal was crucial in determining the direction of change adopted by traditional craft practitioners.

In sum, it was the interplay between collective decision-making and pioneering individuals and firms that led to the revitalization of the kimono cluster. Private – public partnerships sustained the digitalization of cultural heritage, and the creative thinking of artists, graphic designers, and entrepreneurs allowed for a rejuvenation of the kimono cluster, which was made possible through a series of technology-based exaptation processes.

6. Conclusions

This article tells the story of the revitalization of the Kyoto kimono cluster, which was based on the interplay between private and public initiatives oriented toward the revitalization of cultural heritage through digitalization. A narrative approach is taken to illustrate three actors of change: Chiso, Yunosuke Kawabe, and Hosoo. By examining the three cases, we were able to answer our research question: How does exaptation favour path renewal in cultural industries? Technology-based inter-domain exaptations were responsible for revitalizing the kimono cluster. The digitalization of cultural heritage, sponsored by the government, gave rise to a mushrooming of entrepreneurial activities oriented toward the creation of new products, new shopping experiences, and new entrepreneurial opportunities. Visionary graphic designers and innovative entrepreneurs were able to react to the decline of the kimono cluster, pioneering a regional development based on path renewal.

As this article shows, firm-level and system-level agency, both internal and external to the cluster, created a niche environment (Garud and Karnøe 2001) that provided opportunities for path renewal within the declining cluster.

The symbolic value of the traditional kimono is preserved and revisited thanks to the vitality and strong identity (Lazzeretti 2009) of entrepreneurs, professionals, and policy makers in Kyoto. Through the digitalization process, ancient art might find a place in the development of new artifacts (design-based orientation) or new artistic expressions (art-based orientation) through an inter-domain technology-driven exaptation process. The future may see the revitalization of the traditional kimono and a growth in the number of handcraft kimono companies in the Kyoto cluster. Alternatively, we might expect a boost in computer graphics companies, whose business is centred on the application of CG Yuzen to a variety of new products and installations. The emergence of new digital start-ups might be connected with the introduction of new manufacturers of digitally designed products in the cluster. Renewed worldwide attention to Japanese cultural heritage may attract new players from abroad, generating a multiplication of value.

Research on regional development has indicated the need to identify specific evolutionary trajectories based on local resource endowments that can increase the resilience, innovativeness, and economic growth of territories (Cooke 2013). Literature on regional path development (Tödtling and Trippl 2013; Simmie 2013; Isaksen 2015; Isaksen and Trippl 2016; Grillitsch, Asheim, and Trippl 2018; Isaksen, Tödtling, and Trippl 2018; Trippl et al. 2020) has pointed to the interplay between firm-level and system-level agency, which includes resources and drivers external to the cluster. From a regional development perspective, this work adds to the previous literature by showing how new path development trajectories might result from exaptive innovation processes in which knowledge recombination is a key driver for guaranteeing the resilience of clusters. We account for the microfoundations of path development, taking into consideration the case of regional economic adaptability in a non-Western context, called for by Hassink (2017).

One of the most obvious managerial implications of our empirical evidence is that cultural institutions need to undertake and consolidate innovation processes, which can be boosted by digital technologies. It will be necessary to consider both the supply and demand side to understand how digital innovation can be implemented in a cultural ecosystem. Therefore, it will be important to identify a strategic planning path for cultural organizations. Thanks to ICT, designers can rethink and develop cultural heritage fruition projects to be more 'for' and 'with' stakeholders and users originating from different niches, thereby generating a participatory process of mutual exchange and growth. The digitalization of cultural heritage appears to be crucial for revamping the creative and cultural sectors during a period of stagnation (Navarrete 2013; Bertacchini and Morando 2013).

In terms of policy implications, we underline how the rejuvenation process of the Kyoto cluster has been strongly supported by local institutions, which soon began to recognize the importance of the digitalization of cultural heritage and created specific events, which generated opportunities for networking and new business generation. Another important finding of our work is the need to upgrade the competences of artisans through specific training aimed at demonstrating the potential of new technologies and the creation of opportunities for CG designers to learn traditional Nishijin-ori methods of manufacturing.

Moreover, the Japanese attitude to novelty plays a crucial role in this story, where digital innovation is perceived as a natural evolution of traditional craftsmanship and as something that occurs along a continuum from tradition to innovation. Other countries should take this case as an opportunity to reflect on the more widespread attitude of resistance to change, which has hindered the possibilities for new path development processes within traditional clusters in places such as Italy (to mention just a single striking example).

Nevertheless, our discussion has some limitations, as it focuses on only a few case studies. However, it offers room for rethinking cluster development through the leveraging of cultural resources in other geographical contexts and across other industries (such as tourism; see Ma and Hassink 2014), where similar cluster evolution dynamics can be observed. Future research might help to close this gap by providing evidence of the value of the digitalization of cultural heritage for sustaining path renewal through exaptation.

Notes

1. Yūzen is a Japanese resist dyeing technique involving the application of rice paste to fabric to prevent colour transfer of dye to areas of the fabric. Originating in the 17th century, the technique became popular as both a way of subverting sumptuary laws on dress fabrics, and also as a way to quickly produce kimono that appeared to be hand painted with dyes. The technique was named after Miyazaki Yūzen, a 17th century fan painter who perfected the technique.
2. Nishijin-ori is a collective term for silk cloth produced here.

3. Shichi-Go-San is a traditional rite of passage and festival day in Japan for three- and seven-year-old girls and five-year-old (and less commonly three-year-old) boys, held annually on November 15 to celebrate the growth and well-being of young children.
4. Kabuki is a classical form of Japanese dance drama. Kabuki theatre is known for its heavily stylized performances, the often-glamorous costumes and elaborate kumadori make-up worn by performers.
5. Itochu is one of the largest Japanese sogo shosha – general trading companies – operating with six major divisions specializing in textiles, metals/minerals, food, machinery, energy/chemicals, and ICT/general products/real estate.

Disclosure statement

No potential conflict of interest was reported by the author(s).

ORCID

Silvia Rita Sedita http://orcid.org/0000-0002-4589-6934

References

Altork, K. 1998. "You Never Know When You Want to be a Redhead in Belize." In *Inside Stories: Qualitative Research Reflections*, edited by K. DeMarris, 111–125. Mahwah, NJ: Lawrence Erlbaum.
Andrews, M., C. Squire, and M. Tamboukou, eds. 2013. *Doing Narrative Research*. London: Sage.
Asheim, B. T. 2007. "Differentiated Knowledge Bases and Varieties of Regional Innovation Systems." *Innovation: The European Journal of Social Science Research* 20 (3): 223–241. doi:10.1080/13511610701722846.
Asheim, B. T., and M. S. Gertler. 2005. "The Geography of Innovation: Regional Innovation Systems." In *The Oxford Handbook of Innovation*, edited by J. Fagerberg, D. C. Mowery, and R. R. Nelson, 291–317. Oxford: Oxford University Press.
Asheim, B. T., R. Boschma, and P. Cooke. 2011. "Constructing Regional Advantage:Platform Policies Based on Related Variety and Differentiated Knowledge Bases." *Regional Studies* 45 (7): 893–904. doi:10.1080/00343404.2010.543126.
Asheim, B., M. Grillitsch, and M. Trippl. 2017. "Introduction: Combinatorial Knowledge Bases, Regional Innovation, and Development Dynamics." *Economic Geography* 93: 429–435. doi:10.1080/00130095.2017.1380775.
Becattini, G. 2017. "The Marshallian Industrial District as a Socio-Economic Notion." *Revue D'économie Industrielle* 157: 13–32. doi:10.4000/rei.6507.
Belussi, F. 1999. "Policies for the Development of Knowledge-Intensive Local Production Systems." *Cambridge Journal of Economics* 23 (6): 729–747. doi:10.1093/cje/23.6.729.
Belussi, F., and S. R. Sedita. 2009. "Life Cycle vs. Multiple Path Dependency in Industrial Districts." *European Planning Studies* 17 (4): 505–528. doi:10.1080/09654310802682065.
Bertacchini, E., and F. Morando. 2013. "The Future of Museums in the Digital age: New Models for Access to and use of Digital Collections." *International Journal of Arts Management* 15 (2): 60–72.
Boschma, R. 2015. "Towards an Evolutionary Perspective on Regional Resilience." *Regional Studies* 49 (5): 733–751. doi:10.1080/00343404.2014.959481.
Boschma, R. A., and K. Frenken. 2011a. "Technological Relatedness and Regional Branching." In *Dynamic Geographies of Knowledge Creation and Innovation*, edited by H. Bathelt, M. P. Feldman, and D. F. Kogler, 64–81. London: Routledge, Taylor and Francis.
Boschma, R. A., and K. Frenken. 2011b. "Technological Relatedness, Related Variety and Economic Geography." In *The Handbook on Regional Innovation and Growth*, edited by P.

Cooke, B. Asheim, R. Boschma, R. Martin, D. Schwartz, and F. Todtling, 187–197. Cheltenham, UK: Edward Elgar.

Boschma, R., L. Coenen, K. Frenken, and B. Truffer. 2017. "Towards a Theory of Regional Diversification: Combining Insights from Evolutionary Economic Geography and Transition Studies." *Regional Studies* 51 (1): 31–45. doi:10.1080/00343404.2016.1258460.

Chen, Y., and R. Hassink. 2020. "Multi-scalar Knowledge Bases for new Regional Industrial Path Development: Toward a Typology." *European Planning Studies*, 28 (12): 2489–2507. doi:10.1080/09654313.2020.1724265.

Cooke, P., ed. 2013. *Re-framing Regional Development: Evolution, Innovation and Transition*. Abingdon, Oxon: Routledge.

Cooke, P., M. Parrilli, and J. Curbelo, eds. 2012. *Innovation, Global Change and Territorial Resilience*. Cheltenham: Edward Elgar.

Dew, N., S. D. Sarasvathy, and S. Venkataraman. 2004. "The Economic Implications of Exaptation." *Journal of Evolutionary Economics* 14: 69–84. doi:10.1007/s00191-003-0180-x.

Eisenhardt, K. M. 1989. "Building Theories from Case Study Research." *Academy of Management Review* 14: 532–550. doi:10.5465/amr.1989.4308385.

Eisenhardt, K. M., and M. E. Graebner. 2007. "Theory Building from Cases: Opportunities and Challenges." *Academy of Management Journal* 50: 25–32. doi:10.5465/amj.2007.24160888.

Foray, D. 2015. *Smart Specialisation Opportunities and Challenges for Regional Innovation Policy*. New York: Routledge.

Franck, P. 2015. "Kimono Fashion: The Consumer and the Growth of the Textile Industry in Pre-War Japan." In *The Historical Consumer: Consumption and Everyday Life in Japan 1850–2000*, edited by P. Franck, and J. Hunter, 151–175. New York: Palgrave Macmillan.

Frenken, K., and R. A. Boschma. 2007. "A Theoretical Framework for Evolutionary Economic Geography: Industrial Dynamics and Urban Growth as a Branching Process." *Journal of Economic Geography* 7 (5): 635–649. doi:10.1093/jeg/lbm018.

Fujitsuka, Y. 1992. "Burgeon of Gentrification in Nishijin, Kyoto." *Japanese Journal of Human Geography* 44 (4): 495–506. doi:10.4200/jjhg1948.44.495.

Fujitsuka, Y. 2005. "Gentrification and Neighbourhood Dynamics in Japan." In *Gentrification in a Global Context*, edited by R. Atkinson, and G. Bridge, 137–150. Abingdon, Oxon: Routledge.

Garud, R., and P. Karnøe. 2001. "Path Creation as a Process of Mindful Deviation." In *Path Dependence and Creation*, edited by R. Garud, and P. Karnøe, 1–38. London: Lawrence Erlbaum.

Glaeser, E. 2011. *The Triumph of the City: How our Greatest Invention Makes us Richer, Smarter, Greener, Healthier and Happier*. New York: Penguin Books.

Gould, S. J., and E. S. Vrba. 1982. "Exaptation – A Missing Term in the Science of Form." *Paleobiology* 8 (1): 4–15. doi:10.1017/S0094837300004310.

Grillitsch, M., B. Asheim, and M. Trippl. 2018. "Unrelated Knowledge Combinations: The Unexplored Potential for Regional Industrial Path Development." *Cambridge Journal of Regions, Economy and Society* 11 (2): 257–274. doi:10.1093/cjres/rsy012.

Hall, J. 2020. *Japan Beyond the Kimono*. London: Bloomsbury.

Hashino, T. 2015. Luxury Market and Survival: Japan's traditional Kimono Weaving Industry after the 1950s (No. 1507).

Hassink, R., A. Isaksen, and M. Trippl. 2019. "Towards a Comprehensive Understanding of new Regional Industrial Path Development." *Regional Studies* 53 (11): 1636–1645. doi:10.1080/00343404.2019.1566704.

Hassink, R. 2017. "Advancing the Understanding of Regional Economic Adaptability in a Non-Western Context: An Introduction to the Special Issue." *Growth and Change* 48: 194–200. doi:10.1111/grow.12183.

Isaksen, A. 2015. "Industrial Development in Thin Regions: Trapped in Path Extension?" *Journal of Economic Geography* 15 (3): 585–600. doi:10.1093/jeg/lbu026.

Isaksen, A., and S. Jakobsen. 2017. "New Path Development Between Innovation Systems and Individual Actors." *European Planning Studies* 25 (3): 355–370. doi: 10.1080/09654313.2016.1268570.

Isaksen, A., and M. Trippl. 2016. "4 Path Development in Different Regional Innovation Systems: A Conceptual Analysis." In *Innovation Drivers and Regional Innovation Strategies*, edited by M. Davide Parrilli, Rune Dahl Fitjar, and Andrés Rodriguez-Pose, 82–100. New York: Routledge.

Isaksen, A., F. Tödtling, and M. Trippl. 2018. "Innovation Policies for Regional Structural Change: Combining Actor-Based and System-Based Strategies." In *New Avenues for Regional Innovation Systems-Theoretical Advances, Empirical Cases and Policy Lessons*, edited by A. Isaksen, R. Martin, and M. Trippl, 221–238. Cham: Springer.

Lazzeretti, L. 2009. "The Creative Capacity of Culture and the new Creative Milieu." In *A Handbook of Industrial Districts*, edited by G. Becattini, M. Bellandi, and L. De Propris, 281–294. Cheltenham: Edward Elgar.

Lazzeretti, L., F. Capone, and T. Cinti. 2010. "The Regional Development Platform and "Related Variety": Some Evidence from art and Food in Tuscany." *European Planning Studies* 18 (1): 27–45. doi:10.1080/09654310903343518.

Lazzeretti, L., and S. Oliva. 2018. "Rethinking City Transformation: Florence from art City to Creative Fashion City." *European Planning Studies* 26 (9): 1856–1873. doi:10.1080/09654313.2018.1478951.

Lewis, P. J., and R. Adeney. 2014. "Narrative Research." In *Narrative Research. Qualitative Methodology: A Practical Guide*, edited by J. Mills, and M. Birks, 161–179. London: Sage.

Ma, M., and R. Hassink. 2014. "Path Dependence and Tourism Area Development: The Case of Guilin." *China. Tourism Geographies* 16 (4): 580–597. doi:10.1080/14616688.2014.925966.

MacKinnon, D., S. Dawley, A. Pike, and A. Cumbers. 2019. "Rethinking Path Creation: A Geographical Political Economy Approach." *Economic Geography* 95 (2): 113–135. doi:10.1080/00130095.2018.1498294.

Manz, C. C., and H. P. Sims Jr. 1981. "Vicarious Learning: The Influence of Modeling on Organizational Behavior." *Academy of Management Review* 6 (1): 105–113. doi:10.5465/amr.1981.4288021.

Martin, R. 2010. "Roepke Lecture in Economic Geography—Rethinking Regional Path Dependence: Beyond Lock-in to Evolution." *Economic Geography* 86 (1): 1–27. doi:10.1111/j.1944-8287.2009.01056.x.

Martin, R., and P. Sunley. 2006. "Path Dependence and Regional Economic Evolution." *Journal of Economic Geography* 6: 395–437. doi:10.1093/jeg/lbl012.

Menzel, M. P., and D. Fornahl. 2010. "Cluster Life Cycles—Dimensions and Rationales of Cluster Evolution." *Industrial and Corporate Change* 19 (1): 205–238. doi:10.1093/icc/dtp036.

METI-Kansai Bureau of Economy, Trade and Industry. (ed.). 2009. *Kinuorimono no shūsanchi o kaku toshita wasō sen'i sanchi no koteikan renkei ni kansuru chōsa hōkokusho* [Report on linkages between production processes in silk kimono weaving districts with distribution or trading centers].

Moen, T. 2006. "Reflections on the Narrative Research Approach." *International Journal of Qualitative Methods* 5 (4): 56–69. doi:10.1177/160940690600500405.

Nakaoka, T., K. Aikawa, H. Miyaijma, T. Yoshii, and T. Nishizawa. 1988. "The Textile History of Nishijin (Kyoto): East Meets West." *Textile History* 19 (2): 117–141. doi:10.1179/004049688793700537.

Navarrete, T. 2013. "Digital Cultural Heritage." In *Handbook on the Economics of Cultural Heritage*, edited by I. Rizzo, and A. Mignosa. Cheltenham: Edward Elgar Publishing.

Neffke, F., M. Henning, and R. Boschma. 2011. "How do Regions Diversify Over Time? Industry Relat- Edness and the Development of new Growth Paths in Regions." *Economic Geography* 87 (3): 237–265. doi:10.1111/j.1944-8287.2011.01121.x.

Nelson, R. R., and S. G. Winter. 1982. *An Evolutionary Theory of Economic Change*. Cambridge, MA: Harvard University Press.

Pike, A., D. MacKinnon, A. Cumbers, S. Dawley, and R. McMaster. 2016. "Doing Evolution in Economic Geography." *Economic Geography* 92 (2): 123–144. doi:10.1080/00130095.2015.1108830.

Rocchetta, S., A. Mina, C. Lee, and D. F. Kogler. 2021. "Technological Knowledge Spaces and the Resilience of European Regions." *Journal of Economic Geography*. doi:10.1093/jeg/lbab001.

Sedita, S. R. 2012. "Leveraging the Intangible Cultural Heritage: Novelty and Innovation Through Exaptation." *City, Culture and Society* 3 (4): 251–259. doi:10.1016/j.ccs.2012.11.009.

Sedita, S. R., I. De Noni, and L. Pilotti. 2017. "Out of the Crisis: an Empirical Investigation of Place-Specific Determinants of Economic Resilience." *European Planning Studies* 25 (2): 155–180. doi:10.1080/09654313.2016.1261804.

Simmie, J. 2013. "Path Dependence and new Technological Path Creation in the Economic Landscape." In *(2013) Re-Framing Regional Development: Evolution, Innovation and Transition*, edited by P. Cooke, 164–185. Abingdon, Oxon: Routledge.

Simmie, J. 2017. "The Evolution of Economic Resilience in Cities: re-Invention Versus Replication." In *Creating Resilient Economies: Entrepreneurship, Growth and Development in Uncertain Times*, edited by N. Williams, and T. Vorley, 70–88. Cheltenham: Edward Elgar.

Stettenheim, P. R. 1976. "Structural adaptations in feathers." *Proceedings of the 16th International Ornithological Congress*, 385–401.

Sunley, P., R. Martin, and P. Tyler. 2017. "Cities in Transition: Problems, Processes and Policies." *Cambridge Journal of Regions, Economy and Society* 10: 383–390. doi:10.1093/cjres/rsx018.

Tödtling, F., and M. Trippl. 2013. "14 Transformation of Regional Innovation Systems." *Re-framing Regional Development: Evolution, Innovation, and Transition* 62: 297.

Trippl, M., S. Baumgartinger-Seiringer, A. Frangenheim, A. Isaksen, and J. O. Rypestøl. 2020. "Unravelling Green Regional Industrial Path Development: Regional Preconditions, Asset Modification and Agency." *Geoforum; Journal of Physical, Human, and Regional Geosciences* 111: 189–197. doi:10.1016/j.geoforum.2020.02.016.

Yano Research Institute (ed.). 2013. *Kimono sangyō nenkan: 2013-2014* [Kimono industry: 2013–14].

Yin, R. K. 2009. *Case Study Research*, 4th ed. Thousand Oaks, CA: Sage.

Yoshida, M. 2013. "Kimono Kanren Shijo no Mondai Kozo to Kanousei (Structural Problems and the Potential of Kimono-Related Markets)." *Ritsumeikan Keieigaku* 52 (2–3): 429–452.

Anatomy of a techno-creative community – the role of brokers, places, and events in the emergence of projection mapping in Nantes

Etienne Capron, Dominique Sagot-Duvauroux and Raphaël Suire

ABSTRACT
This article aims to study the role of brokers, places, and events in the structuring of a community of innovation whose practice is at the intersection of art and technology – projection mapping. Using an exploratory case study, we observe the relationships between the different actors who form a community, sharing a common interest in a techno – creative practice – but whose collective innovation dynamic is only in its beginnings and remains unstable. We document the critical role of places and events as intermediary platforms for these actors. This reveals preferential circulations – patterns of moves among a set of focal locations in the city for a community – and the crucial role of these locations in communities' emergence.

Introduction

The past two decades have seen a multiplication of regional policies based on cultural and creative industries support (Boix et al. 2016). Related economic sectors (mainly art, media, digital technologies, video games, etc.) have become a major source of employment, yet also produce many external effects for other sectors (Sedita, Noni, and Pilotti 2017). At the same time, they deeply transform territories in three interwoven dimensions: urban transformation through the embellishment of deprived areas; demography of population through the influx of creative and knowledge workers; and economic transformation through convergence toward knowledge intensive economic sectors (Scott 2014). However, the spatial coexistence of (un–)related creative sectors does bring new opportunities for regional cross – specialization (Frenken, Van Oort, and Verburg 2007; Janssen and Frenken 2019), and the co–location of different activities could open up a wider, more sustainable range of anchored possibilities for regional development.

Few studies have documented how some related sectors overlap and produce novelties at their respective knowledge borders, even though there is strong interest in this (Content and Frenken 2016). Furthermore, empirical papers reveal valuable potential in the food industry (Davids and Frenken 2018) and in offshore gas and wind energy (Ingstrup and Menzel 2019) – though very little is known about how Cultural and

Creative Industries (CCI) cross over. Contexts in which STEM (Sciences, Technologies, Engineering, Mathematics) and artistic activities are co-located are rarely studied. Rodríguez-Pose and Lee (2020) provided insights at the city level, showing that cities in which both types of activities are present are particularly innovative when both knowledge fields intersect.

In line with this idea, innovations are increasingly based on both symbolic and synthetic knowledge bases (Asheim 2007). Video games (Grandadam, Cohendet, and Simon 2013) or medias (Martin and Moodysson 2011) are good examples of this tendency. However, studies are mostly conducted at the macro or organizational levels (international, national, regional). This contribution aims to fill some gaps, firstly by specifying the concept of 'techno-creative' activities and innovations – those at the knowledge frontier of arts and digital technologies – and secondly by pointing out the crucial roles played by brokers, places, and events in the emergence of these novelties. Consequently, this paper enriches the literature on community-based knowledge creation and contribute to a recent stream of literature dealing with the role of places and events in the structure and evolution of knowledge communities. By doing this, we offer some perspectives and practical implications for policy makers and creative community managers on the way some communities of innovation can be organized and sustained.

This paper is based on an exploratory in-depth case study (Yin 2013) of the projection mapping community in Nantes (France) as an example of a localized, emergent techno-creative activity. This innovation combines symbolic and synthetic knowledge and is associated with several types of creatives (architects, video-jockeys, artists). Our results identify *preferential circulation* (PC) of community members, which can be defined as the pattern of attendance of innovators among a set of locations in the city. A fragmented community is revealed and to some extent this fragmentation comes with an emerging but also unstable collective dynamic. Our analysis shows that the community attends a multiplicity of places and events (in terms of size, specialization, etc.), and that access to the resources provided by these platforms is not open to all in the same way. Once emerging activities have been detected by public institutions, a policy of material and economic support could benefit their structuring (provision of workspace, logistical assistance, financing of long-term residencies, etc.). Our analysis also confirms the importance of knowledge and geographical brokers located at the intersection of distinct knowledge fields to initiate new techno-creative practices (Sgourev 2015).

The paper is organized as follows: the first part frames the theoretical approach, from which we derive our research questions. The second part is dedicated to methodology, building on semi-directive interviews. The collected data allows us to conduct network analysis. The third part is devoted to the results, which are discussed in the fourth part, and our conclusion highlights implication for policy makers.

Theoretical background

Research on the knowledge-based economy has introduced the notion of knowledge bases in order to specify how innovation processes operate (Asheim 2007). Within this framework, each activity is associated to a knowledge base, according to the industrial sector it belongs to, its degree of tacitness, and the skills it requires (Cooke 2007;

Martin and Moodysson 2011). The literature describes three types of knowledge bases: *analytical*, which is more associated with science-based industries (fundamental research, biotechnology, nanotechnology, etc.) and involves a rational, deductive thinking approach that leads to the creation of highly codified scientific knowledge; *symbolic*, which is related to CCI and art because it refers to the creation of knowledge of high aesthetic value, embedded in cultural systems of interpretation and having a strong tacit dimension – thus, very context–dependent; and *synthetic*, which is based on combining existing knowledge in order to apply solutions to functional, specific problems (e.g. engineering). Depending on the activity, one knowledge base is dominant, and this affects how new knowledge is integrated and created. As pointed out by Rodríguez-Pose and Lee (2020), the amalgamation of activities belonging to both the Science Technology Engineering Mathematics (based on synthetic and/or analytical knowledge) and creative/Art sectors[1] could spur innovation at the city level. To define activities that combine synthetic and symbolic knowledge to produce innovations, we use the term techno–creative. This covers a wide variety of activities that use these two knowledge bases to varying degrees.

While some knowledge is indeed produced by formal organizations (Balland et al. 2020), not all of it is created by them. Indeed, a plurality of actors having an interest in a particular field participate in the creation of knowledge. Scholars define these as communities – sets of individuals who regularly and voluntarily exchange information about a common interest or a shared goal within a knowledge field (Amin and Cohendet 2004). Though these autonomous, informal collectives are not necessarily oriented around market production, they first and foremost share interests, opinions, and practices about whatever it is that brings them together. The role of communities in the processes of knowledge creation is important, because the diverse interactions between members allow for the transfer of (formal and/or informal) knowledge specific to each field and the formation of shared visions (Bathelt and Cohendet 2014; Cohendet, Grandadam, and Suire 2021). Each community has its own cognitive space, constructs in which knowledge and ideas are transferred, translated, and articulated. Cognitive spaces help to guide the future development of a practice or knowledge (Cohendet, Grandadam, and Simon 2010; Capdevila, Cohendet, and Simon 2018).

This broad definition can be refined by distinguishing between two typical types of communities: Communities of Practice (CoPs) focus on sharing best practice in a specific area of knowledge (Lave and Wenger 1991). Because they share the same existing practice, members of these communities also share a common interest in a problem or topic. They use common standards, routines and tools that enable them to understand each other. Thus, we assume CoPs emerge from technological/technical innovations and the various individuals who are interested in them and appropriate them. Epistemic Communities (EC) are focused on the creation, codification and dissemination of new knowledge or ideas (Haas 1992). EC members compare their diverse knowledge sets, to create or update new knowledge and develop a framework with which to interpret it. They therefore share normative frameworks, visions on the validity of knowledge and preferred approaches for its creation. In substance, communities thus refer to networks of individuals who interact regularly, share collective interests and norms. The boundaries of communities are blurred and evolve over time as members become more or less involved. In emerging fields, practices are mostly based on experimentation and prototyping. Bricolage and exploration might be some dominant means of learning (Suire 2019). Theoretically, the difference between CoPs and ECs lies in how they produce knowledge (deliberately for EC, through their practices for CoPs), and in the ability of ECs to create a cognitive space (Capdevila, Cohendet, and Simon 2018). But in reality, members of CoPs and ECs can spill over into a single community, collectively producing something new by combining knowledge, adjusting or initiating practices, developing an interpretative framework, and actively disseminating knowledge through practices (Capdevila, Cohendet, and Simon 2018). For this study, we therefore consider communities that develop both new knowledge and practices, particularly because they combine knowledge from distinct bases (synthetic and symbolic).

From then on, if we consider techno-creative innovation as a combination of synthetic and symbolic knowledge, we explore the dynamics that are driving this process. This requires keeping in mind the embedding of social relations, i.e. belonging to the same social realm (Granovetter 1985). The structure and composition of an actor's social network is important because the social capital it constitutes is an important resource for action (Coleman 1988; Burt 2004). Too much homogeneity could limit access to new ideas or opportunities, whereas ties that are too weak (or even non-existent) could limit confidence – and thus exchanges of tacit knowledge. In addition, the emergence of a techno–creative community implies that its members share the same cognitive space. The capacity of actors to adopt behaviours in line with the established practices, values, or ideals, is therefore crucial. Thus, where actors are strongly interconnected and interact frequently, shared values and understandings emerge (Jones, Hesterly, and Borgatti 1997). But even in a context in which local actors share a single, abiding, geographical space, new combinations involving both synthetic and symbolic knowledge are not guaranteed. We therefore need a more precise investigation of territorial configurations, as these could play a vital role in the emergence and development of communities.

The crucial roles of places, events, and brokers

We analyse the endogenous elements of a territory that can promote crossovers (whether directly or indirectly). We draw on two platforms, places and events, identified in the middleground literature (Cohendet, Grandadam, and Simon 2009, 2010, 2021). Our approach is inspired by the – *grounds* model, but we do not apply this framework, which focuses on platforms of vertical intermediation between informal (*underground*) creative activities and the formal institutions of a territory (*upperground*). However, we focus on places and events in the idea that they can join distinct communities horizontally. We also add brokers (Gould and Fernandez 1989) to develop our own framework.

The first element is *place*: an abiding physical location in which individuals can socialize and share information, and in which social and cognitive flows densify (Rantisi and Leslie 2010). Following the notion of third-places (Oldenburg 1989), these offer a favourable context for social interactions and knowledge exchanges. A wide variety of places can play this role, whether for production or diffusion, niche – or mainstream – oriented (Kloosterman 2014): cafés, restaurants, artist-run spaces, fab-labs, etc. The third–place function is created by the community in making it its focal point, and these places can play a crucial role in the process of creation and/or diffusion of innovations. More precisely, the main function of these places can differ from one location to another: creation/production, social interaction, learning or exploitation of knowledge, etc. We also assume that places may be more or less open to exploitation depending on whether they are institutionalized and highly visible, requiring more accomplished productions for a wider audience, or explorative, niche-oriented places where there are more experimentations.

The second element is *event*: whether regular or not, events act as temporary clusters, gathering actors from different territories for a short period of time (Maskell, Bathelt, and Malmberg 2006; Torre 2008). By allowing face-to-face encounters, events offer an opportunity to create new social relations (Rantisi 2014). Where they have a worldwide audience, these favour global pipelines, and events provide communities with access to new trends, knowledge, and peer reviews, consequently building local buzz (Rantisi 2014). Another crucial characteristic is the field-configuration role an event can have (Schüßler, Grabher, and Müller-Seitz 2015). In those cases, events constitute an important intermediary for creating networks, developing shared standards and visions, and thus have a strong configuring influence for local communities.

Several contributions also emphasis the crucial role played by social networks in the creation and diffusion of creative productions (Burt 2004; Uzzi and Spiro 2005). The ability of some actors to connect individuals with different knowledge can therefore be crucial for innovation (Nedkovski and Guerci 2021). Following Gould and Fernandez (1989), brokers are structurally defined as individuals who connect otherwise disconnected alters, whether or not these people belong to a single organization or field. Moreover, we must take into account their agency and active intermediation effort (Foster and Ocejo 2013). Brokers serve as 'bridges' between different part of a social realm, especially distinct communities, thereby transforming the dynamics of interaction between actors. Thus, depending on the situation, a broker can exploit the disconnection of actors to his advantage (Burt 2004), or conversely connect the different actors in his network (Obstfeld 2005). Brokers' knowledge translation role can also be crucial (Foster and Ocejo 2013). The role of brokers has been studied in contexts of emergence in artistic fields, highlighting the crucial factor of accessing influential actors and bridging different social worlds and views (Sgourev 2015; Lingo and O'Mahony 2010).

The challenge for developing a techno-creative community is to identify the bridges that bring together communities with synthetic knowledge and others with symbolic knowledge. Previous research may have focused on the role of brokers, places, and events independently, or within a particular knowledge domain. Here, we study how these elements all combined contribute to modify the structure of communities, to promote interactions, and ultimately to foster innovation at the intersection of two knowledge fields. We have supposed (1) that places, events, and brokers can both reduce social distance and promote exploration at the frontier of artistic and technological activities. The social embedding leads to the emergence of a cognitive space common to the members of a community. However, (2) the heterogeneity of actors, their values and their approaches to practice can be obstacles to the constitution of an innovation community. We rely on an empirical study to determine their role in structuring a community of mappers within an ecosystem that combines technological and artistic activities.

Methodology and data

Field and object of the study

Since we were observing a social phenomenon *in situ*, we chose to adopt a qualitative research design based on an explorative case study, which allowed us to focus on less-studied phenomenon (Yin 2013). As our field for this study, we chose Nantes – a city located in western France which, over the past 30 years, has developed a strategy of territorial and economic development based on cultural events (Ambrosino, Guillon, and Sagot-Duvauroux 2016). More recently, with the creation of a dedicated cluster (Schieb-Bienfait, Saives, and Charles-Pauvers 2018), the city has focused on attracting the CCI sectors, including digital and tech activities. Nantes was also named European Capital of Innovation in 2019, in recognition of its whole strategy of supporting innovative activities. These two trajectories have recently crossed one another, providing a context that fits the scope of our study.[2] In addition, certain places and events initiated by the city are actively seeking to foster crossovers between arts and technology, underlining the desire to develop activities at the intersection of these sectors.

As we study cases where synthetic and symbolic knowledge must be combined in one way or another, we chose projection mapping – a practice defined as projections of still or moving images onto volumes, using dedicated software and technology (Watier 2018). Mappers are the individuals who create content for projection, but also manage the technical aspect of it. Depending on their practice, they can create specific technological devices to meet their needs. Therefore, innovations of this community can be more aesthetic (based on new symbolic knowledge) or mostly technological (based on synthetic knowledge), but they always combine both types of knowledge. Also, we stress that these innovators are not necessarily intermediaries between a tech community and an artist community. Rather, they are on the edge of the two knowledge fields, using a greater or lesser degree of synthetic and symbolic knowledge in their practices.

Primary and secondary data

Data collection was carried out initially by analysing documents and followed by semi-directed interviews. The analysis of documents from several sources (venues programmes, mappers websites and social media pages) allowed us to identify the local community but not always the links between members. It also allowed us to locate several places and events they attend. Then, we interviewed 17 mappers to obtain more data. The interviews focused on two themes: their individual practice (what tools and processes are used), and the social, spatial, and cognitive resources they mobilize (what places and events they attend and why they do so, with whom they collaborate, etc.). We also asked interviewees to hierarchize places, events, and members of the community as main resources for meeting other members, nurturing their inspiration, learning, experimenting, and sharing their creations. To have an additional view on the community we also interviewed actors having some interest in projection mapping, but whose reasons for participating in the community lie elsewhere: event organization, position in a cultural venue, etc. These five interviews provided us with different, though complementary data about this practice in the local context. The period during which we conducted the interviews spans from September 2019 to March 2020. During this time, new creations were presented, new relations were formed, and integration of these data into our work seemed to be of interest. In total, we conducted 22 interviews and identified 40 individuals, although it was not possible to meet everyone.[3] The data also includes 38 places and 12 events identified with document analysis and cited by interviewees as resources for their practice and/or locations they regularly attend. Finally, through the interview's transcriptions and documents, we found 132 links[4] within the community, 257 links between community members and places, and 96 links between community members and events, which are then used for network analysis.

Network analysis

We chose to divide our analysis into three distinct networks: one devoted to interpersonal relations (social network), another to relations between members of the community and the places they attend (bi–partite network), and the last to relations between members of the community and the events they attend (bi–partite network). In each case, we identify market relationships – that is, when a contract is made regarding the creation, production, or diffusion of projection mapping content (i.e. customer–supplier relationship), and non-market relationships – which can take the form of friendship, exchange of knowledge, ideas or advice, co-creation or collaboration, lending of tools. For analytical reasons, we have separated the types of relationships each time, but in reality they are embedded (Granovetter 1985) and may overlap where two actors have both market and non-market links, since the one may be the consequence of the other. Following Uzzi and Spiro (2005), we consider that a link connects two places or two events if a member of the community attends both places/events. Based on attendance data for the locations identified through interviews and document analysis, and the transformation of the bi–partite graphs into unipartite graphs, we obtain one network made up of places, and another made up of events. This is what we call *preferential circulation* (PC): the individual and collective patterns of attendance among a set of places/events. It reflects the choices, habits, and selection of multiple specific resources (social, economic, cognitive, and material) located in places and events, which are needed to innovate. In total, we come up with six non–directed networks, which we analyse separately and compare based on their structural properties.

Various structural analyses of the network were conducted,[5] starting with degree centrality (the number of links a node has, noted k afterwards), which indicates how well connected a node is in a network, based on whether it has a low or high number of links. We also measured betweenness centrality, which describes the number of times a node is on the shortest path connecting any pair of nodes in the network. This allowed us to identify potential brokers within the social network, as well as intermediary places and events in the other two networks. We also use density – the ratio of the number of existing links to the number of potential links – to specify the cohesion of the network. Lastly, we used degree correlation, which reflects the assortativity of nodes: the idea that nodes having a similar degree connect to each other. A positive coefficient means that nodes sharing the same properties (here, high degree centrality) connect to each other. Assortativity provides a finer understanding of the degree of structural homophily in the network (Crespo, Suire, and Vicente 2014).

Results

Social networks

Actors we interviewed live and work in the same city, have the same techno-creative practice (namely the creation and projection of mappings) and share interests in its development and tools. Thus, we would expect that they constitute a community of practice. However, our interviews highlight that the goals and orientations associated to their practice are not homogeneous – they vary, depending on the actors. For example, a former video editor explains that he *only does it for musicians, with bands, or for live electronic music from time to time* (interview with a video-jockey [VJ], January 2020), whereas an artist will have an approach based on *installations, sometimes interactive, sometimes not. It depends if it makes sense or not for me. […] I work with lasers for example, I do 3D with lasers*. (interview with an artist, November 2019). Representations of the field, aesthetic values attributed to the productions, and conventions regulating the practice are not shared by all.

Instead of a unified network, we have identified three communities, each with a different vision of projection mapping. Links are stronger within than between communities (Burt 2004), especially for those who organize themselves into collectives and meet often to carry out their projects. The first community is made up of mappers from the School of Architecture, mainly former students. Among them, some actors created collectives to carry out their projects. The second is composed of artists (involved in video, digital and lighting arts) and their technical staff, who use projection techniques in their creations. Some of these people are in an art collective and work together regularly. In the whole network, the only engineer we have identified is a member of this collective. His role seems to be crucial in developing technological tools:

> "he is not necessarily going to claim an artistic position, that's not what he is, but at the same time he will share a lot. These days he is developing our own control cards for LEDs that do not exist on the market, we have improved all the systems." (interview with an artist, November 2019).

This assimilation of synthetic and symbolic knowledge is significant for techno-creative innovation. The third community is made of VJs working in clubs and music venues. They mainly use this technique to enhance the festive atmosphere. In their case, there is no collective and relations are more irregular. As one VJ describes his relationship with another mapper: *I was invited, he was invited, and we were already talking a little bit on Facebook before I think. It allowed us to meet in real life. But then we haven't seen each other much since…* (interview with a VJ, November 2019).

We can therefore admit that the logic of similarity is strong within all communities as they share the same frames of reference, but the potential between communities is not necessarily fulfilled. Innovators have a common base of knowledge, basic skills, and interest in projection mapping, but tools, types of collaborations and frames of reference diverge. To some extent, this scattered community is characterized by ambiguity because there are multiple meanings associated with the practice, defended in a non-conflictual way by the actors (Sgourev 2013).

We first analyse market relationships between the actors, plotted in Graph 1. This is represented as follows: a link is created if two have a customer–supplier relationship. We

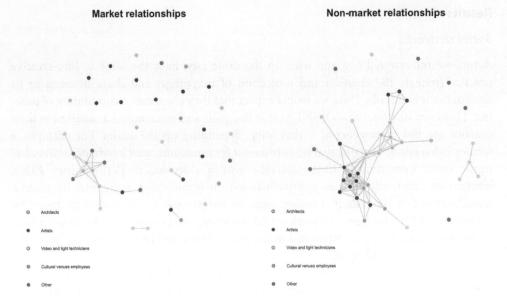

Graph 1 and 2. Market and non-market relationships among local actors.

note that the network is assortative (0.0481872), i.e. positive degree correlation of nodes: here, this means that actors have market relationships with others who also have market relationships. In a word, business goes to business. The degree distribution of nodes indicates that most actors have few market relationships (degree max: 8) but a relatively higher number of non-market relationships (degree max: 15) (Figures 1 and 2).

The second network represents non-market relationships. Here, a link is created if actors interact regularly, exchange knowledge or innovations together. Graph 2

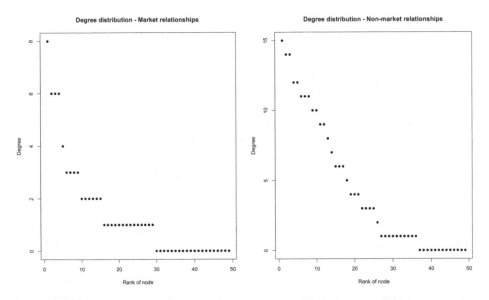

Figure 1 and 2. Actors degree distribution for market and non-market relationships.

highlights three clusters, each representing sub–components of the mappers' network, corresponding to the three communities we identified. Non-market relations account for 82.4% of all relations, revealing a higher number of non-market relationships than market relationships. Moreover, this network is assortative (0.2174976), though to a lesser extent than the previous one, and has a relatively low density (Table 1). This means that actors who are already highly connected have relationships with each other, while those who have few relationships are linked to them but suffer to have few relationships overall. Among identified actors, we identify a broker between the community of architects (to which she belongs) and some artists, as indicated by her high betweenness centrality (291.46 while the second highest score is 159.69). She is a former School of Architecture student who moved to Montreal as part of her training. There, she discovered projection mapping, met the founder of a festival, and later joined the organization team. Following this experience, she returned to Nantes and (along with former student peers) and founded the collective that launched a local version of the festival.[6] To achieve this, she had therefore sought out local mappers, first through her own friendship network (former students at the architecture school) and then beyond. However, we point out that VJs are for the most part disconnected from the main component of the two networks.

Places networks and events networks:

Next, we analyse the network of places attended for market reasons, here defined by the fact that an actor has a paid activity in a place (e.g. a residency or a performance). Thus, when an actor has a market activity in two places, a link is drawn between those two places. Graph 3 illustrates this relatively sparse network (Table 1), revealing that not all actors attend all the same places (if they did, we would get a complete network). Disconnected nodes represent the places where actors have no business activities. Nevertheless, one place seems to be at the core of the network, according to the betweenness centrality: Stereolux, a flagship cultural venue funded by local public institutions. Throughout the year, this venue programmes different types of events (e.g. live music, exhibitions, and performances ... about 180 per year) and hosts artist residencies. However, not all mappers have the opportunity to work there and to be included in the agenda. Having a market relationship with this place allows a strong symbolic resource and is a part of the legitimation process, especially for peripheral actors (Grabher 2018). As one artist with a longstanding relationship with the teams remarked

Table 1. Structural analyses of the networks.

	Density	Assortativity
Social Network		
• Market relationships	0.0289115	0.0481872
• Non-market relationships	0.0901360	0.2174976
Places Network		
• Market relationships	0.0995732	−0.249194
• Non-market relationships	0.2460882	−0.302084
Events Network		
• Market relationships	0.2121212	0.214035
• Non-market relationships	0.4545455	−0.244582

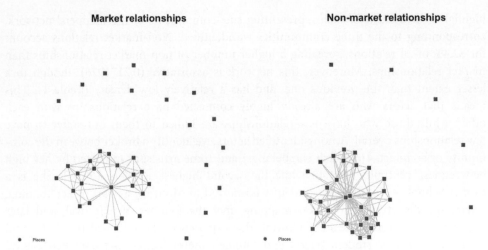

Graph 3 and 4. PC among places for market and non-market relationships.

Stereolux, you go there, you call them and tell them you need a room to work on something, frankly they'll do it. But to programme yourself… (interview with an artist, January 2020).

Regarding non-market relationships (e.g. attending an exhibition, meeting friends, experimenting in a studio), the distribution of degrees (Figure 4) shows that relationships are more dispersed (i.e. are less concentrated around a single place) than for market relationships (Figure 3). However, two places (Stereolux and Lieu Unique, another flagship cultural venue) seem to be at the core of the PCs. The non-market relationships associated with places are visualized in Graph 4.

Regarding the events, we assume that a market relationship exists where a mapper performs during an event. As with places, a link is drawn between two events when an actor has paid activity with both. Results show a reduced number of events attended by

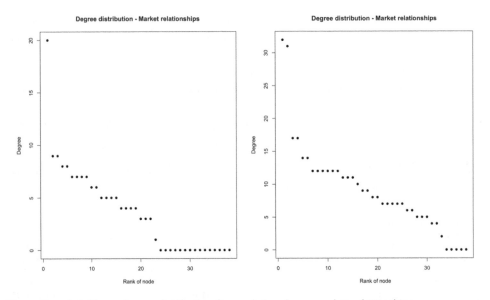

Figure 3 and 4. Places degree distribution for market and non-market relationships.

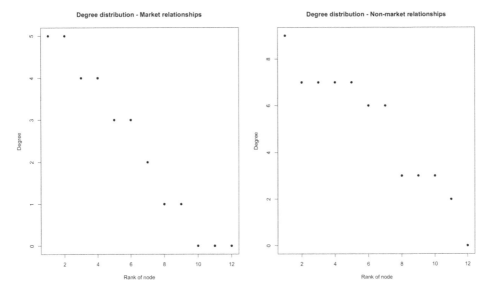

Figure 5 and 6. Events degree distribution for market and non-market relationships.

innovators. Degree distribution indicates few opportunities for mappers to show their work at local events, since they attend few events likely to build market relationships (Figure 5). Actors who mostly have market relations with events are the artists, and these relations are articulated around two events organized by Stereolux's teams, Scopitone and Electrons Libres. This therefore confirms that this place is at the core of their PCs, as summed up by an artist *in Nantes, there is above all Stereolux and Scopitone, who is the main actor, and who offers a lot of advantages to create things.* (interview with an artist, December 2019).

Non-market relations, on the other hand, are more evenly distributed, revealing that actors attend various events (rather than just one), both in terms of size and content. Scopitone seems to be particularly attended by the members of the sample, as indicated by degree centrality (Figure 6). Graph 5 and 6 represents the network of events attended for non-market relationships.

Discussion

The challenges of creating techno–creative communities for territories may be to gain attractiveness, to differentiate, to develop a market, to overcome path dependency (Rodríguez-Pose and Lee 2020; Frenken, Van Oort, and Verburg 2007; Garud and Karnøe 2001). Our questioning about the roles of brokers, places, and events in the emergence of innovative communities by combining art and technology finds several answers in the analysis of the results. It indicates that the actors have compatible heterogeneity, since they are similar on some points and distinct on others. Different actors share the same practices, but we found a dispersion of cognitive spaces, leading to the formation of different epistemic communities. This competition between approaches defended by the different communities is observed in the distinct attendance patterns of places and events (even if they share some). What the results show is the need to jointly study

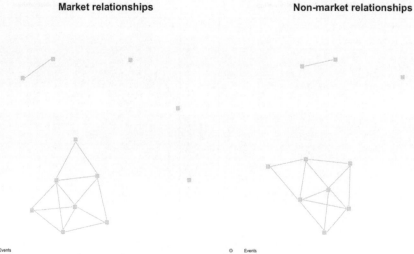

Graph 5 and 6. PC among events for market and non-market relationships.

the bridging or bonding role of brokers, places, and events, since co-presence alone is not enough to develop techno-creative activities.

Observed social networks are fragmented, and we can see that the communities are not well connected to each other. Some links exist between the architects and few artists, though we also note that the sub-component related to events and clubs is disconnected from the main component. As a cohesive network, an integrated community does not really exist. In the phase of emergence, the underlying network of an emerging community is often disconnected and scattered (Lazer and Friedman 2007). Ambiguity related to the more valuable choice for creators and artists (Sgourev 2013) or uncertainty related to the economic opportunity of innovations are usual macro-explanations for this issue. Here, we come with more detailed, micro-founded explanations of the observed fragmentation, which is mainly explained by cognitive distance and symbolic borders (Nooteboom 2007).

Techno–creative innovations require overcoming two main obstacles: the knowledge gap in the use of techniques (synthetic knowledge) and the symbolic gap associated with aesthetic values and references (symbolic knowledge). We show that, between the different communities, even if all share the same practice, the level of deep technical knowledge is not the same, and the fact that some use less advanced techniques might result in negative evaluation by others. More importantly, the aesthetics and the objectives are not the same. Artists use it within the framework of their artistic works, and their discourse is full of artistic references. They situate this in an art world (Becker 1982) that has pre-formed conventions, and refer to this for their productions. Mappers in clubs use mapping to enhance a festive atmosphere already created by music and lights. The aesthetic vision is therefore not the same, and a kind of symbolic border separates club mappers from the others. Thus, a competition between at least two aesthetic visions (artists and club mappers) leads to a strong social bonding within the groups but a weak social bridging. We observe distinct epistemic communities, each with its own cognitive space and homogenous knowledge bases. These symbolic borders seem to be the most difficult to cross, forbidding at the same time the possibilities to share synthetic knowledge from a community to another. In many circumstances, an excess of bonding social capital can conduct to inertia (Antonietti and Boschma 2018) and may hinder collective action (Crespo, Réquier-Desjardins, and Vicente 2014). An integrated projection mapping community probably suffers from a lack of visibility in part for these reasons.

As noted earlier, there is no unified projection mapping community in this territory as there are few relationships among the three communities and a boundary between the communities' cognitive spaces hindering a collective dynamic. Yet, there is a degree of heterophily between these actors that could be optimal for the development and diffusion of innovations (Rogers 1983). There is a certain ambiguity as to the aesthetic framework to be developed and the common standards to be adopted. The fragmented network, with distinct orientations and identities of communities, could be a pre-condition likely to spur knowledge combination and framework reinterpretation (Sgourev 2013), potentially initiating a distinct cognitive space. As previously stated, this structural fragmentation is also the signature of an emerging knowledge field that has typified the battle of standards observed in nascent technological sectors (Suire and Vicente 2014). The question that appears here is related to the stability or instability of this collective dynamic. For projection mapping stakeholders, for local policy makers in charge of cultural sector, for local creative and cultural industry, the answers could be divergent, and this require further investigations.

We identify several elements that could help bring these actors together to gain a level of collective legitimacy and visibility, and by doing this we add some new elements to the literature by distinguishing simultaneously the role of brokers, places, and events relatively to each other and the way they modify structural properties of knowledge networks behind innovation communities. Brokers, places, and events also participate in the formation of cognitive spaces, in their legitimization and in the visibility of techno-creative innovations brought by the communities notably by providing a connection with peers and audience.

Brokers: the main broker we identified has been able to bridge two previously disconnected parts of the network, and is now in a structural hole position (Burt 2004). By linking with Stereolux, she identified other mappers belonging to the artists community. As noted by Foster and Ocejo (2013), the broker position involves a complex process in which an actor may play multiple roles (connecting actors, taking advantage of their position, translating different visions) and where motivation is crucial. In this instance, she has created strategic links with those actors she considers important and whose productions are both relevant and a match for her own vision of projection mapping (i.e. those created by architects and artists) – and would probably include these people in the festival programme. Crucially, through her previous position in Montreal, she has integrated the field and created global pipelines and imports knowledge, which feed the local buzz (Bathelt, Malmberg, and Maskell 2004; Storper and Venables 2004). Beyond her structural position in the network, both her vision of the practice and her role as organizer of the festival are crucial to connecting the two main sub–components of the network, through both strong and weak ties. Through her brokering actions, she transforms the structure of the network and participates strongly in the development of the community by creating new relationships and formalizing a shared cognitive space for members of two communities. This strength is simultaneously a weakness as soon as her disappearance or a decrease in her commitment can maintain a structural status quo. Besides, it does not seem to us to be a coincidence that she belongs to the group of architects. The School of Architecture is a place where both technical (*synthetic*) and artistic (*symbolic*) knowledge are taught. Mastery of these two knowledge bases could facilitate both the other actors' understanding and the interpretation/translation of knowledge. We believe that architects, because of their training, can play a critical bridging role. More broadly, the identification of actors whose practice combines several forms of knowledge seems to be important to decompartmentalize communities that are locked into their spaces.

Places: in this dynamic, places could also play an intermediation role in this context. We have observed different types of venues, with distinct characteristics, and enabling unequal possibilities. On the one hand there are multi–disciplinary, publicly funded and highly visible places. Their programming often relies on artists whose productions interweave the artistic and technological dimensions. Because many actors attend these places for their dense (*there's often something to see*) and varied (*you don't always know what you're going to see*) agenda of artistic events, they have high betweenness centrality in the non–market relationships network. These places, then, are open to a wide audience that includes mappers, allowing for inter–community interactions. These types of places could thus play a crucial role in promoting face-to-face meetings and helping structure a community. Most mappers belonging to the artists community have already worked there in residency and/or performed there – but the same is not true of members of other communities, who perform in niche places. Overall, these places provide fertile ground for a community at the intersection of arts and tech sectors to emerge. But, if interdisciplinary programming with arts and technology is a necessary condition for the development of a common framework and community embedding opportunities (*bridging* role), it is not sufficient in and of itself. The maintenance of a certain heterogeneity of places is however also necessary because this is what allows less visible actors to develop niches, experimentation, and to create stronger links together (*bonding* role). This is what we can observe in the places constituting focal locations for the different communities: a local music venue for VJs; the School of Architecture is a place where current and former students meet and is the venue of the forthcoming projection mapping festival; a shared workspace of a collective of artists, and another one where artists using projection mapping work. These last two are primarily dedicated to creation, as opposed to the dissemination of projection mapping for the two others. These places are at the core of the collective PCs of the different communities. This means that this is where they regularly meet, exchange ideas, do peer reviews, and consequently form their own cognitive space. Since they are not (or rarely) attended by other communities, knowledge spillovers do not happen. We can therefore see that for innovative communities and their spaces to develop (an initial condition for cross–fertilization), there must be focal places where bonding takes place, allowing the actors who attend them to develop their own approach and expertise.

Events: events (especially the forthcoming projection mapping festival, as the other events did not initiate lasting relations between the members of the different communities) could also play an important role locally. Though it has yet to take place, relationships have already been forged as the programme has been put together. As explained above, the organization has sought to combine the artistic and architectural approaches to projection mapping, and to this end has created a programme featuring members of both communities. One could hypothesize from such an event an increase in cross-fertilization of spaces and social bridging between communities even if, as pointed out by Wilks (2011), this structural effect is contrasted. Indeed, if existing relationships can be reinforced during a festival (*bonding*), new relationship are more difficult to build (*bridging*).

The process of drawing up the programme could also be important to the local configuration of this practice. Following the literature focused on field-configuring events (Schüßler, Grabher, and Müller-Seitz 2015), this process links the macro-dynamics of the field (regarding trends and conventions) with local individual actions (building a common cognitive space). This is all the truer given that the person initiating the festival has established strong ties with other actors in the field elsewhere. An event with an editorialized programme can both orient practice in a particular direction, promoting specific aesthetics, and organize moments of encounter for creators. It also offers an opportunity to meet the audience, which can in turn foster recognition and legitimization of the genre (Grabher, Ibert, and Flohr 2008).

Overall, we note that in PCs among the sample of places and events, some places/events are attended by one community and not others, for various reasons (proximity of place of work or residence, cultural tastes, etc.). What this reveals more broadly is the presence on a territory of communities which, in their constitution, are fragmented because of the competition around different spaces. Members of these communities are therefore facing a tradeoff between attending places and events associated specifically to their community's cognitive space (*bonding* logic) and attending places where several communities intersect (*bridging* logic). The former are where innovators belonging to distinct communities can meet and benefit from cross-fertilization. In a situation of co-presence of actors who can potentially collaborate in a techno-creative practice, we show that it is both necessary to have places where niches can structure themselves and places/events whose position on the edges of two knowledge fields allows cross-fertilization. Venues and events should therefore not be thought of as only hosting artistic content, but in places that would interest artists *and* engineers. To this end, arrangements where there would be art/tech hybridization of interest to both communities could stimulate the creation of links. It is in these cases that places and events have an intermediation role. Their ability to bring together network members and complement the role of brokers, therefore, depends as much on the attending habits as on their characteristics. The following figure wraps-up the main learnings of our framework and draws some levers for action for policy makers or community managers when it comes to structuring an innovation community Figure 7.

When two different and related knowledge bases co-exist (KB_1, KB_2), we suggest that supporting ($event_1$, $place_1$) and/or ($place_2$, $event_2$) can help intra-community structuring. These are bonding strategies and help the community related to KB_1 (or KB_2) to be more visible. But we also suggest another way to structure the community by playing with bridging strategies. To this purpose, $event_{12}$ and/or $place_{12}$ can be supported since they are not natural outputs coming from rational behaviours of emerging innovators in search of legitimacy. Indeed, each member can choose to invest time, market and non-market relationships in their respective fields through places and events before attending

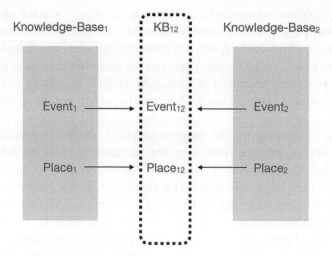

Figure 7. Innovation community structuring.

other places/events associated to distinct fields. This must be considered if a policy maker wants to support techno–creative innovation. At best, these two strategies (bonding and bridging) might be sequential and cumulative, by first letting each community build a structure around their own focal places/events before designing inter–community places and/or events.

The literature has extensively documented the importance of knowledge broker (KB_{12}) and we suggest some new structural brokers with places and events. Obviously, it is beyond this paper to define what these boundary places and events are, but content mixing both knowledge bases are with no doubt a good start to sustain inter-community structuring. Furthermore, the interactions between knowledge brokers and structural brokers have to be investigated more deeply.

Conclusion

The literature has highlighted a strong potential for innovation at the intersection of the arts and technology sectors, but we show in this paper that the interplay of both knowledge and related fields cannot be taken for granted. In the studied case, it does not yet take the form of an integrated innovation community, since different cognitive spaces are in competition. This fragmentation leads to some difficulties and notably those related to critical mass reaching, standardization and external attractivity.

The actors we studied share interests in a practice, with cognitive spaces that can potentially converge, and increasing social embeddedness could allow an innovation community to emerge. In addition to the role of brokers already documented in the literature, we identify the roles of bridging and bonding of places and events. These can play an important role in structuring a collective innovation dynamic, even serving as intra- and inter-community intermediation mechanisms. They allow a community to gain visibility and legitimacy. Places and their articulations in a spatialized network, therefore, appear necessary to facilitating the structuring of communities of innovation.

By developing an ecosystemic vision, and given the bonding or bridging role we identified, our results echo the literature on communities and supports the need to develop places and events where actors evolving in distinct fields of knowledge can meet and develop a shared space.

How can we bring out innovation that crosses arts and technologies? Communities, places, and events are needed, but that is not enough. Brokers at the intersection of different fields of knowledge are necessary, and as such the role of architects is interesting since they manipulate both synthetic and symbolic knowledge. The role of these actors is crucial because it encompasses the embedding of distinct communities and the formation of common cognitive spaces, facilitating the exchange and combination of knowledge. This paves the way for further research on the dynamics of emerging innovative and localized community.

Notes

1. So called, STEAM based Innovation.
2. According to the Agence d'urbanisme de la région nantaise (AURAN), the city has around 26,300 jobs in digital technologies and services (2019), and around 31,000 jobs in the cultural and creative industries (2019).
3. Some mappers could have been overlooked because of being isolated, or invisible to the people we interviewed. We were also unable to interview some for material reasons (they were not in the area, or unavailable during the study period).
4. For more details on the definition of links, see the Appendix.
5. Data analysis was conducted with the *igraph* package of R software.
6. For the moment, the first edition is postponed due to the Covid-19 pandemic.

Acknowledgements

We are also grateful to the participants of the Rethinking culture and creativity in the technological era workshop in Florence, and to the two anonymous reviewers for their insightful comments and suggestions.

Disclosure statement

No potential conflict of interest was reported by the author(s).

Funding

The authors wish to thank the RFI West Creative Industries (RESET project) and the Agence Nationale de la Recherche (SCANEA project - n°ANR-18-CE22-0012) for their financial support.

ORCID

Etienne Capron http://orcid.org/0000-0002-1413-6879
Dominique Sagot-Duvauroux http://orcid.org/0000-0002-2854-7871
Raphaël Suire http://orcid.org/0000-0003-1735-9709

Bibliography

Ambrosino, C., V. Guillon, and D. Sagot-Duvauroux. 2016. "Genius Loci Reloaded, The Creative Renaissance of Nantes and Saint Etienne." In *Tourism and the Creative Industries: Theories, Policies and Practice*, edited by P. Long, and N. D. Morpeth, 116–133. London: Routledge.

Amin, A., and P. Cohendet. 2004. *Architectures of Knowledge: Firms, Capabilities, and Communities.*. Oxford, UK: Oxford University Press.

Antonietti, R., & Boschma, R. 2018. "Social Capital, Resilience and Regional Diversification in Italy." *Papers in Evolutionary Economic Geography (PEEG)*. no. 1804. Utrecht University, Department of Human Geography and Spatial Planning, Group Economic Geography.

Asheim, B. 2007. "Differentiated Knowledge Bases and Varieties of Regional Innovation Systems." *Innovation: The European Journal of Social Science Research* 20 (3): 223–241.

Balland, P., C. Jara-Figueroa, S. Petralia, M. Steijn, D. Rigby, et al. 2020. "Complex Economic Activities Concentrate in Large Cities." *Nature Human Behaviour* 4 (3): 248–254.

Bathelt, H., and P. Cohendet. 2014. "The Creation of Knowledge: Local Building, Global Accessing and Economic Development—Toward an Agenda." *Journal of Economic Geography* 14 (5): 869–882.

Bathelt, H., A. Malmberg, and P. Maskell. 2004. "Clusters and Knowledge: Local Buzz, Global Pipelines and the Process of Knowledge Creation." *Progress in Human Geography* 28 (1): 31–56.

Becker, H. 1982. *Art Worlds (Nachdr)*. Berkeley: University of California Press.

Boix, R., F. Capone, L. De Propris, L. Lazzeretti, and D. Sanchez. 2016. "Comparing Creative Industries in Europe." *European Urban and Regional Studies* 23 (4): 935–940.

Burt, R. 2004. "Structural Holes and Good Ideas." *American Journal of Sociology* 110 (2): 349–399.

Capdevila, I., P. Cohendet, and L. Simon. 2018. "From a Local Community to a Global Influence. How ElBulli Restaurant Created a new Epistemic Movement in the World of Haute Cuisine." *Industry and Innovation* 25 (5): 526–549.

Cohendet, P., D. Grandadam, and L. Simon. 2009. "Economics and the Ecology of Creativity: Evidence from the Popular Music Industry." *International Review of Applied Economics* 23 (6): 709–722.

Cohendet, P., D. Grandadam, and L. Simon. 2010. "The Anatomy of the Creative City." *Industry & Innovation* 17 (1): 91–111.

Cohendet, P., D. Grandadam, and R. Suire. 2021. "Reconsidering the Dynamics of Local Knowledge Creation: Middlegrounds and Local Innovation Commons in the Case of FabLabs." *Zeitschrift Für Wirtschaftsgeographie* 65 (1): 1–11.

Coleman, J. 1988. "Social Capital in the Creation of Human Capital." *American Journal of Sociology* 94: S95–S120.

Content, J., and K. Frenken. 2016. "Related Variety and Economic Development: A Literature Review." *European Planning Studies* 24 (12): 2097–2112.

Cooke, P. 2007. "To Construct Regional Advantage from Innovation Systems First Build Policy Platforms." *European Planning Studies* 15 (2): 179–194.

Crespo, J., D. Réquier-Desjardins, and J. Vicente. 2014. "Why Can Collective Action Fail in Local Agri-Food Systems? A Social Network Analysis of Cheese Producers in Aculco, Mexico." *Food Policy* 46: 165–177.

Crespo, J., R. Suire, and J. Vicente. 2014. "Lock-in or Lock-out? How Structural Properties of Knowledge Networks Affect Regional Resilience." *Journal of Economic Geography* 14 (1): 199–219.

Davids, M., and K. Frenken. 2018. "Proximity, Knowledge Base and the Innovation Process: Towards an Integrated Framework." *Regional Studies* 52 (1): 23–34.

Foster, P., and R. Ocejo. 2013. "Brokerage, Mediation, and Social Networks in the Creative Industries." In *The Oxford Handbook of Creative Industries*, edited by C. Jones, M. Lorenzen, and J. Sapsed, 405–420. Oxford, UK: Oxford University Press.

Frenken, K., F. Van Oort, and T. Verburg. 2007. "Related Variety, Unrelated Variety and Regional Economic Growth." *Regional Studies* 41 (5): 685–697.

Garud, R., and P. Karnøe. 2001. "Path Creation as a Process of Mindful Deviation." In *Path Dependence and Creation (Lawrence Erlbaum Associates)*, edited by R. Garud, and P. Karnøe, 1–40. Mahwah, N.J.: Lawrence Erlbaum Associates.

Gould, R., and R. Fernandez. 1989. "Structures of Mediation: A Formal Approach to Brokerage in Transaction Networks." *Sociological Methodology* 19: 89.

Grabher, G. 2018. "Marginality as Strategy: Leveraging Peripherality for Creativity." *Environment and Planning A: Economy and Space* 50 (8): 1785–1794.

Grabher, G., O. Ibert, and S. Flohr. 2008. "The Neglected King: The Customer in the New Knowledge Ecology of Innovation." *Economic Geography* 84 (3): 253–280.

Grandadam, D., P. Cohendet, and L. Simon. 2013. "Places, Spaces and the Dynamics of Creativity: The Video Game Industry in Montreal." *Regional Studies* 47 (10): 1701–1714.

Granovetter, M. 1985. "Economic Action and Social Structure: The Problem of Embeddedness." *American Journal of Sociology* 91 (3): 481–510.

Haas, P. 1992. "Introduction: Epistemic Communities and International Policy Coordination." *International Organization* 46 (1): 1–35.

Ingstrup, M., and M. Menzel. 2019. "The Emergence of Relatedness Between Industries: The Example of Offshore oil and gas and Offshore Wind Energy in Esbjerg, Denmark." *Papers in Evolutionary Economic Geography* 19: 29.

Janssen, M., and K. Frenken. 2019. "Cross-specialisation Policy: Rationales and Options for Linking Unrelated Industries." *Cambridge Journal of Regions, Economy and Society* 12 (2): 195–212.

Jones, C., W. Hesterly, and S. Borgatti. 1997. "A General Theory of Network Governance: Exchange Conditions and Social Mechanisms." *The Academy of Management Review* 22 (4): 911–945.

Kloosterman, R. 2014. "Cultural Amenities: Large and Small, Mainstream and Niche—A Conceptual Framework for Cultural Planning in an Age of Austerity." *European Planning Studies* 22 (12): 2510–2525.

Lave, J., and E. Wenger. 1991. *Situated Learning: Legitimate Peripheral Participation*. Cambridge: Cambridge University Press.

Lazer, D., and A. Friedman. 2007. "The Network Structure of Exploration and Exploitation." *Administrative Science Quarterly* 52(4): 667–694.

Lingo, E., and S. O'Mahony. 2010. "Nexus Work: Brokerage on Creative Projects." *Administrative Science Quarterly* 55 (1): 47–81.

Martin, R., and J. Moodysson. 2011. "Innovation in Symbolic Industries: The Geography and Organization of Knowledge Sourcing." *European Planning Studies* 19 (7): 1183–1203.

Maskell, P., H. Bathelt, and A. Malmberg. 2006. "Building Global Knowledge Pipelines: The Role of Temporary Clusters." *European Planning Studies* 14 (8): 997–1013.

Nedkovski, V., and M. Guerci. 2021. "When Homophilous Ties Matter: Social Network Brokerage and Individuals' Innovative Behavior." *European Management Journal*.

Nooteboom, B. 2007. Cognitive Distance in and Between COP's and Firms: Where do Exploitation and Exploration take Place, and How are they Connected? Tilburg University - CentER Discussion Paper, 2007-4: 25.

Obstfeld, D. 2005. "Social Networks, the Tertius Iungens Orientation, and Involvement in Innovation." *Administrative Science Quarterly* 50 (1): 100–130.

Oldenburg, R. 1989. *The Great Good Place: Cafés, Coffee Shops, Community Centers, Beauty Parlors, General Stores, Bars, Hangouts, and how They get you Through the day*. 1st ed. New York: Paragon House.

Rantisi, N. 2014. "Exploring the Role of Industry Intermediaries in the Construction of 'Local Pipelines': The Case of the Montreal Fur Garment Cluster and the Rise of Fur–Fashion Connections." *Journal of Economic Geography* 14 (5): 955–971.

Rantisi, N., and D. Leslie. 2010. "Materiality and Creative Production: The Case of the Mile End Neighborhood in Montréal." *Environment and Planning A: Economy and Space* 42 (12): 2824–2841.

Rodríguez-Pose, A., and N. Lee. 2020. "Hipsters vs. Geeks? Creative Workers, STEM and Innovation in US Cities." *Cities* 100: 102653.

Rogers, E. 1983. *Diffusion of Innovations*. New York: Free Press, in press.
Schieb-Bienfait, N., A. Saives, and B. Charles-Pauvers. 2018. "Urban Creative and Cultural Entrepreneurs: A Closer Look at Cultural Quarters and the Creative Clustering Process in Nantes (France)." In *Entrepreneurship in Culture and Creative Industries: Perspectives from Companies and Regions*, edited by E. Innerhofer, H. Pechlaner, and E. Borin, 341–353. Cham: Springer International Publishing.
Schüßler, E., G. Grabher, and G. Müller-Seitz. 2015. "Field-Configuring Events: Arenas for Innovation and Learning?" *Industry and Innovation* 22 (3): 165–172.
Scott, A. 2014. "Beyond the Creative City: Cognitive–Cultural Capitalism and the New Urbanism." *Regional Studies* 48 (4): 565–578.
Sedita, S., I. Noni, and L. Pilotti. 2017. "Out of the Crisis: An Empirical Investigation of Place-Specific Determinants of Economic Resilience." *European Planning Studies* 25 (2): 155–180.
Sgourev, S. 2013. "How Paris Gave Rise to Cubism (and Picasso): Ambiguity and Fragmentation in Radical Innovation." *Organization Science* 24 (6): 1601–1617.
Sgourev, S. 2015. "Brokerage as Catalysis: How Diaghilev's *Ballets Russes* Escalated Modernism." *Organization Studies* 36 (3): 343–361.
Storper, M., and A. Venables. 2004. "Buzz: Face-to-Face Contact and the Urban Economy." *Journal of Economic Geography* 4 (4): 351–370.
Suire, R. 2019. "Innovating by Bricolage: How do Firms Diversify Through Knowledge Interactions with FabLabs?" *Regional Studies* 53 (7): 1–12.
Suire, R., and J. Vicente. 2014. "Clusters for Life or Life Cycles of Clusters: In Search of the Critical Factors of Clusters' Resilience." *Entrepreneurship & Regional Development* 26 (1–2): 142–164.
Torre, A. 2008. "On the Role Played by Temporary Geographical Proximity in Knowledge Transmission." *Regional Studies* 42 (6): 869–889.
Uzzi, B., and J. Spiro. 2005. "Collaboration and Creativity: The Small World Problem." *American Journal of Sociology* 111 (2): 447–504.
Watier, M. 2018. "Video Mapping in Audiovisual Performances: Projecting the Club Scene Onto the Urban Space." *Cinergie – Il Cinema e Le Altre Arti* 7 (14): 69–82.
Wilks, L. 2011. "Bridging and Bonding: Social Capital at Music Festivals.." *Journal of Policy Research in Tourism, Leisure and Events* 3 (3): 281–297.
Yin, R. 2013. *Case Study Research: Design and Methods*. 5th ed. Los Angeles: SAGE Publications.

Appendix

Sample for interviews:
For this study, 22 interviews were conducted, and respondents were divided into communities as follows:

- Architects: 8 (among which 4 belongs to a collective)
- Artists: 5 (among which 3 belongs to a collective)
- VJs : 4

Additional interviews were conducted with two different types of actors: local cultural venues employees and digital art experts (4), and a musical event organizer. For these actors we used another interview guide in order to have a complementary view of the local ecosystem. This allowed us to identify actors involved in this practice, places and events where projection-mapping is regularly used, and better understand the characteristics of the territory in terms of artistic activities.

Finally, informal discussions with an artist and a member of the architects' community, and observation at an event in June 2019 were also used to attest to social relationships.

Coding of the data:

We recorded and transcribed each interview in its entirety. The interview guide is in two parts: the first focuses on the creative process (what type of technology is used, how a project is conducted step-by-step, etc.) and the second focuses on the places and events attended and the respondent's ego-network.

The questions in the first part of the interview guide were used to distinguish between different types of creative processes, and to identify explicit (e.g. "I am an artist") or implicit (i.e. aesthetic sensibilities, artists cited ...) references to categories. Thanks to this and the networks of relationships of each actor, we formed the three communities: architects, artists, VJs.

The second part of the guide allowed us to gather the data necessary for these network analyses. Individuals, locations and events were anonymized for these analyses. The relationships were formatted into a list of links connecting either individuals to each other, places to each other, or events to each other. We distinguish two types of networks:

- the social network, which concerns the relationships between members of the community. We establish a link between two actors when one or both of them claims to have a market or non-market relationship with the other. In addition to interviews (where a previous relationship can be omitted voluntarily or not), we used second-hand data (social media and website pages, event schedules, performance technical descriptions) to attest to a relationship between these actors: collaboration on a project, attendance at the same event, etc.
- the network of places and the network of events. For these networks, we follow Uzzi and Spiro (2005) and consider that a link can be established between two places (or two events) if an actor attends both locations. Here again we distinguish between market and non-market relationships. For example, if an actor A attends both place P1 and P2 to do a performance, a market link is created between these two locations. To proceed, we noted for each actor which places were cited in the interviews. Thus, for each actor, we link together the different places or events he or she attends. Finally, we aggregate these data to produce the final network that will then be studied. We also used second-hand data (social media and website pages, event schedules, work descriptions) to verify and complete these data. Thus, we consider that an individual attends a place if he is on the programming of an event, if he has exhibited in a place, if he has done a performance in a club, etc.

The impact of cultural and creative industries on the wealth of countries, regions and municipalities

Rafael Boix Domenech, Blanca De Miguel Molina and Pau Rausell Köster

ABSTRACT
This paper compares the total impact of cultural and creative industries (CCIs) on per capita income of countries, regions and municipalities. We estimate the total effects of CCIs in 78 developed and developing countries in 5 continents, in 275 European regions and in 518 municipalities in the European region of Valencia, using data obtained from multiple databases and nonparametric local linear least squares. The average effects of CCIs are positive in the three territorial scales, in both low- and high-income locations, and increase in conjunction with increases in development, with high and very high developed places showing greater impacts. CCIs are, thus, a powerful resource for improving the well-being of rich and poor places at all geographic scales; however, they also act as a double-edged sword, as they increase inequalities between places.

1. Introduction

The United Nations Educational, Scientific and Cultural Organization (UNESCO 2013, 2) defines cultural and creative industries (CCIs) as 'those sectors of organized activity that have as their main objective the production or reproduction, the promotion, distribution or commercialization of goods, services and activities of content derived from cultural, artistic or heritage origin'. In a complementary way, the European Parliament (2016:10) defines CCIs as: 'those industries that are based on cultural values, cultural diversity, individual and/or collective creativity, skills and talent with the potential to generate innovation, wealth and jobs through the creation of social and economic value, in particular from intellectual property'.

One of the most important dimensions by which wealth, economic value and well-being are assessed is per capita income (OECD 2018), usually measured through the gross domestic product (GDP) per capita. The study presented in this paper measures the total impact of CCIs on the per capita income of places comparing different territorial scales of analysis: countries, regions and cities, and discusses how it is affected by the levels of development of places.

General evidence on the total impact of CCIs on the per capita income of places is limited. Indeed, the topic has only been examined in a few studies (Rausell, Marco, and Abeledo 2011; De Miguel et al. 2012; Boix, De Miguel, and Hervás 2013; Marco, Rausell, and Abeledo 2014). Those exclusively involved European regions and point estimates. Beyond those studies, no broad data on the total effects of CCIs on the per capita income of countries or localities exists, reflecting an important gap in the empirical literature on CCIs. Moreover, scholars have failed to draw conclusions on whether the impact measurement is affected by the scale of the analysis and the development conditions of the places, because such a comparison has never been made. This constitutes another important gap in the knowledge, which mainly affects well-being and development strategies potentially based on CCIs.

In this study we want to know whether the measurements of the total impact of CCIs on the per capita income differ substantially at each scale of analysis (country, region, city) and whether this impact follow homogenous or heterogeneous patterns within each scale of analysis.

The causal relationship between CCIs and the income of places implies the hypothesis that the average impacts would reflect the same indications and trends and would be within a comparable range for all territorial scales. Certainly, rejection of this hypothesis – or widespread evidence of negative impacts – would lead to a rethink of CCI-based policies. Conversely, solid favourable evidence for all scales would provide important support to policies that address CCIs. We also establish the hypothesis that the impacts are heterogeneous within each scale, although it is difficult to establish a priori if they follow defined patterns. A greater impact of CCIs in places with a lower stage of development would undoubtedly imply a reduction in inequalities between places, while a greater impact in more developed places would lead to the conclusion that CCIs increase inequality between places.

To answer the research questions, an analytical model was estimated for three territorial scales for which data were available: a sample of 78 countries in 2014; 275 regions in 29 European countries in 2008; and 518 municipalities in the European region of Valencia (Spain) in 2015 and 2016.

The data for this study were obtained from multiple databases: United Nations Conference on Trade and Development (UNCTAD), World Intellectual Property Organization (WIPO), Lazzeretti, Boix, and Sánchez (2018), Penn World Table, the World Bank, Eurostat, Orbis (Bureau Van Dijk), Spanish National Institute of Statistics, Spanish Tax Agency, and Spanish National Institute of Social Security. Data source limitations made it necessary to use different years and slightly different empirical definitions of CCIs in this analysis, which enabled a comparison of the sensitivity of the results to the composition of the construct.

The estimates were carried out using the local linear least squares (LLLS) method. The LLLS method is a nonparametric flexible approach that avoids most of the constraints of parametric estimators, providing not only average estimates but also place-specific estimates (Henderson and Parmeter 2015; Racine and Hayfield 2020).

This paper makes three contributions to the literature. First, it presents and compares for the first time simultaneous measurements of the total impact of CCIs on per capita income for three scales of analysis: countries, regions and municipalities, allowing general conclusions to be drawn about these effects and whether they are affected by the scale or the unit of analysis. Second, it presents evidence that the impact of CCIs on per capita income of places are heterogeneous and depends on the development conditions of the places. Third, in contrast to previous research, for which estimates were based on empirical models, we introduce a theory-based analytical model that provides the relevant variables for the estimation, thereby correcting the problem of omitted variables from previous works and providing a causal framework and unbiased impact measurements.

The paper is organized as follows. The next section provides a brief review of the literature on the impacts of CCIs on per capita income and related variables. The third section includes a description of the data. In the fourth section, the methodology is explained. The fifth section provides a comparative study of the impact of the CCIs on the per capita income of countries, regions and municipalities. Finally, the sixth section concludes the paper, introduces some critical remarks and highlights implications for future research.

2. The impact of cultural and creative industries (CCIs) on the per capita income of places

2.1. Nature and type of impacts

The impacts of the CCIs on income can be direct and indirect (Boix and Rausell 2018). Direct impacts, which are the most immediate and visible, are measured by the income directly produced or consumed by the CCIs. However, other impacts of CCIs are indirect, that is, the effects they have on the rest of the economic system (Boix and Soler 2017). The sum of the direct and indirect effects comprises the total impact, which can be negative, neutral or positive (Potts and Cunningham 2008; Boix and Rausell 2018).

A negative impact can be due to a low growth rate of total factor productivity in CCIs (Baumol and Bowen 1965; Potts and Cunningham 2008), to CCIs being underused and other activities making better use of resources at certain stages of the development process (Lazzeretti, Boix, and Sánchez 2018) or to the precariousness of the labour relations model that seems to accompany CCIs (Hesmondhalgh 2010).

Neutral impacts basically involve any direct effect of CCIs that is proportional to the share of CCIs in the economy.

Positive impacts can be due to growth effects and evolutionary changes (Potts and Cunningham 2008). The first type – growth effects – results from the role CCIs play as growth drivers, activating demand or supply-side expansion. Demand-side effects result directly from the expenditures in CCIs, and indirectly from backward-linked industries supplying goods and services to CCIs and income induced effects. Supply-side growth effects come directly from the CCIs own production, and indirectly from other mechanisms:

(a) Multiplier effects generated by the industry life cycle (Boix and Rausell 2018), and industry spillovers disperse through supply chain linkages into other sectors (Bakhshi and McVittie 2009; UNCTAD 2010).
(b) Knowledge spillovers by exporting new ideas to the rest of the economy or by facilitating the adoption, retention and absorption of new ideas and technologies (Potts and Cunningham 2008; Yu et al. 2014; Bakhshi and McVittie 2009).

(c) Amenity influences, attracting skilled and educated people and qualified firms to the area (Florida, Mellander, and Stolarik 2008; Lee 2014).

The second type of positive effect resulting from CCIs is evolutionary change. CCIs are part of a process of economic evolution, and their role is to provide evolutionary services to the innovation system, facilitating change of the entire economic system, resulting in evolutionary change. In this case, all the impact is indirect (Potts and Cunningham 2008).

2.2. Measurement approaches and empirical evidence

UNESCO (2012) identifies two approaches to measuring the effects of CCIs on the economy. The first approach is through its contribution or direct impact on GDP, employment or other variables. Findings on the direct contribution of CCIs to the global GDP and income range from 3% in EY (2015) to 7% in Quartesan, Romis, and Lanzafame (2007). CCIs' direct contribution to the GDP varies depending on the location and the definition of CCIs applied (see UNCTAD 2010). Definitions biased towards copyright activities (e.g. Howkins 2007; WIPO 2014) reflect greater contributions than definitions biased towards cultural activities (e.g. EY 2015).

The second approach focuses on the measurement of the total impact – direct and indirect – of CCIs on the economy, which can be done through input-output analysis and econometric modelling of production and demand functions.

Input-output analysis is a well-known method in which an increase in spending in CCIs produces short-run multiplier effects on the economy (output, added value, employment, taxes) due to their interdependencies with other activities and to induced income processes. Input-output has been used to evaluate the impacts of CCIs in some countries and regions (CEBR 2017; SGS 2013; CRD 2018), obtaining total multipliers of the added value that usually oscillate between 2 and 3. This method also has many limitations (See UNESCO 2012). Its greatest restriction for comparative studies is the difficulty in obtaining input-output tables with territorial and sectoral detail.

Econometric modelling has fewer restrictions on finding comparable data, which makes it more suitable for wide-range comparative studies. It has been used to quantify the total impact of CCIs on the GDP per capita in Rausell, Marco, and Abeledo (2011), De Miguel et al. (2012), Boix, De Miguel, and Hervás (2013) and Marco, Rausell, and Abeledo (2014). These papers are characterized by: (1) the use of samples from multiple European regions, (2) they used econometric estimates based on empirical models with few controls, and (3) they obtained extremely high elasticities for the GDP per capita according to the contribution of CCIs to labour. Rausell, Marco, and Abeledo (2011) found that an increase of 1% in the share of creative industries was associated with about a 0.4% increase in GDP per capita in the Spanish regions. For a sample covering most regions in the EU, De Miguel et al. (2012), Marco, Rausell, and Abeledo (2014) and Boix, De Miguel, and Hervás (2013) demonstrated elasticities between 0.39% and 0.44%. As observed by Boix and Soler (2017), these high elasticities can be attributed to the mis-specification of the empirical models, which reflects the need for robust theoretical models.

Other econometric studies have focused on different variables closely related to the GDP per capita, such as labour productivity, total factor productivity, wages or sales, as well as other scales and economic areas. They uncovered total impacts that were positive, although much more moderate than those of the previously cited studies. Hong et al. (2014) indicated elasticities of the total factor productivity to the specialization in CCI employees of about 0.04% for China's provinces. Boix and Soler (2017) and Boix, Peiró, and Rausell (2021) found elasticities for the impact of CCI services on labour productivity in the European regions ranging from 0.04 to 0.14%. Lee (2014) revealed impacts of the CCIs of 0.047% to 0.066% on the wages of the United Kingdom travel-to-work areas. For the cities in the Miami metropolitan area, Yum (2016) indicated elasticities for city sales relative to the number of CCI firms ranging from 0.048% to 0.074%.

Due to the data limitations, it is difficult to separate direct and indirect impacts in econometric analyses, and those have usually focused on measuring the total impacts. An exception is Boix and Soler (2017) who indicated that, in the case of creative service industries, the indirect impact represents 90% of the total impact on labour productivity.

Some of these papers discuss the implications or sensitivity of the results pertaining to the empirical definition of the CCIs and the partial correlations between GDP per capita or labour productivity and individual CCI sectors. Boix, De Miguel, and Hervás (2013) and Boix and Soler (2017) found robust evidence that only creative service industries have a positive and relevant effect on differences in wealth between EU regions, whereas the aggregated effect of the so-called creative manufacturing industries tends to be null or negative. Boix, De Miguel, and Hervás (2013) disaggregated the correlations of individual creative service sectors with the GDP per capita of European regions, finding a positive correlation for all creative service sectors.

3. Methodology

3.1. Model

To obtain the total effects of the CCIs on the GDP per capita, an econometric estimate of an equation for GDP per capita was used. In a basic identity, the GDP per capita (GDP divided by population P) can be separated into two components: labour productivity (GDP divided by labour L) and the ratio of labour to population (L/P):

$$GDP/P = (GDP/L) \cdot (L/P) \tag{1}$$

Taking logarithms:

$$\ln(GDP/P) = \ln(GDP/L) + \ln(L/P) \tag{2}$$

The effect of the CCIs is introduced through the productivity term. Boix and Soler (2017) measured CCIs' impact on productivity using an adjusted version of a semi-endogenous growth model adapted from Jones (1995, 2001).

The model departs from a multiplicative production function $Y = K^{\alpha}(AL_Y)^{1-\alpha}$, where Y is the output, A is labour-augmenting technology (knowledge stock), K is capital, and α is output elasticity of capital. Working people (L), the source of creativity, can be dedicated to producing ideas (L_A) in the creative sector or, alternatively, producing goods and services in other sectors (L_Y), so that $L = L_A + L_y$. The ideas and designs produced by the creative sector are used by an intermediate sector to transform creative capital into intermediate goods, and then the final sector uses the intermediate goods and labour to produce final goods. The increase in product variety raises productivity by allowing the spread of intermediate production more thinly across a larger number of activities, each being subject to diminishing returns and, hence, yielding an increased average product when operated at a lower intensity.

The general solution of Jones (2001) for the simplest version of the model for a path of balanced growth and a moment of time t can be written as a log-linear equation for the steady state:

$$\ln\left(\frac{GDP}{L}\right) = b \ln \delta + b\lambda \ln s_R + \ln s_y + a \ln s_k - a \ln(n + g_A + d) + b\lambda \ln L \\ - b \ln g_A \quad (3)$$

in which the labour productivity (GDP/L) for a year t depends on the rate at which new ideas are created (δ), the share of persons employed in the creative sector (S_R), the share of persons employed in the rest of the economy (S_Y), the intensity of capital per worker (S_K), the population growth rate (n) and the rate of depreciation of capital (d). In the equation, λ measures the existence of scale economies, $a = \alpha/(1-\alpha)$, and $b = 1/(1-\phi)$, where α is the output elasticity of capital, and ϕ measures productivity (returns) in the production of ideas. The term g_A represents the growth rate of the ideas (See Boix & Soler [2017] for more detail about the derivation of the model).

Substituting the labour productivity term [3] in equation [2], we obtain:

$$\ln\left(\frac{GDP}{P}\right) = b \ln \delta + b\lambda \ln s_R + \ln s_y + a \ln s_k - b \ln g_A + b\lambda \ln L \\ - a \ln(n + g_A + d) + \ln\left(\frac{L}{P}\right) \quad (4)$$

3.2. Estimation

Initial tests on the data revealed non-normality, heteroscedasticity and nonlinearity. The Hsiao, Li, and Racine (2007) test suggested that a nonparametric specification would better capture the nature of the data than parametric specifications.[1]

The estimation of the total effects of CCIs on the income (GDP per capita) was performed using the local-linear least-squares estimator (LLLS) method (Henderson and Parmeter 2015). LLLS is a nonparametric method based on generalized product kernels. Nonparametric kernel regressions are based on the estimation of a flexible functional form, in which the dependent variable (y) is described by a set of explanatory variables (X), and $m(.)$ is an unknown smooth function capturing the conditional relationship between the left- and right-hand side variables in the model. The LLLS estimator is computed using nearby observations in both the left- and right-hand side of the equation, and then these fits are linked to construct the global function:

$$y_i = m(X_i) + u_i, \quad i = 1, 2, \ldots n \quad (5)$$

The LLLS method avoids most of the constraints and strong assumptions of the parametric estimators and, consequently, offers some advantages over traditional parametric methods (see Henderson and Parmeter 2015). The LLLS estimator requires neither a predefined functional form nor a distribution of the error term. Therefore, it does not require normality, and it captures nonlinearities in any part of the distribution. The LLLS technique is based on the values of similar observations in a bandwidth and still produces consistent and asymptotically normal estimations when spatial dependency is present in the data (see McMillen 2010; Jenish 2012).

Furthermore, the LLLS approach provides an estimate, or gradient, for each observation and each variable. Accordingly, it is feasible to report the estimated effects for the mean, the median, quantiles or groups of regions selected by the researcher and based on specific characteristics, allowing for a more detailed analysis than possible when employing parametric methods.

Following recent contributions using the LLLS estimator in a similar context (Boix, Peiró, and Rausell 2021), we used a Gaussian kernel and least squares cross-validation (LSCV) for the bandwidth (see Henderson and Parmeter 2015). For the estimation we used the NP package in R (Racine and Hayfield 2020).

Although our analytical model is supply-oriented and there is no simultaneity between CCIs and GDP per capita, we have verified that there is no endogeneity between the CCIs and the GDP per capita derived from the nature of the data. There are not specific endogeneity tests for LLLs so that we tested the endogeneity and the adequacy of the instruments in a parametric estimation using Wu-Hausman, weak instruments and Sargan tests. We also compare the goodness of fit of the LLLs estimator versus the Su and Ullah (2008) instrumental variables estimator as suggested by Henderson and Parmeter (2015). If there was evidence of endogeneity, the estimates from the Su and Ullah (2008) instrumental variables model would be used.

4. Data

4.1. Units of analysis

The units of analysis used in this paper met three basic conditions of scalability, comparability-replicability and representativeness. First, they corresponded to the three scales of analysis: national, regional and local. Second, sufficient and comparable data were available to allow the same theoretical model to be applied with the same variables. Third, they were representative of a broad economic reality (e.g. developed and developing, rural and urban, etc.).

The national sample covered 78 countries from the 5 inhabited continents and with different levels of development (from low to very high) in 2013 and 2014 (Figure 1). The coverage was good for Europe, America, Eastern and Southeastern Asia, and Australia-New Zealand; the coverage was poor for the rest of Asia and, in particular, for Africa.

The sample of regions included 275 NUTS 2 regions[2] in the 28 countries of the EU (including the United Kingdom) plus Norway (Figure 2). All regions of the 29 countries, except the French overseas areas, were included. This encompassed high and very high-, middle- and low-income regions. We chose the year 2008 because it offered the best coverage related to number of regions due to previous reworkings of the database, and the data were less distorted by the effect of the 2008 crisis, in comparison to data from later

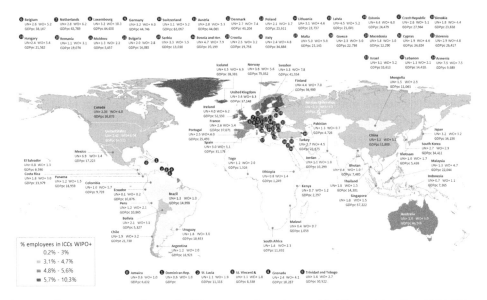

Figure 1. Percentage of employees in CCIs over total employment in 78 countries. Year 2014. UN+ = UNESCO classification of CCIs. WO+ = WIPO classification of CCIs. Source: Elaboration from Lazzeretti, Boix, and Sánchez (2018) and the World Bank.

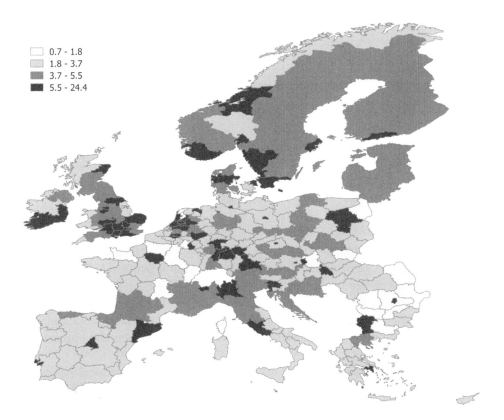

Figure 2. Percentage of employees in CCIs (creative services) over total employment in 275 European regions. Year 2008. Source: Elaboration from Boix, Peiró, and Rausell (2021) and Eurostat.

years. Regions cannot be subdivided into provinces (NUTS 3) because Eurostat data do not allow it for most variables.

The sample of municipalities included 518 of the 545 municipalities in the region of Valencia (Comunidad Valenciana). We excluded 37 micro-municipalities because of the lack of income data. Valencia is a European region located on the eastern coast of Spain and is a representative middle-income region, with an income equivalent to 93% of the European average and 97% of the European median. The data were available for the years 2015 and 2016. The sample contains many small municipalities and, as a sensitivity analysis we also estimated the model only for municipalities with more than 10,000 inhabitants.

The units of analysis and datasets that we used have two limitations. First, the availability and granularity of the statistics prohibit using exactly the same definition of CCIs at all scales of analysis, as well as using data from the same years. Second, the sample of countries was self-selected to include only those countries for which sufficient information on employment in cultural or intellectual property activities was available, and thus, the results must be interpreted with due caution. The regional and local scales do not have the problem of self-selection, although they correspond to European countries and, therefore, represent a specific geoeconomic area.

However, the units of analysis also have some virtues. The most interesting is that when comparing different scales, each with high internal heterogeneity, and using different definitions for CCIs and different years for each scale, a certain randomness is introduced into the experiment. This enabled us to extend much further in our conclusions than previous research allowed.

4.2. Data sources and elaboration of variables

According to the analytical model (Section 3), the dependent variable is the GDP per capita. The explanatory variables include the stock of CCIs measured as the percentage of people employed in CCIs, the share of persons employed in noncreative industries, capital stock per employee, the growth rate of ideas, total employment, the composite term $n + g_A + d$ and the ratio of employees by population.

The correlation matrix describing the relationships among the variables are provided in Appendix 2.

4.2.1. The GDP per capita

The GDP per capita is a proxy variable for income and wealth flow and one of the fundamental dimensions of well-being.

GDP data for countries and regions comes from the World Bank and Eurostat, and is defined as the sum of primary incomes distributed by resident producer units, that is, the 'compensation of employees, plus taxes less subsidies on production and imports, plus gross mixed income, plus gross operating surplus' (OECD 1993, 19).

The data for the municipalities are elaborated by the Spanish National Institute of Statistics (INE) on the basis of personal income tax returns. The data include compensation of employees and mixed income but do not directly capture all the gross operating surplus. This difference should be considered when comparing the results of the municipalities with those of countries and regions.

The average GDP per capita of the countries in the sample in the year 2014 was $23,600, ranging from $1059 for Malawi to $75,600 for Norway. The average global GDP per capita for the same year was less than $11,000. The difference shows a bias towards developed and developing countries, although the less developed are also represented. For regions, the average GDP per capita in the year 2008 was €25,450, ranging from €7500 for Severozapaden (Bulgaria) to €126,700 for inner London. For municipalities, the income data came in the form of an income index. The average income index was about €9400 in 2015 and about €9600 in 2016; it ranged from €5300 to €15,600.

4.2.2. Measurement of the CCIs

The stock of creative industries (s_R) has been measured using the share of persons employed in creative industries over total employment, as requested by the model (equation (4)).

Measurement of CCIs is extremely difficult (UNCTAD 2010; UNESCO 2012). The current statistical classifications (ISIC Rev. 4) require a level of detail at a minimum of a two-digit (Boix, De Miguel, and Hervás 2013) but preferably at a four-digit level of detail (Oxford Economics 2013). This level of detail is difficult to find for developing and less developed countries. Even for developed countries, a two-digit breakdown without gaps for all sectors is difficult to obtain at subnational levels.

Databases of labour statistics with at least two-digit information do not exist for every country in the world. Therefore, the percentage of people employed in CCIs was taken from Lazzeretti, Boix, and Sánchez (2018). Due to data restrictions, they elaborated on two indicators (Table 1): an indicator of CCIs more biased towards cultural activities (based on UNESCO Institute for Statistics data, 2009 and 2014) and another more biased towards intellectual property activities (based on WIPO data, 2014).

For regions, the percentage of people employed in CCIs over total employment was obtained departing from the database of 250 regions developed by Boix and Soler (2017) and expanded to 275 regions by Boix, Peiró, and Rausell (2021), based on Eurostat Labour Force Survey (LFS). Boix and Soler (2017) employed a balanced definition of CCIs, including both creative services and creative manufacturing, although the authors argued that only creative service activities constitute CCIs (see also Boix, De Miguel, and Hervás 2013; UNESCO 2009; WIPO 2014). Consequently, we used creative services as the definition for CCIs but also provided detail for creative manufacturing (Appendix 1).

Data for municipalities came from the Spanish National Institute of Social Security (INSS) and were available at two digits. We used the same definition of CCIs used for the regional scale, although some four-digit sectors used in UNESCO and WIPO definitions were also added using data from the System of Analysis of Iberian Balances (SABI). As in the previous scale, we focused on CCIs as creative services, although we also provided a measurement for creative manufacturing (Appendices 1 and 2).

The details for the ISIC Rev. 4 codes for each scale are depicted in Table 1. The core part of activities, which is common in all definitions for all scales of analysis, includes the following: book and publishing; motion picture with video and television; programming and broadcasting activities; advertising; specialized design activities; photography; creative, arts and entertainment activities; and libraries and archives.

Table 1. ISIC Rev. 4 codes for cultural and creative industries.

Cultural and creative industries	UNESCO	WIPO and OHIM Core	European regions	Municipalities
Manufacture of wearing apparel			14 (m)	14 (m)
Manufacture of leather and related products			15 (m)	15 (m)
Printing and reproduction of recorded media		18	18 (m)	18 (m)
Other manufacturing (jewellery, music instruments, games and toys)	3211, 3220		3211 (m)	3211 (m), 3220 (m), 3240 (m)
Wholesale and retail trade of: other household goods; computers, peripherals and software; music, audio, video books and newspapers in specialized retail stores; second hand goods	4649 (pc), 4761, 4762, 4774 (pc)	4649 (pc), 4651, 4741, 4761, 4762		4742, 4761, 4762
Publishing activities	5811, 5813, 5819, 5820 (pc)	58	58	58
Motion picture, video and television programme production, sound recording and music publishing activities	59	59	59	59
Programming and broadcasting activities	60	60	60	60
Computer programming, consultancy and related activities		62	62	62
Information service activities	6391, 6391	6312, 6391	63	6391
Architectural and engineering activities and related technical consultancy	7110 (pc), 7220		71	71
Research and experimental development	7220		72	72
Advertising and market research	7310 (pc)	7310, 7320 (pc)	73	73
Design, photography and other professional, scientific, and technical activities	7410, 7420	7410, 7420, 7490 (pc)	74	74
Rental and leasing activities of cultural goods	7722	7722, 7729 (pc)		7722
Photocopying, document preparation, and other specialized office and business support activities		8219, 8299 (pc)		
Higher education and cultural education	8530 (pc); 8542			8542
Creative, arts and entertainment activities	90	90	90	90
Libraries, archives, museums and other cultural activities	91	9101	91	91
Activities of professional membership organizations (inc. Copyright collecting societies)		9412 (pc)		

(m) = creative manufacturing, included as a category different from CCIs; (pc) = partial codes as described in UNESCO and WIPO.

Figures 1–3 illustrate the geographical distribution of CCIs in the three scales. The percentage of people employed in CCIs over total employment in the countries of the sample was 2.4% according to the UNESCO data, and 3.8% according to the WIPO data. Figure 1 shows higher values for CCIs in the European countries and North America. For regions, the percentage of people employed in CCIs (creative services) over total employment was 4.5%. CCIs does not follow any defined spatial pattern, although their contribution was greater in highly urbanized regions (Figure 2). For municipalities, the percentage of people employed in CCIs (creative services) over total employment was about 3%, ranging from 0.1% to 65.5% (from 0.5% to 9.6% for the municipalities of more than 10,000 inhabitants); it did not show a defined territorial pattern (Figure 3).

4.2.3. Remaining variables
The rest of variables are defined as follows:

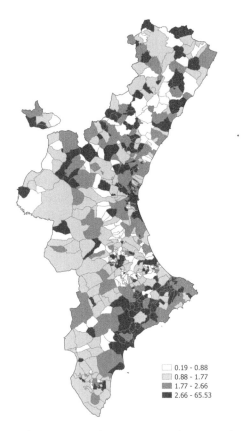

Figure 3. Percentage of employees in CCIs (creative services) over total employment in 518 municipalities in the region of Valencia (Spain). Year 2016. Elaboration from INSS.

(a) The share of persons employed in noncreative industries (S_Y) included the percentage of persons employed in noncreative manufacturing and services over total employment. Agriculture, mining and construction were not included in order to avoid perfect collinearity in the estimates. The data came from the World Bank (countries), Eurostat (regions) and INSS (municipalities).

(b) The sources of capital stock per employee (S_K) data for countries were the World Bank, the International Monetary Fund and Penn World Table. For the European regions, the capital stock data were elaborated following the perpetual inventory method using Eurostat regional capital flows and national depreciations and then divided by the number of employees in the LFS. For the municipalities, the capital stock data were adjusted by multiplying the regional stock of capital per employee of each sector (FBBVA & IVIE 2020) by the number of employees by sector-municipality and then consolidating the results by municipality.

(c) Total employment was measured as the total number of employees. The sources of data were the World Bank (countries), Eurostat LFS (European regions) and the Spanish INSS (municipalities).

(d) The growth rate of ideas (g_A) was measured using the annual average growth rate of patent applications. The ratio was calculated year by year and then averaged. For countries, data from between 1990 and 2014 were obtained from the World Bank and WIPO. For regions, data from the European Patent Office from between 1990 (the first year available in Eurostat with enough number of regions) and 2008 were used. For the municipalities, the data for 1991–2016 came from the Spanish Patents and Trademarks Office, European Patent Office, United States Patent and Trademark Office and World International Property Organization.

(e) The composite term $n + g_A + d$ came from the resolution of the endogenous growth model (see Boix and Soler 2017). It included the growth rate of the population (n), the growth rate of ideas (g_A) and the depreciation rate (d). The periods for each territorial scale were similar to those we used for the growth rate of ideas. The growth rate of population was measured using the annual average growth rate of the working age population (15 to 64 years). The data were taken from the World Bank (countries), Eurostat (regions) and INE (municipalities). The depreciation rate for countries was taken from Penn World Table and OECD. Depreciation data were not available for regions and municipalities, so that factor was measured using OECD data of consumption of fixed capital by country.

(f) The ratio for employment by population was developed using data from The World Bank (countries), Eurostat (regions) and Social Security (municipalities).

4.2.4. Instrumental variables

The instruments we use for CCIs were: (a) countries: the number of UNESCO World Heritage sites per capita in the country; (b) regions: the number of UNESCO World Heritage sites per capita in the region and the public expenditures in culture in the country divided by the number of employees in Arts, entertainment, recreation and other services (NACE groups R-U); (c) municipalities: per capita assets of cultural interest in the municipality. The data came from UNESCO, Eurostat and the Ministry of Culture and Sports of Spain, respectively.

5. Total impacts of the cultural and creative industries (CCIs)

5.1. The average total impact of the CCIs on the GDP per capita is positive and economically significant at all territorial scales

Table 2 contains the detail of the estimates for the CCIs. Complete tables of estimates can be found in Appendix 1. Endogeneity problems were only detected in the estimation for the entire sample of municipalities, for which the results of the IV estimator were also presented. Since the data are expressed in logarithms, the coefficients are interpreted as elasticities, that is, as the relative effect of an increase of the percentage of CCIs on the GDP per capita of places.

The average and median impact of CCIs on the GDP per capita is positive at all scales and the size of the coefficients implies a high response of the GDP per capita to changes in CCIs. The results imply that a 1% increase in CCIs increases the GDP per capita of countries by about 0.13% (UNESCO) and 0.19% (WIPO) average, the GDP per capita

Table 2. Results of the estimates.

	Countries		EU regions	Valencian municipalities	
	(1) LLLS UNESCO CCIs	(2) LLLS WIPO CCIs	(3) LLLS CCIs services	(4) NP-IV[a] CCIs services	(5) LLS Municipalities > 10,000 inhabitants CCIs services
Mean	0.1278*	0.1882*	0.1716*	0.0498*	0.0909*
	(0.015)	(0.000)	(0.000)	(0.026)	(0.000)
Median (2nd quartile)	0.1180*	0.2231*	0.1470*	0.0412*	0.0851*
	(0.029)	(0.000)	(0.001)	(0.057)	(0.000)
Percent positive and negative elasticities[b]					
Positive	100	85.9	95.6	81.6	77.5
Positive and significant	69.2	80.1	93.8	53.7	75.5
Negative	0	14.1	4.4	18.4	22.5
Negative and significant	0	12.8	3.6	9.3	20.4
Percentiles (PE) of GDP per capita (group average)					
Low income ($PE_0 - PE_{25}$)	0.0990*	0.0975	0.1544*	0.0451*	0.0780*
	(0.047)	(0.109)	(0.000)	(0.017)	(0.000)
Medium income ($PE_{25} - PE_{50}$)	0.1177*	0.2375*	0.1622*	0.0497*	0.0796*
	(0.048)	(0.003)	(0.000)	(0.009)	(0.000)
High income ($PE_{50} - PE_{75}$)	0.1776*	0.2806*	0.1670*	0.0531*	0.1233*
	(0.027)	(0.016)	(0.000)	(0.004)	(0.000)
Very high income ($PE_{75} - PE_{100}$)	0.1286*	0.1442	0.2044*	0.0513*	0.0799*
	(0.058)	(0.110)	(0.000)	(0.035)	(0.000)
Human Development Index rank (group average)					
Low human development	0.0899*	−0.2072*			
	(0.056)	(0.000)			
Medium human development	0.0786	0.1390*	0.0898*		
	(0.134)	(0.039)	(0.000)		
High human development	0.1196*	0.2577*	0.1805*		
	(0.040)	(0.002)	(0.000)		
Very high human development	0.1541*	0.2012*	0.1763*		
	(0.036)	(0.042)	(0.000)		
R^2	0.97	0.99	0.97	0.80	0.99
OBS	78	78	275	1036	196

Detail of the coefficients for cultural and creative industries (CCIs) and breakdown of the coefficient by GDP per capita quantiles and by United Nations Human Development Index rank. The dependent variable is the GDP per capita in power purchasing parity. All the variables are in logarithms. The tables of the regressions with all the variables can be found in Appendix 1.
*Statistically significant at 10%. Probabilities are in parenthesis. Standard errors estimated using wild bootstrap.
[a]Nonparametric Instrumental Variables estimation based on Su and Ullah (2008) and Henderson and Parmeter (2015).
[b]Following Henderson and Parmeter (2015), the gradient (g_i) is considered statistically significant when: $g_i \pm 2\,SE$.

of regions by about 0.17% average, and the GDP per capita of municipalities by about 0.05% (entire sample) and by 0.09% (municipalities of more than 10,000 inhabitants).

These results are remarkable, if we consider that they come from three different samples, scales and definitions. They confirm a regularity in the causal effects of the CCIs on per capita income and that they are indeed positive and significant on average.

Both definitions of CCIs, the culture-based (UNESCO) and the intellectual property (WIPO), have positive and economically significant average effects on the income of countries. However, the average effect is 47% higher when the definition is based on intellectual property. The elasticity for regions is 0.17%, almost identical to that of countries in the WIPO definition.

These elasticities are lower than those observed by De Miguel et al. (2012), Boix, De Miguel, and Hervás (2013) and Marco, Rausell, and Abeledo (2014), close to 0.40%. They are closer to the elasticities of CCIs on productivity estimated in Boix and Soler (2017) and Boix, Peiró, and Rausell (2021).

5.2. The individual impact is mostly positive but can also be negative for some places

One benefit of LLLs is that produces observation-specific estimates of each variable. This allowed us to determine in which places the impacts of the CCIs were positive and negative. In Table 2, we calculated the percentage of places (countries, regions, municipalities) in each estimation for which the gradient of the CCIs was positive and the percentage for those that were negative.

The impacts were positive for about 86% of the countries in the sample (80% statistically significant) using the WIPO classification, and for 100% using the UNESCO classification (although in the latter case, they were only statistically significant for 69%). The impact of creative services was positive in almost 96% of the European regions (almost 94% statistically significant) and in 77%-81% of Valencian municipalities (statistically significant in 54%-75% of the cases).

In the rest of the cases, the impact was negative: in up to 14% of the countries, 4% of the regions and up to 22.5% of the municipalities. In those locations, a higher contribution of CCIs in the economy would reduce the GDP per capita, so increasing the contribution of CCIs would not be an appropriate policy.

5.3. Places benefit differently from CCIs depending on their level of development

Table 2 contains the average estimated impact of the CCIs on GDP per capita divided, by income groups and levels of development. Income groups are formed by dividing the GDP per capita of each sample into quartiles. The level of development comes from the national and subnational United Nations Human Development Index (HDI), which measures income, health and education.[3] Both allows to divide the sample into four groups: low, medium, high and very high income (GDP per capita), and low, medium, high and very high human development.

The analysis of income and development groups revealed that the average impacts of the CCIs on GDP per capita increased as we moved from the lower income and development groups to the higher income and development groups (Table 2).

For countries, elasticities increased from about 0.10% average for the lower income quartile to about 0.13%-0.14% average for the higher income quartile. For European regions, CCIs (creative services) elasticity was about 0.15% average for the lower income regions and increased to 0.20% average for the higher income regions. A similar trend was observed for the municipalities of Valencia. The elasticity of CCIs (creative services) was 0.045% average for the municipalities with the lowest income, reaching 0.051% average in the highest income quartile.

This trend is much more marked for the levels of development based on the HDI. For countries, CCIs elasticities increased from about 0.09% to 0.15% (UNESCO CCIs) and from about −0.21% to 0.20% (WIPO CCIs). For European regions, CCIs elasticity was about 0.09% for medium developed regions (no European region was classified as low development) and increased to about 0.18% for the higher developed regions.[4]

It should also be noted that, in some cases the average impact was greater in the high income and developed group than in the top income group. Furthermore, we find countries (e.g. South Africa, Indonesia) and regions (e.g. North Portugal) with low and medium levels of development that show higher than average impacts of CCIs on the GDP per capita.

6. Conclusions and policy implications

In this paper we measured and compared the total impact of CCIs on the per capita income of places for three territorial scales of analysis: countries, regions and municipalities. It is the first time that these impacts have been measured for a broad set of countries and for municipalities and compared with those of the regions.

Based on our findings, we can conclude that: the impact of CCIs on the GDP per capita of places is economically significant on all three territorial scales; that the patterns and trends of the impact are similar on the three scales; and that the impacts are non-linear and heterogeneous within each scale and related to the levels of development of the places.

Based on these results, we can affirm that, in average, policies based on an increase in the share of CCIs increase per capita income or GDP of places and provide a complementary or alternative instrument in the development processes of places.

However, the sign and size of the local impact depends on the characteristics of the place, this is, on the local conditioning. This implies that policies based on CCIs have 'black swans' and are not going to have positive effects in all places; they may be negative or neutral in some places. Moreover, they will have a greater impact in some places than in others. A smart strategy, therefore, implies a fine tuning to the characteristics of each territory.

It is important to note that, as Buitrago and Duque (2013) intuited in their book *The Orange Economy*, the impact of CCIs tends to be positive and economically significant for developing places and even for some less developed areas. In our results, the effect of the CCIs was not small for the medium- and low-developed countries and regions. However, the average impact was significantly larger for high and very high developed places. Thus, CCIs act like a double-edged sword. They serve as an instrument for the development of places but, for the first time, we report that, in average, they also increase inequalities between places, favouring on average the most developed places. Despite this fact, we also found that some places with medium and low levels of development may show high responses to CCIs. Different reasons can explain this behaviour (see Cooke and Lazzeretti 2008; Cooke and Lazzeretti 2018; Lazzeretti, Boix, and Sánchez 2018; Capello and Perucca 2017) that basically depend on the local conditioning, this is, conditions of the environment in which the CCIs interact with the rest of the socioeconomic system.

This research has some limitations, and the results can be interpreted critically. As discussed in the data section, the greatest limitation is the availability and quality of the data, especially in most of Africa and part of Asia. The comparison between different scales, definitions and years partially covers this handicap and allows us to go a little further in the conclusions.

Two additional common criticisms are to what extent the results can be interpreted as causal and whether other controls (e.g. specialization, diversity, density, urbanization and so on) should be added to the estimates. The analytical model in the third section establishes the mechanism through which the CCIs impact GDP per capita, in which there is no simultaneity and endogeneity between CCIs and GDP per capita, and provides variables for the estimates. In addition, residual endogeneity arising from the data was tested and corrected when necessary (municipalities). Since the model is causal, the estimates can be interpreted as causal, and the use of additional controls outside the model can alter the causal paths, distorting the results (See Pearl and Mackenzie 2018). Furthermore, the use of three representative cases involving different scales, definitions and periods introduces a certain randomness in the experiment, reinforcing the causal interpretation of the trends.

We suggest four directions for future research. First, we recommend improvements in the quality and coverage of the data and in the incorporation of time series in order to follow the impacts of the CCIs over a period of time. A second direction is the measurement of impacts for more places for which data may exist, such as metropolitan areas in the United States or municipalities in other regions. A third direction is to advance in the definition of interventions and counterfactuals, which represent an additional step in causal interpretation (Pearl and Mackenzie 2018) and provide relevant information on the effects of simulated changes in CCIs on the income of places. Lastly, the comparative analysis of the effects of CCIs should be expanded to other dimensions of well-being, such as health, environment, education or life satisfaction.

Notes

1. See the results in Appendix 1. The test compares the parametric specification estimated via ordinary least squares (OLS) with the nonparametric scenario.
2. Eurostat's Nomenclature of Territorial Units for Statistics.
3. The categories for countries came from UNDP for 2014. For the regions, the categories are assigned applying the ranks used by UNDP in 2008 to the Subnational Human Development Index 4.0 (Source: Global Data Lab). The HDI is not available for municipalities. The coincidence between GDP per capita quantiles and HDI ranks is below 40%.
4. If regional gradients are analysed by country, the incremental patterns described into this section also holds for most European countries. The exceptions would be Germany and the Netherlands.

Acknowledgements

The authors would like to thank Luciana Lazzeretti, Francesco Capone, the participants in the International Workshop Rethinking Culture and Creativity in the Technological Era, and three anonymous referees for helpful comments to previous versions of the paper.

Disclosure statement

No potential conflict of interest was reported by the author(s).

Funding

This work was supported by Horizon 2020 Framework Programme [grant number 870935].

ORCID

Rafael Boix Domenech ⓘ http://orcid.org/0000-0003-0971-3464
Blanca De Miguel Molina ⓘ http://orcid.org/0000-0002-1267-6070
Pau Rausell Köster ⓘ http://orcid.org/0000-0003-2274-7423

References

Bakhshi, H., and E. McVittie. 2009. "Creative Supply-Chain Linkages and Innovation: Do the Creative Industries Stimulate Business Innovation in the Wider Economy?" *Innovation: Management, Policy & Practice* 11: 169–189. doi:10.5172/impp.11.2.169

Baumol, W., and W. Bowen. 1965. "On the Performing Arts: The Anatomy of Their Economic Problems." *American Economic Review* 55: 495–502.

Boix, R., B. De Miguel, and J. Hervás. 2013. "Creative Service Business and Regional Performance: Evidence for the European Regions." *Service Business* 7 (3): 381–339. doi:10.1007/s11628-012-0165-7

Boix, R., J. Peiró, and P. Rausell. 2021. "Creative Industries and Productivity in the European Regions. Is There a Mediterranean Effect?" *Regional Science Policy & Practice*. doi:10.1111/rsp3.12395.

Boix, R., and P. Rausell. 2018. "The Economic Impact of the Creative Industries in the European Union." In *Drones and the Creative Industry*, edited by V. Santamarina-Campos, and M. Segarra-Oña, 19–37. Cham: Springer.

Boix, R., and V. Soler. 2017. "Creative Industries and Regional Productivity." *Papers in Regional Science* 96 (2): 261–279. doi:10.1111/pirs.12187

Buitrago, P., and I. Duque. 2013. *The Orange Economy: An Infinite Opportunity*. Washington: Inter-American Development Bank.

Capello, R., and G. Perucca. 2017. "Cultural Capital and Local Development Nexus: Does the Local Environment Matter?" In *Socioeconomic Environmental Policies and Evaluations in Regional Science*, edited by H. Shibusawa, K. Sakurai, T. Mizunoya, and S. Uchida, 103–124. Singapore: Springer.

CEBR. 2017. *Contribution of the Arts and Culture Industry to the UK Economy*. London: Centre for Economics and Business Research Ltd.

Cooke, P., and L. Lazzeretti. 2008. *Creative Cities, Cultural Clusters and Local Economic Development*. Cheltenham: Edward Elgar.

Cooke, P., and L. Lazzeretti. 2018. *The Role of Art and Culture for Regional and Urban Resilience*. New York: Routledge.

CRD. 2018. *Ohio's Creative Economy: The Economic Impact of the Arts and Creative Industries 2018*. Bowling Green: Center for Regional Development Bowling Green State University.

De Miguel, B., J. Hervás, R. Boix, and M. De Miguel. 2012. "The Importance of Creative Industry Agglomerations in Explaining the Wealth of the European Regions." *European Planning Studies* 20 (8): 1263–1280. doi:10.1080/09654313.2012.680579

EY. 2015. *Cultural Times: The First Global Map of Cultural and Creative Industries*. France: EY.

FBBVA and IVIE. 2020. *El Stock y los Servicios del Capital en España y su Distribución Territorial y Sectorial (1964–2017)*. Valencia: IVIE.

Florida, R., C. Mellander, and K. Stolarik. 2008. "Inside the Black Box of Regional Development: Human Capital, the Creative Class and Tolerance." *Journal of Economic Geography* 8: 615–649. doi:10.1093/jeg/lbn023

Henderson, D., and C. Parmeter. 2015. *Applied Nonparametric Econometrics*. New York: Cambridge University Press.

Hesmondhalgh, D. 2010. "User-generated Content, Free Labour and the Cultural Industries." *Ephemera* 10 (3/4): 267–284.

Hong, J., W. Yu, X. Guo, and D. Zhao. 2014. "Creative Industries Agglomeration, Regional Innovation and Productivity Growth in China." *Chinese Geographical Science* 24 (2): 258–268. doi:10.1007/s11769-013-0617-6

Howkins, J. 2007. *The Creative Economy: How People Make Money from Ideas*. London: Penguin Books.
Hsiao, C., Q. Li, and J. Racine. 2007. "A Consistent Model Specification Test with Mixed Categorical and Continuous Data." *Journal of Econometrics* 140 (2): 802–826. doi:10.1016/j.jeconom.2006.07.015
Jenish, N. 2012. "Nonparametric Spatial Regression Under Near-Epoch Dependence." *Journal of Econometrics* 167: 224–239. doi:10.1016/j.jeconom.2011.11.008
Jones, C. 1995. "R&D-Based Models of Economic Growth." *The Journal of Political Economy* 103 (4): 759–784. doi:10.1086/262002
Jones, C. 2001. *Introduction to Economic Growth*. New York: WW Norton and Company.
Lazzeretti, L., R. Boix, and D. Sánchez. 2018. "Entrepreneurship and Creative Industries in Developing and Developed Countries." In *Creative Industries and Entrepreneurship: Paradigms in Transition from a Global Perspective*, edited by L. Lazzeretti, 35–57. Cheltenham: Edward Elgar.
Lee, N. 2014. "The Creative Industries and Urban Economic Growth in the UK." *Environment and Planning A* 46: 455–470. doi:10.1068/a4472
Marco, F., P. Rausell, and R. Abeledo. 2014. "Economic Development and the Creative Industries: A Mediterranean Tale of Causality." *Creative Industries Journal* 7 (2): 81–91. doi:10.1080/17510694.2014.958383
McMillen, D. 2010. "Issues in Spatial Data Analysis." *Journal of Regional Science* 50 (1): 119–141. doi:10.1111/j.1467-9787.2009.00656.x
OECD. 1993. *The System of National Accounts, 1993 – Glossary*. Paris: OECD.
OECD. 2018. *OECD Regional Well-Being: A User's Guide*. Paris: OECD.
Oxford Economics. 2013. *The Economic Impact of the Creative Industries in the Americas*. Oxford: Oxford Economics.
Pearl, J., and D. Mackenzie. 2018. *The Book of Why: The New Science of Cause and Effect*. London: Penguin.
Potts, J., and S. Cunningham. 2008. "Four Models of the Creative Industries." *International Journal of Cultural Policy* 14 (3): 233–247. doi:10.1080/10286630802281780
Quartesan, A., M. Romis, and F. Lanzafame. 2007. *Cultural Industries in Latin America and the Caribbean: Challenges and Opportunities*. Washington: Inter-American Development Bank.
Racine, J., and T. Hayfield. 2020. *The np Package*. https://cran.r-project.org/package=np
Rausell, P., F. Marco, and R. Abeledo. 2011. "Sector Cultural y Creativo y Riqueza de las Regiones: en Busca de Causalidades." *Ekonomiaz* 78: 67–89.
SGS. 2013. *Valuing Australia's Creative Industries*. Sydney: SGS & Creative Industries Innovation Centre University of Technology Sydney.
Su, L., and A. Ullah. 2008. "Local Polynomial Estimation of Nonparametric Simultaneous Equations Models." *Journal of Econometrics* 144: 193–218. doi:10.1016/j.jeconom.2008.01.002
UNCTAD. 2010. *Creative Economy Report 2010*. Geneva: UNCTAD.
UNESCO. 2009. *The 2009 UNESCO Framework for Cultural Statistics*. Quebec: UNESCO Institute for Statistics.
UNESCO. 2012. *Measuring the Economic Contribution of Cultural Industries*. Geneva: UNESCO.
UNESCO. 2013. *What do We Mean by the Cultural and Creative Industries? Section for the Diversity of Cultural Expressions, Document No. 11*. Geneva: UNESCO.
UNESCO. 2014. *Summary Report of the 2013 UIS Cultural Employment Metadata Survey*. Montreal: UNESCO Institute for Statistics.
WIPO. 2014. *WIPO Studies on the Economic Contribution of the Copyright Industries*. Geneva: WIPO.
Yu, W., J. Hong, Y. Zhu, D. Marinova, and X. Guo. 2014. "Creative Industry Clusters, Regional Innovation and Economic Growth in China." *Regional Science Policy and Practice* 6 (4): 329–347. doi:10.1111/rsp3.12051
Yum, S. 2016. "The Economic Growth of Creative Industries in the Miami Metropolitan Area." *Creative Industries Journal* 9 (2): 130–145. doi:10.1080/17510694.2016.1206358

Appendices

Appendix 1. Results of the estimates.

	Countries						EU regions				Municipalities				LLLS municipalities with more than 10,000 inhabitants	
	LLLS UNESCO CCIs		LLLS WIPO CCIs		LLLS CCIs services		LLLS CCIs services		LLLS CCIs services		NP Instrumental Variables (Su and Ullah 2008) CCIs services				CCIs services	
	Mean	Median	Mean	Median	Mean	Median	Mean	Median	Mean	Median	Mean	Median	Mean	Median	Mean	Median
Cultural and creative Industries (% on total employees)	0.1278	0.1180	0.1882	0.2231			0.1716	0.1470	0.0365	0.036	0.0498	0.0412			0.0909	0.0851
	(0.015)	(0.029)	(0.000)	(0.000)			(0.000)	(0.001)	(0.030)	(0.046)	(0.026)	(0.057)			(0.000)	(0.000)
Creative manufacturing (% on total employees)							0.0227	0.0099	-0.0134	-0.0186	-0.0138	-0.0183			0.0001	0.0201
							(0.794)	(0.648)	(0.058)	(0.189)	(0.254)	(0.168)			(0.000)	(0.000)
Rest of manufacturing and services (% on total employees)	0.957	1.0145	0.8223	0.8371			0.073	0.0122	0.1482	0.1194	0.1454	0.1136			0.0247	0.0182
	(0.000)	(0.001)	(0.001)	(0.000)			(0.566)	(0.647)	(0.011)	(0.566)	(0.170)	(0.006)			(0.005)	(0.2021)
Capital stock per employee	0.6008	0.5964	0.5273	0.521			0.3928	0.4108	0.164	0.1468	0.1687	0.1513			0.0758	0.1145
	(0.000)	(0.000)	(0.000)	(0.000)			(0.000)	(0.000)	(0.021)	(0.001)	(0.060)	(0.001)			(0.179)	(0.000)
Employees	0.0455	0.0473	0.0463	0.0372			0.0129	0.023	-0.0364	-0.0298	-0.0366	-0.0294			-0.0985	-0.1096
	(0.005)	(0.009)	(0.000)	(0.016)			(0.703)	(0.628)	(0.015)	(0.035)	(0.000)	(0.000)			(0.000)	(0.000)
Growth rate of ideas	-0.0114	-0.0113	-0.0437	-0.044			0.0363	0.0334	-0.0037	0.0082	0.0041	0.0100			-0.1439	-0.2429
	(0.504)	(0.518)	(0.281)	(0.340)			(0.002)	(0.296)	(0.726)	(0.005)	(0.005)	(0.001)			(0.062)	(0.000)
$n + g_A + d$	0.0827	0.0922	0.1697	0.1564			0.0282	0.0132	-0.0272	-0.0854	-0.0392	-0.0845			0.3073	0.5187
	(0.222)	(0.078)	(0.000)	(0.000)			(0.984)	(0.911)	(0.339)	(0.066)	(0.403)	(0.059)			(0.000)	(0.000)
Employees per capita	1.0653	1.1284	1.176	1.2499			0.6494	0.7034	0.1056	0.0972	0.1116	0.1004			0.1822	0.1576
	(0.000)	(0.000)	(0.000)	(0.000)			(0.000)	(0.000)	(0.000)	(0.006)	(0.014)	(0.000)			(0.000)	(0.000)
Dummy year	No		No				No		Yes		Yes				Yes	
Jn statistic (Hsiao, Li, and Racine 2007)	1.445		1.2101				4.7307		7.6046						3.3131	
	(0.037)		(0.022)				(0.000)		(0.000)						(0.000)	
Weak instruments	5.776		7.632				4.465		11.990						2.288	
	(0.019)		(0.001)				(0.012)		(0.000)						(0.132)	
Wu-Hausman	0.072		0.026				1.875		20.260						0.046	
	(0.789)		(0.873)				(0.172)		(0.000)						(0.830)	
Sargan							1.457									
							(0.227)									
R^2	0.97		0.99				0.99		0.82		0.80				0.99	
Observations	78		78				275		1036		1036				196	

The dependent variable is the GDP per capita in power purchasing parity. All variables are in logarithms. Probabilities in parenthesis. n = population growth rate; g_A = growth rate of ideas; d = capital depreciation rate.

Appendix 2. Correlation matrices. Variables in logarithms.*

A) Countries. Unesco classification.   B) Countries. WIPO classification.

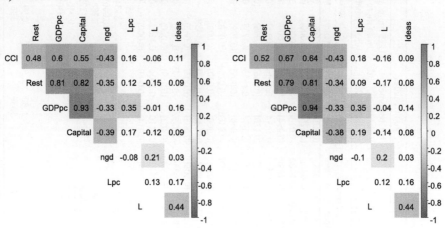

C) European regions.   D) Municipalities of Valencia.

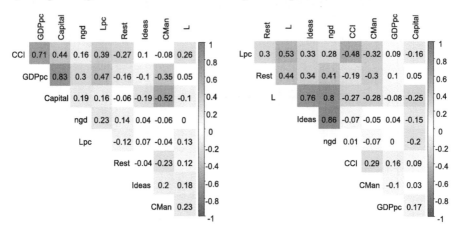

GDPpc = GDP per capita; CCI = cultural and creative industries; CMan = creative manufacturing; Rest = rest of manufacturing and service sectors; Capital = capital stock per employee; L = employees; g = growth rate of ideas; ngd = n+g_A+d; Lpc = employees per capita.

*White cells are statistically nonsignificant at 10%.

Exploiting the technology-driven structural shift to creative work in regional catching-up: toward an institutional framework

Ben Vermeulen and Eleonora Psenner

ABSTRACT
The development and application of technologies such as robots and artificial intelligence drive a shift toward non-routinized, creative work. A stylized narrative is that a few regions dominate the *making* of these technologies and enjoy a virtuous cycle of increasing employment, innovativeness, and in-migration of the creative class. Regions merely *applying* these technologies may get into a vicious cycle of increasing unemployment, out-migration, and decreasing innovativeness. Following the normative governance turn in regional political economics, this theoretical policy paper pitches a framework of three complementary institutions to direct the technology-driven structural change for regional catching-up. Firstly, a system for innovation and entrepreneurial activity creates jobs by supporting exploitation of complementarities of application, co-development activities, and product innovation within mature and emerging sectors. Secondly, education provides creative and entrepreneurial skills to exploit technological opportunities and upskills workers for emerging sectors. Thirdly, labour market and social security institutions are to allow rationalization in mature sectors, incentivize hiring and learning on the job, as well as encourage innovative ventures, notably in emerging sectors. Challenges of implementation of the framework due to path-dependence, co-evolution, and multi-scalarity as well as applicability in different varieties of capitalism are examined.

1. Introduction

The rapid advancement and application of technologies such as robots and artificial intelligence revived a scholarly debate on changes in work, both in terms of employment and skills required. While such technologies are applied in existing sectors to take over routinized tasks and may even outright destroy jobs (see e.g. Frey and Osborne 2017; Brynjolfsson and McAfee 2011; Ford 2015), the introduction also creates new complementary tasks, new skills, new occupations, new jobs, and even new sectors (Acemoglu and

Restrepo 2016, 2017, 2018; Vivarelli 2007, 2013; Mokyr, Vickers, and Ziebarth 2015). Historically, developed economies have seen technological change drive a structural shift in the sectoral composition (Syrquin 2012; Silva and Teixeira 2008) from doing mostly physical work in agriculture to doing mostly work requiring cognitive, creative, and social skills in service sectors (cf. Fisher 1939). The increasing application of labour-substituting technologies reduces demand for workers with physical or cognitive skills for routinized tasks and rather increases demand for knowledge workers with social and creative skills for non-routine ingenuity, improvisation, problem-solving, etc. (cf. Howell and Wolff 1992; Frey and Osborne 2017; Stewart, De, and Cole 2015; Berger and Frey 2016). The premise in this paper is that technological change drives a structural shift toward creative work – broadly defined. Creative work includes work in creative sectors, in creative occupations embedded in firms in other sectors (e.g. in design, marketing), and in occupations structurally engaged in knowledge-intensive complex problem solving, product innovation, etc. However, also in general, there is an increase in the fraction of tasks requiring creativity, ingenuity, improvisation, and complex problem-solving. At present, already more than a quarter of the workforce is doing such creative work (Bakhshi, Freeman, and Higgs 2013, 2015; Florida 2012).

So far, somewhat overlooked in the recent discourse is how this technology-driven structural change may well further exacerbate regional disparities (Feldman and Storper 2018; Moretti 2012). A stylized narrative is that there are few regions in which firms in 'making' sectors agglomerate and that such 'making regions' (e.g. Silicon Valley) enjoy increasing employment for high-wage, high-skilled workers that research, develop, and make the focal advanced technology. At the same time, there is a wide range of regions dominated by firms in mature 'applying' sectors that are rationalizing and automating production and thereby reducing employment for routine tasks. The 'making regions' may forge ahead in a virtuous cycle of in-migration of creative workers (Florida 2002, 2012) subject to positive externalities in creative activities such as innovation (e.g. formation of technological infrastructure, establishment of research and education institutions) (Feldman and Florida 1994; Florida, Adler, and Mellander 2017; Broekel and Brenner 2011). In contrast, 'applying regions' may fall behind in a vicious cycle of increasing unemployment of low-skilled workers doing routinized work, decreasing wages, selective out-migration of high-skilled workers and thereby loss of entrepreneurial and innovation potential. As such, there is an interlocking of the virtuous cycle in making regions in accruing innovation capabilities, increasing product competitiveness and productivity, in-migration of creative workers, etc. with the vicious cycle in applying regions of loss of competitiveness, out-migration of talent, etc. in a multi-regional development process of cumulative causation (see Myrdal 1957; Martin 2017; Fujita 2007).

What can regions that are falling behind in this technology-driven structural shift to creative work do to catch up in economic development? In our view, a way to revert this vicious cycle is not to prevent application of technologies but rather to exploit the labour-creating potential of technological complementarities, co-development of the technologies applied, and exploiting options for product innovation both in the applying sectors as well as in emerging sectors. Following the increasing recognition of the role of institutions in regional development (Rodriguez-Pose 2013; Rodrik, Subramanian, and Trebbi 2004; Acemoglu, Johnson, and Robinson 2006; Amin 2004; Evans 2005) and, more specifically, the role of institutions (such as, e.g. educational institutions, patent laws) in the emerging competitive advantage of industries (Murmann 2003; Nelson 1995), this paper pitches a transformative institutional framework to create a regional development path (cf. MacKinnon et al. 2019). Hinging on existing integrated labour market strategies such as 'flexicurity' (see e.g. European Commission 2007; Forge and Blackman 2010; OECD 2018; Eichhorst and Konle-Seidl 2005), a system of interlocking regional institutions is put forth to direct the regional structural shifts under pressure of technological change. Firstly, a system for regional innovation and entrepreneurial activity is to boost process innovation for productivity and product innovation for competitiveness and job creation. Organizations such as research institutes, competence centres, and knowledge platforms are to be established to acquire and use regional capabilities to generate and exploit technological opportunities. Moreover, entrepreneurial activities and innovation collaboration are to be encouraged, not only to exploit complementarities to technologies, but also to explore breakthroughs giving rise to new sectors. Secondly, a system of educational institutions is to train a labour force with the skills in demand both in making sectors, but also in applying sectors. In our view, the curriculum should emphasize creative work (in the broad sense of what the creative class is doing), so as to create and exploit technological opportunities and to enhance occupational mobility from rationalized to complementary tasks and from declining to emerging sectors. Thirdly, labour market regulations with regard to hiring and firing, social security arrangements and active labour market policies are required for occupational mobility and efficient reallocation across sectors. Sufficient flexibility is required to allow rationalization and automation to bolster the competitive position of labour-intensive sectors and invite firms to hire workers for risky, innovative ventures in emerging sectors. The labour market flexibilization should be complemented with social security arrangements to ensure an income during upskilling of the new unemployed, to entice high-skilled creatives to risk entrepreneurial activities in emerging sectors, and to mobilize public support. As such, the notion in regional political economics that institutions are instrumental in regional development is extended to the idea that an integrated framework of institutions can direct technology-driven structural change for regional catching-up. However, generally, institutions co-evolve with (the industrial organization of) economic activities (Nelson 1995), both within and across regional boundaries and at other spatial scales (Gong and Hassink 2019; Benner 2021; Grillitsch 2015). Effective implementation of the proposed institutional framework requires regional governance capabilities to transform the existing institutions, to overcome the complementarities with existing economic activities, and to ensure embedding in and compliance with institutions at (inter)national level. So, although the transformative institutional framework is arguably conducive to structural change in any region, the applicability may be restricted. After all, the required capabilities for institutional transformation reside particularly in *advanced* political economies (cf. Streeck and Thelen 2005). In addition, particular functions of the proposed institutions (e.g. providing unemployment benefits or public support for human resource development), are more compatible with particular varieties of capitalism (see Hall and Soskice 2001).

The structure of the remainder is as follows. Section 2 elaborates on how technological change affects structural developments in employment and skills required across the different types of sectors. Section 3 describes the impact on regional development of such technology-driven structural change. We hereby focus on 'applying regions', i.e. regions hosting mostly mature sectors that have to apply the focal technologies to remain competitive. These technologies are produced in 'making regions', i.e. regions hosting the rapidly growing high-tech sectors producing the technologies. Section 4 describes the framework of institutions governing the regional catching-up given the technology-driven structural shift. It also examines the challenges in implementing the institutional framework, the compatibilities with different varieties of capitalism, and thereby limits to applicability. Section 5 provides conclusions and directions for further research.

2. Technology-driven shift to creative work by sector

Over the last centuries, developed economies have evolved from having a labour force doing mostly physical work in agricultural sectors to doing mostly work requiring cognitive and social skills in service sectors (cf. Fisher 1939). Such structural change, i.e. the long-term persistent shift in composition and relevance of sectors in an economy, is attributed to changes in demand and technological change (Syrquin 2012; Silva and Teixeira 2008). Similar to previous waves of technological change (e.g. mechanization, computerization), the ongoing robotization and AI-driven automation is likely to bring about substitution of a large part of the current labour force (see e.g. Frey and Osborne 2017; Brynjolfsson and McAfee 2011; Ford 2015). However, it also increases (at least relative) demand for (i) creative work requiring creative skills, ingenuity, symbolic thinking, and coping with high knowledge intensity, (ii) work hinging on human interaction skills (e.g. regarding emotions such as empathy, sharing personal experiences, companionship and care), and (iii) physical work requiring nimble and dexterous physical manipulation and motoric skills (e.g. hairdressing, machine repair), physical improvisation, and adaptation to highly dynamic environments (cf. Howell and Wolff 1992; Frey and Osborne 2017; Stewart, De, and Cole 2015; Berger and Frey 2016). So, the application of technologies such as robots and AI may decrease employment in particular sectors (e.g. manufacturing) but increase it in others (e.g. software engineering). Notably, this structural change takes place in conjunction with a shift in skills in demand, not only in the sectors in which the technology is applied, but also in emerging sectors (e.g. renewable energy, health care, biotechnology, mobility, ICT).

2.1. Creative work, definition

Widespread technological change drives a structural shift toward work requiring creative skills. Such 'creative work' does not refer to occupations in creative sectors per se. After all, these sectors also employ workers engaged in supporting, non-creative activities. Moreover, there are 'embedded creatives' in other industries that do creative work (Higgs and Cunningham 2008; Hearn and Bridgstock 2014; Cunningham and Potts 2015). As such, definitions relying on occupation or sector encodings are either including or excluding too much, and are in any case uninformative on the shifts in the *fraction of tasks* requiring creative skills in occupations and sectors. Here, we refer to 'creative work' not as occupation, but rather as the tasks that require creative skills. With 'creative skills', we refer to the ability to come up with ideas or objects deemed original by experts in the field, which generally requires ingenuity, inventiveness and improvisation in solving problems related to the materialization or expression (so-called 'functional creativity', see Cropley and Cropley 2010). We distinguish those engaged in (i) creative work – narrowly defined – which requires a particular talent for creative expression (e.g. performer, visual artist, composer), (ii) applying artistic creativity for product and service enrichment (e.g. website developers, product designers, advertisers & marketers), (iii) applying ingenuity and problem-solving without artistic purpose *stricto sensu* (e.g. product innovators, research & development personnel), (iv) using improvisation and cognitive processing in tasks that are complements to using technology (e.g. non-scripted repairs). The latter categories of creative work may well be done by embedded creatives, i.e. fixed staff of firms active in non-creative sectors (see Hearn and Bridgstock 2014). The broad definition of 'creative work' that we use in this paper is thus close to the work done by the 'creative class' (Florida 2012). All the workers engaged in (a) creative activities around innovation, engineering, etc., including design, media and arts, and (b) problem-solving drawing on complex bodies of knowledge to come up with new solutions.

That creative work is on the rise can be seen even from rough indicators. For one, there is an increase in economic significance of the cultural and creative sectors (van der Pol 2008), which is an indicator of employment in creative work – narrowly defined. Moreover, there is an increase in employment in scientific, technical and research work requiring human ingenuity, problem-solving skills, and creativity. Florida computes that roughly 30% of the labour force belongs to the creative class. Even detailed quantifications of (changes in) occupational task sets using laborious expert assessment (Bakhshi, Freeman, and Higgs 2013) possibly in combination with a machine learning approach (Bakhshi, Frey, and Osborne 2015) indicate that nearly a quarter of the labour force is involved in creative work. In this paper, quantification is not required: we rather make plausible that making and applying of technologies drive a structural shift toward creative work.

2.2. Technology-driven structural shift toward creative work

To understand where and how creative work matters and how this evolves with technological change, we distinguish three *types* of sectors based on the relationship with the focal technologies (cf. Vermeulen, Pyka, and Saviotti 2020; Vermeulen et al. 2018). In 'applying' sectors, competition drives firms to apply these technologies for rationalization and automation of production, thus having technology take over routine tasks of workers, or using these technologies to facilitate product or service innovation. In 'making' sectors, firms research, develop, and produce these technologies. In 'spillover' sectors, there is no direct relationship with the focal technologies, but part of the discretionary income earned in the other sectors is spent there. Importantly, innovation culminates into new industrial and service activities that may ultimately give rise to new occupations and even entirely new sectors. As described below and summarized in Figure 1, the making, applying and spillover sectors experience a shift in skills in demand and notably toward creative skills.

2.2.1. Complementary, co-development, product innovation in applying sectors

In applying sectors, automation and other productivity-enhancing technologies take over routinized tasks and may thus 'destroy jobs'. However, technologies such as computers

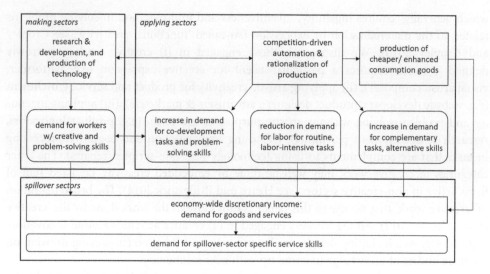

Figure 1. Structural shifts in skills in demand across making, applying, and spillover sectors.

(see e.g. Levy and Murnane 2004) and robots (see e.g. Ford 2015) do not only *substitute* but also *complement and augment* human tasks. So, there are various ways in which the decline in employment is compensated, for instance by emergence of complementary tasks and new occupations in which new (higher) skills are required (Acemoglu and Restrepo 2016, 2017, 2018; Vivarelli 2007, 2013; Mokyr, Vickers, and Ziebarth 2015). There may not be just a *relative* increase for workers doing non-routine tasks, there is also an absolute increase for workers with skills to leverage the complementarities (Acemoglu and Autor 2011; Autor, Levy, and Murnane 2003), which are particularly higher skills at higher wages (see e.g. Machin and van Reenen 1998; Pianta 2004; Acemoglu 2002). In addition, workers may shift attention to other tasks, such as process improvement, product design, social interaction with customers, etc. Notably, such product and service innovations, in turn, are likely to create new jobs. In addition, there may be requirements specific to the context of application or to ways of using, which offer opportunities for technology co-development activities. In the process of co-development, technological knowledge is transferred, capabilities are developed, new directions for development unlocked, etc. Wages for jobs retained (but transformed) may go up due to the higher productivity using advanced technologies and the higher skills required for non-routinized tasks.

2.2.2. Research & development work in making sectors

Sectors researching, developing and producing technology and machines (so, not only robots, AI, but also 3D printers, CAD/CAM/CNC, production equipment, for instance) employ large numbers of high-skilled workers with problem-solving skills in knowledge intensive engineering tasks. These creative workers are not only involved in understanding and engineering the sector's core technologies themselves, but often also in finding creative solutions to rationalize the production or provide opportunities for product innovation in the sectors in which these technologies are or may be applied.

With maturation of the focal technologies, further modularization generally divides research, development, and production activities into specialized sectors of their own. For instance, modularization of computer technology spawned many new occupations such as software developers, hardware and architectural designers, consultants in enterprise management software, specialists in computer repair, etc. Many of these occupations became industrial sectors of their own. Clearly, many of the tasks conducted in these sectors require creative skills such as conducting research, solving complex problems, designing elements, etc.

2.2.3. Local multiplier effects
There is a 'multiplier effect' that has each new high-skill, high-tech job result in several additional jobs in the region (cf. Moretti 2010; Goos, Konings, and Vandeweyer 2015). The changes in the employment rate, skills required, and wages paid in the making and applying sectors also affect demand for goods and services outside of these sectors (see e.g. Autor 2015). For one, the changes in total discretionary income (through employment rate and wages paid) 'spills over' to sectors such as culture and performance arts (see e.g. Baumol and Bowen 2006; Withers 1980), leisure & tourism (see e.g. Crouch 1995) and sports (see e.g. Løyland and Ringstad 2009). And these sectors in turn also contribute to economic growth and employment (see e.g. Bucci, Sacco, and Segre 2014; van der Pol 2007 on creative and cultural subsectors). In each of these sectors, there are service-specific skills, e.g. social interaction skills in health care and hospitality.

2.2.4. Progressive differentiation and rise of new sectors
Creative work not only emerges in existing sectors. In capitalistic economies, competition drives product and service innovation, and hereby boosts not only employment in research & development work, but also gives rise to product and process innovations in mature sectors that ultimately culminate in entirely new sectors. These new sectors initially often boast labour – and knowledge-intensive work focusing on product and service innovation, development of production technologies, etc. So, the process of diversification of economies also drives the emergence of creative work. In addition, products and services become technologically more complex, *grosso modo*, thus requiring more creative work. Moreover, we conjecture that there is a process that we have coined *escalation of competitive dimensionality* (see Vermeulen, Pyka, and Saviotti 2020) in which firms increasingly incorporate more product and service features (e.g. from price, to quality, to time-to-market) such as aesthetics, design, and image. Products and services as well as their marketing become more aesthetically adorned or require to be more creative to stand out (Scott 1997). This calls for functional creativity (Cropley and Cropley 2010) and gives rise to more and more prominent embedded creatives (Hearn and Bridgstock 2014).

3. Technological change and regional development

Technology-driven structural change exacerbates regional disparities. A manifestation thereof is, for instance, the growing digital divide (Moretti 2012). Given the prior sectoral make-up of regions, some regions with mature sectors competing globally experience job destruction, out-migration, and deskilling, while other regions with world-leading emerging sectors enjoy job creation, in-migration, and upskilling. To study structural shifts in employment and skills, we discern three main types of regions with interrelated dynamics. In 'making regions' (e.g. Silicon Valley in the U.S.A., Germany's ICT cluster in the Rhine-Main-Neckar area), firms are researching, developing, and producing technology for automation, process rationalization, computerization, etc. In 'applying regions', firms in the dominant sectors merely apply the focal productivity-increasing technology. Although there are a few major 'making regions' and many 'applying regions', a region may be both making and applying technology. In fact, firms in applying regions may seek to collaborate in co-developing specific applications. Typical, purely applying regions are those that mostly exploit geographically-bound natural endowments, such as e.g. rural areas supplying agricultural commodities, or other industrial capital, e.g. old manufacturing areas. A last category that would not be applying but nonetheless experience the impact of technological change are 'off-/ de-shoring regions'. In these regions, dominant sectors offer labour-intensive, low-wage production capabilities upstream in a global production chain. The introduction of advanced production technology downstream in the global production chain in another region may offshore activities to or reshore activities away from the focal region.

3.1. Making regions and positive externalities

Firms and institutes tend to cluster due to a variety of agglomeration externalities, such as formation of a shared labour pool, scale economies for specialized suppliers, and technological knowledge spillovers (Glaeser et al. 1992). Particularly the tacit component of knowledge and importance of face-to-face collaboration drives the agglomeration of knowledge-intensive activities in research, development, and production of technologies. Moreover, innovativeness of (the output of) regions depends on a range of institutions (e.g. technological infrastructure, production system, research and education institutions), many of which coincide with agglomeration and urbanization externalities (Feldman and Florida 1994; Florida, Adler, and Mellander 2017; Broekel and Brenner 2011). Once innovative, accumulated technological capabilities and human capital, attractive labour market conditions, presence of well-developed institutions, and a range of other positive economies ease keeping ahead of other regions (Iammarino, Rodriguez-Pose, and Storper 2019). Indeed, bigger agglomerations not only attract more skilled workers, the proximity of workers also drives upgrading of skills and productivity of entrepreneurs (Glaeser and Resseger 2009). With the in-migration of high skilled workers, the innovation and entrepreneurial potential increases. Hereby also the opportunities for product and service innovations increases, by which new sectors may arise. All in all, the progressive accumulation and recombination of technological knowledge contributes majorly to regional economic development (cf. Feldman and Storper 2018).

3.2. Applying regions, polarization, and a vicious cycle

Technological change affects employment most in regions dominated by mature sectors (see e.g. Gagliardi 2014). In line with the topical debate on polarization, substitution of routinized tasks (more present in mature sectors) may culminate in loss of middle-skilled jobs and subsequent crowding around jobs with non-routinized but low-skilled tasks (e.g. requiring physical dexterity or social skills) and – to lesser extent – around jobs requiring cognitive skills and creativity of human workers (Acemoglu and Autor 2011; Autor 2015; Autor and Dorn 2013; Autor, Katz, and Kearney 2006; Goos, Manning, and Salomons 2009, 2014). Given that labour mobility is particularly low for jobs requiring skills with lower wage prospects (Manning and Petrongolo 2017; Amior 2015), selective out-migration is actually high-skill and high-wage biased. As such, the rationalization of production in mature sectors may cause selective out-migration and thus exacerbate the unequal access to skilled labour, technological capabilities, etc. (see e.g. Fratesi and Percoco 2014). The labour market polarization manifests itself as a digital divide between regions with low-skilled, low-wage labour and high unemployment, and regions with high-skilled, high-wage labour and low unemployment. In a circular causal process, progressive deskilling of regions reduces demand for local products, causing depressed regions to fall behind even further.

For regional development, it is of vital importance to retain the (potentially) high-skilled creative workers 'freed up' by rationalization either by local exploitation of complementarities and co-development tasks or product innovation activities in the mature applying sectors themselves or by creation of and reallocation to high-skilled creative jobs in emerging sectors.

3.3. Off-/ de-shoring regions

In global production chains, firms across various regions are executing different stages of production. Production rationalization may well coincide with modularization of the products being produced and may lead to offshoring of labour-intensive production steps to low-wage countries. The low-skilled, labour-intensive work done by firms in developing regions does not only increase employment and wages, but builds production capabilities, and allows to catch up with developed countries. Automation may well diminish the cost-economic rationale of offshoring. Indeed, the introduction of new advanced production technology (such as robotics) in applying regions in downstream stages of the production chain may trigger reshoring of production tasks (De Backer et al. 2016), thus throwing developing regions off of their development path. The polarization due to technological change is explicitly also geographical, where reshoring removes routinized, low-skilled labour from developing regions and adds less-routinized, high-skilled labour to developed regions. As such, technological change may also inhibit formation of a high-skilled labour force in developing regions (Shen and Zheng 2020; Nomaler, Verspagen, and van Zon 2020). Automation may thus exacerbate interregional inequalities along value chain relationships.

3.4. Connected cycles increasing regional disparity

In general, prior inequalities in economic development of regions tends to self-reinforce due to increasing returns, positive scale economies, externalities, etc. (Myrdal 1957; Martin 2017; Fujita 2007). Our conjecture is that the making regions experience a virtuous cycle (in part) due to vicious cycle that applying regions undergo. On the one side, making regions enjoy a 'virtuous cycle' of (i) in-migration of and local accumulation of high-skilled and creative workers doing non-routinized work such as research and development of technology, (ii) employment creating effects of innovation by and entrepreneurial activities of those creative workers, (iii) acquisition of technological capabilities and thereby innovation potential, and (iv) increasing wages with local multiplier effects contributing to regional development. At the same time, there is, on the other side, a wide-range applying and deshoring regions dominated by sectors hosting a substantial share of workers doing routinized, low – to medium-skilled physical/ cognitive work. These regions befall a 'vicious cycle' if (i) the employment destroying effect of automation and productivity-increasing technologies (developed in making regions), (ii) selective out-migration of skilled workers, (iii) decline in technological capabilities and innovation potential, and (iv) decrease in discretionary income causing a falling behind of regional development. Indeed, at the extreme sides of the continuum, there are urbanized, high-tech making regions hosting high-skilled knowledge workers doing creative work, while the applying regions may be rural or middle-to-small metropolitan areas hosting workers doing predominantly low – or middle-skilled physical work such as in agriculture or manufacturing or and service work such as in tourism (cf. Iammarino, Rodriguez-Pose, and Storper 2019). This interlocking virtuous cycle in the making regions and vicious cycle in the applying regions is depicted in Figure 2.

Two critical notes on this narrative. Firstly, the variety of applying regions is large and the potential applicability depends on the automatability of production work, the relative wages, the institutional framework in place, skill level of the labour force, technological absorptive capacity, etc. So, although regions produce the same, they may still have different incentives to innovate. Moreover, the job loss due to application may also be compensated locally in various ways (see Vivarelli 2007; Acemoglu and Restrepo 2018). For one, by exploiting complementarities in product or service propositions (e.g. maintenance, product improvement, customer interaction). Moreover, the application may be so specialized that local domain experts are required to formulate

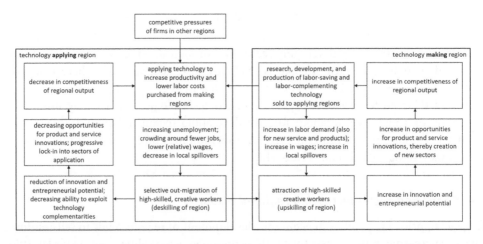

Figure 2. Interlocking of the vicious cycle of progressive unemployment, deskilling, and dwindling innovation and entrepreneurial potential in applying regions and the virtuous cycle of increasing demand for high-skilled labour, upskilling, and increasing innovation and entrepreneurial potential in making regions.

specifications, co-develop and customize technologies, train employees, establish technology transfer, etc. Secondly, it is not so that urban, high-tech regions are exclusively making and rural or low/medium-tech areas are exclusively applying technologies; it depends on the type of technology. For example, artificial intelligence augments high wage cognitive tasks that may be more present in cities, while robotics replaces low wage physical tasks that may be more present in rural areas (Frank et al. 2019). As such, the applying and making region may be the same, such that the net effect on employment due to structural shifts in making, applying, supporting, and spillover sectors is more involved.

4. Institutional framework for regional catching up

There is an increasing recognition that institutions play a pivotal role in regional development (Rodriguez-Pose 2013; Rodrik, Subramanian, and Trebbi 2004; Acemoglu, Johnson, and Robinson 2006; Amin 2004; Evans 2005) and competitive advantage of industries (Murmann 2003; Nelson 1995). As such, institutions are among the regional assets that are instrumental in catch-up pathways (see e.g. MacKinnon et al. 2019). Here, we take a disaggregated conception of an institution as *the (system of) organization(s) regulating human interaction in providing a specific societal function (e.g. education, labour, security, business transaction)*. How then to reform institutions to revert the vicious cycle in a region in which firms are rationalizing or even moving away production steps subject to technological change? A reflex may be to inhibit production rationalization and secure employment, in spite of thus locking in the region on a development path in labour-intensive, routinized work. Instead, a more comprehensive framework of institutions is necessary to accommodate structural change toward high-skilled creative work both as source of immediate employment and as future engine to create jobs.

Under competition, a necessary (but not sufficient) condition for regional development is the timely, efficient allocation of labour across sectors, including education and reskilling for job opportunities. Arguably, this is the foundation of flexicurity (European Commission 2007; Forge and Blackman 2010) and integrated labour market strategies (see e.g. OECD 2018). These strategies combine (i) labour market flexibility (through deregulation) and incentives for hiring inexperienced or low-skilled employees for training on the job, (ii) training and education for upskilling and upward occupational mobility, and (iii) social security to sustain demand and social cohesion during education and finding a new job. Following an evolutionary economic perspective on technological change, this flexicurity framework focusing on the labour market and educational institutions is extended with institutional provisions to stimulate innovation and entrepreneurial activities to create and reap employment opportunities and ensure regional competitive output. Moreover, this is to build capabilities to exploit the complementarities of technological change and create high-skilled jobs even at the expense of the loss of lower-skilled jobs. To this end, we propose a comprehensive framework of institutions that provides three interlocking functions for regional development subject to technological change: create jobs in emerging sectors (or by exploiting opportunities in existing sectors facing rationalization and automation), free up workers bound to be substituted, and enable upskilling and vocational training for workers engaged in routinized tasks, outdated skills, and sectors in decline to realize occupational and sectoral mobility. These three institutions are now described in more detail.

4.1. Innovation and entrepreneurship

For regions falling behind, it is commendable to support firms to improve their existing product and service propositions. Beyond the micro-level interests of firms, a regional innovation system aids in setting the region on a catch-up path (see e.g. Lundvall et al. 2009). Such a regional innovation system is to enhance networking and matching of firms and research institutes within and across regional boundaries and to stimulate interactive learning and collaborative innovation of the various actors in the region. Doing so, it develops the product and service innovation capabilities and boosts entrepreneurial activities that renew existing and draw in emerging sectors for new, higher-skilled jobs. The orchestration of collaboration between government, industry, public and private research institutes, etc. is to leverage regional (technological) capabilities in sectors that the region has traditionally been doing well in (Asheim, Moodysson, and Tödtling 2011). For practical application, regions will have set up institutions that provide particular functions and define interactions that support accumulation of innovative potential (see e.g. Doloreux and Parto 2005). A range of organizations contribute in transferring and absorbing technological knowledge developed elsewhere, exploiting complementarities in technology applications locally, or even co-developing in process innovation. Practically, regions are to stimulate entrepreneurial activities (e.g. through incubation, stimulating spin-off), build problem-solving capabilities (e.g. through a knowledge & competence centre), stimulate innovation collaboration (e.g. through public funding of joint research projects), aid in inter – and intra-regional knowledge transfer (e.g. through training centres, transfer centres), etc. Particularly for catch-up regions, regional technology transfer centres may focus on (supraregional) network formation and involvement of expert consultants to deal with scarce financial and human resources in building local technological capabilities (see e.g. Esparcia 2014). The operational institutional development path and concrete (multi-scalar) knowledge sourcing strategy may further depend on the type of (technological) knowledge involved (Bellandi, Chaminade, and Plechero 2020; Chen and Hassink 2020). Problematic for regions that are trying to catch up is that many of the institutions in a regional innovation system (notably technological infrastructure, research facilities, educational institutions) typically reside in cities due to the agglomeration externalities (Feldman and Florida 1994; Florida, Adler, and Mellander 2017; Broekel and Brenner 2011). Given the challenges in and timeframe required for building or renewing capabilities in new technologies, the involved process of transformation of institutions, it seems commendable to stimulate establishment of slender institutions for localized innovation activities highly focused on co-development of the technologies being applied and exploiting complementarities, notably also in social and creative work.

Complementary to enhancing the regional innovation system to create new job opportunities and thus boost structural change, a more general method is to attract and retain the creative class. The creative class is conducive to further innovativeness and entrepreneurial activities and thus to outright regional economic development and employment growth (Florida 2012; Boschma and Fritsch 2009). Despite the association of the creative class with metropolitan areas, there is mounting evidence that this strategy is also suitable for rural areas (McGranahan and Wojan 2007) and small to medium-sized cities (Selada, Vilhena Da Cunha, and Tomaz 2012).

4.2. Education

Education institutions have a multifaceted role in catching up, both in increasing the competitiveness of sectors currently dominant in the region as well as in supporting the emergence of sectors in which the region has a (potential) competitive advantage. With changes in the technologies, the knowledge, and material or information transformations to be executed, the skills in demand on the labour market and the education thus to be provided will also change (see e.g. Adams and Demaiter 2008). On the one hand, education institutions are to train workers in the existing sectors to exploit technological complementarities and co-development tasks. This may concern more specific vocational skills augmenting existing occupations to work with new technologies but also developing more general skills with regard to complementarities such as problem-solving, product/ process innovation, customer service, etc. On the other hand, the education institutions are to train workers to create and exploit opportunities in emerging sectors. This may concern more generic skills in entrepreneurship, networking, and business development, as well as product and service related problem-solving skills, creativity, and the like. Importantly, whenever the number of jobs created in complementarities and other forms of compensation in existing sectors is insufficient, there is ramping unemployment. Innovation then has to generate labour demand in emerging sectors, and education then has to provide the necessary occupational mobility from work in the old to work in emerging sectors. There may be a considerable gap between the skills of the (newly) unemployed that used to work in the old sectors and the skills required for existing and notably emerging jobs. The unemployed from applying sectors may have been doing routinized tasks in predictable environments, while emerging jobs may consist of non-routine, high-skilled tasks in unpredictable environments. Clearly, the newly unemployed may actually have lost their jobs for lacking these skills. Particularly in periods of rapid and pervasive structural change, there may be a considerable pool of such newly unemployed with outdated skills. As such, ironically, it seems critical particularly for catch-up regions to be able to exploit complementarities in creative work.

So, education contributes to (i) exploiting complementarities and co-development activities in the sectors of application, (ii) development of entrepreneurial and creative skills that boost product innovation (and thereby creation of new jobs and sectors), and (iii) increasing occupational mobility between the applying and emerging sectors. In general, the dynamic efficiency of labour mobility is not only moderated by geographical stickiness or sensitivities to wage differentials, but also by educationability of the unemployed and the rate at which the curriculum of (vocational) studies adjusts to (foreseen) labour market demand. However, given the substantial uncertainty about specific technologies as basis for future regional development paths, picking concrete directions for e.g. vocational studies is challenging. As such, there are substantial risks in pursuing a *pro*active education system in isolation. However, the education system should at least be more *re*active to labour market demands on workers in the light of (pending) technological change (Chatterton and Goddard 2000). Moreover, despite the fact that concrete directions for vocational or engineering studies may be hard to pick, there is a general contention that creative, entrepreneurial, and social skills are least susceptible to automation (see Frey and Osborne 2017; Berger and Frey 2016). So, from a long-term perspective, curricula best also teach future-proof skills required for creative work such as creativity, ingenuity, problem-solving, etc. Indeed, workers need to be trained in creativity-focused technology fluency rather than algorithmic, programmatic thinking (Cropley 2020). To this end, education is to be reformed from rewarding obedience, memorization, etc., toward enhancing creative thinking (Strom and Strom 2002; Cropley 1995). Contrary to popular belief, aspects of creativity and ingenuity are not innate, but present in everyone and can be trained, e.g. by training in metaphorical and analogical thinking (Schlee and Harich 2014).

In general, regions may have to resort to an education-intensive occupational mobility programme to move workers between sector-specific (vocational) skills upon external, technology-driven structural change. However, regions benefit from a pool with workers that have entrepreneurial and creative skills and thus are able to engage in job – and sector-creating service and product innovation. Not only are these workers more prone to be employed in emerging sectors, their entrepreneurial activities are also conducive to regional development.

4.3. Labour market flexibility and social security

In catching up in technology-driven structural change, the roles of institutions for job creation (through innovation and entrepreneurial activities) as well as those for occupational mobility (through education) seem rather uncontested. In contrast, there is an ongoing debate about the role of labour market institutions on the development of regional employment (see e.g. Elhorst 2003; Freeman 2007; Betcherman 2012). In neoliberal perspective, regulating wages, dismissal protection, social security, etc. distort the allocative efficiency of the labour market and thus cause un – and underemployment. As such, regional development would benefit from market flexibilization by progressive deregulation, decentralization of wage bargaining, abolishing minimum wages, and market liberalization (see e.g. OECD 2005). This, however, overlooks ample cases of low unemployment under alternative institutional setups (Howell 2005; Baker et al. 2005).

To accommodate the necessary structural change in regional catching up, both the interests of mature sectors losing competitiveness and (potentially) emerging sectors have to be served. Firstly, the labour market institutions should allow firms in existing sectors competing globally to rationalize and automate production to lower unit costs and thereby keep products in demand. High wage rates and dismissal protection would unduly sustain high product prices and thus cause unemployment in the long run. *Opponents* of labour market flexibilization argue that weak bargaining power and labour market regulation have firms substitute workers that are already disadvantaged on the labour market. Those being fired may be medium – and low-skilled workers doing routinized work and with limited educationability. These newly unemployed may have difficulty in finding work in new occupations (e.g. due to skills, age) and become dependent on social security. Labour market flexibility may thus induce unemployment, a widening skill gap, and increase inequality in incomes and wages. As such, application of technologies may worsen the marginal position for the most vulnerable, e.g. migrant labour in agriculture in rural regions (Rotz et al. 2019; Sorenson et al. 2019). Instead, dismissal protection would incentivize firms to invest in upskilling these disadvantaged workers and to exploit potential complementarities. *Proponents* of flexibilization argue that powerful dismissal protection keeps workers tied up in obsolete jobs, consolidates automatable tasks, and sustains labour-intensive routinized skills. When rivaling firms in other regions actually do engage in rationalization and product innovation, firms in the focal regions soon produce products that are outdated or uncompetitively expensive. An additional effect is that firms in these sectors do not acquire technological capabilities in new process technology, nor engage in product innovation. So, ironically, dismissal protection, high wages, and strong labour unions thus ultimately cause demand to dwindle, workers to become unemployed, and firms to go bankrupt. We argue that the institutional form has to allow rationalization of uncompetitive sectors and at the same time incentivize hiring and learning on the job for those needing to be upskilled. Together with training by educational institutions and social security, this facilitates occupational mobility.

Secondly, the labour market institutions should stimulate firms and entrepreneurs to engage in ventures that exploit opportunities in existing and create opportunities in emerging sectors. To this end, firms should have access to skilled, educated creative workers that exploit technological and social & creative complementarities to automation, use of new technologies to upgrade products and services, etc. The combination of labour market flexibilization to reduce the reservations to hire people for entrepreneurial endeavours as well as incentives to hire people and train them on the job will increase chances of the take-off of new sectors. In addition, social security boosts dynamic efficiency of the labour market as it sustains regional demand during upskilling and entices the high-skilled worker to engage in risky endeavours even under the prospects of few job opportunities when fallback options are limited.

Given that rights for workers and duties for employers are generally laid down at (inter)national level, the mandate for differentiation of regional labour market policies or regional discretionary measures may be limited compared to that for other institutions (e.g. those pertaining to the innovation system, education). The functions fulfilled by these national institutions in turn derive from the particular 'variety of capitalism' adhered to nationally (Hall and Soskice 2001), i.e. to a particular set of complementary ideologies on roles of the market and government. See Section 4.5 for further implications of multi-scalarity and restrictions on applicability of our institutional framework in certain varieties of capitalism.

4.4. Interlocking system of institutions

The framework of institutions to direct technology-driven structural change is depicted in the Venn diagram in Figure 3. Subject to global competition, the labour market institutions are best to allow rationalization and automation of the production system in mature sectors, even if this reduces labour demand (or face long-run unemployment due to falling behind regardless). Active labour market policies and incentives are to support mobility between sectors and hiring of unemployed. In conjunction, social

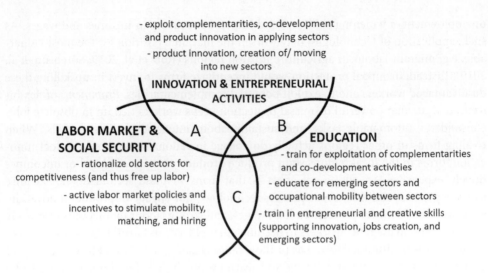

Figure 3. Three interlocking institutions for technology-driven structural change.

security measures are to retain democratic support for the labour market flexibility required for dynamic efficiency of the structural change. The regional system to support innovation and entrepreneurial activities boosts leveraging the potential complementarities in and co-development of the productivity-enhancing technologies being applied. In addition, it increases product and service innovation potential, and thereby the emergence of new sectors with new employment opportunities. The educational system trains the newly unemployed as well as labour market entrants to exploit opportunities arising in the application of the focal technologies, in creative and entrepreneurial skills in general, or in skills in demand in emerging sectors. This boosts employment in existing as well as emerging sectors and increases occupational mobility between sectors.

The complementarity between these functions for regional development subject to technological change becomes obvious when omitting one of these functions. Inadequate education (A) hampers upskilling of workers to exploit opportunities in existing or emerging sectors. Rationalization and automation of the production system would free-up labour, but the newly unemployed remain insufficiently skilled to exploit complementarities and co-development opportunities, and likely also lack the skills to create or reap potential job opportunities in emerging sectors. These newly emerging jobs remain un – or underexploited or are filled by high-skilled migrants, which leaves low-skilled locals un – or underemployed. In case of inefficient or inadequate allocation of labour (B), innovation would create opportunities for high-skilled creative work which are un(der)exploited due to local workers being stuck in low-skilled work. In the long run, the faltering rationalization and automation would cause a decline in regional competitiveness, thus causing unemployment in old sectors. This may cause polarization by having high-skilled work in new sectors notably filled by migrants, und low-skilled unemployed. An ineffective innovation system (C) hampers the creation of jobs in emerging sectors and the exploitation of complementarities and co-development of technologies in the sector of application. So, although the newly unemployed are upskilled by the adequate education systems, there are insufficient job opportunities in the region, thus creating high-skilled unemployed likely to migrate out of the region.

In general, institutional impediments to labour mobility and product innovation as well as (fundamental) limitations to educationability and transferability of creative skills hamper catching up and will cause unemployment and inequality. Given that res-killing is required to 'mop up' the low-skilled newly unemployed, any limit to educationability may be particularly impactful in regions with predominantly applying sectors. Moreover, institutional impediments and technological limits (such as due to the prior mix of capabilities in the region) to innovativeness may stifle the creation of jobs and notably the creation of new sectors. This seems certainly the case for regions predominantly applying technology and/ or regions relying on emerging sectors to catch up. Innovativeness is not only required to just create jobs, but particularly for creative work that curbs selective out-migration of high-skilled workers. As such, facing the rapid technology-driven shift toward creative work, the catching up path requires a well-functioning triad of institutions engaged in innovation and entrepreneurial activities for job creation and exploitation of opportunities, education for upskilling and occupational mobility, and labour market regulation for hiring and firing in the process of structural change.

4.5. Path-dependence, co-evolution, and multi-scalarity

The institutional framework to direct the technology-driven structural change in the focal applying region is not implemented *ex novo*: there are institutions readily in place. However, institutional change often follows a path of incremental rather than radical steps (Mahoney and Thelen 2009; Streeck and Thelen 2005) such that decisions made earlier feed forward in decision to be made later. Such path-dependence poses a challenge for institutional transformation, if required. In addition, the new regional institutional framework is not only to be developed from the existing institutions, but also to be embedded in the institutional architecture at higher spatial scale. Moreover, the institutions are not structuring economic activities unidirectionally, but the interests and activities of economic actors also drive institutional change. So, ultimately, there is co-evolution of institutions and industries (Nelson 1995) both within and across regions as well as at other geographical scales (cf. Gong and Hassink 2019; Grillitsch 2015; Benner 2021). The following paragraphs describe these three challenges (path-dependence in institutional transformation, co-evolution with economic activities, multi-scalarity) to the implementation of our institutional framework, a brief examination of limits to applicability, and how this calls for additional governance measures for institutional change.

Firstly, institutions *tend to persist over long periods of time and constrain the range of options available to actors in the future, including those that may be more efficient or effective in the long run* (Campbell 2010). While institutions develop and often do so endogenously (e.g. through layering, drift, conversion, see Streeck and Thelen 2005), the 'new' institutional framework is not necessarily on the development path of the existing institutions. Since various mechanisms consolidate the institutional development path (see e.g. Rixen and Viola 2015), active governance is required to branch into alternative paths (Ebbinghaus 2005). Such path-changing institutional transformation requires strong governance capabilities, political mandate, development vision, and quality of government. However, regions that are falling behind often lack such governance capabilities (see e.g. Rodríguez-Pose and Ketterer 2020). Arguably, particularly the applying regions falling behind require a further bolstering of governance capabilities to transform the institutional framework for structural change.

Secondly, on top of endogeneity in institutional development, there is co-evolution with the activities and interests of economic actors in the region (Gong and Hassink 2019; Benner 2021). Certain complementarities between institutions and industry may have emerged that lock-in the region in the vicious cycle. For example, the bargain power of workers in historically large labour-intensive sectors has given rise to labour market institutions that inhibit rationalization (e.g. dismissal protection, unions). Another example is that both research and educational institutions are serving the production system of existing sectors (see e.g. Thelen and Kume 1999). Such complementarities further consolidate the institutional architecture and may thus inhibit the emergence of radically new sectors at the expense of existing sectors.

That said, the actors across the various sectors also partly operationalize the functions of the institutions and may as such drive institutional change. For instance, entrepreneurs in emerging sectors may provide intensive training on-the-job, spur the establishment of training programmes in labour activation programmes, call for changes in the curriculum of vocational studies of apprentices, etc. Generally, the 'institutional entrepreneurship' of these actors would thus drive the emergence and change of institutions to their needs (Garud, Hardy, and Maguire 2007). So, on the one hand, institutions structure the economic activities, and on the other hand, the operationalization of the functions of these institutions are evolving subject to institutional entrepreneurship as well as active reforms. Since endogenous institutional change generally caters to the interests of powerful incumbents and their interests may well be conflicting with the actors in sectors yet to emerge, reform of institutions is not granted, let alone effectively coaxing the structural shift.

The implementation of the integrated framework pitched in this paper thus requires proactive governance to create corporate, political, and public support for the reforms of institutions in favour of sectors that have yet to emerge.

Thirdly, while the focus in this paper is *regional*, the change in technology and competitive position generally is global. For one, given that the economic actors in the region in question are merely *applying* the focal technology, the main technological developments driving the (global) structural change are largely taking place elsewhere. The shift in regional economic activities thus requires access to technological knowledge elsewhere and possibly available through actors operating at different spatial scales (Bellandi, Chaminade, and Plechero 2020; Chen and Hassink 2020). In addition, regional institutions are also embedded in an institutional architecture at higher spatial scale (and embedding those at lower spatial scale). Regional governance of multi-scalar institutional embedding may result in several types of change in the institutional architecture at both the regional and (inter)national level, e.g. by conversion, layering and recombination (see e.g. Hermelin and Persson 2021). In general, the organizational form of institutions such as the innovation system (e.g. open research collaboration in tech parks) and human resource management notably in the private sectors (e.g. on-the-job training to cope with scarcity) may have considerable regional specificities even within one and the same country (see e.g. Saxenian 1994). However, the operationalization and organization of institutional functions as well as the implementation and transformation of these institutions may also well be shaped by (inter)national institutions. There are different varieties of such national institutional architectures, notably based on ideologies on governance of market economies. There are groups of countries that have more liberal market economies (with emphasis on competition, deregulation, entrepreneurship, flexibility, etc.) or rather more coordinated market economies (with emphasis on collaboration, governance, social security, etc.) (Hall and Soskice 2001). Clearly, these ideologies may be more or rather less compatible with principles underlying the institutional framework proposed in this paper. For example, the implementation of a mix of social security, financial support for entrepreneurial activity, and public provisions for training at the regional level is bound to encounter more objections in a country with national institutions rooted in free-market ideologies. That said, in the ongoing process of devolution, more autonomy is granted to regional authorities to be able to address specific local and regional problems with tailored instruments. Even in countries with liberal market ideologies or in economic unions with variation in ideologies there is room for regional differentiation in policies, see e.g. Structural and Investment Funds in the E.U., and the Empowerment Zones in the U.S.A. (Cook et al. 2008). Moreover, also for labour market policies, which typically abide by national or even international laws (with regard to e.g. social security, worker rights, minimum wage, dismissal protection), there is freedom for local discretionary measures such as budgets for training, search assistance, job creation (see e.g. Doeringer, Sum, and Terkla 2002). In fact, such regional differentiation may be a necessary instrument in reducing inequality and increasing cohesion (Iammarino, Rodriguez-Pose, and Storper 2019). As argued, though, effective implementation of the institutional framework conducive to structural change requires capabilities for institutional transformation dealing with multi-scalar co-evolution. Typically, these capabilities may be found in advanced political economies, which thus also limits the applicability of our institutional framework.

5. Conclusions

The ongoing technology-driven structural shift away from routinized physical and cognitive work toward non-routinized, creative work is bound to exacerbate regional disparities. A tendentious narrative is that, on the one hand, there are 'making regions' that experience a virtuous cycle of increasing employment for and in-migration of high-skilled, high-wage creative workers that research, develop, and make the focal technologies and, on the other hand, there is a wide range of 'applying regions' that befalls a vicious cycle of decreasing competitiveness, increasing unemployment of low-skilled workers, and out-migration. This paper addressed how to reverse the falling behind of a region in which dominant sectors are becoming increasingly uncompetitive. It is argued that the focal region has to embark on a development path of structural change away from automatable routinized work toward creative work. Firstly, existing sectors have to fend off an imminent decline in product demand by rationalizing production, even if possibly displacing workers. The emerging opportunities in co-development, complementarities, and product innovation are then to be exploited. In this, there is an increasing demand for workers with creative, problem-solving and technology-complementary skills and opportunities for entrepreneurs. Secondly, product innovation is to be nurtured to give rise to emerging sectors with job opportunities for the unemployed and to retain high-skilled workers. Lastly, with further rise of discretionary income, there is local multiplication of employment in otherwise unaffected sectors. This paper provided outlines of an institutional framework to provide three complementary functions that direct this technology-driven structural shift toward creative work – broadly defined. Firstly, a regional innovation system is to support the acquisition and building of capabilities, exploit complementarities, assist in co-development of the focal technologies, enhance reaping technological opportunities, and facilitating product innovation. Moreover, institutions should encourage entrepreneurial activities and innovation collaboration, not only to exploit existing technologies, but possibly also to explore breakthroughs giving rise to new job opportunities, new occupations and possibly even emerging sectors. An entrepreneurial and innovative culture may curb selective out-migration of high-skilled labour and rather attract the creative class to the region. Secondly, educational institutions are to provide a labour force with the skills in demand to exploit new opportunities and to enhance occupational mobility. Education is to be reformed to stimulate creativity and train people to use methods for creative thinking. Thirdly, labour market institutions should be flexible to (i) facilitate automation for competitiveness and (ii) incentivize firms to hire workers for training on the job and for risky ventures, notably for emerging sectors. The labour market liberalization should be complemented with social security arrangements during upskilling of the newly unemployed and enticing high-skilled creatives to risk entrepreneurial activities in emerging sectors. Arguably, in applying regions education and innovation may seek to focus on building capabilities (co-development, transfer) and exploiting complementarities of regional, specialized sectors with a competitive edge. A meta-level challenge in implementation for the applying region falling behind is to build and wield capabilities to transform institutions readily in place, thereby coaxing the co-evolutionary feedback from existing sectors, nurturing institutional entrepreneurialism from emerging sectors, as well as embedding into institutions at higher levels.

There are several avenues for further research. So far, the institutional framework presented in this paper is a theoretical concept. Although there are real-world implementations of closely related frameworks (e.g. 'flexicurity' is implemented in Denmark and The Netherlands), encompassing integration (notably with the innovation system) for governance of structural change as advocated in this paper is limited. Further analysis is to reveal how real-world implementations are to be differentiated to regional specificities such as the existing state of institutional arrangements (e.g. poor social security, absence of higher education institutions), different varieties in the (inter)national institutions at higher spatial scales, and the prior sectoral composition (e.g. rural agricultural regions, old industrial districts). Moreover, analysis is to elucidate the relationship of the transformative institutional framework with other (supraregional) development strategies (e.g. smart specialization). As the latter may also specify education, labour market, or innovation policies, there may be synergies or conflicts. A last avenue is to study the implications for institutional governance whenever there are fundamental limitations to structural change such as bounded educationability of creativity or whenever technology ultimately indeed may replace the vast majority of the labour force.

Acknowledgements

We thank two anonymous reviewers, Greg Hearn, Marco Vivarelli, Pier Paolo Saviotti, Smita Srinivas, Erkan Erdil, Iciar Dominguez Lacasa, Beata Woźniak-Jęchorek, Anastasia Constantelou and other participants of the Annual Conference of the European Association for Evolutionary Political Economy 2019 in Warsaw and 2021 in Napoli, and the International Workshop Rethinking Culture and Creativity in the Technological Era 2020 in Florence for their valuable input on earlier versions of this paper and presentations thereof.

Disclosure statement

No potential conflict of interest was reported by the author(s).

Funding

Ben Vermeulen gratefully acknowledges European Union Horizon 2020 Research and Innovation programme, [grant number 731726]. Eleonora Psenner gratefully acknowledges European Union Horizon 2020 European Training Networks programme, [grant number 955907], and financial support from IDM Südtirol for the project *A Strategy for the Creative Industries South Tyrol*.

ORCID

Ben Vermeulen http://orcid.org/0000-0001-6563-2568

Bibliography

Acemoglu, D. 2002. "Technical Change, Inequality, and the Labor Market." *Journal of Economic Literature* XL: 7–72. doi:10.1257/jel.40.1.7

Acemoglu, D., and D. Autor. 2011. "Skills, Tasks and Technologies: Implications for Employment and Earnings." In *Handbook of Labor Economics*, edited by David Card, and Orley Ashenfelter, vol. 4, 1043–1171. Elsevier. http://www.sciencedirect.com/science/article/pii/S0169721811024105

Acemoglu, Daron, Simon Johnson, and James Robinson. 2006. "Understanding Prosperity and Poverty: Geography, Institutions, and the Reversal of Fortune." In *Understanding Poverty*, edited by Abhijit Vinayak Banerjee, Roland Bénabou, and Dilip Mookherjee, 19–36. Oxford: Oxford University Press.

Acemoglu, D., and P. Restrepo. 2016. *The Race Between Machine and Man: Implications of Technology for Growth, Factor Shares and Employment*. Cambridge, MA. https://www.nber.org/papers/w22252 National Bureau of Economic Research NBER Working Paper Number: 22252. doi:10.3386/w22252

Acemoglu, D., and P. Restrepo. 2017. *Robots and Jobs: Evidence from US Labor Markets*. Cambridge, MA. https://www.nber.org/papers/w23285 National Bureau of Economic Research NBER Working Paper Number: 23285. doi:10.3386/w23285

Acemoglu, D., and P. Restrepo. 2018. "Artificial Intelligence, Automation and Work." In *NBER Working Paper* (24196). doi:10.3386/w24196

Adams, T, and E. Demaiter. 2008. "Skill, Education and Credentials in the new Economy: The Case of Information Technology Workers." *Work, Employment and Society* 22 (2): 351–362. doi:10.1177/0950017008089109

Amin, A. 2004. "An Institutionalist Perspective on Regional Economic Development." In *Reading Economic Geography*, edited by Trevor J. Barnes, Jamie Peck, Eric Sheppard, and Adam Tickell, 48–58. Oxford, UK: Blackwell Publishing Ltd.

Amior, M. 2015. "Why are Higher Skilled Workers More Mobile Geographically?" The role of the job surplus. LSE Centre for Economic Performance (Discussion Paper, 1338).

Asheim, B., J. Moodysson, and F. Tödtling. 2011. "Constructing Regional Advantage: Towards State-of-the-Art Regional Innovation System Policies in Europe?" *European Planning Studies* 19 (7): 1133–1139. doi:10.1080/09654313.2011.573127.

Autor, David. 2015. "Why Are There Still So Many Jobs? The History and Future of Workplace Automation." *Journal of Economic Perspectives* 29 (3): 3–30. doi:10.1257/jep.29.3.3.

Autor, D., and D. Dorn. 2013. "The Growth of Low-Skill Service Jobs and the Polarization of the US Labor Market." *In American Economic Review* 103 (5): 1553–1597. doi:10.1257/aer.103.5.1553.

Autor, D., L. Katz, and M. Kearney. 2006. "The Polarization of the US Labor Market." National Bureau of Economic Research. Cambridge, MA (NBER Working Paper Series, 11986).

Autor, D., F. Levy, and R. Murnane. 2003. "The Skill Content of Recent Technological Change: An Empirical Exploration." *The Quarterly Journal of Economics* 118 (4): 1279–1333. doi:10.1162/003355303322552801

Baker, D., A. Glyn, D. Howell, and J. Schmitt. 2005. "Labor Market Institutions and Unemployment: Assessment of the Cross-Country Evidence." In *Fighting Unemployment. The Limits of Free Market Orthodoxy*, edited by D. R. Howell, 72–118. Oxford, NY: Oxford University Press.

Bakhshi, H., A. Freeman, and P. Higgs. 2013. A Dynamic Mapping of the UK's Creative Industries. NESTA.

Bakhshi, H., C. Frey, and M. Osborne. 2015. Creativity vs Robots: The Creative Economy and the Future of Employment. NESTA. London (April).

Baumol, W., and W. Bowen. 2006. *Performing Arts - the Economic Dilemma. A Study of Problems Common to Theater, Opera, Music and Dance. Repr.* Aldershot: Ashgate. (Modern revivals in economics).

Bellandi, M., C. Chaminade, and M. Plechero. 2020. "Transformative Paths, Multi-Scalarity of Knowledge Bases and Industry 4.0." In *Industry 4.0 and Regional Transformation. 1st*, edited by L. De Propris, and D. Bailey, 62–83. London: Routledge (Regions and cities).

Benner, M. 2021. "Retheorizing Industrial–Institutional Coevolution: A Multidimensional Perspective." *Regional Studies*, 1–14. doi:10.1080/00343404.2021.1949441.

Berger, T., and C. Frey. 2016. "Digitalization, Jobs, and Convergence in Europe: Strategies for Closing the Skills Gap." Report for Executive Agency for Small and Medium-sized Enterprises (EASME); the European Commission. DG Internal Market, Industry, Entrepreneurship and SMEs.

Betcherman, G. 2012. "Labor Market Institutions. A Review of the Literature." The World Bank (Policy Research Working Paper, 6276).

Boschma, R., and M. Fritsch. 2009. "Creative Class and Regional Growth: Empirical Evidence from Seven European Countries." *Economic Geography* 85 (4): 391–423. doi:10.1111/j.1944-8287.2009.01048.x.

Broekel, T., and T. Brenner. 2011. "Regional Factors and Innovativeness: An Empirical Analysis of Four German Industries." *The Annals of Regional Science* 47 (1): 169–194. doi:10.1007/s00168-009-0364-x.

Brynjolfsson, E., and A. McAfee. 2011. Race Against The Machine. How The Digital Revolution Is Accelerating Innovation, Driving Productivity, and Irreversibly Transforming Employment and The Economy.

Bucci, A., P. Sacco, and G. Segre. 2014. "Smart Endogenous Growth: Cultural Capital and the Creative use of Skills." *International Journal of Manpower* 35 (1/2): 33–55. doi:10.1108/IJM-08-2013-0193.

Campbell, J. 2010. "Institutional Reproduction and Change." In *The Oxford Handbook of Comparative Institutional Analysis*, edited by G. Morgan, J. L. Campbell, C. Crouch, O. K. Pedersen, and R. Whitley, 87–115. Oxford, NY: Oxford University Press. (Oxford handbooks).

Chatterton, P., and J. Goddard. 2000. "The Response of Higher Education Institutions to Regional Needs." *European Journal of Education* 35 (4): 475–496. doi:10.1111/1467-3435.00041

Chen, Y., and R. Hassink. 2020. "Multi-scalar Knowledge Bases for new Regional Industrial Path Development: Toward a Typology." *European Planning Studies* 28 (12): 2489–2507. doi:10.1080/09654313.2020.1724265.

Cook, B., W. Mitchell, V. Quirk, and M. Watts. 2008. Creating Effective Local Labour Markets: A New Framework for Regional Employment Policy. Centre of Full Employment and Equity. Callaghan, Australia.

Cropley, A. 1995. "Fostering Creativity in the Classroom: General Principles." In *The Creativity Research Handbook*, edited by M. Runco, 1, 83–114. Cresskill, NJ: Hampton Press.

Cropley, A. 2020. "Creativity-focused Technology Education in the Age of Industry 4.0." *Creativity Research Journal* 32 (2): 184–191. doi:10.1080/10400419.2020.1751546.

Cropley, D., and A. Cropley. 2010. "Functional Creativity: "Products" and the Generation of Effective Novelty." In *The Cambridge Handbook of Creativity*, edited by J. C. Kaufman, and R. J. Sternberg, 301–317. New York: Cambridge University Press.

Crouch, G. 1995. "A Meta-Analysis of Tourism Demand." *Annals of Tourism Research* 22 (1): 103–118. doi:10.1016/0160-7383(94)00054-V.

Cunningham, S., and J. Potts. 2015. "Creative Industries and the Wider Economy." In *The Oxford Handbook of Creative Industries*, edited by C. Jones, M. Lorenzen, and J. Sapsed, 1st ed., 387–404. Oxford: Oxford University Press ([Oxford handbooks]).

De Backer, K., C. Menon, I. Desnoyers-James, and L. Moussiegt. 2016. Reshoring: Myth or Reality? OECD Publishing. Paris (OECD Science, Technology and Industry Policy Papers, 27).

Doeringer, P., A. Sum, and D. Terkla. 2002. "Devolution of Employment and Training Policy: The Case of Older Workers." *Journal of Aging & Social Policy* 14 (3-4): 37–60. doi:10.1300/J031v14n03_03.

Doloreux, D., and S. Parto. 2005. "Regional Innovation Systems: Current Discourse and Unresolved Issues." *Technology in Society* 27 (2): 133–153. doi:10.1016/j.techsoc.2005.01.002.

Ebbinghaus, B. 2005. "Can Path Dependence Explain Institutional Change?" Two Approaches Applied to Welfare State Reform. Cologne: Max Planck Institute for the Study of Societies (MPIfG Discussion Paper, 05/2).

Eichhorst, W., and R. Konle-Seidl. 2005. "The Interaction of Labor Market Regulation and Labor Market Policies in Welfare State Reform." Institute for Employment Research. Nürnberg (IAB-Discussion Paper, 19/2005).

Elhorst, J. 2003. "The Mystery of Regional Unemployment Differentials: Theoretical and Empirical Explanations." *Journal of Economic Surveys* 17 (5): 709–748. doi:10.1046/j.1467-6419.2003.00211.x.

Esparcia, J. 2014. "Innovation and Networks in Rural Areas. An Analysis from European Innovative Projects." *Journal of Rural Studies* 34: 1–14. doi:10.1016/j.jrurstud.2013.12.004.

European Commission . 2007. *Towards Common Principles of Flexicurity: More and Better Jobs Through Flexibility and Security*. Luxembourg: Office for Official Publications of the European Communities.

Evans, P. 2005. "The Challenges of the Institutional Turn: New Interdisciplinary Opportunities in Development Theory." In *The Economic Sociology of Capitalism*, edited by V. Nee, and R. Swedberg, 90–116. Princeton, NJ: Princeton University Press.

Feldman, M., and R. Florida. 1994. "The Geographic Sources of Innovation: Technological Infrastructure and Product Innovation in the United States." *Annals of the Association of American Geographers* 84 (2): 210–229. doi:10.1111/j.1467-8306.1994.tb01735.x

Feldman, M., and M. Storper. 2018. "Economic Growth and Economic Development: Geographical Dimensions, Definition, and Disparities." In *The new Oxford Handbook of Economic Geography*, edited by G. L. Clark, M. P. Feldman, M. S. Gertler, D. Wójcik, and A. Kaiser, 1st ed, 143–158. Oxford: Oxford University Press.

Fisher, A. 1939. "Production, Primary, Secondary and Tertiary." *Economic Record* 15 (1): 24–38. doi:10.1111/j.1475-4932.1939.tb01015.x

Florida, R. 2002. "The Economic Geography of Talent." *Annals of the Association of American Geographers* 92 (4): 743–755. doi:10.1111/1467-8306.00314.

Florida, R. 2012. *The Rise of the Creative Class*. New York: Basic Books, a member of the Perseus Books Group.

Florida, R., P. Adler, and C. Mellander. 2017. "The City as Innovation Machine." *Regional Studies* 51 (1): 86–96. doi:10.1080/00343404.2016.1255324.

Ford, M. 2015. *Rise of the Robots. Technology and the Threat of a Jobless Future.* New York: Basic Books.

Forge, S., and C. Blackman. 2010. *A Helping Hand for Europe. The Competitive Outlook for the EU Robotics Industry.* Luxembourg: Publications Office. EUR. Scientific and technical research series, 24600.

Frank, M., D. Autor, J. Bessen, E. Brynjolfsson, M. Cebrian, D. Deming, et al. 2019. "Toward Understanding the Impact of Artificial Intelligence on Labor." *Proceedings of the National Academy of Sciences of the United States of America* 116 (14): 6531–6539. doi:10.1073/pnas.1900949116.

Fratesi, U., and M. Percoco. 2014. "Selective Migration, Regional Growth and Convergence: Evidence from Italy." *Regional Studies* 48 (10): 1650–1668. doi:10.1080/00343404.2013.843162.

Freeman, R. 2007. "Labor Market Institutions Around the World." National Bureau of Economic Research. Cambridge, MA (NBER Working Paper Series, 13242).

Frey, C., and M. Osborne. 2017. "The Future of Employment: How Susceptible are Jobs to Computerisation?" *Technological Forecasting and Social Change* 114: 254–280. doi:10.1016/j.techfore.2016.08.019.

Fujita, N. 2007. "Myrdal's Theory of Cumulative Causation." *Evolutionary and Institutional Economics Review* 3 (2): 275–283. doi:10.14441/eier.3.275

Gagliardi, L. 2014. "Employment and Technological Change: On the Geography of Labour Market Adjustments." Spatial Economics Research Centre (London: SERC Discussion Paper, 165).

Garud, R., C. Hardy, and S. Maguire. 2007. "Institutional Entrepreneurship as Embedded Agency: An Introduction to the Special Issue." *Organization Studies* 28 (7): 957–969. doi:10.1177/0170840607078958.

Glaeser, E., H. Kallal, J. Scheinkman, and A. Shleifer. 1992. "Growth in Cities." *Journal of Political Economy* 100 (6): 1126–1152. doi:10.1086/261856.

Glaeser, E., and M. Resseger. 2009. "The Complementarity Between Cities and Skills." National Bureau of Economic Research (Cambridge, MA: NBER Working Paper Series, 15103).

Gong, H., and R. Hassink. 2019. "Co-evolution in Contemporary Economic Geography: Towards a Theoretical Framework." *Regional Studies* 53 (9): 1344–1355. doi:10.1080/00343404.2018.1494824.

Goos, M., J. Konings, and M. Vandeweyer. 2015. Employment Growth In Europe - Role of Innovation, Local Job Multipliers and Institutions (Utrech: U.S.E. Discussion Paper Series, 15-10).

Goos, M., A. Manning, and A. Salomons. 2009. ": Job Polarization in Europe." *The American Economic Review: Papers and Proceedings* 99 (2): 58–63. doi:10.1257/aer.99.2.58

Goos, M., A. Manning, and A. Salomons. 2014. "Explaining job Polarization: Routine-Biased Technological Change and Offshoring." *American Economic Review* 104 (8): 2509–2526. doi:10.1257/aer.104.8.2509

Grillitsch, M. 2015. "Institutional Layers, Connectedness and Change: Implications for Economic Evolution in Regions." *European Planning Studies* 23 (10): 2099–2124. doi:10.1080/09654313.2014.1003796.

Hall, P., and D. Soskice, eds. 2001. *Varieties of Capitalism: The Institutional Foundations of Comparative Advantage.* New Tork: Oxford University Press.

Hearn, G., and R. Bridgstock. 2014. "The Curious Case of the Embedded Creative: Creative Cultural Occupations Outside the Creative Industries." In *Handbook of Management and Creativity*, edited by C. Bilton, and S. Cummings, 39–56. Cheltenham, UK: Edward Elgar Publishing.

Hermelin, B., and B. Persson. 2021. "Regional Governance in Second-Tier City-Regions in Sweden: A Multi-Scalar Approach to Institutional Change." *Regional Studies* 55 (8): 1365–1375. doi:10.1080/00343404.2021.1896693.

Higgs, P., and S. Cunningham. 2008. "Creative Industries Mapping: Where Have we Come from and Where are we Going?" *Creative Industries Journal* 1 (1): 7–30. doi:10.1386/cij.1.1.7_1.

Howell, D. 2005. *Fighting Unemployment. The Limits of Free Market Orthodoxy.* Oxford, NY: Oxford University Press.

Howell, D., and E. Wolff. 1992. "Technical Change and the Demand for Skills by US Industries." *In Cambridge Journal of Economics* 16 (2): 127–146. doi:10.1093/oxfordjournals.cje.a035197.

Iammarino, S., A. Rodriguez-Pose, and M. Storper. 2019. "Regional Inequality in Europe: Evidence, Theory and Policy Implications." *Journal of Economic Geography* 19 (2): 273–298. doi:10.1093/jeg/lby021.

Levy, F., and R. Murnane. 2004. *The New Division of Labor: How Computers are Creating the Next Job Market*. Princeton: Princeton University Press.

Løyland, K., and V. Ringstad. 2009. "On the Price and Income Sensitivity of the Demand for Sports: Has Linder's Disease Become More Serious?" *Journal of Sports Economics* 10 (6): 601–618. doi:10.1177/1527002509334231.

Lundvall, B., J. Vang, K. Joseph, and C. Chaminade. 2009. "Bridging Innovation System Research and Development Studies: Challenges and Research Opportunities." In. 7th Globelics Conference: Georgia Institute of Technology.

Machin, S., and J. van Reenen. 1998. "Technology and Changes in Skill Structure: Evidence from Seven OECD Countries." *The Quarterly Journal of Economics* 113 (4): 1215–1244. doi:10.1162/003355398555883.

MacKinnon, D., S. Dawley, A. Pike, and A. Cumbers. 2019. "Rethinking Path Creation: A Geographical Political Economy Approach." *Economic Geography* 95 (2): 113–135. doi:10.1080/00130095.2018.1498294.

Mahoney, J., and K. Thelen, eds. 2009. *Explaining Institutional Change. Ambiguity, Agency, and Power*. Cambridge: Cambridge University Press.

Manning, A., and B. Petrongolo. 2017. "How Local Are Labor Markets? Evidence from a Spatial Job Search Model." *American Economic Review* 107 (10): 2877–2907. doi:10.1257/aer.20131026

Martin, R. 2017. "Cumulative Causation, Endogenous Growth, and Regional Development." In *International Encyclopedia of Geography: People, the Earth, Environment and Technology*, edited by D. Richardson, N. Castree, M. F. Goodchild, A. Kobayashi, W. Liu, and R. A. Marston, 1–13.

McGranahan, D., and T. Wojan. 2007. "The Creative Class: A Key to Rural Growth." *Amber Waves* 5 (2): 16–21. doi:10.22004/AG.ECON.125533.

Mokyr, J., C. Vickers, and N. Ziebarth. 2015. "The History of Technological Anxiety and the Future of Economic Growth: Is This Time Different?" *Journal of Economic Perspectives* 29 (3): 31–50. doi:10.1257/jep.29.3.31.

Moretti, E. 2010. "Local Multipliers." *The American Economic Review* 100 (2): 373–377. doi:10.1257/aer.100.2.373

Moretti, E. 2012. *The New Geography of Jobs*. Boston: Mariner Books; Houghton Mifflin Harcourt.

Murmann, J. 2003. *Knowledge and Competitive Advantage: The Coevolution of Firms, Technology, and National Institutions*. Cambridge: Cambridge University Press.

Myrdal, G. 1957. *Economic Theory and Under-Developed Regions*. London: Duckworths.

Nelson, R. 1995. "Co-Evolution of Industry Structure, Technology and Supporting Institutions, and the Making of Comparative Advantage." *International Journal of the Economics of Business* 2 (2): 171–184. doi:10.1080/758519306.

Nomaler, O., B. Verspagen, and A. van Zon. 2020. "The Role of Innovation in Structural Change, Economic Development, and the Labor Market." In *Handbook of Labor, Human Resources and Population Economics*, edited by Klaus F. Zimmermann, 1–14. Cham: Springer International Publishing.

OECD (Ed.). 2005. *OECD Employment Outlook 2005*. Paris: OECD Publishing.

OECD. 2018. *Good Jobs for All in a Changing World of Work: The OECD Jobs Strategy*. Paris: OECD.

Pianta, M. 2004. "Innovation and Employment." In *The Oxford Handbook of Innovation*, edited by J. Fagerberg, D. C. Mowery and R. R. Nelson, 568–598. Oxford University Press.

Rixen, T., and L. Viola. 2015. "Putting Path Dependence in its Place: Toward a Taxonomy of Institutional Change." *Journal of Theoretical Politics* 27 (2): 301–323. doi:10.1177/0951629814531667.

Rodriguez-Pose, A. 2013. "Do Institutions Matter for Regional Development?" *Regional Studies* 47 (7): 1034–1047. doi:10.1080/00343404.2012.748978.

Rodrik, D., A. Subramanian, and F. Trebbi. 2004. "Institutions Rule: The Primacy of Institutions Over Geography and Integration in Economic Development." *Journal of Economic Growth* 9 (2): 131–165. doi:10.1023/B:JOEG.0000031425.72248.85

Rodríguez-Pose, A., and T. Ketterer. 2020. "Institutional Change and the Development of Lagging Regions in Europe." *Regional Studies* 54 (7): 974–986. doi:10.1080/00343404.2019.1608356.

Rotz, S., E. Gravely, I. Mosby, E. Duncan, E. Finnis, M. Horgan, et al. 2019. "Automated Pastures and the Digital Divide: How Agricultural Technologies are Shaping Labour and Rural Communities." *Journal of Rural Studies* 68: 112–122. doi:10.1016/j.jrurstud.2019.01.023.

Saxenian, A. 1994. *Regional Advantage. Culture and Competition in Silicon Valley and Route 128.* Cambridge, MA: Harvard Univ. Press.

Schlee, R., and K. Harich. 2014. "Teaching Creativity to Business Students: How Well Are We Doing?" *Journal of Education for Business* 89 (3): 133–141. doi:10.1080/08832323.2013.781987.

Scott, A. 1997. "The Cultural Economy of Cities." *International Journal of Urban and Regional Research* 21 (2): 323–339. doi:10.1111/1468-2427.00075

Selada, C., I. Vilhena Da Cunha, and E. Tomaz. 2012. "Creative-Based Strategies in Small and Medium-Sized Cities: Key Dimensions of Analysis." *Quaestiones Geographicae* 31 (4), doi:10.2478/v10117-012-0034-4.

Shen, C., and J. Zheng. 2020. "Does Global Value Chains Participation Really Promote Skill-Biased Technological Change? Theory and Evidence from China." *Economic Modelling* 86: 10–18. doi:10.1016/j.econmod.2019.03.009.

Silva, Ester, and Aurora Teixeira. 2008. "Surveying Structural Change: Seminal Contributions and a Bibliometric Account." *Structural Change and Economic Dynamics* 19 (4): 273–300. doi:10.1016/j.strueco.2008.02.001.

Sorenson, J., K. Zawieska, B. Vermeulen, S. Madsen, S. Trentemøller, A. Pyka, et al. 2019. *Perspectives on Robots: A Reality Check on Imagined Futures.* Copenhagen: Aarhus University.

Stewart, I., D. De, and A. Cole. 2015. Technology and people: The great job-creating machine. London: Deloitte.

Streeck, W., and K. Thelen. 2005. "Introduction: Institutional Change in Advanced Political Economies." In *Beyond Continuity: Institutional Change in Advanced Political Economies*, edited by W. Streeck, and K. Thelen, 3–39. Oxford University Press.

Strom, R., and P. Strom. 2002. "Changing the Rules: Education for Creative Thinking." *The Journal of Creative Behavior* 36 (3): 183–200. doi:10.1002/j.2162-6057.2002.tb01063.x.

Syrquin, M. 2012. "Two Approaches to the Study of Structural Change and Economic Development: Kuznets and Pasinetti." In *Structural Dynamics and Economic Growth*, edited by R. Arena, and P. L. Porta, 69–87. Cambridge: Cambridge University Press.

Thelen, K., and I. Kume. 1999. "The Rise of Nonmarket Training Regimes: Germany and Japan Compared." *Journal of Japanese Studies* 25 (1): 33. doi:10.2307/133353.

van der Pol, H. 2008. "Key role of cultural and creative industries in the economy." In: *Statistics, Knowledge and Policy 2007: Measuring and Fostering the Progress of Societies*, 343–353. Paris and Washington, D.C: OECD.

Vermeulen, B., J. Kesselhut, A. Pyka, and P. Saviotti. 2018. "The Impact of Automation on Employment: Just the Usual Structural Change?" *Sustainability* 10 (5). doi:10.3390/su10051661.

Vermeulen, B., A. Pyka, and P. Saviotti. 2020. "A Taxonomic Structural Change Perspective on the Economic Impact of Robots and Artificial Intelligence on Creative Work." In *The Future of Creative Work. Creativity and Digital Disruption*, edited by G. Hearn, 57–76. Cheltenham, UK: Edward Elgar Publishing.

Vivarelli, M. 2007. Innovation and employment: Technological unemployment is not inevitable—some innovation creates jobs, and some job destruction can be avoided. IZA. Bonn, Germany (IZA Technical Report).

Vivarelli, M. 2013. "Innovation, Employment, and Skills in Advanced and Developing Countries: A Survey of the Economic Literature." *Journal of Economic Issues* 48: 123–154. doi:10.2753/JEI0021-3624480106

Withers, G. 1980. "Unbalanced Growth and the Demand for Performing Arts: An Econometric Analysis." *Southern Economic Journal* 46 (3): 735–742. doi:10.2307/1057143

Uses and practices of digital services in a situation of mobility: evolution versus revolution? The case of the Champs Elysées

Marie Delaplace, Leïla Kebir, Marjolaine Gros-Balthazard and François Bavaud

ABSTRACT

The ongoing digital revolution is transforming economic production systems as well as our daily lives. If the expectancies in terms of innovation and opportunities are very high on the supply side, little is known about the effective uses of digital tools by customers and the impact on them and their consumption patterns, especially in a situation of mobility. Tourism for example has been tremendously impacted by the digital transformation. It has changed the way people plan, book and travel, but also the way the stakeholders communicate on their destination. But it is also expected that mobile and wireless technologies change the tourist experience of the destination. Mobile devices could induce change in tourist behaviour at the last minute *in situ*. By using an analysis in terms of services, we suggest that suppliers and tourists in territories coproduce M-tourism services. These services depend on the tourist behaviour but also on the supply, which is available in the destination. Drawing on a survey conducted on the Champs Elysées in Paris in 2018, this paper analyses how different types of people (tourists, residents, workers, etc.) are using these digital services.

1. Introduction

The use of computer has progressively changed the whole tourism sector since 1950s (Buhalis 2020) and the subsequent development of digital tools has totally altered tourist practices (Buhalis and Law 2008; Gretzel, Fesenmaier, and O'Leary 2006; Law, Chu Chan, and Wang 2018). First, the digital transformation that occurred in this sector fundamentally changed the way people plan their travel. Online collaborative platforms (hospitality, transport, etc.) challenged the way tourism is produced and organized. Social media and customer reviews have had a powerful impact on tourist information and, through a knock-on effect, on the organization of production promotion and advertisement. More recently, mobile and wireless technologies (smartphones and connected tablets) have become ubiquitous, and with them the proliferation of apps designed to promote and enrich the tourist experience (from extra information to augmented reality). As Buhalis and Law pointed out already in 2008, these mobile technologies have opened new avenues for development through the potential they offer. Actors in the tourist sector are now developing such tools (virtual tours, virtual reality, etc.). New tools will also be created in the future, with the 5G technology (immersive visits, ultra-smooth augmented reality and virtual reality, etc.) (Chen et al. 2021). While there have been numerous studies on the spread of these technologies and the promise they offer on the supply side (see Chen et al. 2021 for a recent review), there has been little research on how they are actually used by tourists (Dorcic, Komsic, and Markovic 2019; Law, Chu Chan, and Wang 2018) especially *in situ*. In addition, tourist destinations are also places that are used by people, whether to live, for temporary activities or for work. What then are the respective activities of these populations? Do the mobile technology practices of tourists differ from those of the other users? How far does-it change the experience of any destination?

The purpose of this article is to analyse how these devices and the associated services (geolocation, augmented or overlap reality, instant messaging about destinations on social media, immediate feedback on experiences, etc.) are actually used by the different types of users. Do these uses have an impact on the activities pursued *in situ*? Which services are actually used?

By using an analysis in terms of services, we suggest that suppliers and tourists coproduce M-tourism services in the destination. These services depend on the tourist behaviour but also on the supply, which is available in the destination. Drawing on a survey conducted on the Champs Elysées in Paris with different types of users (tourists, residents, workers, etc.), the aim is more specifically to see whether these uses are specific to tourism or whether they are simply an extension of ordinary digital practices (Wang, Xiang, and Fesenmaier 2016).

In the first section, we provide a literature review on the topic. Then, we draw on the survey to identify how these tools are used and by whom. Finally, we show that if the digital devices, contrary to the expectations of the tourist operators, affect these practices they ultimately remain conventional, with regard to the Champs-Elysées where supplying conventional experiences seem to be already sufficient.

2. The issue of the appropriation of innovation linked to M tourism

2.1. Mobile revolution and tourism

Tourism is a sector in which many authors have looked at the impact of digital technology. It is widely recognized as one of the sectors in which the digital transformation has happened the fastest (McKinsey 2014). Profoundly affected since the 1990s (Buhalis and Law 2008), the tourism sector is also in many respects a pioneer (Cabrespines and Wargnie 2017) in the adoption of these new tools. In 2019, the leading use of online shopping worldwide was related to travel (including accommodation), with an estimated expenditure in that year of $750.7 billion.[1] This digital transformation grew with the development and spread of mobile technologies, where the smartphone can be considered, according to Liang et al. (2017) 'as the symbol of this technological superstorm'

(732). Applications, tablets and mobile Internet have become ubiquitous in our day-to-day experiences and practices. Since the early 2000s, therefore, much research has been done into the implications of these technologies for tourism and the hospitality industry (Dorcic, Komsic, and Markovic 2019; Kim and Law 2015; Law, Chu Chan, and Wang 2018; Liang et al. 2017). By facilitating access to the information needed before (organization, preparation, decision-making, purchases, etc.), during (connection, browsing, decision-making, local transactions) and after (sharing, documentation, re-experiencing, attachment) the travel, these technologies are transforming the tourist experience (Gretzel and Jamal 2009). The spontaneity and ubiquity they offer have changed our relations to time and space (Dickinson et al. 2014; Tussyadiah and Wang 2014). They make it possible to perform tasks on the spot that were previously done before or after: deciding here and now what activities to choose (with less advance planning), revising an itinerary, sharing experience, information and opinions in real time with friends and family on social media (Tussyadiah and Wang 2014; Wang, Xiang, and Fesenmaier 2016). They can also help to resolve problems and to increase our sense of security (Schroeder et al. 2013; Wang, Xiang, and Fesenmaier 2016). Armed with these technologies, tourists are better informed and more autonomous. They become coproducers of the content of their journeys, but also and increasingly, of their destinations (Dorcic, Komsic, and Markovic 2019; Molz 2014; Naramski and Herman 2020). As Sundbo, Rubalcaba, and Gallouj (2021) put forward in the case of creative and cultural industries 'experiences via social media and the internet, mobile phones, etc., have turned the power toward users'. As a result, their practices are evolving. Mourtazina (2019) explains, for example, that digital photography is today 'a form of being-in-the-world and of making the world around with these elements' (own translation, 3), and no longer just as a way of seeing it. On the other hand, these technologies (e.g. digital tourist guides) can also standardize or mark out the tourist experience in the sense that they can recommend 'the best location for capturing the best view with one's mobile phone' (Bideran and Fraysse 2015, 84).

While many articles look at the effects of these technologies on demand, and in particular at the factors that drive or inhibit it (Law, Chu Chan, and Wang 2018), it should be noted that not much is known on the way they are effectively used and how practices are impacted. In other words, have tourist practices deeply changed?

Visitors of a destination are using digital tools to plan the journey, to find a hotel and so on. But when they are in the destination, they can also use new services we call M-tourism services.

2.2. M-tourism, an analysis in terms of services

2.2.1. The characteristics-based definition of services

Besides their intangibility, what distinguishes services from goods is their relational character, i.e. the interaction between the provider and the user (Howells 2010).

Taking into account these specificities and using previous analysis (De Vries 2006; Gallouj and Weinstein 1997; Lancaster 1966), Gallouj and Savona (2010) present a theoretical representation of a service. A service can be presented as a mapping of interlinked vectors of characteristics: a vector of technical characteristics [T] behind the vector of services characteristics [Y] which describes the utilities provided to the user; a vector of

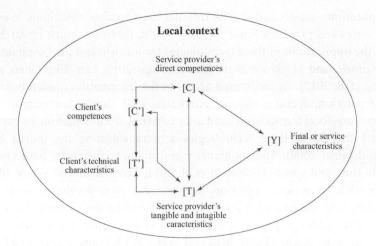

Figure 1. M tourism services. Source: the authors based on Gallouj and Savona (2010).

competencies of the provider(s) [C]; a vector of competencies of the client [C'] and lastly a vector of technical characteristics [T'] for the client (see Figure 1).

Like other services, M-tourism is coproduced by the interaction between the provider(s) and the client. In the case of M-tourism, various types of agents can handle the M-tourism services: the different developers of the applications, but also the city, a museum; etc.

For M-tourism, the technical characteristics [T] involve the technical components of the destination (infrastructures, museums, wifi terminal, etc.). The vector of final or services characteristics [Y] corresponds to distance communication, finding a restaurant, a theatre, etc. Each type of provider mobilizes its own vector of competencies [C]. Clients also need some competencies (a vector of competencies [C']) to coproduce M tourism services. Indeed, they must be able to use their smartphone or their tablets, to take a picture, to see the augmented reality provided by an application, etc. Moreover, as suggested by De Vries (2006), the co-production of the service also requires adding a vector of technical characteristics for the clients themselves [T']. Indeed, especially in the pervasive digital economy, clients will need to use their own technical tools in order to interact with the technical characteristics of the service provider(s). This is the case, for example, when clients are using their phone to book their museum tickets.

Last, because the service relationship characterizing M-tourism takes place in time and in places, M-tourism services, also heavily depend on the local contexts. M tourism services are coproduced in territories (Figure 1). Digitalization of practices and the servitization of tourism depends on the way the territory and its actors allow it.[2]

2.2.2. M tourism services as co-produced services in territories

As mentioned above, new services have been developed to be used on digital tools. The first concerns geolocation applications. These applications are already present in mobile terminals but must be activated by the user. They allow users to geolocate themselves in real time, to find a shop, a monument, a place and to define how to get there. Google Maps is the best-known example. The advantage of these applications is that they identify places to visit *in situ* and display additional information on the terminal more or less automatically (location of nearby amenities, tourist sites, sometimes illustrated with photos, videos, etc.).

The second type corresponds to the QR codes (Quick Response Code) which appeared in Japan in 1994. This square pictogram gives access to information when scanned by a mobile terminal with a previously downloaded application. In the field of tourism, QR codes can be attached to a monument to indicate, for example, practical information (opening hours, prices, etc.).

The third type corresponds to dedicated applications offering specific information *in situ* (practical information, images, explanatory texts, user recommendations, etc.). For example, Foursquare allows users to recommend places (restaurants, hotels, shopping, nightlife, etc.) and in so doing, earn points to benefit discount or gift. Among dedicated applications, the augmented reality allows information to be displayed on a terminal, added to reality: for example, images of old buildings that no longer exist appear in their original location. Numerous museums have developed such applications since 2012 (Lesaffre, Watremez, and Flon 2014).

Finally, superimposed reality applications allow the viewing of videos or archive images, which can be considered as a second reality, superimposed on the reality you are looking at. Sky Boy, for example, adds virtual information on the image wherever it is available. Arromanches with the D-Day beach has also developed this type of application. After downloading the application and activating the geolocation, the tourist can, by pointing the terminal towards a spot indicated on the ground, be immersed in an action taking place where he is standing. The action can be to take a virtual tour of the place, to visit the place following a guide that appears on the screen … ; these applications are often supplied in several languages.

But are these new technical characteristics that are sometimes developed by providers used by the clients?

2.3. M tourism services in act

In 2013 Brittany's Regional Tourism Committee (CRT Bretagne – FNCRT 2013) published a study – the only one existing in France to our knowledge – on the uses of smartphones by European tourists. The study shows that tourist's practices are quite conventional in the region. Smartphones are mainly used to do actions previously done with a tourist guide, or, at other times, through tourist information services (obtain practical information, look for nearby restaurants, hotels, shops, etc.). The next most commonly used function was the sharing of opinions and photos on social media. This study also suggests that other uses, in particular those associated with applications, apart from GPS, seem not to have developed far. For example, QR code scanning is not much used (5% regularly and 14% fairly often). Likewise, virtual tours of cultural sites are used regularly by less than 5% of the respondents and fairly often by 18%. Only few tourist have used digital tools such as augmented and virtual reality. Nevertheless, it should be noted that at the time of the study, the level of smartphone ownership were lower than today, according to the CREDOC (French research centre for the study and observation of living conditions) (Albérola et al. 2017) and the supply in Brittany was also lower than today.

Moreover, the study focused on tourists only. It did not consider the other users of the destination. In order to understand the way mobile tools are effectively used *in situ* by tourists and if these uses are specific to tourism, one should take into consideration the other users of the place and not only the tourists category.

The survey conducted on the Champs Elysées in Paris shed light on these issues.

3. Uses of mobile technologies on the Champs Elysées: background and methodology of the survey

3.1. Background of the survey

A survey was conducted in 2018[3] in order to identify how mobile devices are used on the Champs Elysées. Avenue des Champs Elysées is located in the 8th arrondissement of Paris, between Place de la Concorde and the Champs-Élysées-Marcel-Dassault roundabout where the Arc de Triomphe stands (see Figure 2).

Avenue des Champs Elysées is a major spot of Paris. According to the Paris Convention and Visitors Bureau,[4] it attracts 300,000 visitors per day. It is a prestigious area frequented by international high society since the 1900s (Aufrère 1950): The Champs Elysées is home to well-known shops (luxury boutiques, many flagship stores), restaurants, culture and leisure sites (cinema, theatre, exhibitions) as well as a plethora of events, official (a military parade to celebrate the National Day) and festive.

As it is increasingly the case in numerous large cities and at tourist sites, the avenue enjoys good digital coverage. In 2016, the Champs-Elysées Committee,[5] who is in charge of promoting the avenue installed a free and unlimited high-speed Wi-Fi connection via 58 Wi-Fi access points placed along the whole length of the avenue.[6]

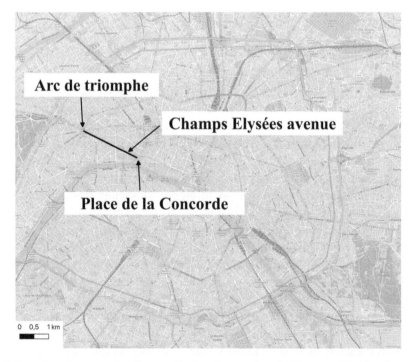

Figure 2. Location of avenue des Champs Elysées. Source: Google Maps modified by the authors.

However, few applications specifically linked with the Champs Elysées exist. For example, out of the 20 practical applications for Paris included in July 2018 in the SortiraParis.com guide,[7] one of them the 'Welcome to Paris' mobile app,[8] developed by the Tourist office and Congrès de Paris organization, in cooperation with the mobile phone operator Orange, referred to the Champs Elysées. On the other hand, other apps, like 'Paris au fil de la Seine' developed by Paris Musées[9] or Foxie[10] did not include the Champs Elysées. With regard to shopping, to the best of our knowledge no retail outlet or institution offered specific services based on QR codes at the time of the research. The last store offering this type of service closed in 2013.

3.2. Methodology

The survey was conducted on Avenue des Champs Elysées during the last two weeks of May 2018 and during the second and third weeks of June 2018. Were excluded the days with special events on the Avenue or in Paris. The questionnaires were administered face-to-face at different times of day, and to a lesser extent in the evening up to 9 pm and sometimes 11 pm, every day of the week, including weekends. The interviewers were positioned on specific spots, on both sides of the Avenue. People were interviewed randomly, without any criteria for age, sex, social category or nationality. Each questionnaire took approximately 10 min. Once the questionnaire was completed, the next new person who passed the interviewer was asked to participate. 408 questionnaires were completed (in some cases partially) in English or in French.

Information was collected on the respondent's characteristics (age, sex, gender, socioeconomic category, place of residence). They were asked about the duration and the main purpose of their presence on the Champs Elysées. Six main reasons were considered: 'tourism', 'leisure', 'on the way to another place', 'work', 'shopping' and 'other reason'. We consider as tourists those who declared being in the Champs Elysées for tourism purpose.

Next, respondents were asked several questions about their smartphone and Internet use before coming to the Champs Elysées (did they search for information online before coming? If so, what was the nature of the information? Had they made any reservations?) and *in situ* (did they access the Internet while on the Champs-Elysées? Did they use an online app? Did they share information?).

Statistical analyses were carried out in order to understand which different digital practices were used and the links between these practices and the characteristics of the respondents, in particular their reason for being on the Champs-Elysées. The data were analysed using the entire sample (with a few exceptions). In order to identify whether the personal characteristics of the visitors determined their use of ICT, bivariate analyses[11] were conducted. Gender, age, place of residence and purpose of presence[12] were associated to Internet use before arrival and *in situ*. Then a linear discriminant analysis was used to identify different digital profiles. Finally, a multiple correspondence analysis was conducted to examine to which extent the reason for presence and/or the place of residence were associated with specific digital practices and, if so, which ones.

3.3. Characteristics of the sample

Out of the 408 people interviewed, more than the majority (69.4% of visitors) were residents in France (Figure 3). 26.7% were from Île-de-France (the Paris region, but outside the city of Paris), 28.4% from Paris (including 3.2% from the Champs Elysées) and 13% from other French cities (0.5% of the interviewees did not answer). International visitors accounted for only 30.6% of the sample, with a majority from European countries, then from the U.S., Brazil, China and Morocco.[13]

The majority of the population present was less than forty, with 29.9% aged between 25 and 39, and 21.8% between 20 and 24. The extreme age groups were less represented, with 7.4% of respondents aged between 15 and 19, and 7.6% aged over 65. As regards the socio-economic categories (SEC), the majority were office workers (25.2%) and students (23.8%), followed by people from higher managerial/administrative/professional categories (16.7%) and then from intermediate occupations (13%). 30.6% of interviewees were present on their own. The others were accompanied mainly by family (23%), friends (18.4%), their partner (16.6% were in a couple) or by colleagues (5.9%).

The reason for being on the Champs Elysées, was, first tourism (30.6%),[14] and then work (20.3%), shopping (16.4%) and leisure (15.7%). As might be expected, people who lived on the Champs Elysées and in the city of Paris were present for reasons other than tourism (mainly work, leisure and shopping). Almost all the people present for tourism come from other French regions or from abroad (on 125 coming for tourism only 3 came from Île-de-France). In contrast, some non-resident people were on the Champs not for tourism (leisure, work, shopping, passing through).

In order to establish links between personal characteristics and to determine the profiles of individuals present on the Champs Elysées, we conducted a multiple correspondence analysis on variables such as gender, age, place of residence, SEC, being alone or in company, and the reason for being there. Three main profile types can be identified (Figure 4):

- Senior tourists: the first type consists of people aged over 50, present for purposes of tourism. Travelling in tour groups, in families or in couples, they are retired, self-

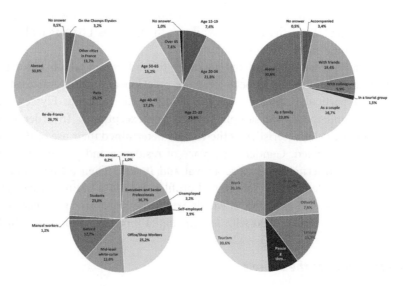

Figure 3. The characteristics of the sample (a: residence; b: age; c: accompaniment; d: socio-economic category; e: reason of presence).

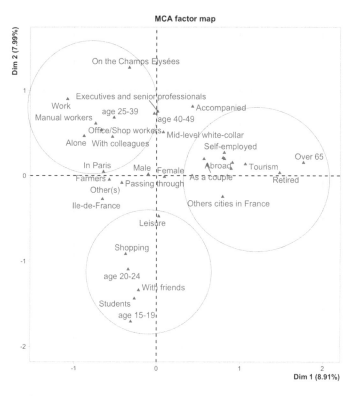

Figure 4. Profiles of the people interviewed.

employed or unemployed, and come from the rest of France (excluding Île-de-France – the Paris region) or from abroad.
- Young shoppers from Île-de-France: the second profile consists of people aged under 25, often students, in the company of friends and present for shopping.
- Parisian workers: the third group corresponds to people aged between 25 and 50, present for work purposes, often alone or with colleagues, and resident in Paris.

The diversity of the visitors and their reasons for being there are a reminder that, while the Champs Elysées is a tourist destination, it is also a district in the city of Paris. As must-see and much visited tourist destination, it is nevertheless a multifunctional and iconic space (Deroy and Clegg 2012; Gravari-Barbas and Violier 1998) that brings together a wide variety of people.

4. Results

The survey enabled us to construct broad digital profiles that we compared with the different types of people present, especially according to their residence and their reasons for being there. Then we specifically analysed their use of the Internet before coming to the Champs Elysées, then the use of these technologies *in situ*.

The first question we had was: could we identify digital profiles among the visitors of the Champs Elysées[15]? We conducted a linear discriminant analysis[16] and then we used confusion matrix[17] (see also Appendix, Figures A1 and A2, and Tables A1 and A2) to evaluate the predictability of these profiles. Two indicators appeared relevant to determine profiles: the place of residents (in the Paris region, in other French regions or abroad) and the reason for being on the Champs Elysées (Shopping, Leisure, Passing Through, Tourism, Work or other). The analysis showed that international and regional visitors (Ile de France and Paris) have specific and predictive digital profiles. The same is true for individuals present for tourism (main activity of international visitors) and work (main activity of regional visitors).

4.1. Use of digital tools to prepare the venue

184 visitors (45.1%) used the Internet to prepare their visit to the Champs Elysées. The Internet was the only source of information for most of them (121 visitors[18] including 52 international visitors and 14 people from French regions excluding Île-de-France). The analysis (Table 1) unsurprisingly shows that there is no correlation between Internet use before visiting and gender. On the other hand, there is a correlation with age and a stronger correlation with place of residence and reason for visiting.

The extreme age brackets (15–19, over 65) and the 40–49 age group used the Internet less than the other age groups. It was the 50–65 age group (55%) and the 20–24 age group (51%) that used it the most (49% on average for the sample as a whole). People who were not resident in France also used the Internet more before visiting that the others (73% compared with 45% of the sample on average). This was the case for 39% of people resident in Île-de-France (outside the city of Paris) and 45% of visitors from other French cities. People present for reasons of tourism (69%), and to a lesser extent for leisure (48%), also used the Internet more than people present for other reasons (Shopping, Passing Through, Work).[19]

To investigate further if the practice of preparing a venue using digital tools is related to the place of residence and the reason for visiting the Champs Elysées, we conducted a multiple correspondence analysis on the 184 visitors who did prepared their venue. We chose the following variables likely to characterize these digital practices prior to visiting the Champs Elysées: search for information on transport, accommodation, eating out, weather, shopping, leisure, to which we added the reason for visiting as an additional variable (Figure A3 in Appendix) then the place of residence (Figure A4 in Appendix).

People present for reasons of tourism and leisure tend to prepare their visit notably on transport, restaurants/food, leisure and tours, weather and shopping. Non-residents have similar behaviour. This result is not surprising as tourists, people coming for leisure purpose, and non-residents have, a priori, less knowledge on the place than others.

Table 1. Links between individual characteristics and Internet use before visiting.

	Individual characteristic	Dependency of variables	Intensity of the association[a]
Internet use before visiting	Gender	Not significant	/
	Age	Significant	Low
	Place of residence	Significant	High
	Reason for visiting	Significant	Moderate

[a]As measured by Cramer's V, the square of which measures the proportion of variability of one variable that is explained by another. The intensity here was qualified as 'low' for $V < 0.2$, 'moderate' for $0.2 < V < 0.4$, and 'high' for $V > 0.4$.

Visitors present for other reasons tend not to prepare their venue, alongside people resident in France, whether in the Paris region or outside.

Dedicated websites (32% respondents) are most consulted, then to a lesser degree are complemented by – consultation of online guides (14%), and finally Facebook, Twitter, forums and/or blogs (17%). When accommodation websites were consulted (20%), visitors looked more for hotels (65%) than other types of accommodation such as AirBnB (39%).

It should be noted that international visitors favoured the former (21 hotel searches) and visitors from other French regions looked almost exclusively for AirBnB accommodation (six searches as compared with 0 for hotels). This is probably largely explained by the cost of hotels in Paris. 18% of the visitors who prepared their visits looked for restaurant, 50% were residents (Paris Region), 42% international visitors, 8% domestic visitors. The subject that generated the most searches was unsurprisingly transport beginning with itineraries by public transport (115), then by car (63), then on foot (23). However, there was very little use of the Internet to book a transport solution. Only 12 visitors made reservations before coming.

4.2. The use of digital tools in situ

The use of mobile technologies depends first of all on ownership of a device (smartphone or tablet) and secondly on the possibility of connection.

85.0% of the individuals interviewed said that they had a smartphone or tablet. The only variable associated with ownership seems to be the age of the individuals, with the highest level of ownership among the youngest (Table 2).

Among the individuals with mobile devices (85.0% of the sample), 71.5% used their web connexion during their visit to the Champs Elysées. There is no correlation between connection and either gender or reason for presence (Table 3). There is, however, a (very small) correlation with the place of residence and a greater one with age. Connection rates were lower among the people over 50. As for the link with the place of residence, the incidence of people connecting on the Champs Elysées was greater for people non-resident in Île-de-France: 66.7% of international visitors went online there and 63.6% of French visitors living in other parts of France (as compared with 62.8% on average for the sample as a whole).

The large majority of the respondents, whether international or French, connected using their own phone data. The free Wi-Fi services available on the Champs Elysées or in the particular places visited (restaurants, shops) were also used, but to a lesser degree.

Table 2. Links between individual characteristics and ownership of a mobile device.

	Individual characteristic	Dependency of variables	Intensity of the association[a]
Ownership of a mobile device	Gender	Not significant	/
	Age[c]	Significant	Moderate
	Place of residence[b]	Not significant	/
	Reason for visiting	Test not valid	

[a]As measured by Cramer's V, the square of which measures the proportion of variability of one variable that is explained by another. The intensity here was qualified as 'low' for V < 0.2, 'moderate' for 0.2 < V < 0.4, and 'high' for V > 0.4.
[b]For the test to be valid (enough theoretical subjects), the place of residence 'On the Champs Elysées' was combined with 'In Paris'
[c]For the test to be valid (enough theoretical subjects), the 50–65 and the over-65 age group were combined.

Table 3. Links between individual characteristics and Internet connection on the Champs Elysées.

	Individual characteristic	Dependency of variables	Intensity of the association
Internet connection on the Champs Elysées	Gender	Not significant	/
	Age	Significant	Moderate
	Place of residence[a]	Significant	Very low
	Reason for visiting	Not significant	/

[a]For the test to be valid (sufficient theoretical numbers), the place of residence 'On the Champs-Elysées' has been grouped with 'In Paris'.

Finally, some people used both their phone data and the free Wi-Fi. Neither device ownership nor connection facilities, therefore, seem to inhibit the use of mobile devices.

4.3. Sharing information: the main practice on the champs

About 60% of the visitors connected themselves to the Internet with their mobile device when visiting the Champs. Among them, 40% shared information and only 3% downloaded applications.

4.3.1. Digital tools: not the drivers for in-situ change of plans

Among the visitors who used their mobile device, very few said that they had used it to look for information *in situ* with specialised/dedicated applications.[20]

Whereas Wang, Xiang, and Fesenmaier (2016) showed that the smartphone offers greater flexibility when travelling and helps people to alter their plans if the trip does not live up to expectations, none of the visitors said that they had changed their tour programme on the basis of information obtained *in situ*. So the use of a mobile device is not associated with a last-minute *in situ* change to the visit to the place.

4.3.2. Sharing information main digital practice

While the visitors' experience seems to have been little changed by searching for information *in situ*, what may on the other hand have changed is the sharing of photographs, information, etc.

More than 25% of the visitors (129) declared having done this. 67% of them had exchanged only photos or videos, 17% had shared photos or videos and opinions or impressions and 12% had posted opinions and localization (4% didn't indicate what they had shared). These interchanges, and in particular photos and videos, are carried out *in situ* and, with a few exceptions, after the visit.

Sharing information via an online application is not related to gender nor to place of residence. There is however a strong relationship with age and the reason for visiting the Champs (Table 4).

Considering age, younger respondents, i.e. those in the 15–19 and 20–24 age groups, use more their mobile devices to share information than older age groups. 60.7% of the 15–20 age group and 47.5% of the 20–24 age group have declared having done it, although it was the case 33% of the 25–39 age group and around 28% for the 40–49 age group and over 50s.

As for the reason for being on the Champs, the people present for leisure and to a lesser degree for tourism, used their mobile devices to share information more than

Table 4. Links between individual characteristics and sharing information on mobile devices on the Champs Elysées.

	Individual characteristic	Dependency of variables	Intensity of the association
Sharing of information on apps	Gender	Not significant	/
	Age[a]	Significant	Moderate
	Place of residence[b]	Not significant	/
	Reason for visiting	Significant	Moderate

Notes: For a more detailed analysis, a second MCA was conducted based on variables that may characterize digital practices during presence on the Champs Elysées: application downloads, sharing of photos or videos, sharing of opinions, sharing of location or other information, time of sharing. To answer our research questions, we added reason for presence and then place of residence as additional variables. Here again, only individuals who said that they had gone online on the Champs Elysées were included ($N = 245$). Three individuals who did not answer all the questions included in the analysis were withdrawn.
[a]For the test to be valid (enough theoretical subjects), the 50–65 and the over-65 age group were combined.
[b]For the test to be valid (sufficient theoretical numbers), the place of residence 'On the Champs-Elysées' has been grouped with 'In Paris'.

the others. 57.9% of the visitors present for leisure purposes did this, and 37.6% of the visitors present for tourism (which is a few more than the average of the sample). In comparison, 36% of visitors passing through, 35% of visitors present for shopping and 22% of visitors present to work did it.

5. Discussion and conclusion

There is an abundant literature which takes the view that digital technology and mobile devices, insofar as they alter practices, offer numerous opportunities for rethinking tourist destinations, for innovating in order to build the destinations of tomorrow, smart destinations (Chen et al. 2021; Gretzel et al. 2015). As a result, some stakeholders in the tourist sector are investing in these technologies by creating apps, being present on social media, interacting with tourists. Others do not do much or don't need to do much, perhaps because the proposed experience is already fulfilling. It doesn't necessary worth the investments. As the service analysis shows M tourism in act depends on the supply of digital tools and on the use made by people. M tourism services are coproduced in place. Both ends must be taken into consideration. However, excepted for social networks, the literature on the effective uses of these technologies, and the conditions for it, is much sparser. The example of the Champs Elysée is, in that sense, instructive.

Our question, therefore, was: whether the people present in a tourist location use M tourism and, if so, in what ways? In particular, we wanted to identify in the case of Champs Elysées whether these practices were specific to the reasons for visiting (leisure, tourism, work, etc.) or to the status of the visitor (a resident of Paris or the Paris region, international tourists or tourists from other French regions). More broadly we intend to identify whether ultimately the mobile technologies were simply an extension of standard digital practices, as argued by Wang, Xiang, and Fesenmaier (2016).

The different statistical analyses (bivariate analyses, discriminant analyses, multiple correspondence analyses) that we conducted, based on the survey carried out on the Champs Elysées, produced several findings that provide answers to these questions.

First, our results confirm part of the analysis advanced by De Reuver, Nikou, and Bouwman (2016): there is no link between gender and the use of digital technologies, at any given moment, but age influences uses.

However, the lack of significant statistical associations between income levels and socio-economic category, and digital practices, prevent us drawing conclusions on this point.

We identified whether the reason for presence (tourism or others) and/or the place of residence were associated with specific digital practices and, if so, which ones, distinguishing between uses before and after arrival on the Champs Elysées.

Before arrival on the Champs Elysées, the places of residence and the reasons for visiting explain the use of the Internet to search for information of different kinds. They also influence the type of information sought. We showed therefore that the Internet was above all a tool used to plan the visit before arriving on the Champs Elysées in particular for international tourists. International visitors and individuals present for tourism (two categories that partly overlap) went online before coming and searched for information about accommodation.

In situ, our research also shows – if it needed proof – the spread of the smartphone as a tool. Most of the people present on the Champs Elysées were equipped with a mobile device, regardless of age. Nonetheless, it confirms that age still plays an important role in their use of digital tools *in situ*. So the mobile digital divide exists here *in situ*. On the other hand, place of residence has little or no impact on *in situ* practices. For its part, the reason for visiting has a modest influence on the sharing of information through online applications, but not at all on the *in situ* use of digital tools. More fundamentally, whether international or from other French regions, tourists go online *in situ* no more than individuals present for work purposes when visiting this major tourist site, the Champs Elysées. Nor do they seem to demonstrate specific uses of their mobile devices there. Whatever the reason for being present on this site, smartphones and the Internet are used to exchange videos and photos, i.e. to share a view on an experience. So *in situ* digital practices do not seem to be mostly specified by the reason for being there (tourism, work, etc.).

This absence of a link between Internet connection, *in situ* practices and the reason for visiting is a surprising result. Whereas an abundant literature is developing on tourist use of mobile phones at tourist destinations, our study shows that use of a mobile device is ultimately not specific to the status of being a tourist in a tourist location. It corroborates the findings of Wang, Xiang, and Fesenmaier (2016). Behind the reasons for presence, there are individual characteristics, especially age, which influence digital practices. And, while some reasons for presence are very different (tourism and work), others are more similar (tourism and leisure) and blur the associated digital practices. In addition, Facebook access, bookings for transport, hotels, restaurants or tours, are not very much used, neither are the most innovative possibilities (dedicated apps, QR code, etc.). In the end, mobile devices seem not to be a tool of behavioural change. If, as the literature reveals, smartphones enrich people's experience by enabling them to exchange photos and pictures remotely *in situ*, they do not alter the activities that people plan before reaching their destination. Ultimately, digital practices on the Champs Elysées remain fairly conventional.

This raises the question of the reasons for the lack of specific digital practices on the Champs Elysées. As we show before M tourism services are coproduced between users and providers. If Wi-Fi connexion is available on the Champs Elysées avenue, the services supplied on the Champs Elysées are scarce limiting the possibility to coproduce M-

Tourism services. The reputation of what has been called the world's most beautiful street perhaps makes the development of specific applications superfluous. In addition, because tourists prefer to discover the Champs Elysées and their atmosphere as a total experience, tools of this kind could be less useful in this specific context: it is less important to have information about the Champs Elysées or to discover it with an augmented reality, than it is at other tourist sites.

If Chen et al. (2021) argue that the number of related studies (Mobile Communication Technology Research in Hospitality and Tourism) 'is predicted to continue to increase in the future', research should therefore be focused on less well-known places or places where extensive information is needed to appreciate them in all their dimensions. This will allow to explore whether more innovative digital practices are developed and used more on such sites. The research must focus on the way users actually experience the mobile technology and in particular its new tools in different types of places. This will allow to identify the type of places where mobile technology and its new tools add value and are useful to enhance the tourism experience.

Notes

1. Source: https://datareportal.com/reports/digital-2019-global-digital-overview, consulted on the 10 March 2020, 15h20, page 196.
2. See servitization analysis of creative and cultural industries by Sundbo, Rubalcaba, and Gallouj (2021).
3. This survey is part of a research programme conducted by the Ville Tourisme Transport et Territoires cross-disciplinary group of the Labex Urban Futures at the University of Paris-Est and the University Gustave Eiffel.
4. https://www.parisinfo.com/decouvrir-paris/balades-a-paris/tout-savoir-sur-les-champs-elysees, consulted on the 22 August 2020, 18h20.
5. Created in 1916, it is responsible for the promotion, the development and the international reputation of Avenue Champs-Elysées and its district in Paris.
6. https://www.lesechos.fr/2016/06/du-wifi-gratuit-sur-les-champs-elysees-208323, consulted on the 20 March 2020.
7. https://www.sortiraparis.com/arts-culture/balades/guides/25144-top-20-des-applications-pratiques-pour-votre-sejour-a-paris.
8. This app helps visitors to plan a tour programme by providing addresses, events, itineraries and practical information. It can also be used to buy a museum ticket and to find out about nearby events or places.
9. Which prompts visitors to discover GPS located paintings and photographs from different museums, thereby retracing the surroundings of the River Seine through history.
10. Which suggests visits to quirky and lesser-known streets.
11. A Pearson's chi-square test was applied. For each of the analyses, we chose a significance level of 5%. Cramer's V tells us about the intensity of the association between the two variables under consideration.
12. The socio-economic category and accompaniment variables could not be studied here because the numbers in the contingency table were too low.
13. However, as is the case with all face-to-face surveys, the true number of international visitors is likely to be greater. Indeed, the number of responses from international visitors is probably lower than from others, as they are reluctant to respond to a face-to-face questionnaire, in particular people from Asian countries who often travel in group.
14. Only one answer was allowed.
15. These profiles were built from scores on 16 quantitative binary predictive variables: Internet connection before visiting, searching for information on transport, searching for

accommodation, a restaurant, weather information, climate information, information on shopping, on leisure, on tours, or other information, searching for information off-line, ownership of a connected device, connection on the Champs Elysées, application downloads, the time of information sharing, and information shared (photos, videos, on the one hand, opinions on the other hand, sharing of location information, and finally sharing of other types of information). The analysis was made over 406 individuals (two individuals for whom answers were missing were withdrawn from the analysis). Then we analysed how far the distribution of these digital profiles differed according to the type of people present, looking first at their residence and secondly their reasons for being there.

16. The differences in profile between the three groups are very significant. Pillai trace, the multivariate analogue of the proportion of variance explained by the groups (the 'eta-squared' coefficient), is .51, with a p-value $< 2.2 \times 10^{-16}$. The digital profile of the respondents can, conversely be used to predict their origin by the standard linear discriminant procedure.
17. With a kappa index (measuring the improvement from a random assignation) of .47.out of 125 individuals from abroad, 74 (i.e. 59%) are correctly classified as being from abroad on the basis of their digital profile. This rate of correct classification even rises to 90% (203 out of 225) for people coming from Île-de-France: their digital profile can be used to identify them very accurately. Conversely, this is not the case for individuals from other French regions, who are similar in profile to the respondents from Île-de-France.
18. 23.1% of visitors also use other sources of information (word-of-mouth, family, friends, the press and guidebooks).
19. The average use of internet before visiting is 45% in the sample.
20. 11 of them, 6 international, 2 from Île-de-France (the Paris region excluding Paris) and 3 Parisians. Those who did had calculated routes for getting from one place to another and/or to download GPS maps (9), look for a restaurant, a bar or a cafe on the Champs Elysées (6), check the weather (6 foreigners and 2 Parisians). Four international visitors had also looked for practical information (police station, doctor, post office and bank), two had looked at the Champs Elysées Calendar and checked for recommendations. The visitors were not interested in searching for special offers available in the shops on the Champs Elysées or for feedback on places to visit.

Disclosure statement

No potential conflict of interest was reported by the author(s).

Funding

The authors would like to thank the Labex Futurs Urbains of the University of Paris-Est and the University Gustave Eiffel which funded this research.

References

Albérola, E., I. Aldeghi, L. Brice-Mansencal, P. Croutte, R. Datsenko, N. Guisse, and S. Hoibian. 2017. *Baromètre Du Numérique 2017*, Rapport du CREDOC réalisé pour le compte du Conseil Général de l'Economie, de l'Industrie, de l'Energie et des Technologies (CGE), l'Autorité de Régulation des Communications Electroniques et des Postes (Arcep) et l'Agence du numérique.

Aufrère, L. 1950. "Introduction à l'étude morphologique et démographique de l'Avenue des Champs Élysées." *Annales de Géographie* 59 (313): 13–37. https://doi.org/10.3406/geo.1950.12858

Bideran, J., and P. Fraysse. 2015. "Guide numérique et mise en scène du territoire, entre médiation patrimoniale et stratégie de communication touristique." *Études de communication* [En ligne], 45. consulté le 28 juin 2020. http://journals.openedition.org/edc/6464.

Buhalis, D. 2020. "Technology in Tourism-from Information Communication Technologies to eTourism and Smart Tourism Towards Ambient Intelligence Tourism: A Perspective Article." *Tourism Review* 75 (1): 267–272. doi:10.1108/TR-06-2019-0258.

Buhalis, D., and R. Law. 2008. "Progress in Information Technology and Tourism Management: 20 Years on and 10 Years after the Internet—the State of eTourism Research." *Tourism Management* 29 (4): 609–623. doi:10.1016/j.tourman.2008.01.005.

Cabrespines, J., and R. Wargnie. 2017. "Tourisme et numérique." Les avis du CESE, 26 décembre 2017.

Chen, S., R. Law, M. Zhang, and Y. Si. 2021. "Mobile Communications for Tourism and Hospitality: A Review of Historical Evolution, Present Status, and Future Trends." *Electronics* 10: 1804. doi:10.3390/electronics10151804.

CRT Bretagne – FNCRT. 2013. *M-Tourisme et réseaux sociaux: les pratiques des clientèles européennes*. Rennes: CRT Bretagne FNCRT.

De Reuver, M., S. Nikou, and H. Bouwman. 2016. "Domestication of Smartphones and Mobile Applications: A Quantitative Mixed-Method Study." *Mobile Media & Communication* 4 (3): 347–370. doi:10.1177/2050157916649989.

De Vries, E. 2006. "Innovation in Services in Networks of Organizations and in the Distribution of Services." *Research Policy* 35: 1037–1051. doi:10.1016/j.respol.2006.05.006.

Deroy, X., and S. Clegg. 2012. "Contesting the Champs-Elysées." *Journal of Change Management* 12 (3): 355–373. doi:10.1080/14697017.2012.673075.

Dickinson, J., K. Ghali, T. Cherrett, C. Speed, N. Davies, and S. Norgate. 2014. "Tourism and the Smartphone App: Capabilities, Emerging Practice and Scope in the Travel Domain." *Current Issues in Tourism* 17 (1): 84–101. doi:10.1080/13683500.2012.718323.

Dorcic, J., J. Komsic, and S. Markovic. 2019. "Mobile Technologies and Applications Towards Smart Tourism – State of the art." *Tourism Review* 74 (1): 82–103. doi:10.1108/TR-07-2017-0121.

Gallouj, F., and M. Savona. 2010. "Towards a Theory of Innovation in Services: A State of the Art." In *The Handbook of Innovation and Services, a Multi-Disciplinary Perspective*, edited by F. Gallouj and F. Djellal, 27–48, Cheltenham (GB): Edward Elgar Publishing.

Gallouj, F., and O. Weinstein. 1997. "Innovation in Services." *Research Policy* 26 (4–5): 537–556. doi:10.1016/S0048-7333(97)00030-9.

Gravari-Barbas, M., and P. Violier. 1998. Les espaces. Norois, n°178, Avril-Juin. *Villes et tourisme*. 171–173. https://www.persee.fr/doc/noroi_0029-182x_1998_num_178_1_6862.

Gretzel, Ulrike, Daniel R. Fesenmaier, and Joseph T. O'Leary. 2006. "Chapter 2 - The Transformation of Consumer Behaviour." In *Tourism Business Frontiers*, edited by Dimitrios Buhalis and Carlos Costa, 9-18. Oxford: Butterworth-Heinemann. https://doi.org/10.1016/B978-0-7506-6377-9.50009-2

Gretzel, U., and T. Jamal. 2009. "Conceptualizing the Creative Tourist Class: Technology, Mobility, and Tourism Experiences." *Tourism Analysis* 14 (4): 471–481. doi:10.3727/108354209X12596287114219.

Gretzel, U., M. Sigala, Z. Xiang, and S. Koo. 2015. "Smart Tourism: Foundations and Developments." *Electronic Markets* 25 (3): 179–188. doi:10.1007/s12525-015-0196-8.

Howells, J. 2010. "Services and Innovation and Service Innovation: New Theoretical Directions." In *The Handbook of Innovation and Services, a Multi-Disciplinary Perspective*, edited by F. Djellal and F. Gallouj, 68–83. Cheltenham (GB): Edward Elgar.

Kim, H., and R. Law. 2015. "Smartphones in Tourism and Hospitality Marketing: A Literature Review." *Journal of Travel & Tourism Marketing* 32 (6): 692–711. doi:10.1080/10548408.2014.943458.

Lancaster, K. 1966. "A New Approach to Consumer Theory." *Journal of Political Economy* 74 (2): 132–157. doi:10.1086/259131

Law, R., I. Chu Chan, and L. Wang. 2018. "A Comprehensive Review of Mobile Technology Use in Hospitality and Tourism." *Journal of Hospitality Marketing & Management* 27 (6): 626–648. doi:10.1080/19368623.2018.1423251.

Lesaffre, G., A. Watremez, and E. Flon. 2014. "Les applications mobiles de musées et de sites patrimoniaux en France: quelles propositions de médiation?" *La Lettre de l'OCIM* [on line] 154. doi:10.4000/ocim.1423. http://ocim.revues.org/1423.

Liang, S., M. Schuckert, R. Law, and L. Masiero. 2017. "The Relevance of Mobile Tourism and Information Technology: An Analysis of Recent Trends and Future Research Directions." *Journal of Travel & Tourism Marketing* 34 (6): 732–748. doi:10.1080/10548408.2016.1218403.

McKinsey France. 2014. *Accélérer la mutation numérique des entreprises: un gisement de croissance et de compétitivité pour la France*.

Molz, J. 2014. *Travel Connections: Tourism, Technology and Togetherness in a Mobile World*. London: Routledge.

Mourtazina, E. 2019. "Photographier Zermatt: les pratiques photographiques des touristes à l'épreuve du numérique." *Mondes du Tourisme* [En ligne], 15. mis en ligne le 01 juin 2019, consulté le 26 juin 2020. doi:10.4000/tourisme.2148. http://journals.openedition.org/tourisme/2148

Naramski, M., and K. Herman. 2020. "The Development of Mobile Tourism in the Upper Silesian Metropolitan Area of Poland." *Sustainability* 12 (1): 44. doi:10.3390/su12010044.

Schroeder, A., L. Pennington-Gray, H. Donohoe, and S. Kiousis. 2013. "Using Social Media in Times of Crisis." *Journal of Travel & Tourism Marketing* 30 (1–2): 126–143. doi:10.1080/10548408.2013.751271.

Sundbo, J., L. Rubalcaba, and F. Gallouj. 2021. "Servitization in the Creative and Cultural Industries." *International Journal of Quality and Service Sciences* 14 (1): 65–85. doi:10.1108/IJQSS-01-2021-0017.

Tussyadiah, I., and D. Wang. 2014. "Tourist's Attitudes Towards Proactive Smartphone Systems." *Journal of Travel Research* 55 (4): 493–508. doi:10.1177/0047287514563168.

Wang, D., Z. Xiang, and D. Fesenmaier. 2016. "Smartphone Use in Everyday Life and Travel." *Journal of Travel Research* 55 (1): 52–63. doi:10.1177/0047287514535847

Appendix

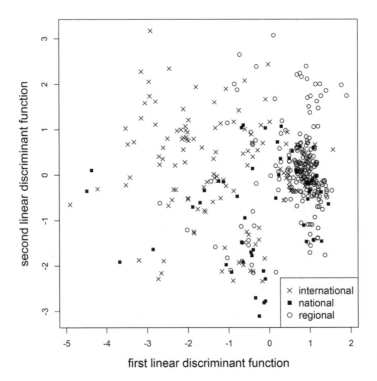

Figure A1. Linear discriminant analysis on the origins of the visitors.

The digital profiles, therefore, differ according to the place of residence. The confusion matrix (see Table A1) confirms the existence of this link by indicating the level of predictability of digital behaviour that can be expected on the basis of people's place of residence.

Table A1. Confusion matrix.

Actual origin	Origin predicted by digital profile		
	International	National	Regional
International	**74**	13	38
National	13	**13**	30
Regional	12	10	**203**

The confusion matrix (see Table A2) shows that the established digital profiles can be used

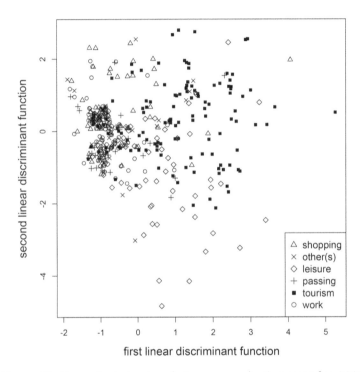

Figure A2. Linear discriminant analysis on respondent's reasons for visiting.

effectively to identify people present for Tourism (66% correctly classified) and for Work (74%), whereas the other categories are more difficult to identify. Unlike the other categories, the people present for Work and those present for Tourism are quite easy to identify from their digital profile.

Table A2. Confusion matrix.

Actual reason	Predicted reason from the digital profiles					
	Shopping	Other	Leisure	Passing through	Tourism	Work
Shopping	13	1	4	11	9	29
Other	2	1	2	5	5	16
Leisure	2	1	17	7	21	16
Passing Through	3	0	7	10	3	15
Tourism	4	2	13	6	**83**	17
Work	4	1	6	6	5	**61**

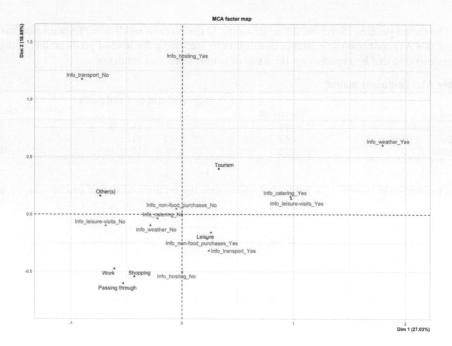

Figure A3. Biplot: digital practices before visiting versus reason for visiting.

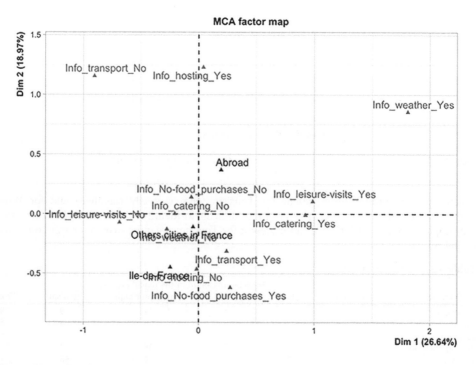

Figure A4. Biplot: digital practices before visiting versus place of residence.

Index

Note: Figures are indicated by *italics*. Tables are indicated by **bold**. Endnotes are indicated by the page number followed by 'n' and the endnote number e.g., 20n1 refers to endnote 1 on page 20.

AARON program 18
Abeledo, R. 183
Adobe Illustrator software 136
Agence d'urbanisme de la région nantaise (AURAN) 165n2
agglomeration externalities 198, 202
Albert, A. 32
algorithmic art 18
algorithmic society 3–4, 11, 12–14, 19, 20, 24–6; cinema industry 19; cultural transformations of 14; culture *17*; digital revolution and advent of 15; opportunities and risks of culture *17*; rise of 12–14; smart city model 18
Alone Together 21
Amazon 16–17
analytical framework 57–62
Anchors of Memory 15
Angelina (video game) 19
anthropomorphous robot 18
Apple 16–17
applying sectors 193–4, 198, 209; complementary, co-development and product innovation 195–6
Arc de Triomphe stands 222
archaeological museum of Naples (MANN) 20
Arendt, Hannah 12
artefacts 4.0 18
ARTEMREDE project 56, 66n11
artificial intelligence (AI) 139–41, 191, 201; application of 10; cultural markets 34–5; development of 12; online platforms 3; woven textile 139
artistic knowledge 162
arts and cultural organizations (ACOs): audience relationship 37–9; challenges, data analytics adoption 42–4; conceptual framework 35–7; data analytics 32; data-driven innovation 31; digital technologies to data analytics 33–5; innovation in business models 40–2; networked technologies 32; public and private value creation 39–40; stakeholders and customers 4
ARTSBANK project 50, 54, 55, 65, 66n12
Arvanitis, K. 32

Asheim, B. 131, 132
assortativity 154, **157**
attention economy 3
Australia 19

Bakhshi, H. 4, 32, 35
Balkin, J. 12
Banker, R. 93
Barca, F. 24
Barker, A. 34
Bavaud, F. 6
behavioural micro-targeting system 23
Belfanti, C. 114
Berners-Lee, T. 13
Bertacchini, E. 4, 39, 75
bias-corrected efficiency scores **97**
Bi-gram analysis 120, 123
bio-art 18
biotechnology 139–40
bi-partite network 154
Boden, M. 18
Bodo, C. 94
Bodo, S. 94
Boix, R. 171, 174, 179, 183
Bonini Baraldi 4
bootstrap truncated regression: DEA 89, 92; ICT services **100**
Bootstrap Truncated Two-Stage Estimation **100**
Boschma, R. 132
Bouwman, H. 229
Boyd, D. 42
British Newspaper Archive, The 111, 117, 123
British/US articles *120*
brokers 5–6, 149, 152, 161–2; places and events 15–163
Brown, Thome 140
Brusco, S. 112
Buitrago, P. 185
Bulgari 140
Bush, George W. 23
business model 2, 4, 31–3, 36, 45, 55, 62, 70–2, **73**, 74–8, 80–2, 88, 138; innovation 40–2
Buying Offices 120, *122*, 123

California 13
Camarero, C. 38
Canada 19
capital stock per employee data 181
Capron, E. 5
Carroll, S. 23
Carta Musei Piemonte 40
Carù, A. 37
catching-up 6, 193, 194
Cazals, C. 102n10
Centro Arte e Cultura 20
CERN 13
Champs Elysées 222; background of the survey 222–3; characteristics of the sample 223–5; Internet connection **228**; linear discriminant analysis 225–6; location of *222*; methods 223; mobile devices **229**
Champs-Elysées: Committee 218, 222, 223
Chanel 140
CHCfE Consortium 57
Chen, H. 231
China 140
Chiso Co., Ltd. 133, 134–6
Coachella Valley Music and Arts Festival 38
co-evolution 207–9
cognitive geography 16
Communities of Practice (CoPs) 150–1
Compas software 22
computerization 194
computer 'makes art' 18–19
concrete (multi-scalar) knowledge 202
Constant Returns of Scale (CRS) 93, 97
core arts field 32
corpus 119
Cova, B. 37
COVID-19 pandemic 20–1, 70, 133
Crawford, K. 42
creative milieu 13
Creative Mind: Myths and Mechanisms, The (Boden) 18
creative skills 194
creative work 2, 6, 35, 192, 193, 199–207, 209, 210; definition 194–5; sector 194; by sector 194; technology-driven structural shift 195–7
CREATOUR project 50, 55, 56, 65
Cristianini, N. 11, 23
criticisms 3, 23, 113, 185
cross-fertilization processes 13
cultural and creative industries (CCI) 2, 3, 6, 14, 15, 31, 50–2, 112, 148–9, 153, 170; approaches 173–4; capita income of places 171–2; employees *177*, *181*; GDP per capita 174, 178–9, 182–3; individual impact 184; instruments 182; level of development 184–5; measurement 179–80; nature and type of impacts 172–3; variables 180–2
cultural heritage 2, 3, 5, 21, 32, 54, 58, 75, 79, 90, 92, 102n3, 110, 112, 113, 118, 124, 129–30, 132, 133, 136, 137, 140–2
cultural policy 32, 40

culture: conservation and technological enhancement of 14–16; creative technology-driven sectors 19–20; digital art and digitalization of assets 18–19; digital, physical and virtual ecosystems 17–18; digital revolution 16–17; legitimacy and soft power 20–1; social enhancement of 15
Culture 1.0 14, 52
Culture 3.0 14, 51
culture-driven economic development 11–12, 129–30
Culturomics 111
customer lifetime value (CLV) 38
customer relationship management (CRM) 38
customer–supplier relationship 154, 155–6
cyber-physical systems 17

Dafydd, J. 79
DAHMUSE research project 82n1
Daily American, The 118
Dallas Museum of Art (DMA) 41–2
data analytics 4, 31, 32, 34, 36, 38–40, 45; Arts and Cultural Organizations 35; challenges 42–4; cultural policy 40; digital technologies 33–5
data analytics innovation: Arts and Cultural Organizations 35
data-driven strategy 32, 33, 36, 38, 42, 44, 45
Data Envelopment Analysis (DEA) 89, 91–3
DCMS Model 16–17, 23
decentralization 204
Decision-Making Units (DMUs) 92
Delaplace, M. 6
De Miguel, B. 183
Democratizing Innovation 11
Denmark 38–9
density 154, 157, 185–6
De Reuver, M. 229
destination 6, 218–21, 225, 229, 230
dialectic relationship 11
differentiated knowledge base 132, 140
DigiCult report 74–5
digital business ecosystems (DBEs) 76
digital communities 2
Digital Culture Report 43, 44
digital heritage 82n3
digital innovation 34, 70–2, 76, 77, 80, 81, 143
digital insurrection 12, 24
digitalization 5, 20, 23, 24, 36, 44, 130, 136, 220; assets of 18–19; cultural heritage 129–30, 142
digitalization of culture 5, 129, 130, 133, 141–3
digital literacy 33, 78
digital maturity 71
digital practices: before visiting *vs.* place of residence *236*; before visiting *vs.* reason for visiting *236*
digital professionals 77, 82n6
digital revolution 2, 15; biases and hidden errors 22–3; dark side of 21; economic, digital and recognition inequalities 24; loss of memory

and fundamental rights 23–4; risk of alienation and impoverishment of natural language 21–2
digital strategy 79–80
digital technology 1, 2, 4, 18, 32, 33, 37, 69–71, 74–6, 78, 80, 82n6, 90, 92, 130, 133; data analytics 33–5
digital transformation 2, 3, 12, 71, 217
DINAMIA'CET-ISCTE 50, 55, 65
Dior 140
Di Pietro, L. 37
Disney+ 19
diversity 185–6
documedial capitalism 12
domestic kimono market in Japan *135*
Duque, I. 185

education 203–4
E-Governance model 23
Electrons Libres 159
Ellerton, C. 44
emergent bias 22
Empowerment Zones 209
entrepreneurial activity 193
entrepreneurship 202–3
Enumerate Core Survey 102n3
Epistemic Communities (EC) 150–1
Europeana 102n8
European Erasmus Plus programme 77
European Mu.SA project 79
Eurostat 171
Eurostat LFS 181
Eventbrite 75
events 152, 158–9, 162–3
exaptation 130–2, *132*, 142, 143; taxonomy *132*

Facebook 13, 16–17, 21, 227
fashion boutique 113–15, 124
fashion industry 5, 110–11, 117, 118, 120, 123, 124; determinants **116**; Made in Italy 111–13 (*see also* Made in Italy)
Fashion Show 120, *122*, 123
fast fashion *(pronto moda)* 124
Ferilli, G. 14
Fernandez, R. 152
Fernández, Teresita 140
Fesenmaier, D. 228, 229
Firenze (Florence) 119
First Italian High Fashion Show 114
Five Sisters (Google, Apple, Facebook, Amazon, Microsoft) 16–17
Flaounas, I. 22
flexicurity 193, 210
Fortis, M. 112
Foster, P. 161
Foundation Zegna 112
France 76, 141
functional creativity 195

Garrido, M. 38
generative antagonist network (GANs) 18

Geneva 13
geography of discontent 24
Getty Museum, Los Angeles 21
Gilmore, A. 32
Giovanni Battista Giorgini (GBG) 5, 111, 114, 116, **116**, 117, 118, **118**, 120, 123–4, 124n1, 125n1–125n3
global and innovative business model 76
Google Art Project 102n8
Google Books 111, 124
Google Books N-gram Viewer 118
Gould, R. 152
Grillitsch, M. 131, 132
Gros-Balthazard, M. 6
gross domestic product (GDP) 170
growth-oriented model 75–6
5G technology 218
Gucci boutique 121–2
Guccio, C. 5

Halevy, A. 11
Handke, C. 32
Hararim, Y. 21
Harper's Bazaar 122–3
Hassink, R. 143
Haute Couture 114, 115–16
Heldman, C. 23
Henderson, D. 176
Hervás, J. 183
heterogeneity 159
Hidalgo, C. 25
hieroglyphics 21
High Fashion 115, 120, *121*
high-skilled workers 192, 207
Homus Abilis 25–6
Homus Deus 25–6
Hosoo 133, 138–40
Hsiao, C. 175
Human Development Index (HDI) 184
humanology 11
Human Resources 15
Hyatt Regency Kyoto Hotel 140

Île-de-France 223–5
image banks 102n8
impact assessment 51, 53, 56, 57
IMPACTOSAR project 50, 54, 55
IMPACTOSARTEMREDE 65
Imperial Data Bank 133
Indonesia 184
industrial district 13, 18, 25, 112, 113, 134, 210
Industrial Internet of Things (IIoT) 18
industrial revolution 11
Industry 4.0 14, 18
inequality 24, 171, 204–5, 207, 209
information and communication technology (ICT) 33, 36, 71, 88, 97, 99; bivariate analyses 223; and digital business practices 76; extent of **107**; museums 89–91, 98–100; second

stage estimation **101**; and technical partners 76; V's (volume, variety, velocity and veracity) 34
innovation 202–3; community *164*
'in situ' services 96–9
Instagram 13
interlocking system of institutions 205–7, *206*
Internet of Everything (IoE) 18
Internet of Things (IoT) 10, 18
ISIC Rev. 4 codes **180**
Italian articles *119*
Italian Fashion 120, *121*
Italian fashion industry **116**, 123–4
Italian Ministry of Cultural Heritage and Activities and Tourism (MiBACT) 21
Italian Museums and Cultural Institutions *(Indagine sui musei e le istituzioni similari)* 94
Italian National Statistical Office (ISTAT) 89, 96, 98, 101, 102n13
Italian Renaissance 112
Italy 138, 141
ITOCHU 138, 144n5
iTunes 102n8

Japan 130, 133, 138, 140; Crafts Association 140; domestic kimono market *135*
Jobs, Steve 13
Jones, C. 175

Kabuki 137, 144n4
Kaplan, J. 11
Kebir, L. 6
kimono cluster 130, 133, 134–5, 142; firm-level and system-level agency 142; rise and decline of 133–4; transformation of 133
Kitchin, R. 43
Kiyomizu pottery 140
knowledge bases: analytical 150; symbolic 150; synthetic 150
knowledge broker (KB_{12}) 163, 164
knowledge stock 174
Kyoto Chamber of Commerce and Industry 136, 137
Kyoto City University Town Center 136–7
Kyoto Digital Archive Promotion Organization 137
Kyoto Digital Archive Research Center (KDARC) 136–7
Kyoto Premium 138
Kyou Ka Sui Getsu (Mirror Flower Water Moon) 135
Kyungwon, Moon 140

labour-augmenting technology 174
Labour Force Survey (LFS) 179
labour market 193, 203–4, 210; flexibility and social security 204–5; opponents of 204–5; proponents of 205
labour mobility 207

labour-substituting technologies 192
La Nazione 118
L'arte ti somiglia 21
Lazzeretti, L. 3, 17, 131–2, 171, 179
least squares cross-validation (LSCV) 176
Lee, N. 149, 150
Leica Gion Store 140
Lester, R. 3
Lieu Unique 158
linear discriminant analysis: origins of the visitors *234*; respondent's reasons for visiting *235*
Li, Q. 175
liquid capitalism 12
local communities 2
local linear least squares (LLLS) method 171, 175–6, 184
local multiplier effects 197
Los Angeles Times 118
Louis Vuitton 140
Louvre Lens museum 76
Louvre Museum 39, 75, 80
low-skilled workers 192

Made in Italy 5, 18, 110–11, 117, 118, 120, 123–4; concept 111–13; first Italian fashion show 113–16; Italian fashion show 113–16
Maison et Objet 138
making sectors 194, 198, 209; research and development work 196–7
Marco, F. 183
Margem Sul 66n12
market and non-market relationships: actors degree distribution *156*; events degree distribution *159*; PC among events *160*; PC among places *158*; places degree distribution *158*
marketing intelligence 32
Martin, R. 131
Martorana, M. 5
mass-marketing phase 37
Matias Duarte 13
Mazza, I. 5
McCain, John 23
measurement bias 22
Measuring the Social Dimension of Culture (MESOC) project 55
mechanization 194
medias 149
Michel, J. 116
Microsoft 16–17
Mikimoto Stores 140
Ministry for Heritage, Cultural Activities and Tourism (MIBACT) 89, 94, 96, 101, 102n9
MNEMONIC research project 82n1
mobile devices 222, **227**, 227–9, **229**, 230
modularization 197
Morando, F. 39, 75
Morrison, A. 79

M-tourism 229; act 221–2; characteristics-based definition of services 219–20; co-produced services in territories 220–1; mobile revolution and tourism 218–19
multimedia devices 96
multiplier effect 197
multi-scalarity 207–9
Museo dell' Opera del Duomo 20
MUSE of Trento 20
Musetech model 79
museums 39–41, 70, 72, 77, 79; business models 74; digital transformation 4–5; efficiency of 91–2, 97; fundamental 88; ICT 89–91, 100; implications for 81; list of **108–9**; 'minor' 95; national art galleries 94; technical efficiency of 88–9
Museum Sector Alliance project 77

Nantes (France) 149, 153, 157
National Institute of Agrobiological Sciences (NIAS) 139
National Museum of China, Beijing 41
National Museum Poles *(Poli Museali Nazionali)* 94
Natural Resources 15
Navarrete, T. 75
Nelson, R. R. 130
net-art 18
Netflix 19
networks 154; analysis 149, 154; places and events 157–9; structural analyses **157**
Neuromation 19
new sectors, progressive differentiation and rise of 197
Newspapers.com 111, 118
N-grams analysis 123; Buying Offices *122*; Fashion Show *122*; High fashion *121*; Italian Fashion *121*
Nikou, S. 229
Nishijin brocade 140
Nishijin-ori technology 138–9, 143
Noir Kei Ninomiya 140
non-creative industries 181
non-creative sectors 195
non–market relationships 156–8, 162
nonparametric kernel regressions 175
Norvig, P. 11
Nuccio, M. 4
NUTS 2 regions 176

Ocejo, R. 161
off-/ de-shoring regions 198, 199
Oliva, S. 131, 132
Olson, S. 23
OPAC 73
open licensing models 75
operationalization: citizenship and participation dimension 62, *64*; cultural dimension 58, *59*; economic dimension 58, *60*; environmental dimension 62, *63*; social dimension 58, *61*

Orange Economy, The 185
Orbis (Bureau Van Dijk) 171
orchestration 202
ownership of a mobile device **227**
Ozeki, T. 5

Paba, S. 112
Paris au fil de la Seine 223
Parmeter, C. 176
Parry, R. 70
path renewal 5, 129–32, 142, 143
path transformation *141*
patronage 14, 51, 52, 134
PC/tablet devices 96
Peiró, J. 183
Penn World Table 171
Pereira, F. 11
Peukert, C. 34
Piccialli, F. 40
Pignataro, G. 5
Pinchuk Art Center, Kiev 21
Piore, M. 3
Place de la Concorde 222
places 151–2, 162
PlayStation 13
poetic portraits 19
policy makers 33–6, 54, 55, 81, 142, 149, 161, 163–4
pragmatic self-assessment framework 55–7
pre-existing bias 22
preferential circulation (PC) 149, 154
pre-industrial model 14
Price, K. 79
product-variety marketing 37
proprietary imagelicensing model 75
Psenner, E. 6

QRcodes 96

Racine, J. 175
Rausell, P. 183
regional development 52, 130–2, 142, 148, 192, 193, 199–201, 203, 204; technological change 197–8
regional innovation system 193, 202, 210
rejuvenation 142, 143
RESHAPE project 50, 53–5, 65, 65n7, 66n10
revitalization 142
Rizzo, I. 5
robotic art 18
robots 191
Rodríguez-Pose, A. 149, 150
Roth et al. (2017) 116

Sacco, P. L. 14
Sagot-Duvauroux, D. 5
Sala della Balena 20
Sánchez, D. 171, 179
Santagata, W. 112
Scantamburlo, T. 23

scholars 81–2
Sciences, Technologies, Engineering, Mathematics (STEM) 148–50
Scimago Journal & Country Rank (SJR) platform 72
Scopitone 159
Scott, Alan 52
Sedita, S. 5, 131
segmentation marketing 37
Severozapaden (Bulgaria) 179
Shichi-Go-San 135, 144n3
Shokunin (artisan) 137
Silicon Valley 13, 18, 198
Simar, L. 93, 95
Siu, N. 38
smartphone 21, 96, **96**, 99, **100**, **101**, **107**, 217–18, 220, 221, 223, 227, 228, 230
social disparities 2
social media 3, 20, 33–4, 217
social networks 2, 155, 160
social security 171, 179, 182, 193, 201, 204, 205, 209, 210
socio-economic categories (SEC) 224
soft power 20, 21
Soler, V. 174, 179, 183
SortiraParis.com 223
South Africa 184
Spanish National Institute of Social Security (INSS) 171, 179, 181
Spanish National Institute of Statistics (INE) 171, 178
Spanish Tax Agency 171
Special Issue 3–6
specialization 112, 131, 148, 149, 174, 185–6, 210
spectacularization 3
spillover sectors 195, *196*
Spiro, J. 154
Stepan, P. 32
Stereolux 157–9
stopwords 119
stricto sensu 195
structural change 58, 192–4, 197, 201–10
Suire, R. 5
Su, L. 176
Sunley, P. 131
Super Potato 140
symbolic knowledge 153, 155, 160, 162, 165
synthetic knowledge 153, 155, 160–2, 165
System of Analysis of Iberian Balances (SABI) 179

tablet apps 96
Table vivant 21
TaoBao 41
Taormina 4
Tatras 140
Tavano Blessi, G. 14
technical bias 22
technical knowledge 162

techno-creative innovation 151, 155, 161
technological change 2, 34, 192–5, 199, 201, 203–4, 206; and regional development 197–8
TEIKOKU DATABANK 133, 140
territories 13, 15, 16, 21, 24, 25, 51–4, 56, 58, 65, 129, 142, 148, 152
Territories of the Mind 16
textile industry 114, 115, 124
textual analysis 5, 111, 118–20, 122
thematic domain, primary and additional sources 72, **73**, 74
Throsby, D. 4, 32, 35
tm package 117, 119
Towse, R. 32
traditional craftsman 137, 143
Traps of Imagination 15
Trippl, M. 131, 132
Turkle, S. 14
Tussen Kunst en Quarantine 21
Twitter 13, 21, 227

ubiquitous 13
Uffizi Gallery 75, 76, 80
Ullah, A. 176
uncorrected efficiency scores **97**
Understanding, Capturing and Fostering the Societal Value of Culture (UNCHARTED) project 55
unicum 11
United Kingdom 40, 176
United Nations Conference on Trade and Development (UNCTAD) 171
United Nations Educational, Scientific and Cultural Organization (UNESCO) 25, 170, 179, **180**, 182–4
United States 19, 121, 122
urbanization 185–6
use of digital tools: prepare the venue 226–7; sharing information 228–9; *in situ* 227–8
user-generated digital content models 75
Uzzi, B. 154

Valencia (Comunidad Valenciana) 178
variable returns to scale (VRS) 93, 97, 98
variables in logarithms 190
Vermeulen, B. 6
vicarious learning 134
vicious cycle 199–200, *200*
video games 20, 149
Vietnam 12–13
virtual museum 70
virtuous cycle 199–200
visualization: British/US articles *120*; Buying Offices *122*; Fashion Show *122*; High fashion *121*; Italian articles *119*; Italian Fashion *121*
vocational skills 204
Vogue 118

Wang, D. 228–9
Ward, J. 34

Web Strategy Scheme (WSS) 79
Welcome to Paris mobile app 223
well-being 15, 51, 58, 171, 178, 186
Whale Hub project 20
Wikipedia 102n8
Wilks, L. 163
Wilson, P. 93
Winter, S. G. 130
Women's Wear Daily (WWD) 118
Wordcould package 117, 119
working people 174
World Bank 171, 181
Worldcat 73
World Intellectual Property Organization (WIPO) 171, 179, 181–3

Xiang, Z. 228, 229

Yasuaki Kakehi Laboratory 139
Yasuhiro, Mihara 140
Yoshida, M. 134
Yoshimura, Y. 39
YouTube 75
YouTubeRed 19
Yunosuke Kawabe 133, 136–8, 140
yuzen dyeing 133–8, 140, 143n1

Zegna, Anna 112
ZOZO Technologies Inc. 139
Zuckerberg, Mark 13